Dearest Daddy-
Merry Christmas! I hope you
get a kick out of this and
perhaps a little inspiration...
I love you lots!

♡ Claire

MOUNT McKINLEY

Icy Crown of North America

MOUNT
McKINLEY

Icy Crown of North America

FRED BECKEY

THE MOUNTAINEERS

Published by The Mountaineers, 1011 SW Klickitat Way, Seattle, Washington 98134

Published simultaneously in Canada by Douglas & McIntyre, Ltd., 1615 Venables Street, Vancouver, B.C. V5L 2H1

Published simultaneously in Great Britain by Cordee, 3a DeMontfort Street, Leicester, England, LE1 7HD

Manufactured in the United States of America

Edited by Dana Fos
Maps by Carla Majernik (pages 16, 17, and 53) and Dee Molenaar (page 27)
Cover design by Watson Graphics. Typesetting by The Mountaineers Books
Frontispiece: Mount McKinley's ice walls, and ski-wheel aircraft (photo by Olaf Sööt)

Library of Congress Cataloging-in-Publication Data
Beckey, Fred W. 1921–
  Mount McKinley: icy crown of North America / Fred Beckey.
      p.   cm.
  Includes bibliographical references and index.
  ISBN 0-89886-362-7
  1. Mountaineering--Alaska--McKinley, Mount--History. 2. McKinley, Mount
(Alaska) I. Title.
  GV199.42.A42M322   1993
  796.5'22'097983--dc20   93-26422
                                                                CIP

Permissions
The following publishers and individuals have generously granted permission to use extended quotations from copyrighted works: Excerpts from *Surviving Denali,* by Jonathan Waterman, are reprinted with permission of the author; ©Jonathan Waterman. Excerpts from *The Conquest of Mount McKinley,* by Belmore Browne, copyright 1913, ©1956 by Houghton Mifflin Co., are reprinted with permission of Houghton Mifflin Co. Excerpts from *Minus 148⁻: The Winter Ascent of Mt. McKinley,* by Art Davidson, are reprinted with permission of the author. Excerpts from *Mountain Man: The Story of Belmore Browne,* by Robert Bates, are reprinted with permission of The Amwell Press, Clinton, New Jersey, 1988. Monica Sullivan/Editor. Excerpts from "McKinley's Centennial Wall," by Graham R. Thompson (*Summit* magazine, March 1968) are reprinted with permission of *Summit* magazine and the author. Excerpts from "Denali, the Lion, Sleeps," by Paul Stoliker (*Canadian Alpine Journal* 72, 1989) are reprinted with permission of the *Canadian Alpine Journal,* Alpine Club of Canada. Excerpts from "Billy Taylor, Sourdough," by Norman Bright (*American Alpine Journal,* 1939); "The Mount McKinley Cosmic Ray Expedition," by Edward P. Beckwith (*American Alpine Journal,* 1933); "McKinley, Northwest Buttress," by Donald McLean (*American Alpine Journal,* 1955); "Mount Deborah and Mount Hunter, First Ascents," by Fred Beckey (American Alpine Journal, 1955); "The First Traverse of McKinley," by Morton S. Wood (*American Alpine Journal,* 1955); "The South Face of McKinley," by Riccardo Cassin (*American Alpine Journal,* 1962); and "The Southeast Spur of Mount McKinley," by Boyd Everett, Jr. (*American Alpine Journal,* 1963), are all reprinted with permission of the *American Alpine Journal,* American Alpine Club. Excerpts from *Airborne to the Mountains* are reprinted from the book by James Mills, Thomas Yoseloff, Ltd., 1961. Excerpts from *Old Yukon Tales, Trails, and Trials* are reprinted from the book by James Wickersham, Washington Law Book Company, 1938.

CONTENTS

Part III: Routes, Accidents, and Logistics

Heinrich Harrer Reminisces

Legendary climber Heinrich Harrer reminisces about his first meeting with author Fred Beckey:

When my book Seven Years in Tibet *was published in the United States I was invited to tour the country on a lecture circuit. During the following summer, when there were no lectures scheduled, I decided to visit Alaska. In particular, I wanted to see Mount McKinley—not only the highest and most legendary mountain in North America, but one with an amazing and unique human history.*

In my luggage I carried a copy of National Geographic *magazine and some maps from Bradford Washburn. Some of the photographs showed Mount Foraker and other notable peaks, but what fascinated me were the ones with captions such as: "in the background Mount Hunter, unclimbed" or "in the background Mount Deborah, unclimbed" or even "the highest unclimbed mountain in America." These unclimbed mountains sounded incredible to me, and I tore out the pages from that magazine to keep.*

I bought an old Packard in New York City for $1,600 and headed for Alaska. The gravel covering the Alaska Highway caused a number of tire blowouts, but by the end of May I reached Fairbanks. I met the naturalist George Schaller and made the first ascent of Mount Drum with him. I also met the mountaineers Fred Beckey and Henry Meybohm. Meybohm was a German immigrant who had a physique proving good conditioning. Both had just returned from a successful new climb on Mount McKinley. I was glad to have met two comrades who showed interest in climbing Mount Deborah and Mount Hunter.

We made preparations for the climbs. When an expedition lasts only a few weeks I'm not very particular about food, and so I told my new friends that they should buy provisions to their tastes. The weight had to be taken into consideration, since Don Sheldon, the famous bush pilot from Talkeetna, had only a small plane to fly us to the base camp. The landing was quite spectacular. Snow was already soft and some of the bridges across crevasses opened up when crossed. After Sheldon, with some difficulties turning about, had left us, we began to sort our provisions. With some astonishment I saw the labels on the cans of food. Nearly all of them read "...contains only xxx calories." My friends had brought the highest amount of weight with the lowest possible amount of calories!

We planned to climb Mount Deborah during the colder midsummer night, when the snow was a little frozen, and sleep during the noon hours when the slopes were avalanching. We had two unforgettable, wonderful climbs, but most impressive was the ridge to the summit of Deborah. There was an enor-

Fred Beckey, Heinrich Harrer, and Henry Meybohm on summit of Mount Hunter, July 1954 (photo by Heinrich Harrer)

mous high and large cornice. Appearing bizarre, like some cornices in the Andes of Peru, the cornice was a little wider than our rope length for belaying. I thought of my two friends, Herman Buhl and Fritz Kasparek (one of my Eiger companions), who both fell to their deaths from a cornice.

Normally I wouldn't take any risks, but in mountaineering there are moments when the target is near and action makes one forget danger. All went well; there was even a horizontal crack that made it easier to cross quickly. The pictures on that cornice are the most impressive of all my climbs. The last rope length to the summit was more like a channel, a vertical chimney through the soft ice. Happily, we stood on the summit, safely atop an Alaskan mountain new to all of us.

Heinrich Harrer
Huttenberg, Austria 1993

PREFACE

The height and immensity of Mount McKinley, today the best known of Alaska's thousands of icy alpine peaks, has only been recognized within the last 200 years. Now held in awe as a magnificent rock and ice colossus of isolation and frigid conditions, the polar mountain had only a minor legendary aura among early Native Americans and fur traders.

Europeans discovered Mount McKinley not from the Alaskan landscape, but from an inlet adjacent to the Pacific Ocean. In search of a legendary waterway to bypass North America, the famed British navigator Captain James Cook set the pace for revealing the mysteries of the coastal frontier and sighting some of Alaska's high peaks. Captain Cook was unsuccessful in finding a water passage to Hudson Bay, but in the course of a single summer, 1778, he accomplished many times as much as all previous navigators of the Northwest Coast. The vague and haphazard reports of earlier voyagers were replaced by Cook's concise charts and accurate observations, which proved there was no land connection with Asia. While Cook became convinced of the futility of seeking a waterway to the Atlantic Ocean, it remained for George Vancouver, one of his officers, to put an end to this vision.

While surveying Knik Arm of Cook Inlet in 1794, Vancouver wrote that the vista to the north was bounded by distant and stupendous snow mountains "apparently detached from each other."[1] There can be little doubt that he saw Mount McKinley and probably its neighbors Mount Foraker and Mount Hunter.

Alaska, believed to be an Aleut word meaning "the Great Land," was the original North American frontier. Perhaps as long as 40,000 years ago, and possibly at other times, when a land bridge connected Asia and North America, early peoples came in search of game and new territory. The indigenous humans of the Americas can trace their origins to this crossing, a passage that left many fossil remains. These early hunters followed Ice Age mammals migrating westward from Siberia, stalking such large fauna as the mammoth, which thrived until about 8,000 years ago, and other species such as the moose, which still survives. The Eskimos who settled in the Bering Sea region fared particularly well as hunters and today are the most numerous of the Native American groups in Alaska.

When Vitus Bering, a Dane in the employ of the Russian czar, made the European discovery of Alaska, some fifty-six miles of ocean water separated Siberia's Chukchi Peninsula from Alaska's Seward Peninsula. Bering sailed from Okhotsk in 1741 (his third voyage). In mid-July he sailed near Mount Saint Elias and apparently landed on what today is known as Kayak

Island. In his haste to return to Asia, Bering did not find the time for an adequate exploration of the southern coast and its spectacular inlets and therefore never sighted Mount McKinley.

Settlement took place in Alaska before the end of the eighteenth century, when the Russian fur traders established themselves on the shores of the Bering Sea. Certainly the desire to exploit and obtain control of the fur trade was the motivation for the early land exploration. Because the Aleutian Islands are mostly intervisible, the traders could follow this archipelago eastward to the mainland. As a result, they became familiar with the Alaska Peninsula and the Iliamna Lake region. To the Russians who followed Bering, the new continent promised a fortune in furs.

Russia was to owe the success of her American colony to the initiative and enterprise of private individuals, for the Court of St. Petersburg paid little attention to its American possessions for over a half century after Bering. Siberian fur hunters in crude boats sometimes became murderous traders, and they made no permanent settlement in Alaska by the time the English and Spanish first appeared on the southeast and southern coasts. But by the beginning of the nineteenth century the fur trade had left the hands of individuals and came under the control of the strong monopolistic Russian–American Company.

Meanwhile, in the era of Catherine the Great, who took a real interest in Russian America, Grigorii Shelikhov ("the man who would own America") founded a settlement on remote Kodiak Island in July 1784. As others besides Shelikhov sought their fortune in a new land, the Russian–American Company brought its various explorers to hunt for furs and trade. In 1839 Governor Ferdinand von Wrangell published the first volume of an encyclopedia of the Russian Empire. An enclosed map depicted the words *Tschigmit* and *Tenada* in the position of the unknown Alaska Range and marked the *Sushitna River.*

The most successful of the Russian inland explorations was that of Lieutenant Lavrenti Alekseevich Zagoskin of the Imperial Navy. In the spring of 1843, Zagoskin ascended the *Kvichpak* (Yukon) River as far as the Tanana and explored the lower stretches of the Koyukuk. He made track surveys and astronomical determinations of his positions and also took careful notes on resources and native populations, which he published in a book. His map, however, omitted the mountain names bestowed by von Wrangell.

In 1844 Zagoskin was accompanied by Ivan Simonsen Lukeen, a Creole, during a journey along the Kuskokwim River to near the present site of McGrath. Along his route, Zagoskin sighted the 600-mile Alaska Range—a different vantage than that from the Susitna River.

Prior to 1867 little was known of the Great Land's interior. Lukeen had ascended the Yukon River from the sea to the Porcupine River, the Kuskokwim some 500 miles, and the Susitna and Copper rivers a short distance, but little of the details were made public.

In March 1867, Secretary of State William H. Seward persuaded a skeptical Congress to pay $7.2 million for a great peninsula of the North American continent, then Russian America. Critics howled back epithets such as "Icebergia" and "Walrussia," calling the land worthless. Its great distance from the contiguous states and territories shrouded Alaska in myth. Even the boom of the Klondike gold rush did not bring its qualities to public light. Only a few early literate explorers and scientists, such as Frederick Schwatka, William H. Dall, Edwin F. Glenn, Alfred H. Brooks, Henry Allen, and George Davidson, left vital chronicles that affected politics and opinion.

No systematic exploration of Alaska was put into motion by the United States until 1882, and after the purchase, the only thread of continuity in investigations of the new territory was provided by Dall. Involved with the Western Union telegraph in 1865, Dall was more than a regional specialist. Representing the Coast Survey, the Smithsonian Institution, and the U.S. Geological Survey, Dall undertook the first systematic examination of the territory and wrote a useful book, *Alaska and Its Resources.*

The first military reconnaissance in Alaska was made by Charles P. Raymond, captain of engineers, in 1869. He was directed to ascertain the amount of trade being carried out by the Hudson's Bay Company within Alaskan territory, to obtain all information he could on the resources of the Yukon and its tributaries, and to determine the latitude and longitude of Fort Yukon.

The role of the famed Chilkoot Trail, from the coast to the Yukon watershed, began long before the days of the gold prospectors. The Chilkat and Chilkoot tribes had pioneered trail routes from Lynn Canal to the interior: concerned about the loss of their trading rights, these vigilant Native Americans killed the first white man to cross Chilkoot Pass on their trail. Prospectors who attempted to force the route were frustrated, but the efforts of Commander L. A. Beardslee of the U.S. Navy ship *Jamestown* in 1879 were fruitful. Beardslee had befriended Chief Klotz-kutch of the Chilkats, assuring him that the gold potential would enrich his people; soon a party of thirty friendly Chilkats was sent to the interior to grant concessions for the passage of white traders and miners.

The Klondike gold rush was ushered by prospecting activity in the Cassiar region, which by 1875 produced about $1 million in gold. Men swarmed into the Dease Lake area and then were lured to the Yukon region. A trading post had been established only six miles from the historic Klondike River by 1873.

The vanguard of Alaskan frontiersmen was composed of trappers, explorers, and prospectors who left few diaries and scarce records. Most of the forgotten men left with thoughts and adventures that remain with them alone. But we are indebted to them for exploring virgin regions and passing knowledge on to others—much of the land that they penetrated was so inhospitable that it was only superficially known until well after the gold rush had subsided.

After Alaska became a U.S. possession, there was a lull in its exploration, although the Coast Survey began to chart the complex coastline. Except for Raymond's venture up the Yukon and the efforts of fur traders and prospectors, no attempt was made at gaining knowledge of the interior until Arthur and Aurel Krause of the Geographical Society of Bremen crossed Chilkoot and Chilkat passes in 1882. The first chapter of scientific exploration in Alaska began the following year with an awakening of army interest, an expedition secretly championed by General Nelson Miles. The somewhat clandestine expedition of Lieutenant Frederick Schwatka across Chilkoot Pass and down the Lewes and Yukon rivers resulted in the first survey of a principal route to the Klondike gold fields and the first complete investigation of the over-2,000-mile length of the Yukon. The subsequent publicity of this expedition, which liberally distributed new feature names with disregard for customary usage, caught the fancy of armchair geographers. Whereas the Krause report had drawn little fanfare, Schwatka, a man on a mission, in 1895 published an account, *Along Alaska's Great River,* that did much to arouse interest in the Yukon.

The army established military posts in Alaska to preserve order and extend assistance to many ill-prepared argonauts and also built trails and telegraph lines. Spurred by the Schwatka expedition, the army conducted determined explorations, a formidable task because of the magnitude of the territory, and because mountain ranges guarded the Alaskan interior like concentric walls of a medieval fortress. In the summer of 1885, Lieutenant Henry T. Allen bravely pioneered his way up the Chitina and Copper rivers; he crossed the watershed of the Tanana River and continued to the Koyukuk— probably the first white man to see the Brooks Range.

Later, Lieutenant John C. Cantwell ascended the Kobuk River flanking the Brooks Range on the south, and Captains Edwin F. Glenn and William R. Abercrombie led expeditions into the Copper River valley.

During most of the nineteenth century, the American public was primarily interested in technological progress and economic achievement. The rapid industrialization of the nation promised a good life to those who remained at home; therefore, Americans were less interested in the wilderness frontier as a source of opportunity. Political, institutional, and intellectual attitudes influenced the intensity and character of scientific exploration in Alaska. Certainly national policy of the times relegated exploration to the background, and in science there was a policy of laissez faire. Strangely, Mount McKinley—the continent's highest peak—was one of the last great mountains in the world to be discovered. White men barely recognized the peak as a significant feature in 1865, when Switzerland's Matterhorn was first scaled.

But attitudes toward Alaskan exploration changed. When settlement increased and gold prospecting became relatively successful at the end of the century, mapping became a high priority as the public took interest in finding gold and the location of mines. To answer this new need, in 1898 the U.S. Geological Survey began its systematic surveys and explorations in the Alaskan interior, to eclipse the army's efforts. One of the most ardent of the Survey's explorers, Frank C. Schrader, spent six field seasons investigating the territory's interior, and in 1901 he crossed the Brooks Range to the Beaufort Sea. The geologist Alfred H. Brooks made quite notable explorations, the most adventurous being his crossing of the Alaska Range and the first visit to the glaciers of Mount McKinley in 1902. Despite the many natural obstacles, government exploration compiled an admirable record, especially when taken in light of social attitudes then prevailing in the United States.

In the Coast Mountains and the Icefield Ranges of the Yukon and Alaska, nearly unheralded topographers surveyed the rugged peaks and immense glaciers for the International Boundary Survey, often persevering well beyond the call of duty. One of science's most ambitious explorers, Israel C. Russell, conducted the pioneer explorations of the vast Malaspina Glacier, and his efforts nearly brought him to the summit of that coastal mountain giant, Mount Saint Elias. Long considered to be Alaska's highest, the peak was climbed in August 1897 by the brother of the Italian king, the Prince Luigi Amadeo di Savoia, Duke of the Abruzzi, with a strong party of guides and porters.

With such an abundance of mountain riches in the Far North, and with so many remote mountain ranges, the quest for Mount McKinley was not begun until after 1900, when both Alaskans and outsiders exhibited a proprietary zeal for its summit. Only at the close of the eighteenth century, exploration's last great age, did men begin to consider mountaineering a pleasure in its own right. The early alpinists, such as Russell and the Duke of the Abruzzi on Mount Saint Elias and James Wickersham, Dr. Frederick Cook, the Sourdough Expedition, Belmore Browne, and Hudson Stuck on Mount McKinley, all had style and vision, climbing with an intensity of effort and an obsessive dedication.

▲ ▲ ▲

I was inspired to write this book after many years of climbing in Alaska. I've tried to portray the mountain through the history of its stunning countenance: its formation, geography, and regional flora and fauna; and through a selection of significant, definitive events. North America's highest mountain has such a rich, intricate legacy with a cast of characters, ranging from gold prospectors to bold alpinists, that the choice of what to include here was almost overwhelming. This book doesn't cover all facets of history, exploration, and mountaineering on Denali. Included herein are those events and daring adventures that seem uniquely of the mountain, some well known and others largely forgotten. I hope you enjoy the narrative that follows as much as I have enjoyed researching and writing it.

Fred Beckey
Seattle, Washington 1993

▲ ▲ ▲

ACKNOWLEDGMENTS

The scope of my indebtedness to historians and researchers who have focused on the lore and science of both Alaska and Mount McKinley is immense. My facts, themes, anecdotes, and interpretations have come partly from this base and are complemented with my personal experience in Alaska's ranges, rather than with primary manuscript research.

Because this discourse concentrates on one particular mountain massif—a great icy crown—my indebtedness ranges from the extensive written literature to friends and sometimes mere acquaintances who have kindly assisted me in various ways in its preparation. Unfortunately, I cannot be completely inclusive, but the following persons deserve my gratitude.

Craig and Phyllis Tillery have provided encouragement, research, and endless hospitality in Anchorage. Roger Robinson, Renny Jackson, and Kathy Sullivan of the National Park Service, Steven Nelson of the U.S. Geological Survey, Bradford Washburn, Brian Okonek, Dave Johnston, Robert H. Bates, Charles R. ("Bucky") Wilson, William D. Hackett, Gray Thompson, Chip Faurot, Heinrich Harrer, Henry Meybohm, John S. Edwards, Henry Abrons, Mark Bebie, Matt Culberson, Dennis Eberl, Art Davidson, John Roskelley, Jim Wickwire, Jon Krakauer, and Phil Ershler have all provided first-hand recollections, research assistance, route descriptions, opinions, or manuscript review. Sybil Goman, Doug Stufflebeam, and Roy Ratliff read and criticized preparatory stages of the manuscript. Robert B. Schoene, M.D., graciously lent his expertise on high-altitude medicine. Jim Okonek of K2 Aviation and Charles Rigden flew me on aerial reconnaissances. Debbie McKinney of the Anchorage Daily News researched newspaper files, and John Pollock provided gracious assistance in library research. James Smith and Kevin Swan expertly negotiated for release of the title in a contractual disagreement.

Many librarians courteously assisted me in my probe for history, technical information, and photography—in particular, the staffs of the Alaska State Library and the U.S. Geological Survey libraries, Susan L. Hengel of the Hagley Museum and Library, and Patricia Fletcher, the librarian of the American Alpine Club.

This book is greatly enriched by the excellent photography and artwork within its pages. I am most appreciative of the skilled contributions by Charles R. Wilson, Bradford Washburn, Dee Molenaar, Heinrich Harrer, Olaf Sööt, David Johnston, Roger Robinson, Brian Okonek, Charles Sassara, James Balog, Dennis Eberl, Jim Okonek (K2 Aviation), Mark Bebie, Scott Fisher (Mountain Madness), Randall D. Miller, AeroMap U.S., Inc., Theodore Koven, Belmore Browne, Dr. George Wichman, Glenbow Museum Collection, Historical Photograph Collection and Charles E. Bunnell Collection (University of Alaska Archives, Fairbanks), Merl LaVoy (courtesy Belmore Browne Collection, Dartmouth College Library), Austin Post (U.S. Geological Survey), Hudson Stuck, Donald McLean, and the American Alpine Journal.

INTRODUCTION

The huge ice-corniced granite cliffs rise in successive tiers out of a gold-strewn low country, over which wander bear, moose, caribou, and other big game animals. The middle slopes are swept by a sea of storm-driven clouds, and above, far above the usual cloud line, there is a new world of silent glory and snowy wonder. Peak upon peak, range upon range, the great uplift continues to rise into the blackness and mystery of the arctic heavens.

Frederick A. Cook
To the Top of the Continent, 1908

GEOGRAPHIC SETTING

Viewed from the coastal plain, Mount McKinley is one of the world's most magnificent mountains. Rising to an ice-crowned height of 20,320 feet (6,194 meters), this great alpine massif, *Denali* to the Athabascans, seems synonymous with Alaska. The great granite massif acts as a magnet to thousands of sightseers, many mountaineers, and countless fascinated readers. Located at 63°04'15" north latitude (just over 3° south of the Arctic Circle), Mount McKinley is a befitting figure for the Great Land.

All of earth's other mountains above 20,000 feet are spread between 43° north and 32° south of the equator; in fact, the nearest higher mountain is Gongga Shan in central China at a latitude of near 30° north. Possibly only Nanga Parbat, which sweeps 23,000 feet from the Indus River at its northern base, surpasses the immense northern relief of Mount McKinley, which rises from nearly 2,000 feet in the upland tundra.

Most of the great mountain uplifts in Alaska—the Saint Elias, Chugach, Wrangell, and Alaska ranges—are part of the Pacific Mountain System, where the largest glaciers in North America are located. Farther inland, the Rocky Mountain System sweeps northward from Canada, the Brooks Range extends east to west, and a chain of volcanos, both active and extinct, extends southwestward from the Alaska Peninsula into the Pacific Ocean to form the mountainous, bleak Aleutian Islands.

The vast arc of the Alaska Range, culminating in Mount McKinley, has been most influential in shaping the nature and location of the surrounding ecosystems as well as human activities on the land. The range is part of a broad, continuous mountain belt oriented parallel to the Pacific Coast of Alaska which forms a natural barrier between the coastal lowlands and the northern interior. On the west, the range's drainage flows to the Bering Sea

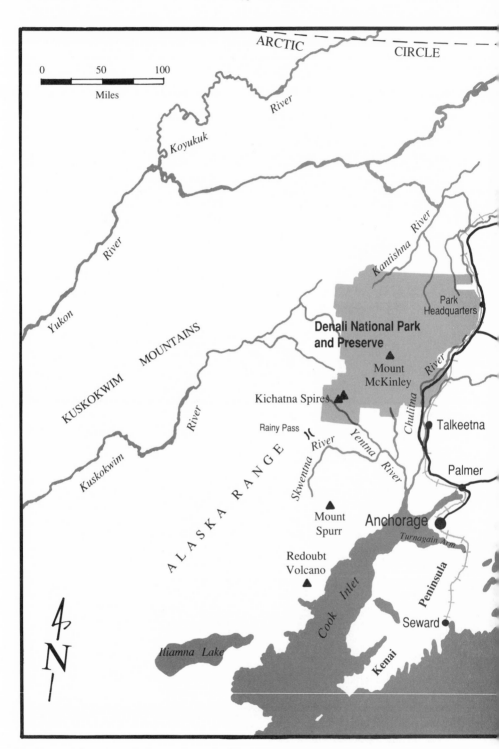

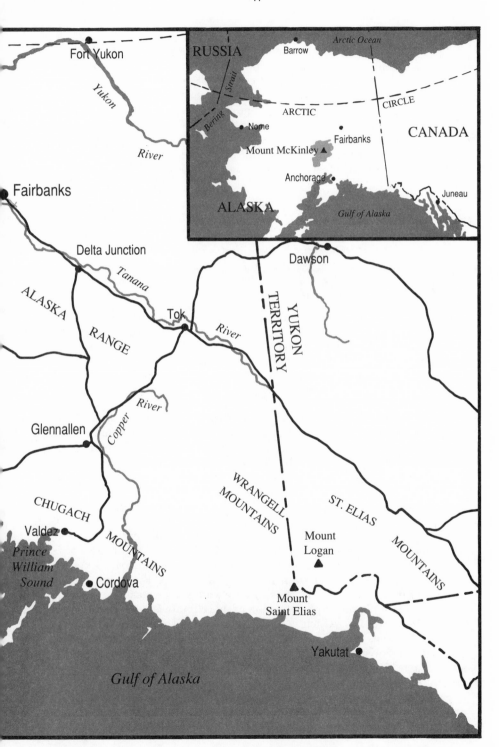

and, on the south and southwest, to the Gulf of Alaska.

The Alaska Range includes not only the highest mountain on the North American continent but also a wilderness of immense peaks and rock ridges still locked into a replica of the Pleistocene Ice Age. All of the higher valleys of the range, regardless of exposure, are occupied by glaciers. Surrounding Mount McKinley and its court of great adjacent peaks—Mount Foraker, Mount Hunter, and Mount Huntington—and stretching far to the southwest are crowns of glacier ice, massive rock walls, spectacular gabled peaks, and gigantic razorback ridges that continue into the Aleutian Range. The early explorer and geologist Alfred H. Brooks portrayed this grandiose vista:

> The great crescentic sweep of Alaska's southern coast line is broken at its most northerly point by Cook Inlet, an embayment which penetrates the mainland for nearly 200 miles. The drainage basin tributary to this embayment is cut off from the Yukon and Kuskokwim waters on the north and west by a chain of rugged mountains called the Alaska Range. At the heart of this chain stands Mount McKinley, the highest peak of North America, and its sister peak, Mount Foraker.[2]

Well marked along the western and northwestern front of the Alaska Range is what Brooks termed a piedmont gravel plateau—an extensive feature some 2,500 to 3,000 feet above sea level. With a surface mostly above the regional timberline, it is underlain by sands and gravels, covered with moss and grasses, and deeply dissected by streams.

▲▲▲

Alaska is spectacular, superlative, and varied. It is a vast land of midnight sun and midday darkness, the aurora borealis, glaciers and twisting rivers, tundra and muskeg, moose and caribou, salmon and salmon-eating bears, oil and gold. Alaska, the Aleut translation of "the Great Land," indeed seems fitting. Alaska's width alone extends for 21° of longitude and spans four time zones. One-fifth the size of the remainder of the United States, its terrain totals 586,000 square miles—even dwarfing the adjoining Yukon Territory.

Alaska is a collage of gentle landscapes and meandering rivers, sometimes set in boreal forest, sometimes in upland tundra, amid some of the most rugged alpine rock and ice ranges on the face of the earth. Extensive regions of Alaska are underlain by deposits that are the result of mass wasting or frost action in a rigorous climate widely known as the periglacial. A widespread and unique phenomenon of this climate is permafrost (perennially frozen ground), which is present throughout eighty-two percent of Alaska and exists where summer heat fails to penetrate to the base of the frozen ground layer; it is a soil layer at variable depths beneath the earth's surface in which the temperature has been below freezing from a few to several thousands of years.

Permafrost is continuous in the Arctic and then discontinuous as one proceeds southward. This frozen substratum of earth and ice is responsible for the seemingly endless muskeg bogs that cover the interior lowlands.

Mount Foraker and Herron Glacier from the west (August 26, 1969) (photo by Austin Post, U.S. Geological Survey)

Shallow ponds and lakes of this environment are a transitional feature: mats of tangled vegetation around the borders of the water bodies encroach on the open water and slowly reduce it to muskeg.

Taiga and tundra are specialized terms describing vegetation in the Far North. The taiga is the woodland or forest, an endless assemblage of dark spruce dominating the ecosystem, mixed with deciduous birch, aspen, and willow. This subarctic forest with its frequent ponds is associated with some 450 species of low shrubs and herbs, including blueberry, wild rose, Labrador tea, cranberry, mosses, and lichens. A thin soil layer covers the lower elevations, much of it a coarse gravel found where drainage is poor, often overlying permafrost. Where sphagnum and bog plants accumulate, the soil is rich in organic material.

Because of Alaska's climate, some fifty percent of the land is treeless, much of it being the tundra. The tundra (meaning "barren land") is a term applied worldwide to windswept treeless areas and to the high vegetated elevations above timberline—usually above 2,700 feet in Alaska. The dominant tundra plants are willows, dwarf birch, various shrubs, and mosses; unique flowers come to life in June. Plants in this zone tend to grow in clumps or mats. Here the tussock tundra, both above and below timberline, is waterlogged and most cumbersome for the hiker.

Despite its almost-overwhelming alpine mountain ranges, roughly one-third of Alaska is relatively flat. The greatest rivers, the Yukon and the Kuskokwim, for much of their courses loop slowly in great meanders, frozen in winter, and set in a terrain of countless thawed lakes in summer. Flowing from the Yukon Territory, the Yukon River at 1,979 miles in length is the third longest in North America (after the Mississippi and Mackenzie River systems).

Alaska can be considered to be primarily a subarctic peninsula attached to the northwest shoulder of North America, bordered with an arctic fringe on the north and west and a temperate panhandle wedged against British Columbia along the southeast coast. The great peninsula is bounded on the south by the North Pacific Ocean, on the west by the Bering Sea, and on the north by the Arctic Ocean.

▲▲▲

The effective geography of Alaska has made it a global crossroads rather than an outlying province, partly because seventy-seven percent of the world landmass (excluding Antarctica) is located north of the equator. In this landmass—from 25° to 65° latitude—is most of the world's modern industry and concentration of civilization. With the development of long-range jet aircraft, Alaska has become a keystone area in world air-travel routes. Great circle routes (the shortest distances) are deflected to the north in the northern hemisphere, the consequence being that communication lines cross the Arctic.

In addition, Alaska has become a commercial success, hardly envisioned when the questionable purchase was negotiated with Russia in 1867. Its once-unknown resources have proven a vast richness in oil, minerals, fisheries, and tourism. Because large sections of Alaska are covered with vegetation of economic importance, its timber resources continue to provide a large export market. Alaska's forests are a reflection of its precipitation, which varies from the sparse inland subarctic forest to the dense rain forest of the south and southeast coastal regions.

GEOLOGY

The first portions of what would later become Alaska were added to the North American continent when it formed a supercontinent with Africa and South America. Then, from about 200 million years ago to about 50 million years ago, terranes[3] were grafted piecemeal onto the ancient western edge of North America, including southern Alaska. Much of the greater region now consists of a collage of oceanic crustal fragments and island arcs that were tacked onto the older, more inland continental margin. The Mount McKinley terrane itself is composed of the eroded remains of a volcanic island arc.

In the entire Alaska Range, Jurassic and Cretaceous rocks that were deposited in a deep oceanic trough have been strongly compressed and deformed to a fraction of their original width and have been overridden by various oceanic terranes on the south along a major thrust fault. The continual accretion of thrusted sheets along the ancient continental margin created a new belt of thickened continental crust. This accretion and sliding of the Pacific plate under southcentral Alaska may still be lifting the Alaska Range. These actions and the resultant contortions created suffi-cient heat to form melts of granite in the core of the range. Some of the magma, which cooled at great depths, intruded into older, tightly folded sedimentary and metamorphic rocks, mostly south of the extensive Denali Fault System.

The intrusive masses of the Alaska Range, making up some 9,600 square miles, form a southwest–northwest linear arrangement; a massive oval-shaped granitic batholith of eighteen miles in length and fourteen miles in width includes most of Mount McKinley and Mount Foraker and all of Mount Hunter. Data indicate that the granite is about 60 million years old,[4] cooled from its molten state to form beautiful pink crystalline rock (pre-dominantly quartz monzonite), eventually exposed at the surface by uplift and erosion, and contrasting sharply with dark-colored older rocks. Near Mount McKinley's summit can be seen areas where the molten material met an overlying layer of black slate (which once formed a sea bottom).

The Denali Fault System, the longest weakness in the crust of North America, is an elongate zone of fracture and displacement slicing through the Alaska Range, passing across Denali National Park and Preserve and, for 1,300 miles in a great arc across Alaska, separating its oldest rocks from much younger ones. The fault system juxtaposes the younger Mount McKinley terrane against an older Yukon crystalline terrane on the north in the park area. Here the mountain-building forces caused by plate movements has produced an 18,000-foot rise from the piedmont region flanking the mountain on the north, where Wonder Lake occurs. The Denali Fault, whose movements two million years ago may have affected the uplift of Mount McKinley, controls the course of Muldrow Glacier for fifteen miles. Parts of this glacier, and the Peters and Foraker glaciers, follow the zone of weak rocks along this major fault.

The complexly faulted Alaska Range was continuously uplifted during Pleistocene time, and about 10,000 years ago the landscape with its extensive glaciers began to take on the aspects we see today. Because of the uparching, most streams in the range have a dendritic drainage system. Many follow narrow canyons through east-trending ridges of pre-Tertiary rocks and then cross broad plains and lowlands.

CLIMATE AND THE NORTHERN LATITUDE

Alaska's great climatic range is caused by a varied topography, different conditions of the oceans bounding Alaska on three sides, and a great geographical span—some twenty percent of the area of the forty-eight contiguous states. It is significant that the northernmost point of Alaska is within 18° of the latitude of the North Pole and the southernmost tip of southeastern Alaska is close to the latitude of Copenhagen, Denmark.

Alaska's climatic zones are to a great extent a consequence of the positions of the oceans in relation to the land. The three oceans that surround Alaska differ markedly in their physical characteristics and, hence, in their effects on the climate. To the north, the Arctic Ocean has year-round sea ice, and in winter the ice blanket over the water can chill to extremely low temperatures, in which respect it becomes almost an extension of the continent. The seas to the west are seasonally ice-covered, and those to the southwest and south are largely free of sea ice even in winter. The major North Pacific warm current, the Kuroshio, does not penetrate as far north as the Atlantic's Gulf Stream, but it does provide some warmth to the Gulf of Alaska's waters.

Alaska weather tends to arrive from the North Pacific. Prevailing atmospheric flow usually brings warm moist air, which as it lifts on striking the land's first mountain masses causes precipitation as it is rapidly chilled. However, the climate of the vast Alaskan interior, bordering the Alaska Range on the north, is dry and continental, with an immense contrast between summer and winter temperatures—ranging from minus 70 degrees to over 100 degrees Fahrenheit during the brief summer when the sun almost never sets.

While southeastern Alaska is one of the wettest portions of the world— with up to 300 inches of annual precipitation on the outer islands—the rainfall diminishes to only 4 inches at Point Barrow on the Arctic Coastal Plain, where the mountain systems have intercepted the rainfall and the cool Bering Sea and Arctic Ocean are poor sources of moisture.

The predominant storms reach Alaska from the southwest, originating in the western Aleutians and traveling across the Gulf of Alaska. Disturbances of exceptional violence and turbulence may occur with high-pressure gradient characteristics. When the Hawaiian High moves north and invades the lower Gulf, the Aleutian storm centers are shunted to the northeast; the storms then travel into the Kuskokwim valley and pass over Mount McKinley and the Alaska Range.

Alaska's mountain ranges influence the climate, acting as barriers to free circulation of oceanic air. The numerous ranges set up impediments to allow such unmodified oceanic air to reach the Alaskan interior only from the west. Mount McKinley and Mount Foraker rise so abruptly from sea level that they create their own microclimate, catching the frequent storm systems crossing the Gulf of Alaska and the Alaska landscape itself. Weather changes and barometric pressure fluctuations tend to be severe and rapid. Fierce storms and winds can develop within hours—often catching mountaineers by surprise.

Alaska's mountain regions have lower summer temperatures than the adjacent lowlands, and their yearly precipitation (mostly in the form of snow) is more abundant. In winter, however, the mountain temperatures may not differ much from those in the lowlands, and in clear weather all but the highest peaks are actually warmer than the valleys.

In Denali National Park and Preserve, the clearest weather is always in the winter, when the temperature drops markedly—sometimes falling below minus fifty degrees Fahrenheit. The weather usually remains dry throughout May and also sometimes in June. The seasonal progression of Alaska's climate is closely associated with the seasonal general circulation changes of the atmosphere. In the seasonal precipitation variations, April is the driest month and August is the wettest for most of Alaska (except the Pacific coastal zone). The principal reason for this pattern is that during April and May a strong arctic cyclonic ridge usually develops over the Yukon and Alaska. Mountain barriers block moisture transport from south to north into the interior. As the season progresses, the onshore flow becomes less intense and the ridge flattens. By August the flow is usually southwesterly, almost parallel to the mountain barriers, and ideally aligned to bring moisture up Cook Inlet and around the west end of the Alaska Range. Summer rains, in fact, account for most of the fifteen inches of annual precipitation in Denali National Park and Preserve.

In fall, when migratory birds begin flights southward, snowfall blankets the tundra. This is a time when mammals don their winter coats. The landscape takes on autumn hues; deciduous trees and shrubs turn into their orange and yellow colors. Certainly Alaska's climate enhances its beauty.

▲▲▲

On an annual basis, Alaska receives a small bonus in sunlight and a large bonus in twilight. The sun, in rising and setting, crosses the horizon at a shallow angle at the northern latitudes, to slightly lengthen the day and greatly increase the twilight. In addition, refraction (the bending of the sun's rays by the atmosphere), lengthens the day by making the sun visible even when it is below the horizon (refraction is minimal in the tropics but significant in Alaska, particularly in winter). Alaska receives most of its sunlight during the summer, but the sun is never overhead. During the longest day of the year, the sun only reaches $23^1/_2°$ north latitude. Because the sun's rays strike the ground at an angle in higher latitudes, the energy received on the ground surface is less than that if they struck from overhead. However, the total daily summer radiation is approximately equal to that of lower latitudes. The Arctic Circle (66½° north) separates the area to the north, which receives continuous sunlight during part or all of the summer and no sunlight during part or all of the winter, from the area to the south, which has long summer days and winter nights but in which neither reaches twenty-four hours.

The northern latitude of the Alaskan interior makes it a favorite location to admire the aurora borealis, which is Latin for "northern goddess of dawn." Especially in winter, the northern lights enliven the dark skies with their glowing, waving displays. Like giant searchlights, the northern lights streak the night-time polar skies to display a shimmering variety of patterns, such as pulsating luminous arcs and multiple sweeping bands. The aurora borealis frequently dances above the tree-hemmed campus of the University of Alaska near Fairbanks, a major center for studying the solar-originated phenomenon of these luminescent fingers of light.

From the ground the aurora borealis appears to be a horizontal curtain of lights streaked with narrow vertical rays. As the aurora becomes more active, folds develop in the curtain. The curtain begins at an altitude of several hundred kilometers and ends about 100 kilometers above the ground, where the atmosphere becomes so dense that it stops most of the incoming electrons. The sheet is estimated to be less than a kilometer thick, whereas it extends laterally for thousands of kilometers.

Past observers of the aurora borealis imagined that these Arctic displays resulted from sunlight refracted by atmospheric ice crystals. The shimmering undulations, they speculated, were caused by the movement of air above the earth's polar regions. Physicists today know that auroras are lights emitted when atoms and molecules in the upper atmosphere collide with negatively charged electrons blowing in from the sun. These auroral emissions occur because the ionosphere is bombarded by electron beams generated by a complex interaction between the solar wind and the earth's magnetic field. The apparent motion of the auroral curtain is caused not by atmospheric turbulence but by changes in the electromagnetic conditions that propel the electrons.

GLACIERS

It was the great masses of glacier ice, especially those that discharge to the sea, that captured the imagination of the early navigators who first explored the Alaska coast. Their discoveries were brought to public notice through reports that contributed to the slogans of a frozen northland—the "Icebergia" of an American political purchase.

The number and immensity of Alaska's glaciers have perpetuated this myth and hindered Alaska's early exploration—despite the fact that glaciers occupy only an estimated five percent of Alaska. But snowfall, which is among the world's greatest amounts, have formed immense icefields in the southern and southeastern coastal mountains. Bering Glacier (over 100 miles in length) is the longest, and Hubbard Glacier fronts six miles of calving ice at tidewater. The famous piedmont glacier, the Malaspina, is alone larger than the state of Rhode Island.

The Frenchman La Pérouse, who in 1786 studied Lituya Bay in the Alaska coastal ranges, where glaciers discharged into the sea, was the first to use the word *glacier* in his account and chart. He was also probably the first to comprehend their nature, for his expedition included scientists who were familiar with glaciers in the Alps. At the entrance of Glacier Bay, Joseph Whidbey, master of the *Discovery* on Captain George Vancouver's voyage in 1794, described them as solid mountains of ice rising perpendicularly from the water's edge. The calving of tidal glaciers, however, was described in such vague terms that one wonders whether or not such mariners understood what they saw. Vancouver, for instance, was puzzled by the nature of glaciers, speculating that they were rivers of ice.

Not until after the Alaskan purchase did the naturalist John Muir, from 1879 to 1899, make his observations in Glacier Bay in the Saint Elias Mountains. Muir's vivid accounts of the large glaciers led to a series of scientific expeditions that culminated in the Harriman Expedition of 1899: by 1900 all of the principal glaciers along Alaska's southern coast had been located and their lower sections marked on field maps. Still, virtually nothing was known of the interior glaciers. After Alfred Brooks studied the Alaska Range in 1902, he stated that its glaciers form the most extensive ice sheets of inland Alaska. He noted that those with sources on Mount McKinley and Mount Foraker extend to the inland front of the range.

Modern studies have shown that the combined Saint Elias and Wrangell mountains contain the most glacier ice in North America (8,700 square miles in Alaska and additional ice masses in Yukon Territory) and the most in the world except for the continents of Greenland and Antarctica. The more inland Alaska Range has been estimated to contain 5,300 square miles of glacier ice, the largest glaciers located on the range's southern slope. In the Mount McKinley area alone, some twenty glaciers exist with lengths over five miles—the largest of these, the forty-five-mile-long Kahiltna, is fed by the moist Gulf of Alaska air mass.

The largest glacier on the northern slope of the Alaska range is the thirty-nine-mile-long Muldrow, with its additional Traleika and Brooks Glacier feeders. Four other Mount McKinley glaciers—the Ruth, Eldridge, Tokositna, and Yentna-Lacuna—are each over twenty-five miles in length. The Ruth Glacier system, which has carved a gorge that scientists by sonar measurements have recently proven extends almost 9,000 feet in depth (as measured from the glacier bed to the peak of Mount Dickey), is now considered to be the world's deepest, according to cartographer Bradford Washburn.[5]

A consequence of climatic factors and the high coastal mountain barriers, late Pleistocene glaciers were much more extensive in southern Alaska than in northern Alaska and much larger on the southern flanks than on the northern flanks of individual mountain ranges. Troy Péwé, in "Quaternary Geology of Alaska," stated the following: "Glaciers have covered about 50 percent of the present area of Alaska at one time or another, but large areas in central and northern Alaska have never been glaciated.... The extents of the late Tertiary and early Pleistocene glacial advances remain almost unknown, but [later] advances are well established."[6]

Climatic fluctuations during the slowly warming Quaternary Period,

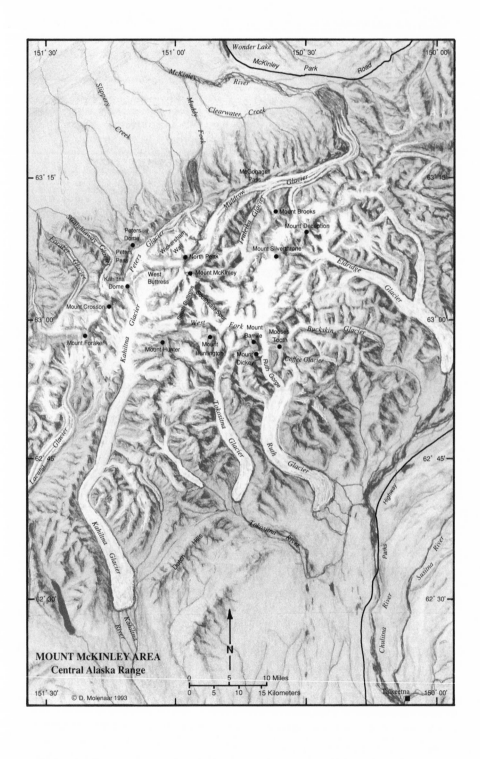

MOUNT McKINLEY AREA
Central Alaska Range

© D. Molenaar 1993

N

| 0 | | 5 | | 10 Miles |

| 0 | | 5 | | 10 | | 15 Kilometers |

which began at least three million years ago, were responsible for the formation and disappearance of glaciers and permafrost and changes in the distribution of plants and animals. Scientists now believe that in much of Alaska the Wisconsin climate (late Pleistocene) gradually warmed to a postglacial thermal maximum between 3,500 and 7,500 years ago.[7] In central and western Alaska, however, solid evidence indicates that a warming period began 10,000 years ago. Glacial retreats and thermal records from permafrost indicate a distinct very recent warming during the past 100 years.

Such immense glaciers as those that emanate from Mounts McKinley, Foraker, and Hunter not only capture the wonder of the casual visitor, but their features have long fascinated the body of specialized observers. The moraines of great glaciers from these mountains form patterns indicating how the ice masses flow. Most moraines on the larger glaciers stand as sharp ridges 50 to 200 feet above the clean glacier ice surfaces. The moraine debris often is only a few feet thick, protecting the underlying ice from ablation.

Medial moraines are composed chiefly of angular and frost-riven material that has tumbled onto the ice surfaces on the upper glacier reaches and then, as the glacier broadens from its tributary additions, form a striking visual lane. On the great glaciers there are usually several prominent medial moraines in their broadest realms. Erratics (rocks from a distant location) are typically found on Mount McKinley glaciers—notably on the Ruth and Kahiltna. In the lower glacier reaches, individual moraine ridges coalesce into a chaotic jumble of irregular hummocks and hollows—often with a local relief of as much as several hundred feet.

Nearer to glacier snouts are one or more terminal moraines, deposited within the last few hundred years. Most are unmodified by erosion and often are underlain by stagnant glacier ice. An outer set of terminal moraines often contains grass and moss, or even trees, while the inner set shows little or no vegetation.

Even the casual observer of a glacier snout will be impressed by the turbid glacial streams emptying from the great Alaskan glaciers. The Muddy River, coming from Peters Glacier, is a typical braided stream flowing on an outwash plain located between morainal hills. Outwash fans deposited during glacial advances have been traced here and elsewhere on Mount McKinley glaciers miles beyond their terminal moraines.

While all geographic aspects--mountains, rivers, lakes, glaciers, the coastline--change their features and shape in due time, it is certain that glaciers have made the most spectacular alterations. In past centuries, some Alaskan glaciers have uniquely advanced in a period of general glacier recession. While such gradual changes, not always in tune with climatic fluctuations, rarely capture public attention, it is the catastrophic advances, or surges, that have brought some glaciers into sharp scientific scrutiny. Glacier surges are periodic, large-scale, short-lived movements within a glacier. These surges, sometimes humorously referred to as "galloping glaciers," usually make ice movements 10 to 100 times faster than their normal flow rate. The U.S. Geological Survey has identified 204 surging glaciers in North America—two-thirds of them are in Alaska.

Mount Foraker, showing southwest, south (Talkeetna), and south (French) ridges (August 31, 1967) (photo by Austin Post, U.S. Geological Survey)

Because of its association with Mount McKinley, the erratic flow characteristics of Muldrow Glacier have focused attention on this phenomenon, one still not fully comprehended by glaciologists. The Muldrow has surged twice in the past 100 years, most recently in 1956–57. This exceptional advance was reviewed in 1960 by Austin S. Post: "The Muldrow Glacier, after many years of quiescence and slow retreat, suddenly and unexpectedly made a spectacular advance, with ice movements down the glacier amounting to 6.6 km (4.1 mi) taking place within a few months."[8] The midsection underwent rapid flow, and the upper end sank.[9] At its peak in the summer of 1957, the glacier's velocity was recorded at 1,150 feet per day.[10] The surge was similar to movements witnessed in Black Rapids Glacier in 1936–1937.

In 1956 a British mountaineering expedition on the Muldrow's branch, Traleika Glacier, found that the increasing number of crevasses made a descent of their route nearly impossible. The surface level of the ice on the Traleika may have dropped sixty feet in the interval from May to early July. In 1957 observers noted that the lower Muldrow had drastically transformed. Active ice overrode stagnant, debris-laden ice and established a terminal position within three miles of Denali National Park road. But today, ablation moraines cover the surface of much of the glacier's lower five miles. Here soil sometimes covers the stagnant ice up to four feet thick, and large kettles and ice caves exist in old moraines. The largest Muldrow moraine is visible from Eielson Visitor Center and the Park road. It was formed by sixteenth- and nineteenth-century advances—the maximum advances of Neoglacial time.

Studies of Muldrow Glacier have suggested that the erratic flow was the result of dynamic conditions within the glacier and not any pervasive external cause (such as extensive recent avalanching or earthquake activity). Such advances are not a normal reaction to climatic changes; similar flows seem to have occurred in the past. A possible connection to these surges is the fact that the Alaska Range glaciers that surged are located along the same fault system.

THE PLEISTOCENE ICE AGE

Eight times within the past one million years of the earth's history, climatic equations have changed to allow snow in the northern latitudes and elsewhere in alpine regions to remain where it had previously melted. In a chilling climate, snow steadily compacted into ice, eventually forming glaciers and ice sheets. Over tens of thousands of years, some of these ice sheets reached thicknesses of several kilometers, and they scoured and scarred the landscape as far south as the midwestern United States and central Europe. Both the vegetation and the animal herds were slowly planed and starved from existence in a deathlike silence. After each glacial cycle came to an abrupt end, the ice sheets shrank back to near their present-day configurations.

As the Swiss scientist Louis Agassiz hypothesized in 1837 when he proposed his glacial theory—a concept in raging dispute for a quarter century—the advancing ice sheets destroyed all organic life at the earth's surface. With his imagination, bold assertions, and vigorous prose, Agassiz soon captured a wide audience. Yet such new ideas encountered vast resistance because they ran quite counter to religious and scientific conviction.

Scientists more recently have shown that ice volume climbs gradually for about 100,000 years and then falls abruptly in Pleistocene Ice Age terminations that correspond to episodes of increasing summer sunshine at northern latitudes. It has been shown quite conclusively that astronomical cycles are the pacemaker of glaciation, the cycles appearing to be 23,000 to 100,000 years in length. These cycles affect the eccentricity of the earth's orbit, the orientation of its spin axis and axial tilt (and introduce the periodic earth "wobbles"), and ultimately the solar radiation that the planet receives. These orbital changes affect summer temperatures in the higher latitudes.

The Pleistocene Epoch began about 2.5 million years ago, as advancing ice sheets marked the onset of one of the coldest climatic interludes ever experienced during the earth's presumed seven major ice eras. As climatic fluctuations repeatedly produced large land glaciers, ice covered some thirty percent of the world's landmass (it now covers only ten percent).

The most recent advance of the Pleistocene Ice Age began an estimated 120,000 years ago and reached an extreme from 50,000 to 15,000 years ago, as many millions of cubic miles of the world's water was transformed into glacier ice. When temperatures plummeted, frigid strongholds flowed inexorably southward, deforming the surface of the earth as they buried the landscape. Concurrently, so much water was drawn from the oceans to form these relentless ice sheets that sea levels worldwide fell an estimated 350 to 400 feet, exposing large areas of the continental shelves: the Persian Gulf dried, Ireland was linked to Great Britain, which was linked to France, and a land bridge emerged between North America and Eurasia. A reduction of 100 meters of sea level, it has been shown, would expose almost the entire Bering–Chukchi continental platform, which extends some 500 miles on either side of the Bering Strait.

It seems plausible that between 65,000 and 31,000 years ago such a broad continuous land bridge existed to connect these continents. After submergence and severance in response to fluctuations in water volume as stored in continental glaciers, the bridge was reestablished during late Wisconsin time—roughly 25,000 years ago—then the advancing seas submerged it by 10,000 years ago as a worldwide climatic warming period ensued and the continental glaciers melted. This broad Eurasian–North American land connection is now covered by a shallow sea, one first sailed by Vitus Bering in August 1728.

The existence of the extended Bering Land Bridge at intervals as an ice-free region resulted from a low precipitation regime. In glacial times the colder air masses had a lower moisture-carrying capacity and were less successful in crossing mountain ranges and releasing precipitation. The combined low precipitation and cold climate of the Bering Strait region and interior Alaska during the last (Wisconsin) glaciation inhibited forest growth and encouraged the formation of tundra and grasslands. With a tundra environment much more widespread than at present, the treeline was lowered 450 to 600 meters in central Alaska.

During glacial advances of the late Pleistocene epoch, when Alaska was sealed off from the remainder of North America by intensive glacier complexes, it was open to the west. Large unglaciated portions of Alaska met the Bering landmass, across which animals, plants, and early man migrated into the New World. A wide area of tundra and steppe occupied eastern Siberia and the greater Yukon Valley, hundreds of miles in width, and was inhabited by a relatively rich and large mammalian fauna.

When this land bridge existed, glacier sheets covered the landscape south of Mount McKinley and prairielike grasses existed to the north. During the height of continental glaciation, there was simultaneously an ice-free corridor through central Alaska, which extended beyond the Yukon River and along the eastern flank of the Canadian Rockies.

At times during the Pleistocene Ice Age, glaciers covered as much as one-

Looking westward to tundra and streams from high on West Buttress of Mount McKinley (photo by Olaf Sööt)

half of present Alaska. Like their modern counterparts, ancient masses of ice were most extensive close to the moisture sources in the Gulf of Alaska. Researchers believe that the peak of glaciation came some 19,500 years ago; land ice in southeastern Alaska extended beyond the present coastline in some places because the sea level was lower. While glaciers south of the Alaska Range expanded to form the northern portion of the Cordilleran ice sheet, those in northern valleys of the range were free to expand until they fanned out. Denali National Park and Preserve now lies at the north edge of Pleistocene Ice Age glaciation. Both the northern ice sheets and the mountain glaciers in both hemispheres began their retreat from the last glacial maximum at about 14,000 years ago. The continental glaciers took about 7,000 years to melt away, whereas the mountain glaciers shrank more slowly.

It is believed that the climate warmed to a postglacial thermal maximum between 7,500 and 3,500 years ago in much of Alaska; however, in central and western Alaska, strong evidence indicates that a warmer period began about 10,000 years ago.

▲▲▲

Alaska was not always the same. At times the land has risen, the uplift being greatest near the close of the Tertiary Period. In a slow evolutionary change, complex events through the ages have affected the geological, biogeographical, and climatological history of Alaska. At times the land was forested, glaciers being mere pockets of ice on high mountains. In such interglacial times, forests re-invaded the valleys and low hills—an environment not very different from that of today. During colder interludes, massive piedmont ice sheets spread across the lowlands; some of the land was then dominated by a tundra-type vegetation, disrupted by wide, braided glacial streams from which sand and dust were blown.

As rivers left their floodplains high and dry, great amounts of glacial sediment and gravel remained in place, a periglacial landscape affected by the margin of continental and cordilleran glaciers. Much of this landscape of broad, level plains became fertile dusty loess steppes and rich grasslands, which owed their existence to huge amounts of mineral-rich rock flour, a sediment resulting from glacial abrasion of bedrock, and spewed out with meltwater. After being dried by the sun, strong winds carried the fine-grained sediments far from the ice sheets to be deposited as loess. Much of this finely ground rock flour was blown throughout the interior north of the Alaska Range.

The wide floodplains of the major rivers, low terraces, and well-drained soil were ideal locations for a productive grassland habitat. Especially in winter, this environment of loess and grassland was the ideal home of the best food supply for the late Pleistocene grazers. In colonizing such landscapes later within historic times, man began to inhabit this ecosystem.

As far back as the early Quaternary Period (two million years ago), the Bering Strait region was a principal avenue for the territorial spread of cold-resistant mammals. The complex chronological sequences of the openings and closings of the land bridge worked as one-way valves, allowing the flow of biota in one direction but limiting the reversal. Scientists have estimated that during the past few millions of years, about twice as many species of fauna dispersed from the Old to the New World as the reverse. The fluctuating waters of the shallow Bering Strait provided the sole avenue for overland migrations that permitted the colonization of North America.

When the sea level was lower, broad tundra-covered continental shelves were exposed, which provided a rich pasturage. The Pleistocene steppe vegetation—a mosaic of productive habitats and cold-climate floras—attracted various herbivorous mammals, along with carnivores that preyed upon them. Researchers have proposed that the great size of these mammals was due to a high-quality plant diet, a result of the periglacial environment and extensive glacial abrasion that ensured a new supply of mineral nutrients annually.

The strange mixture of species that once cohabited in Alaska's interior steppe grassland included mammoths and mastodons with their long, curved tusks, and bison, moose, musk ox, horse, camel, and yak—that Asiatic colonizer that is the hairy relative of cattle—all good grazers and well adapted to a diet of poor-quality roughage.[11] Large herbivores such as these survived the hostile winters by feeding on dried sedges, grasses, and shrubs in protected valleys.

During these times, a diversity of carnivores also existed. Fossils indicate that there were lions, sabre-toothed tigers, giant short-faced bears, northern wolves, and grizzlies. The diverse mammal population occupied the unglaciated refugia throughout Wisconsin time. Near the end of this last episode of the ice advances, however, when the forest began to return, vegetational patterns must have changed radically to hasten the disappearance of many mammals about 10,000 years ago.

Quaternary specialist Troy Péwé made the following summary of the faunal changes in the Far North: "Many mammals became extinct in Alaska at the end of Pleistocene time, and most of the species were grazers. It is thought that the loss of grassy habitat alone did not cause the extinction of the grazers at this time; rather, the restriction of ideal habitat plus additional stress in the form of man probably caused the demise of these species."

THE ARRIVAL OF MAN

Cro-Magnon (Ice Age) man populated Asia, and by 25,000 years ago probably crossed the Bering Land Bridge, a contemporary of the late Pleistocene fauna. Although man evolved during the glacial advances of this epoch, Alaska and the New World were one of the final locations he reached.

It is now believed that the Bering Strait region saw two waves of human migration. As the last ice sheet began to retreat 15,000 to 10,000 years ago, an ice-free corridor established itself east of the Alaska Range and the Rocky Mountains. At this time nomadic tribes migrated southeast toward the North American interior. The severe interior conditions restricted the wanderers, who probably became ancestors to the Native Americans.

The robust Stone Age hunters of Alaska followed herds of mammoth and reindeer across the tundra. Using spears, these hunters probably also killed moose and auroch. With their tools and weapons made by flaking stones and sharpening sticks, these hunters could kill and dismember animals and prepare clothing and shelter. Reindeer supplied hides for clothing, and their bones were carved into harpoons, fish hooks, and needles. To stave off the winter cold, fires were built with mammoth bones.

It is conjectured that Cro-Magnon man may have used some of the same hunting techniques of that superpredator, Neanderthal man—who killed mammoths at close quarters at an earlier time in Europe. The amazingly powerful Neanderthal's kill patterns slanted to the heavy-bodied grazers with long hair, such as the mammoth and horse, and also the carnivores. Archaeologists have theorized that these humans were so strong in muscu-, lature that they could use their large hands and firm arms to cling to hair in close-quarter hunting techniques. Groups of hunters might attack an animal, and then, using spears, a few would pierce an animal's sides, where the most damage could be inflicted.

The land bridge also provided routes for humans who remained in Alaska through late Wisconsin time during a period of changing climate, environments, and game resources. Those who migrated to the coastal areas, becoming ancestors of the Aleuts and Eskimos, found conditions more genial for occupation than in the interior.

When encountered by early explorers, the Athabascans of the interior were an impoverished race of nomads lacking the wealth of the coastal Tlingits and the ingenuity of the Eskimos and Aleuts.[12] Living in small bands, they moved with the seasons in search of game, using lances and arrows to kill caribou. The first sites of human habitation in the Alaska Range, between the coast and the interior, date between glacial advances 9,500 and 6,000 years ago, although man had reached the boundary parameters much earlier.

▲▲▲

The taiga and tundra is a bountiful habitat for the wide variety of mammals that populate the Alaskan interior. This rich periglacial environment north of the Alaska Range, a consequence of retreating ice sheets, was the food source for late Pleistocene grazers. As during those distant times, when the grazers found a rich pasturage in prairielike grasses, the turf today erupts with grasses, shrubs, and flowers.

Fauna

Early explorers of the Alaska Range were astounded at the "game paradise" they encountered. In late summer of 1903, when Dr. Frederick A. Cook and his party pitched camp at a stream fourteen miles northwest of Mount McKinley, wildlife was rampant. "The bears were so numerous that we never felt safe without firearms at hand," he wrote. One wolf was so bold he came into camp. "Caribou grazed about like domestic cattle, and moose were always expected in the willows."[13] A family of black foxes followed the party at long range.

Dr. Cook urged protection of the mountain sheep, caribou, and moose, calling this region "the finest games preserve in all the world." He felt that the game laws in Alaska then in effect were a farce: "It behooves us to protect these splendid animals against the cruel slaughter which blots the history of wild life,"[14] he penned.

No mammal of the Far North has captured the imagination of all early exploring parties more than the Dall sheep (*Ovis dalli*), which graze on high, snow-free meadows and climb precipitous crags to escape their enemies—wolves, coyotes, bears, lynx, wolverines, and golden eagles. These delightful white-coated sheep have soft, concave hoof centers that enable them to move with agility on the high rocky slopes. These sheep follow the retreating snow in spring, feeding on succulent plants, grasses, sedges, lichens, and willows.

Rams, who wander separately from ewes much of the year, make a distinctive pose with their grand, gold-toned curved horns—which can be over forty inches in contour length. The Dall sheep, whose mature rams weigh 150 to 160 pounds, inhabit all major Alaska mountain areas, including the Brooks, Kenai, Chugach, and Wrangell mountains, and also the Yukon and Northwest territories in Canada. They are currently estimated to number 50,000.

The naturalist Charles Sheldon, who came to Alaska in 1906 to study them, remarked that no fewer than seven bands of sheep were feeding or resting nearby, with their winter coats nearly shed. All the mature ewes were swollen with young, their necks stretched out on the ground. It appeared that they fed exclusively by pawing away the gravel or broken rock.

Sheldon was equally fascinated by the habits of the barren ground caribou (*Rangifer arcticus*)—the northern counterpart of the elk and antelope, which often dotted the land in their erratic migrating pattern. Their brown color, with a white neck, rump, and feet, make the caribou unforgettable. On one of Sheldon's study trips, caribou were constantly in sight, both on the mountainsides and on the rolling plateau—even on the river bars. In scattered bands of four to twenty, some 200 were casually observed. When Sheldon approached a band with the wind, and still a long distance away, both the adults and the calves would throw up their tails and trot off. If the wind were favorable, the pack-train would only excite their curiosity, and usually they either came trotting up to it, or ran off a short distance and came to a stand. Sometimes they would gallop a short distance. Once, two young bulls trotted up to the horses and stampeded them.

Sheldon observed the caribou's response to a seasonal urge to migrate for feed, the spring movement of this herd animal normally beginning in March. In their habitat of thin soils where plant growth is slow, these social members of the deer family require relatively undisturbed tundra and boreal forest, where they forage on sedges, lichens, and grasses. Their trails show that the cottongrass shoots on the upland tundra calving areas are the caribou's most important food item during late May–late June calving. Near the end of winter, caribou dig out vegetation from below the shallow snow of the boreal forest.

Studies indicate that the caribou's nomadic movements vary from year to year, but all herds have a strong tendency to return annually to traditional calving grounds. The calving area is therefore a critical habitat. The calving of the large Porcupine herd takes place after long migrations on the

Arctic Plain, and the Denali herd, now numbering some 2,600 animals, similarly moves some distance from the summer to winter range.

To facilitate their movements, large concave hooves readily support the caribou, which can gallop thirty miles per hour in soft tundra and on snow. Despite their mobility, caribou calves fall easy prey to wolves and grizzlies. During the fall, caribou-watchers may witness the bulls engage in spectacular rutting battles.

No northern mammal is as astonishing as the ungainly moose (*Alces alces*), whose North American habitat spans from Maine to Alaska. Its short body, perched on long, spindly legs, gives the moose a comical appearance, especially in ponds and shallow lakes when it dunks its head underwater in search of aquatic plants. Sometimes consuming forty pounds of willow twigs daily, moose forage on new deciduous leafy growth, sedges, and wetland plants. In winter its diet is composed of great quantities of twig shrubbery and bark. The largest member of the deer family, the imposing bull moose may stand seven feet at the shoulder and weigh 1,000 to 1,600 pounds, with massive antlers that may measure eighty inches across. Its large hooves equip the moose well for footing and rapid gait in forest and boggy terrain.

Of all Alaska's mammals, it is the great brown grizzly (*Ursus arctos*) that is most feared—although it is smaller than the coastal brown bear, which may weigh up to 1,500 pounds. It is estimated that there are 5,000 to 10,000 grizzlies in Alaska. At Denali National Park and Preserve, the Toklat grizzly is sometimes seen on the upland tundra slopes; strangely, these bears have been seen crossing glaciers in their large habitat range. These puzzling bears are feared for their "charge," which may be real but is usually a bluff.

The grizzlies vary in color from dark brown to a blonde cream; the prominent hump or shoulder always distinguishes them from the black bear. Most of the grizzlies' diet is roots, plant material, and berries, but they regularly dig for ground squirrels with their curved four-inch claws, and they may kill young sheep, caribou, and moose. The female bear may give birth to up to four cubs, these being born in winter dens. The cubs remain with the mother for two or three summers.

The black bear of the interior (*Ursus americanus*), which is generally black with a yellow-brown muzzle, is usually a harmless clown in comparison to the much-larger grizzly. Like the latter, they are omnivorous, although sometimes these bears seem to subsist on garbage dumps. Adults weigh up to 200 pounds, making them light enough to be competent tree climbers.

More ferocious than any bear is the wily wolverine (*Gulo gulo*), a member of the weasel family that weighs twenty-five to thirty-five pounds. Although it tends to feast on carrion, the wolverine, like the bear, will eat berries. In the Alaskan interior, this animal has a wide range; its tracks have been seen high on Mount McKinley.

The shy wolf (*Canis lupus*), a carnivore with highly social characteristics, roams in packs varying from two to thirty individuals. The wolf can sprint a mile at a speed of twenty-five miles per hour and maintain a fast hunting gait for hours. No other animal in Alaska has such endurance.

Wolves consume an amazing amount of food (an estimated four to seven pounds per day), and it is no wonder that when seen they may be stalking game. Wolves will kill Dall sheep, mountain goats, deer, caribou, beavers, hares, and even the vastly larger moose (which they hunt in packs); they generally prey on old, young, and injured animals.

The red fox (*Vulpes vulpes*), found throughout Alaska, largely feeds on rabbits and rodents. The fox, distinguished by a bushy tail with a white tip, is a secretive creature that is not as social as the wolf.

The porcupine (*Hystrico morpha*), whose heavy coat of quills is a superb defense against the wolf, is a solitary animal, often active at night. The Athabascans, who could kill the porcupine with bow and arrow, long used the quills for decoration. Much desired for its beautiful fur is the marten (*Martes americana*), a member of the weasel family whose habitat is the taiga spruce forest.

The beaver (*Castor fiber*), whose valuable fur helped provide the Russian impetus to explore Alaska, is the largest of North American rodents. The average adult weighs thirty-five pounds and is nearly four feet in length. With its scaly tail assisting in swimming performances, the beaver's sharp teeth cut deciduous trees to form dams—often to the consternation of the wilderness traveler.

In contrast to the beaver, which is seen in lakes, ponds, and streams, is the hoary marmot (*Marmota caligata*) of the hillside tundra. This large burrowing squirrel must beware of the golden eagle and grizzly to survive. Its forte is a piercing whistle that warns others in its colony (and other creatures) of imminent danger. Another prey of the grizzly, wolf, wolverine, and weasel is the arctic ground squirrel (*Spermophilus parryii*), which sets up colonies on the mountain slopes, often in conjunction with the marmot.

Perhaps the Far North's most amusing creature is the harmless white snowshoe hare (*Lepus americanus*). It calls on its disguise, agility, and light weight to escape from predators. Depending on its white winter camouflage, this evasive hare, with its long, wide-spreading toes, can travel over powder snow surfaces more rapidly than a skier. Co-habitants of the mountain and forest winters are the willow and white-tailed ptarmigan and the snowy owl. Both are commonly seen from November to May in their white plumage above the timberline region.

In Denali National Park and Preserve, 37 mammal species and 155 species of birds have been noted. These include the golden eagle, hawk owl, horned owl of the forest, raven, jaeger of the uplands, gyrfalcon, arctic tern, and woodpecker plover. The smaller animated birds include the water ouzel, kinglet, chickadee, snipe, jay, pipit, warbler, thrush, sparrow, swallow, and shrike. Often seen on lakes of the rolling tundra is the green-winged teal, and frequently seen on ponds and lakes west of the Susitna River are the beautiful trumpeter swans—which are now on the increase. In the woodland ponds, the small wood frog is Alaska's only amphibian.

▲▲▲

PART I

MOUNT
McKINLEY
ENTERS
HISTORY

View down the west ridge from summit of South Peak of Mount McKinley (photo by Olaf Sööt)

CHAPTER 1

The European Discovery of Alaska and Mount McKinley: Russian Fur Traders Yield to American Settlement

May 6, 1794
The shores we had passed were compact; two or three small streams of
fresh water flowed into the branch between low steep banks; above these
the surface was nearly flat, and formed a sort of plain, on which there was
no snow, and but very few trees. This plain stretched to the foot of a
connected body of mountains, which, excepting between the west and
north-west, were not very remote; and even in that quarter the country
might be considered as moderately elevated, bounded by distant stupen-
dous mountains covered with snow, and apparently detached from each
other; though possibly they might be connected by land of insufficient
height to intercept our horizon.

> George Vancouver
> *Voyage of Discovery to the North Pacific Ocean,*
> *and Round the World,* vol. 3, 1798

Vitus Bering, the Danish naval officer who served in the Imperial Navy of Peter the Great, made voyages in 1728 and 1741 that resulted in the discovery of the Bering Strait and of Alaska; thus began the Russian domination of northwestern America. Historians accept the traditional view that Peter initiated both voyages to determine the geographical relationship of Asia and America, but recent Soviet scholars have projected the thesis that a route to America, not the discovery of a strait, was the intended objective.

On his first voyage, Bering sailed through the strait that now bears his name, but having kept close to the Siberian coast he failed to detect the close approximation of the two continents (at its narrowest point, the strait is fifty-five miles in width). In June 1741 Bering set out from Siberia to find lands and riches. He bypassed the 1,200-mile Aleutian Island chain to the south, and his two ships became separated in the fog-shrouded islands. Eventually, the captain of the *St. Paul,* Alexei Chirikov, lost most of his crew to warlike Tlingits and to scurvy. From the *St. Peter* Bering sighted the Alaska mainland on July 16 when the ice-clad peak of Mount Saint Elias came into view; four days later he landed on Kayak Island.

As the eighteenth century progressed, the questions of a possible northwest and a northeast passage, and the separation of Asia and America, remained alive in Europe. Certainly Peter took seriously the notion that America was close to Kamchatka, but he knew nothing about the American coast south of the Alaska Peninsula. Meanwhile, reports of thick-furred sea otters in Alaska precipitated the coming era of Russian fur traders. It was not until 1784, however, that the Siberian Grigorii Shelikhov landed on Kodiak Island and established the first Russian colony in North America.

During his exploration of Alaska's southern coast in 1778, the British navigator Captain James Cook discovered a great embayment and explored it from May 26 to June 3. Believing it to be a great river, he called the future Cook Inlet "River Turnagain." With the prevailing poor weather, the mariner saw only outlines of mountains to the west, and if he sighted Mount McKinley and its neighbors, there is no record of it.

Three years later the British captains George Dixon and Nathaniel Portlock visited Cook Inlet, and Captain John Meares skirted the embayment. Nothing in their journals indicated that high mountains caught their attention. In spring 1794 Captain George Vancouver spent one month in the inlet's waters, making a detailed chart and proving that Turnagain Arm was not a great river.[15] The historical first European sighting of Mount McKinley took place on May 6, when Vancouver was surveying Knik Arm at the upper end of Cook Inlet. In his journal he noted "distant stupendous mountains covered with snow." The captain made no attempt to bestow names (as he had previously done when in Puget Sound in 1792), but there can be little doubt that he was referring to Mount McKinley and Mount Foraker.

Like the later Americanization of Alaska, the early Russian explorations were borne by the sea. The *promishlenski* (fur traders) wanted the sea otter, which abounded on the Aleutian Islands. Meanwhile, the Russian establishment apparently had no interest in extending the surveys of the British seafarers.

After the colonization of Kodiak, the Russian–American Company was given exclusive trading rights under a charter signed by Paul I in July 1799. This merchant company effectively became the only government in the Alaskan colonies, wielding economic, political, and military control over a vast monopoly. As could be expected, this company came into competition with American mariners for the fur trade. American ships from New England had taken most of the furs from Alaska's south coast and competed with the Russians by selling them in China.

Russian explorations up the important Kuskokwim River began in 1832, when Alexander Kolmakov, a Russian–American Company explorer, made a pioneering trading journey. His assistant, the Creole Semyon Lukeen, went farther, reaching near present McGrath, where the western front of the Alaska Range is in full view.[16] The Creoles, persons of mixed Russian and Alaskan native blood, were the leading fur traders and explorers of the interior. Lukeen's noteworthy ventures are not fully recorded; later his son

Ivan became the first to trace the Yukon River from the sea to the Porcupine River. Chosen by the chief Russian trader at St. Michael to learn more
about British operations on the upper Yukon, he alone finished a journey
to the company's post at Fort Yukon.

Enterprising early Russian–American Company explorers, who had sailed
eastward from Eurasia, certainly saw Mount McKinley at various times and
made crude maps. The most interesting early exploration came in the winter
of 1834, when Andrei Glazunov, who had been the first to enter the lower
Yukon River, made an adventurous journey overland from the Yukon to the
Kuskokwim River in an attempt to open a trading route to Cook Inlet. During
the dog-team journey Glazunov entered in his journal under March 7, "Saw a
great mountain called Tenada, to the northeast, at a distance of 70 to 80
versts (about 50 miles)."[17] According to Glazunov, the natives were unwilling
to guide him up a tributary, the Tschalchuk (Stony River), for further exploration. Starvation forced his retreat, the hunger becoming so serious that the
men had to eat all their dogs—and even the harnesses. Glazunov and his companions barely reached a Kuskokwim settlement alive.

In the interests of fur trading, the Creole Pyotr Malakoff made an ascent
of the Susitna River (at the head of Cook Inlet) in 1834. However, if he
reported on the high mountains of the Alaska Range, which he must have
seen while dragging his clumsy boat up the river, it was not included in
Mikhail Tebenkoff's 1852 atlas of Russian America. In March 1838 Malakoff pushed the Yukon frontier farther upstream and reached the Nulato
River (just below the Koyukuk River's entry), where he established a
trading post.

Baron Ferdinand P. von Wrangell, an admiral in the Russian Navy
distinguished for his Siberian arctic explorations, drew on Malakoff's journey up the Susitna as well as on information compiled by Kolmakov,
Lukeen, and Glazunov to obtain data for his map completed in 1839. On von
Wrangell's map, the coastal waters largely follow the British charts, but the
interior features are Russian originated. Dividing the Susitna and
Kuskokwim River watersheds are mountain clusters that must be Mount
McKinley, Mount Foraker, and satellite peaks. The map shows *Tenada*
encircled and *Tschigmit,* more linear, for the range.[18]

The Russian explorer who launched the first scientific exploration of the
Yukon River was an observant amateur naturalist. At the age of thirty-two,
Lieutenant Lavrenti Alekseevich Zagoskin's interest in exploring the Alaskan interior coincided with that of von Wrangell, now director-in-chief of
the Russian–American Company. Zagoskin was a naval academy graduate,
having served on both the Baltic and Caspian seas, and in 1838 transferred
his services from the Old World to New Archangel (present Sitka). While
Robert Campbell (a Scotch trader) explored the upper Yukon tributaries
under orders of Sir George Simpson (governor of the Hudson's Bay Company) in 1843, Zagoskin took on the grandiose task of exploring and mapping the interior—finally setting forth from Saint Michael Redoubt for the
Yukon on December 4, 1842.

The energetic officer was destined to leave a lasting imprint on Russian
maps. He traveled by dog team in winter and skin boat in summer, covering
thousands of miles and collecting the first significant information on the

environment during the three years of surveying. Zagoskin mapped the Yukon nearly to its junction with the Nowitna (a southern branch west of the Tanana River). From the lower Kuskokwim River, he had a grand, though distant, view of the great Alaska Range—learning from the Native Americans that these mountains were known as the *Tschigmit*, but he omitted details of the Mount McKinley region—the *Tenada* of von Wrangell— because he did not enter the range and because he could not survey its features. On his map of 1847, Zagoskin only entered the streams he followed and the key locations he determined astronomically for latitude and longitude.

Information about the mountains at the headwaters of the Kuskokwim River was known to the Russian fur traders only from reports brought by Native Americans. They must have been aware of high mountains between the Kuskokwim and Susitna River drainages. Constantin Grewingk, who in 1850 summarized the geography of Alaska, indicated on his map the axis of such a range—which like von Wrangell he titled *Tschigmit Mountains*.

The Russian literature has few references to the Tschigmit Mountains, but there was a name for the future Mount McKinley—*Bulshaia Gora,* meaning "big mountain." The geologist Alfred Brooks believed the name for the culminating point of North America came from Pyotr Doroshin, the Russian mining engineer who named it while seeking gold on the Kenai Peninsula.[19]

The names Tschigmit and Tenada later disappeared from Russian and American maps. Terris Moore, in *Mt. McKinley,* stated that

> when Wrangell returned to Russia at the end of his term as Governor, he continued his interest in the mapping of the huge unknown territory. It seems to have been through his influence that in 1842 a young naval officer, Lieutenant Lavrenti Zagoskin, was sent out by the Russian–American Company to carry out scientific mapping of the Kwikpak (Yukon), and if possible to make the crossing, which Glazunov had attempted, from the Kuskowim [sic] across the mountains to Cook Inlet.[20]

Captain Mikhail D. Tebenkov became director of the Russian–American colonies from 1845 to 1850. During his stay in North America, Tebenkov was active in surveying Alaskan coastal waters. Between 1848 and 1850, some 39 maps were compiled under his direction at New Archangel, later published in Russia in 1852 under the title *Atlas of the Northwest Coast of North America.*

Before the close of Russian occupation of Alaska, the young scientist William H. Dall, who succeeded Robert Kennicott as chief of the scientific corps of the Western Union Telegraph Expedition in 1866, and the English artist Frederick Whymper (brother of Edward Whymper of Matterhorn fame) canoed up the Yukon River in a skin boat—noting the range of high snowy mountains to the south. They may have seen Mount McKinley some 150 miles away, but neither singled it out nor made any estimate of its probable height. Dall still assumed, as others did, that Mount Saint Elias was the highest on the continent. Dall, however, suggested the name Alaska Range for these mountains at a scientific meeting in Boston in 1868. He seems to have taken a literal translation of the German *Gebirge von*

Alaeksa from the geographer Constantin C. A. Grewingk—who in 1850 at St. Petersburg published a map of northwestern America.

The ambitious Western Union project, which envisioned a telegraph line to pass through western Canada, then through Russian Alaska, across the Bering Strait by cable, and then through Siberia to Europe for thousands of miles of largely unexplored wilderness, did a great deal to publicize the Far North. With the approval of the British and Russian governments, the Western Union Telegraph Company, which anticipated an immense profit, began its surveying in 1865. The project was suspended, however, in the summer of 1867 because the transatlantic cable began its operation.

The winter of 1866–67 found Dall and Whymper at Nulato collecting and preparing specimens. In his fascinating book *Travel and Adventure in the Territory of Alaska,* Whymper described boating past the "Rapids" of the Yukon (below Fort Yukon) in early June. He related how the river abounded with moose, a mammal that could not stand the scourge of mosquitoes:

> *He plunges into the water, and wades or swims as the case may be, often making for the islands. This is therefore a favourite part of the Yukon for the Indian hunter. The moose are scarce below Nuclukayette, and never known as low as Nulato.... In winter, it is said, the Indians can, by following them on snow shoes, tire them out, and so get near enough to kill them.*[21]

During the years of Russian occupation, it can truthfully be stated that virtually nothing was known of the Great Land. The Russians seemed to have had no concept of its economic potential, and seemed to care little about the quest for geographic and resource knowledge. They barely knew where the great rivers carved into the terrain, and they knew nor cared nothing about the mountain ranges. In fact, the immense area between Cook Inlet and the Yukon River was as unknown to the world at large as central Africa was at the time of David Livingstone's travels. The Russians had ascended the Yukon for about 1,000 miles and the Kuskokwim some 500 miles; they had traveled the Susitna River a short distance and made one abortive attempt to explore the Copper River.

As Morgan Sherwood stated in *Exploration of Alaska 1865–1900,* "The pace and extent of Russian and American exploration in Alaska were intimately related to the social and political atmosphere in the parent nations."[22] Certainly during this period, political attitudes in St. Petersburg did not foster the promotion of science or inland exploration. When the sea otter became depleted and the quick profits vanished, the Russian interest in Alaska waned except as a pawn in international politics. Russian science was uncoordinated and piecemeal, and exploration was in the same vein.

Considering the realities of geographical separation, it is amazing that the United States did acquire Alaska, for its policymakers and the State Department knew no more. Fed on ignorance, the public misconceptions of the climate and geography—the "icebox myth"—outweighed all the facts. It was a stroke of fate when the possible sale came into the open during 1854, only eight years after the 49th parallel became the final northern boundary between American and British possessions in North America, when England was on the verge of entering the Crimean War against Russia.

Only a few years earlier the United States was ringing with oratory on Manifest Destiny. James Polk's presidential campaign climaxed with the slogan "Fifty-Four-Forty or Fight," threatening Britain with war unless she released the entire Oregon Country. Although Polk finally compromised with the British, there were those who spoke about taking Alaska as well.

The Russian–American Company, realizing its motherland was too weak to defend Alaska, concocted a bizarre scheme to sell Alaska to a San Francisco distribution concern called the American–Russian Commercial Company. But with the Russian defeat in a gloomy 1856, realistic officials approached Washington on the subject of the sale of its North American colony, knowing America's passion for expansion. Alaska might be a useful trade for money to pay war debts. At a time when the United States still licked its Civil War wounds, Baron Edouard de Stoeckl, the urbane Russian minister in Washington, met with Secretary of State William H. Seward. The two diplomats labored the entire night of March 30, 1867, to write the purchase agreement, one that was consummated with an uncaring cabinet.[23]

Czar Alexander approved the treaty between the two nations, which gave the United States a territory of 586,400 square miles (twice the size of Texas) at a price of close to two cents an acre. The treaty also added some 30,000 indigenous peoples and 900 more Americans (most of them were at Sitka). Congress endorsed the Alaska measure early that summer, despite grumblings by critics that "Seward's Ice Box" was worthless. The Russians added $7.2 million to their needy coffers when in the following year Congress appropriated funds for the purchase.

Both members of Congress and the skeptical American press made the invidious appellation "Seward's Folly" the butt of popular jokes. Critics howled back epithets such as "Icebergia" and "Walrussia," calling the land useless.

The initial press response was bewilderment. A principal journalistic opponent was the *New York Tribune,* which claimed the administration was attempting to divert attention from domestic difficulties and asserted that the nation was seeking alliance with a power not friendly to England. Cartoonist Thomas Nast lampooned Seward and Alaska, characterizing the region as mostly icebergs and polar bears.

But Seward had his allies, including the Far West senators. Support came from the *Boston Herald,* which reminded its readers of the abundance of furs, forest, and minerals. The Boston press, in fact, was singular in its favor toward the purchase, emphasizing the growing importance of fisheries, furs, minerals, and forestland. The *Philadelphia Inquirer* was another advocate of the purchase. Its pages conjectured on the potential of now commanding over the Pacific.

Time would validate Seward's optimism. Within three months of the purchase there were signs that the wise Secretary of State would be vindicated. As fur traders exploited the new territory, an invention found a method to remove the outer layer of the bristly guard hairs from the skin of the fur seal, an operation formerly done by hand. By 1870 the demand for trimmed pelts reached new heights, while the numbers of the fur seal plummeted. By 1877 New England whalers had brought back news of seal furs and walrus ivory.

When the United States purchased Alaska in 1867, the map included by Petr A. Tikhmenev in his *History of the Russian American Company* was regarded as the most reliable of the interior. But he left the entire Alaska Range region a blank, to effectively eliminate the early Russian explorers' mappings of the Tschigmit Mountains with "Tenada" as the high peak.

But the Russian fur traders, with no care or respect for the Native Americans and their culture, used the term easier for them to pronounce, *Bulshaia Gora*. After the purchase of Alaska, the native names and even the Russian term for Mount McKinley fell into disuse. Various American prospectors in the 1860s and 1870s explored the Yukon, then the Tanana, as had Dall and Whymper. Such traders and prospectors were aware of the great mountains between the seacoast and interior, but the terrain was a mystery, waiting for reliable explorers to penetrate it. Thoughts about the great mountains of the region were seldom passed on, for few early pioneers kept diaries or even wrote informal travel reports, let alone made maps.

After the Alaska purchase, the increasing number of prospectors meant more of them would see the great mountain of the interior. In 1878 two traders, Alfred Mayo and Arthur Harper, ascended the Tanana. On their return, they mentioned to others that an enormous ice mountain was visible to the south. Near the end of the next decade, the well-known pioneer Frank Densmore, who prospected near Lake Minchumina, enthusiastically kept referring to this immense feature to the south: gold seekers informally began calling it "Densmore's Mountain."

The full appreciation of Mount McKinley's magnificence and height was not brought to public attention until William Dickey—a thirty-four-year-old New Englander who had prospected the sands of the Susitna River for gold in 1896, all the while being awed by the immensity of the ice mountain—made a report to the *New York Sun* on January 24, 1897: "We named our great peak Mount McKinley, after William McKinley of Ohio, who had been nominated for the Presidency."[24] Dickey, who was head of his class at Princeton in 1885, and who became a well-known curve-ball pitcher in Seattle, added, "and that fact was the first news we received on our way out of that wonderful wilderness. We have no doubt that this peak is the highest in North America, and estimate that it is over 20,000 feet high."

Dickey indeed made a remarkably accurate estimate of the mountain's height, one not confirmed by surveyors until after the turn of the century. Until then 18,000-foot Mount Saint Elias was believed to be the continent's highest, and Mount Logan was still unknown.

Dickey, who ascended Mount Susitna while in southern Alaska, endured numerous vivid experiences while prospecting. Once he came to a small village of the Kuilchaul (Copper River) Indians. The Kuilchaul, who had no permanent homes and lived in Russian tents, were catching and drying salmon when Dickey arrived. In his newspaper account, he described them as

tall and fine looking, and great hunters. Throughout the long and arduous winter they camp on the trail of the caribou. They build huge fires of logs, then erect a reflector of skins back from the fire, between which reflection and the fire they sleep, practically out of doors, although the temperature reaches 50° below zero.

Dickey learned that he could venture no further with boats, as the Susitna entered an impassable canyon—with a high waterfall at the far end blocking all passage, one not even the Indians had gone to its source. Dickey recalled their exclamations of "Bullshoe" as they raised both hands high above their heads in describing the waterfall.

At the farthest reach of the river, Dickey found a deep, "millrace" current. As he descended the river at "race-horse speed" the bulging waves threatened to swamp their boats. What took one day to ascend took only one hour of rapid descent.

Dickey, whose skills as a raconteur became apparent in his newspaper account, brought the perils of the Alaskan wilderness to the urban reader:

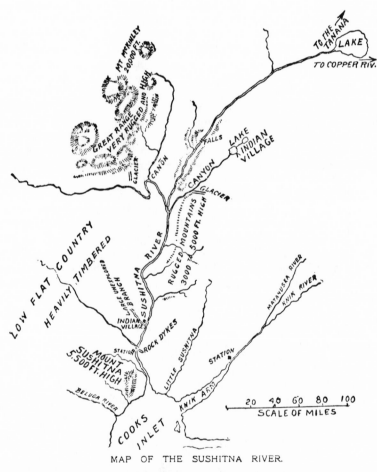

MAP OF THE SUSHITNA RIVER.

Dickey's 1897 map depicts the first appearance of the name "Mt. McKinley." His distances were not to scale, but his effort was admirable.

Many Indians were killed or seriously wounded by the great brown bear, which they hold in great respect. They never bring in the head or claws, although they would bring higher prices at the store with them left on the skin. At Kuskutan last spring a hunter did not return to the village after his daily trips of inspection to his traps. The next morning another brave, axe in hand, went to search for him. He also failed to return, and the next day the whole village went in search of the missing. They found nothing except the axe and huge bear tracks. A few days later an enormous bear chased some of the natives to their very doors, notwithstanding the many wounds inflicted by rifles of the pursued. After that he hung about the village, and although shot many times he would soon return. Just after dark one evening he suddenly appeared at a window of one of the cabins, smashed in the glass, and gave the lamp inside a knock that sent it across the room. Without further ceremony the monster proceeded to climb into the room. Luckily all escaped through the door, and the men finally drove the bear away with no further damage than the wrecking of the furniture. All were now afraid, for surely this must be an evil spirit or shaman, and not an ordinary bear, as bullets seemed to have no effect on him. As a last resort they took some bullets to the church, had special prayers recited and holy water sprinkled over them.

Mount McKinley, then, not Denali, Traleika, or Doleika, stayed in the public eye and on maps. As Hudson Stuck wrote in *The Ascent of Denali,* "No voice was raised in protest, for the Alaskan Indian is inarticulate and such white men as knew the old name were absorbed in the search for gold."[25]

But as Alfred Brooks later wrote in a U.S. Geological Survey Professional Paper,

The world at large paid little heed to Dickey's high peak, for his report was classed as only another of the wild tales which emanated from Alaska; but another discovery about the same time—the Klondike gold— was destined to alter the status of Alaska in the public mind. Then, at last, the Government began to realize its long neglect of this vast possession. Money was appropriated for its development, and among other agents the United States Geological Survey was enabled to begin the series of explorations and surveys which have extended to some of the remotest parts of the Territory.[26]

▲▲▲

Because the Icefield Ranges could be seen from the sea, the standard approach to Alaska late in the century, it was logical that the high coastal mountains would be noticed and explored first. Even the ambitious Israel C. Russell, an explorer-alpinist who had style and vision—one who crossed the Malaspina and Seward glaciers on National Geographic Society expeditions in 1890 and 1891 to Mount Saint Elias—appears to have known little of the early reports of high ranges farther west and north. In his book *Glaciers of North America,* Russell wrote, "In the interior of Alaska and of the adjacent portion of Canada, there are many mountains that reach elevations of at least four or five thousand feet above the sea ... and no glaciers are known to exist upon them."[27] But Russell and others soon learned differently, although Mount McKinley still had no identity.

Russell, however, appreciated Alaska's natural wonders. He wrote, "In purchasing Alaska the United States not only acquired a vast territory rich in natural resources, but added new wonders to her already varied scenery."[28] Seward's wisdom in sighting Alaska's potential in economic resources was compounded by Russell's sense that Alaska's beauty would eventually create a great series of parklands and tourism. Its great distance from the contiguous states shrouded Alaska in myth and, later, even the boom of the great Klondike gold rush did not bring its grand qualities to light.

▲ ▲ ▲

Even though the army had withdrawn from Alaska in 1877, ten years after the purchase, General Nelson A. Miles (Commander of the Department of the Pacific) believed that Alaska fell under his military jurisdiction. Without Congressional approval, Miles funded the expedition undertaken by Lieutenant Frederick Schwatka in 1883 to explore and map the Alaska interior, seizing upon the rumor of native discontent as the pretext.

Although Schwatka was a West Point graduate, he was hardly a typical officer. After receiving a medical degree and admittance to the bar, Schwatka outfitted an expedition in 1879 under the auspices of the American Geographical Society to search for Sir John Franklin (missing in the Arctic since 1847).

After completing the longest sledge journey in history during the two-year quest, Schwatka welcomed Miles' Alaskan support. He climbed over the Chilkoot Pass and then built a raft and floated the Yukon to finally arrive at Fort Selkirk (at the junction of the Pelly). At the Tanana's mouth, the small expedition abandoned its battered raft for a vessel with a jib sail. At some place along the great river, Schwatka must have sighted North America's highest mountain.

The success of Schwatka's expedition inspired General Miles to plan an even more ambitious reconnaissance of the Alaskan interior. For this assignment he chose Lieutenant Henry T. Allen. In seven months during 1885 the ardent officer overcame hostile Native Americans and the dangerous waters of the Copper, Chitina, and Tanana rivers in traveling nearly 2,500 miles. Allen even noted the absence of glacial evidence north of the Alaska Range, and he observed the language similarities between the Copper River natives and the Apaches of the American Southwest. The remarkable Allen certainly saw the high summits of the Wrangell Mountains (such as Mount Sanford, Mount Wrangell, and Mount Drum) but never mentioned the unnamed Mount McKinley in his report. He may have distantly sighted the great Icy Crown as he descended the Tanana River.

It is indeed unfortunate that Denali, Doleika, Tenada, Traleika, or some other euphonious name was not retained for North America's highest mountain. *Denali* is the original Athabascan name, the one used by the Native Americans of the Yukon, Tanana, and Kuskokwim, the ones who hunted the caribou well onto the mountain's flanks. The Susitnas used the name *Doleika,* meaning "the big mountain," and the Aleuts called it *Traleika.*

The Native Americans near Lake Minchumina called Mount Foraker *Sultana*, meaning "his wife."

Alfred Brooks, a geologist by profession, was among the best gatherers and recorders of Alaska's early history. In his impressions concerning Native American names, he wrote,

> *No one can know how many generations of natives have wandered over this region, but it seems certain that the indigenous population was greater at the first coming of the white man than it is now. As the natives depended largely on the chase for subsistence, they must have frequented the slopes of the Alaska Range, and the adjacent lowlands, for this is one of the best game regions in the Northwest. Much of the range formed an almost impassable barrier between the hunting ground of the Cook Inlet natives and that of the Kuskokwim Indians. It does not seem to have been named, for the Alaska Indian has no fixed geographic nomenclature for the larger geographic features. A river will have half a dozen names, depending on the direction from which it is approached....*
>
> *The immense height of Mount McKinley must have impressed the Indian. It was used as a landmark in his journeys. With its twin peak, Mount Foraker, it is interwoven in the folklore of the tribes living within sight of the two giant mountains. The tribes on the east side of the range, who seldom, if ever, approached it, termed it Traleyka, probably signifying big mountain. Those on the northwest side, who hunted the caribou up to the very base of the mountain, called it Tennally.[29]*

The purchase of Alaska from the Russians was made before Yellowstone—the world's first national park—was signed into law in 1872, to serve as a precedent for some 1,200 American national parks. The national parks, which have been called "the best idea America ever had," did not come to Alaska until the second decade of the twentieth century. It was naturalist Charles Sheldon who proposed a national park to surround Mount McKinley, and in 1916 legislation sponsored by Judge James Wickersham was signed by President Woodrow Wilson early the following year. Mineral entry and development was allowed under the national mining laws, a defect in the wilderness aspect of the protected parkland.

Congress expanded Mount McKinley National Park in both 1922 and 1932 and then again in 1980 with an expansion to total six million acres (an area slightly larger than Massachusetts). With a new name, Denali National Park and Preserve to honor the native tradition, the park was enlarged from 3,353 to 9,418 square miles. No other of the world's protected parks have such an altitude differential, ranging from 160 meters (500 feet) to 6,194 meters (20,320 feet).

This last major expansion of the national park system in 1980 came when the U.S. Congress directed additions in Alaska totaling some forty-seven million acres. Still largely remote and unspoiled, they constitute America's greatest promise of a wilderness legacy, one unimpaired for the enjoyment of future generations.

▲▲▲

CHAPTER 2

The Wilderness Explorers of the Alaska Range

Alaskan exploration, under the best of conditions, is a severe strain on the endurance of the average man.
Alfred H. Brooks
"The Mount McKinley Region, Alaska," 1911

The exploration of the Alaska Range was not seriously considered until after gold had been discovered in the Cook Inlet district and the madness of the Klondike Stampede had ended. When Israel C. Russell was making his two gallant attempts on Mount Saint Elias in the 1890s—then believed to be the apex of North America—a mountain of even greater stature in central Alaska, known to the Athabascans as *Denali,* or "the Great One," was ignored by the Russian and American fur trappers, gold seekers, and other pioneers. High mountains held no interest to those with economic or life-support pursuits.

For the pioneering explorers of the Alaska Range, there were immense psychological barriers, including the lack of reliable maps and travel through virtually unknown wilderness such as forests with their taxing muskeg bogs, fearsome river crossings, dangerous canyons, and the torturous mosquitoes. The early explorers who ventured into this mountain range represented an enduring testament to human spirit.

In 1898, more than thirty years after the territorial acquisition, the U.S. Geological Survey began its extensive Alaskan explorations—ranging in scope from the Copper River to the Yukon River and Bristol Bay. Of six parties sent that year, all had memorable adventures, and some were classic epics that relied on ingenuity simply to survive.

The government expedition that came nearest to Mount McKinley that year was that led by George H. Eldridge and Robert H. Muldrow, who made the first triangulated determination of the height and position of the mountain. With five camp hands these hardy men made their way along the difficult Susitna River, dragging loaded canoes against the swift cur-

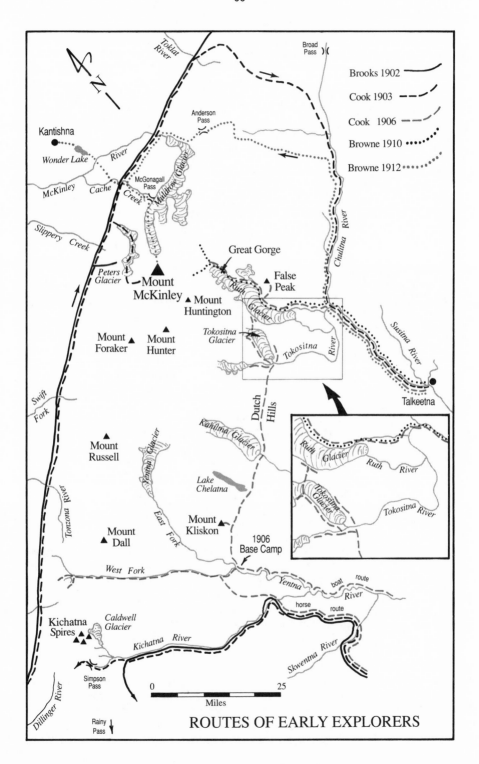

ROUTES OF EARLY EXPLORERS

rent just as Malakoff had a half century before. At the head of navigation (Indian Creek), the party pushed on overland, crossing to the Nenana River while investigating routes for a railroad or wagon road. The topographer Muldrow made a professional instrumental determination of Mount McKinley's altitude—settling on 20,464 feet.[30]

Also in that summer, the geologist Josiah E. Spurr[31] and topographer William S. Post of the Survey undertook the first crossing of the great Alaska Range. These men, with three others, ascended the Skwentna River (a western fork of the Susitna) and then the Yentna River to cross the range at Simpson Pass (not far from some of Alaska's most stupendous collection of granitic spires and monoliths, today known as the Kichatna Spires). Like others later, Spurr and Post found the wilderness route filled with spruce bogs, swamps, endless ponds, and stream oxbows. Their canoes repeatedly overturned in the wild, rushing rivers. As provisions ran low, the party portaged two canoes, finally reaching the Kuskokwim drainage. Boldly chancing the unknown waterways, they entered a rocky canyon where a boulder upset a canoe; the men only barely escaped. The party finally reached Bristol Bay and the Bethel mission; they then crossed the Aleutian Range via Katmai Pass to Cook Inlet. This episode, lasting from May to November, was a daring and historic exploration, but its course was well southwest of Mount McKinley.

Another official expedition of 1898 was that led by Willard J. Peters, with Alfred H. Brooks attending as geologist. While traversing the Tanana River, the expedition members sighted the icy peaks of the Alaska Range and the glittering Mount McKinley 150 miles away. The enterprising Brooks would return in four years.

Some inkling of what was required for the government surveyors is given in an unpublished history of the U.S. Geological Survey. The first prerequisite was a sturdy physique and experience in backpacking heavy loads. The next necessity was a familiarity with camp life, horses, and small boats. The men would have to cope with unexpected problems in the Alaskan wilderness, so dedication and good sense was important. The field party chief was traditionally the geologist, with his assistant chief the topographer.

The Survey work did possess attractions. The field season, although quite strenuous, was only some three months long, with relaxing ocean voyages along the coast at both ends of this tenure. In addition, the men could expect six to seven months of comfortable office work in Washington, D.C.

▲▲▲

For sheer determination and miraculous survival, it would be difficult to surpass the exploit of Lieutenant Joseph S. Herron of the 8th U.S. Cavalry in the summer of 1899. Herron crossed the Alaska Range via Simpson Pass, as had Spurr and Post, to the Kuskokwim River and then explored in a different direction—northward to the Yukon. En route he named the mountain known to the natives as "Denali's wife" Mount Foraker, for Ohio Senator Joseph Foraker.[32]

Lieutenant Herron's exploration was prompted by army headquarters to locate an "American" route from Pacific Ocean ports to the interior gold fields of the upper Yukon River. The army explorer took six men, two native guides, and a pack train of fifteen horses from Cook Inlet into the boggy muskeg forest to the Yentna and Kichatna rivers, with part of the outfit coming by launch to the upper Yentna. As others before and after him on this difficult traverse to the river's headwaters, Herron had to search for river crossings, make dangerous fords, and find passages through canyons and swamps. The party had to chop out a pack train trail in the timber and brush, sometimes build spar bridges for the horses, and lay out corduroy log trails in the boggy and muddy going. It was imperative to find dry campsites. Each day the horses had to be packed and unpacked, allowed to graze, and rounded up. One of Herron's statements from his report is from June 30:

> *The steamboat left us [on the upper Yentna].... The fifteen pack horses, tied on a picket line, were fed their last ration of oats and over 3,000 pounds of our rations and other impedimenta were piled up on the ground.*

At night, after unpacking and washing backs, the packers had to oil the ears, eyes, "and other favorite mosquito resorts" of the horses. The morning roundup was not easy, for the animals' wanderings in search of feed and relief from mosquitoes involved much tedious trailing ... and scouring the country for miles. Each morning, axes had to be sharpened for the day's trail cutting, and each night wet blankets and clothes had to be dried.

Lieutenant Herron's first objective was to cross the Alaska Range, which, as he explained it, was "a mass of enormous peaks and glaciers about 70 miles wide extending across Alaska and constituting the chief barrier to the interior. The task of crossing the range required the month of July." Herron's report continued:

> *The first day's march was through dense timber and over soft ground. The packs were heavy, the lash ropes stiff, and the horses frolicsome. They stampeded back on the trail at every opportunity, raced through the woods, knocked off packs, plunged into mud holes, bogged down, and it required eleven hours of patient toil to make that short march.*[33]

On July 10 Herron's Native American guides informed him that it would be impossible to push the horses over the divide, "that it consisted of vertical rock cliffs, and that the Indians who crossed had to use their hands in climbing over. I told them we should make efforts to get over."[34] One of the animals fell that day, knocking down a man and both rolling down a steep bluff, but luckily the event caused no serious injury.

"During the following six days," Herron wrote, "the Indians informed me that they 'saveyed' (knew) the country no further."[35] Despite his proposal that they climb to the summit of the mountains for a reconnaissance, which they did on the 16th, the natives still wanted to go back. Their repeated warning was "one month snow." Daily efforts were made to persuade the expedition to abandon its course.

The monotony of progress was relieved on the 19th with the discovery of the pass over the divide (Simpson's Pass, as Herron later mapped the location). "I camped in the last clump of trees, our elevation now being at the timber line, and prepared to reconnoiter the pass," Herron wrote.

Stepan shot, about a mile from this camp, a large bull moose. The animal was not far from 20 hands high and very fat, the antlers in velvet state. The fresh meat was welcome after a diet of bacon. The Indians consider the soft outer edge of the horns a great delicacy, likewise the nose, the sole of the hoof, the intestines, and the marrow of the bones....

While in this pass I came upon two enormous brown bears, asleep.... Led by the Indian Slinkta, I crawled around to the leeward, and then approached them, too near, I thought to myself, as I had a poor gun, only a few cartridges, and the nearest tree was 5 miles away. Slinkta whistled and awoke the bears, while I fired and shot the larger one in the head, but only staggered him. He arose and passed a swinging right-hander at the other bear, but missed him. They got away. The same day Jones and Webster were chased by a brown bear, near the glacier at the end of the Keechatno....

The 22nd of July we crossed the crest of the divide and started down the other side of the watershed. East of the divide the drainage is into the Pacific Ocean; west of it into Bering Sea.[36]

In the camp's vicinity on July 23, hundreds of mountain sheep were seen near the divide above. Three of Herron's men climbed the mountains and shot two of them. Five days later the two Native American guides deserted the expedition.

Having exhausted all their arguments to persuade me to turn back, Slinkta and Stepan, theretofore faithful and energetic, slipped out of camp, deserted, and went back to the coast. There being no other Indians in that section of the country at that time, the loss of my natives was a severe blow to the expedition. It was not unexpected, however. I had previously considered the question of putting a guard over them day and night, but had decided it to be impracticable.... I proceeded, all of us redoubling our efforts, did my own guiding, and traveled by compass and the sun.[37]

In early August, as the men traversed the piedmont plateau northeastward, they found three deserted Indian villages. On August 18 they discovered Chedotlothno:

It consisted of two cabins of hewn logs, a cache, and a graveyard. In one cabin was a sled, a pair of snowshoes, a stove, a knife, spearhead, and some pictures of Russian divinities and prophets.

August 25, I lost two pack horses by their having been snagged, one in the abdomen and one in a lung. I was obliged to abandon the canvas canoe here on that account. August 25 to September 1 brought us to higher and firmer ground.

About September 1st frosts at night killed off the mosquitoes; also the grass and leaves.... A violent earthquake occurred at 2 p. m. on the 3d. A sack of evaporated potatoes was punctured and leaked out on the trail about this time, which ended our potato diet.[38]

On September 4, Herron cached some food and supplies in order to reconnoiter from higher ground. While the men were gone, a bear knocked down the cache and devoured their remaining fifty pounds of bacon. Unknown to Herron, a native crossed the bear's trail, tracked the animal to its hole, and killed it. After discovering that the bear had "been indulging in bacon," the native went out to search for the expedition, whose presence was unknown to him. Herron wrote, "We owe much to that bear, and as we helped to eat him we were not out much by the loss of the bacon."[39]

Rations proved so low on September 8 that Herron finally ordered the pack saddles and equipment permanently cached, turned out the horses to fend for themselves, and started to explore down the river on rafts. The early frost had killed the grass, the horses were starving, and the party was lost in the timbered lowland of the upper Kuskokwim River. Rafting would hopefully lead to the Tanana and native villages. The river, however, was "crooked, full of snags and sweepers, and dangerous for rafting. Eight miles down began a series of log jams extending entirely across the river. Rafting was a succession of collisions and clashes," Herron recounted.[40]

Predictably, the rafting venture ended in failure, and the men had to continue on foot, "making packs so large and heavy that progress was a continuous performance of wrestling, the pack having the advantage of a double-Nelson hold and the assistance of the brush and timber." The first snowfall had loaded the trees until they bent under its weight. "Then, as we pushed through the brush, each tree dropped a small avalanche on our heads and kept our clothes wet, while snow on the ground added to the labor and discomfort of walking and kept our feet wet."[41]

On the 16th, fresh blazes on the trees and other signs led Herron and his men to believe they were now near natives—and in three days they met one,

> who, I later learned, was the one who had killed the bear that had robbed our cache.... It is needless to say that we gave him a welcome, sincere if not verbose, our mutual vocabulary consisting of three words, "yes," "no," and "good," and the Indian seemed to think them synonymous at times, but the deficiency was made good by pantomime. I learned his name to be "Shesoie."[42]

The negotiations to hire him as a guide and setting a time to start forward required eight days; then they packed some twenty-five miles to Shesoie's village, Telida (on the Tatlathna River). Here Herron and his men set up camp for two months, making winter clothes and socks out of their horse blankets and procuring mitts, fur caps, moccasins, and snowshoes from the natives. Herron continued his narrative:

> Our food during this period was chiefly moose, bear, beaver, fish, and tea. The Indians were hospitable, but childish, requiring careful management. In our condition we were in their power and we knew it, but they were our prisoners and they did not know it. There was to be no deserting us this time. Before the two months had elapsed, however, I had gained their entire confidence and friendship.[43]

On November 25, with four native guides, the party resumed their travel, the conditions now favorable for snowshoeing. On December 11 they reached Fort Gibbon on the Yukon River, at the mouth of the Tanana River, to end a "summer" expedition that had taken more than five months.

▲▲▲

In the summer of 1902, the unforgettable geologist Alfred H. Brooks and his colleague, the topographer Dewitt L. Reaburn, both thirty-one years of age, made a historic reconnaissance through the unexplored Alaska Range, discovering and crossing Rainy Pass and then passing along the western and northwestern flank of the range. They were the first white men to come near Denali. The Brooks journey has since come to be considered one of the classic explorations in Alaska, and his report in a U.S. Geological Survey Professional Paper was a scholarly and thorough review of the history, topography, and geology of the great range.

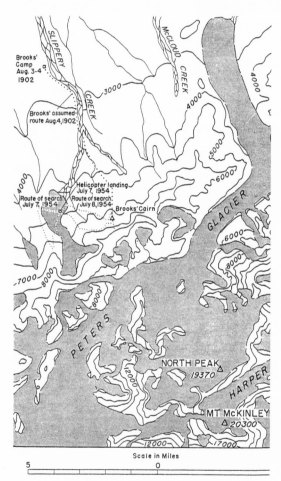

The official Survey expedition which Brooks headed also included Louis M. Prindle to cooperate in geological investigations, Fred Printz and W. W. von Canon as packers, and George Revine as cook. Unlike Lieutenant Herron, Brooks did not rely on native guides. The contemplated journey was longer than any similar one yet made in Alaska with packhorses; therefore, it was important to select horses with endurance.

Reaburn was placed in charge of obtaining the best animals he could find—located in North Yakima (eastern Washington). Of twenty horses, eighteen were buckskins, bays, and sorrels—all fitted with sawbuck pack-saddles, strong breeching, and breast straps. Once in the field, with a load totaling 3,500 pounds, bags were used to pack provisions; three horses carried light wooden boxes as side packs.

This modern map displays the 1902 route of Alfred H. Brooks to his cairn northwest of Mount McKinley, and the route taken during the search for this monument in 1954 by John C. Reed, Jr. (courtesy American Alpine Journal*)*

Most of the expedition's food was dried, the allocation being 3½ pounds per man per day. In addition to the usual staples of flour, bacon, beans, rice, and sugar, there were evaporated peaches, pears, apricots, plums, and nectarines. Other nourishing items to provide variety to the diet were currants, raisins, cheese, dried eggs, condensed soup, chocolate, coffee, condensed cream, and tea.

Most of the provisions were packed in paraffin bags each holding fifty pounds of food. These were inserted into heavy canvas bags and tied in a manner so that no water could enter if the pack was submerged, "a wisdom," Brooks later wrote. During the 3½-month journey, the horses often rolled into the water. With such careful packing, only once were provisions ruined.

Each man had two hiking shoes, a head net, and gauntlet gloves. Twelve-pound sleeping bags were made up of two woolen bags with a duck cover. The Brooks expedition took three cotton wall tents that weighed ten pounds each and one eight-by-ten-foot cook tent. There were numerous axes, two .30-30 carbines, a .22 caliber rifle, 750 rounds of ammunition, and a folding canoe with oars (an awkward load for a horse).

Each geologist carried a Brunton pocket theodolite, an aneroid barometer, a hammer, a camera, and Zeiss field glasses. For the extensive topographic program, there was a plane table, a tripod fitted with new movement, a telescope alidade, a theodolite, a barometer, and a thermometer. Reaburn's sightings and later computations resulted in a reliable measurement of Mount McKinley: his figure of 20,300 feet was accepted for the next fifty-two years.

The Brooks expedition left Seattle on the *Santa Ana* on May 13, 1902, arriving at Tyonek on the 27th. While the horse party toiled through muskeg and swamp to a camp on the Skwentna River, a boat took some supplies up the river systems. During this initial portion of the expedition, Reaburn made a plane-table station on the summit of Mount Susitna. From here he was able to take the azimuth of Mount McKinley (almost due north), which helped his accuracy in determining the longitude all season.

A week after leaving Tyonek, "the good traveling came to an end all too soon, and we plunged into the thick growth of timber covering the floor of the Yentna Valley," wrote Brooks in *Journal of Geography*. On June 18, upon reaching the Yentna's banks,

> the turbulent, silt-bearing waters, coursing through a score of channels, did not look inviting, and we had grave doubts whether a crossing could be made.... Mounted on two of the stronger horses, from which the saddles had been stripped, Fred and I managed to ford some of the streams, though the horses barely kept their footing in the rushing waters which reached their shoulders.... The unwilling animals were urged into the first [channel] and in a moment were swept off their feet by the muddy torrent, which for an instant engulfed both riders and horses and bore them down stream at a terrific rate. By almost instinctive movement, we threw ourselves from the struggling brutes, seized them by their manes and swam alongside, thus at length guiding them back to the bank. We dragged ourselves out, both we and the horses shivering from our ducking in the icy water.[44]

After much trail cutting, Brooks and his pack train arrived at the Kichatna River, here finding the men with the boat waiting.

The Keechatna was a less turbulent stream than the Yentna, and with the aid of the boat a crossing was effected without difficulty.

We now parted with Eberhardt and Anderson, who returned to Tyonok, taking the last letters we should be able to send out. Thenceforth until we reached the Yukon, about three months later, we were to be entirely cut off from the rest of the world.

The outlook was not encouraging, for we had nearly 700 miles of practically unknown territory to traverse, and the incessant labor of toiling through the swamp, added to the continual annoyance from mosquitoes and horse-flies, was having a serious effect upon the strength of our horses. Night after night we would hear the tinkle of the bell-horse as he led the band of horses, maddened by the insects, back and forth. Though we blanketed them and built large fires as smudges, they seldom got relief for more than two or three hours of the twenty-four. It was terrible to see their suffering and be powerless to help them. They would frequently crowd into camp as if to implore us to relieve them from their misery.

The men, too, were becoming worn out by the mosquito pest, which harassed them continually during the day, though they found relief at night in the mosquito-proof tents. The soft blanket of moss, usually saturated with moisture, which nearly everywhere covers the face of the country, offers a breeding-ground for myriads of the insects. They are ever active, both day and night; on the mountain-tops far above timber as well as in the lowlands. Five years of Alaskan travel have convinced me that there is no hardship so difficult to bear as this insect pest. I have seen horses, fairly maddened by the torment, blindly charge through the forest, oblivious to the trees and branches encountered, until they wore themselves out; then, in utter hopelessness, drop their heads and patiently endure the suffering. I have seen strong men, after days and nights of almost incessant torment, when they were too weary to offer further resistance to their relentless foes, weep with vexation. No part of an Alaskan traveler's outfit is more important than his mosquito-proof headdress and gloves. The former is made to fit closely around the rim of his hat and to his shoulders, for the mosquitoes will find the smallest opening. Unfortunately, the headdress has only too often to be discarded. When pushing through the undergrowth, using a surveying instrument, sighting a rifle or chopping a trail, the traveler is at the mercy of the mosquitoes, which follow him in clouds. While every other hardship of Alaskan travel is often grossly exaggerated, it is hardly possible to do this one justice. Men capable of enduring heat and cold, hunger and fatigue without murmuring, will become almost savage under the torture. However, the story told me by an old prospector of the days on "Fortymile," when he could wave a pint cup over his head and catch a quart of mosquitoes, did seem somewhat beyond the bounds of probability.[45]

The swamps and muskeg drained the vitality of the horses. Just when the supply of fresh meat was getting low, a convenient shot by Printz's carbine at a moose that walked into camp "gave us a welcome supply." At last the men found a pass long used by the natives—one Brooks called Rainy Pass simply because of the dismal wetness of the crossing on July 15.

This defile, which leads to the waters of the Kuskokwim, is about 2,950 feet above sea level and some twelve miles southwest of where Spurr and Lieutenant Herron crossed.

In another twenty miles the Brooks party veered to the northeast into territory completely unknown to white men. The party traversed along the inner margin of a gravel plateau for 100 miles to the base of Mount McKinley with relative ease. Here they found good footing for the horses on the smooth, moss-covered surface of the plateau, which was covered by glacial outwash. There was ample grass for the animals and always enough dry willow for cooking.

On August 3 Brooks made camp along Slippery Creek, some thirteen miles northwest of the summit of Denali (the location was three miles northeast of Peters Dome). In *Journal of Geography,* Brooks noted that the camp was located "in a broad, shallow valley incised in the piedmont plateau." He decided to allow one day's delay to set foot on the mountain's slopes, although his "mission was exploration and surveying, not mountaineering." But Brooks lamented, now that he was close to its glaciers, "It ... seemed very hard to us that we had neither time nor equipment to attempt the mastery of this highest peak of the continent." He continued,

> The next morning dawned clear and bright. Climbing the bluff above our camp, I overlooked the upper part of the valley, spread before me like a broad amphitheatre, its sides formed by the slopes of the mountain and its spurs. Here and there glistened in the sun the white surfaces of glaciers which found their way down from the peaks above. The great mountain rose 17,000 feet above our camp, apparently almost sheer from the flat valley floor. Its dome-shaped summit and upper slopes were white with snow, relieved here and there by black areas which marked cliffs too steep for the snow to lie upon.
>
> A two hours' walk across the valley, through several deep glacial streams, brought me to the very base of the mountain. As I approached the top was soon lost to view; the slopes were steep and I had to scramble as best I could. Soon all vegetation was left behind me, and my way zigzagged across smooth, bare rocks and talus slopes of broken fragments. My objective point was a shoulder of the mountain about 10,000 feet high, but at three in the afternoon I found my route blocked by a smooth expanse of ice. With the aid of my geologic pick I managed to cut steps in the slippery surface, and thus climbed a hundred feet higher; then the angle of slope became steeper, and as the ridge on which the glacier lay fell off at the sides in sheer cliffs, a slip would have been fatal. Convinced at length that it would be utterly fool-hardy, alone as I was, to attempt to reach the shoulder for which I was headed, at 7,500 feet I turned and cautiously retraced my steps, to find the descent to bare ground more perilous than the ascent.
>
> I had now consumed all the time that could be spared to explore this mountain which had been reached at the expense of so much preparation and hard toil; but at least I must leave a record to mark our highest point. On a prominent cliff near the base of the glacier, which had turned me back, I built a cairn in which I buried a cartridge-shell from my pistol,

containing a brief account of the journey together with a roster of the party....
    *As I sat resting from my labors, I surveyed a striking scene. Around me
were bare rock, ice and snow; not a sign of life,—the silence broken now
and then by the roar of an avalanche loosened by the midday sun,
tumbling like a waterfall over some cliff to find a resting-place thousands
of feet below. I gazed along the precipitous slopes of the mountain and
tried to realize again its great altitude, with a thrill of satisfaction at being
the first man to approach the summit, which was only nine miles from
where I smoked my pipe. No white man had ever before reached the base,
and I was far beyond, where the moccasined foot of the roving Indian had
never trod. The Alaskan native seldom goes beyond the limit of smooth
walking and has a superstitious horror of even approaching glacial ice.[46]*

The Brooks party now continued to skirt the base of the Alaska Range
as far as the Nenana River (then called the Cantwell). They then descended
to the Tanana River to reach the Yukon at the village of Rampart on
September 18. After being in the wilderness for 105 days, Brooks and his
party made a vast contribution to the knowledge of the Alaska Range.
Certainly the geologic information he obtained, the pioneering exploration,
and the mapping by Reaburn was a monumental achievement for only one
season's labor.

▲ ▲ ▲

In July 1954 John C. Reed of the U.S. Geological Survey searched for
Brooks' visitation, aided by a helicopter. Climbing above the "slippery
glacier" and then traversing slopes to its east, he located the cairn at an
elevation of about 6,500 feet. The cairn consisted of four or five rocks piled
over a small hollow in the large boulder which contained a .30-30 cartridge,
wrapped in a cloth tobacco sack (Maryland Club Mixture). Since the cairn
had been erected by Brooks on August 6, 1902, at least an inch of moss had
grown between the rocks.

In less than one year, the geologist Brooks would be followed by another
expedition, led and organized by Dr. Frederick A. Cook, whose aspirations
were to scale Mount McKinley. Cook traveled 5,000 miles from New York
to find that the enormous task of getting to the base of the mountain had
just begun. Despite all the later condemnation given him, Cook undertook
a dauntless journey, taking only nine weeks to reach Peters Glacier—
essentially guided by that expert packer Fred Printz. Cook's pen captured
the essence of the Alaskan wilderness challenge, one faced by all the early
explorers from Spurr to Brooks:

*The thick underbrush, the endless marshes, and the myriads of vicious
mosquitoes bring to the traveller the troubles of the tropics. The necessity
of fording and swimming icy streams, the almost perpetual cold rains, the
camps in high altitudes on glaciers in snows and violent storms bring to
the traveller all of the discomforts of the arctic explorer.[47]*

▲ ▲ ▲

CHAPTER 3

Judge Wickersham Discovers Gold and Finds a Glacier on Mount McKinley

The oftener one gazes upon its stupendous mass, the stronger becomes the inclination to visit its base and spy out its surroundings.
James Wickersham
Old Yukon Tales, Trails, and Trials, 1938

Judge James Wickersham, who in 1898 was elected to the legislature by the people of Alaska, and who oversaw the American courts delve into the rough-and-tumble wilderness disputes of miners and frontiersmen, wanted to "spy out the surroundings" of Mount McKinley after he had repeatedly seen the great mountain during his territorial travels. During his encounters in the Alaska "floating court," he had been advised by the Tena Indians, a branch of the Athabascans, that to best reach Denali he should travel up the Kantishna River to its glacier source and make the ascent from there. The Native Americans, of course, saw Denali as a background to a plentiful hunting paradise like no other on earth and had no need to venture onto the mountain's bodies of ice.

During Wickersham's diverse courtroom trials as U.S. District Judge for Alaska, he encountered men and women of many sorts, including vagabond prospectors, dishonest gamblers, harlots, Native Americans, homesteaders, and even the good Archdeacon of the Yukon, Hudson Stuck.[48] Once, after holding a week of court in Eagle City, the former Illinoisan met Captain Barnette, a Fairbanks merchant and miner.[49] The captain asked Wickersham to accompany him on his return to Fairbanks on sleds, taking the wintry trail via Circle City. Wickersham related a bizarre encounter on its streets in his unforgettable story of these times, *Old Yukon Tales, Trails, and Trials:*

While walking down the street to the A. C. Co.'s Circle City store, to purchase some supplies for our trip over the mountains to Fairbanks, I met two handsomely dressed young Russian Indian creole girls. As they passed, the younger beauty smiled at me most bewitchingly with the evident purpose of attracting my attention. Judicial dignity and male vanity fought it out as their unfortunate subject strode down the street. An hour later as I left the store, they slowly approached me again; they were certainly lying in wait to make my acquaintance! A short time later they again confronted me, this time on a quiet side street. As they approached the little charmer looked me full in the face with such an entrancing smile as to be irresistible. As they drew near, she sidled away from her companion and barred my passage. I was so flustered that a soft and mellow voice made but little impression upon my receptive faculties, for my reply to her inquiry was an astonished "Huh?" She drew closer as she repeated it— "How much you charge for deevorce?"—The impudent little hussy! So that's what she wanted! The very idea of chasing a judge around a Circle City block three times to ask such a question. I suppose she thought I carried a ready-made supply of "deevorces" around in my pocket to sell to desirous and desirable young ladies on the street. I advised her to go hire a lawyer, but learned later that she had run away with a husky mate off one of the A. C. Co.'s steamboats without troubling to get a "deevorce." "Oh, ho, hum" said the judge, when he saw Maud Muller making hay.[50]

From the moment Wickersham reached the Tanana Valley, he longed to approach the mountain, and now the opportunity was finally at hand. In the small mining communities, word of the planned ascent spread rapidly. Finding mountaineers during those times was impossible, but there were many hardy and athletic candidates. In the judge's words,

Many adventurous persons offered to go, but only the young and vigorous were accepted—men who were physically sound and would go from love of adventure and pay their share of the expense. George Jeffrey, court stenographer and a good amateur photographer, his friend, Mort Stevens, six feet tall and an all-round athlete, and Charlie Webb, packer and woodsman, were accepted. They chose the fourth and last man, John McLeod, the interpreter for Da-yin-nun, the medicine man of Too-whun-na. McLeod was the son of a Hudson Bay Company trader and was born on the Liard river in British America. He had spent the greater part of his life on the lower Mackenzie river, principally at Fort McPherson, from which point he crossed Rat portage and thence down the Porcupine to Fort Yukon the previous year. He spoke the Tena languages—all the northern Tena dialects. He was hunter, canoeman, and trapper and knew the wilderness as well as his foster-brothers, the Indians. He, too, wished to go to the great mountain and we accepted him. The two other members of the party were Mark and Hannah, so named in honor of Hon. Marcus Alonzo Hanna, of Ohio, the friend of President McKinley, after whom Dickey had named the mountain. Billie Robertson had driven Mark at the head of his double-ender sled from Dawson to Fairbanks that spring, and Hannah, too, had hauled a grubstake load over the same trail. They were thoroughbred Kentucky mules, young and strong, yet learned in the ways of pack-saddles and mountain trails, and their owners, in their enthusiasm, had offered them as transporters and carriers of packs. They were the only mules to be had in the Tanana valley and were, of course, gladly accepted. The personnel of our party was thus completed![51]

When the ice broke on the Tanana River, the Wickersham party could progress to the Kantishna River by boat. A chronicler of the time related how the party departed from Fairbanks on May 16, 1903, on the *Isabelle* with considerable fanfare. At Chena, the last outpost of civilization along the route, the party disembarked to obtain additional supplies (the purchase was financed by the judge).

Wickersham noted, "The people of Fairbanks are greatly interested in our expedition, and more than a hundred came with us to the lower town on the *Isabelle*. They escorted us with flags flying and the dance hall band."[52] Privately, he suspected that the true purpose of this enthusiasm was to let it be known that the expedition was from Fairbanks, not Chena, and also that the river between the two towns was navigable all the way to the former. His narrative from *Old Yukon Tales* continued:

> *Our supplies consisted of flour, bacon, beans, dried apples, prunes, three hundred feet of good rope, alpenstocks, footwear, and one hundred pounds of rolled oats and a bale of hay for the mules. After stowing our equipment we had a good dinner, cooked on a real stove by a real Yankee woman from Massachusetts, after which we cast off and started down the Tanana river at 9:30 p. m., though the sun was yet above the horizon. The Chief is pushing a small barge into whose open hold we loaded our packs and the mules.*
>
> *May 17, 1903. We passed the Indian village of Tawtilla, at the mouth of the Nenana or Cantwell river, early this morning. Some years ago a famous prospector and hunter by the name of Frank Dinsmore reached this point on a prospecting trip and explored the Nenana up to the gorge. He reported the existence of large coal seams in that neighborhood and told his friends at Circle of a high mountain to the southwest, which was called Dinsmore's mountain until Dickey gave it the name of Mount McKinley. We overtook a small flat-bottomed steamer called the Jennie M. belonging also to Hendricks and Belt. That enterprising firm put their freight from Weare or Tanana, on the north bank, across the Yukon and a few miles up the Tanana river early in the spring while the Yukon winter ice was solid, and now hope to make a quick return to Chena and enjoy big profits thereon before other freight can reach camp. Ducks and geese are resting on every sand bar, and clouds of these summer visitors are winging their way to their northern nesting places.*[53]

When the judge's party reached the Kantishna's mouth, Captain Hendricks agreed to take them upriver another day's distance. Continuing in *Old Yukon Tales*, Wickersham penned, "Owing to the swift current at the mouth of the Kantishna ... we had much trouble and delay in getting into the side stream, but finally after much puffing and smoking our craft worked up to the point where the current was more confined and regular, the river deeper and navigation easier."[54] The steamer plied along during the night hours and at 6:00 A.M. arrived at a large expanse of quiet water.

> *[The Kantishna] shores are well timbered and fertile. It is a beautiful virgin country, and our boat is the first to enter its waters. It is a glorious spring day; birds sing in the birch and spruce forests along the river*

banks; innumerable waterfowl—ducks, geese, and swan—are in the sky. Far across the evergreen valley ahead of us the distant summits of the snowy range sparkle in the sunshine. The landscape nearby bears no resemblance to an Arctic land; it more nearly resembles a scene in the lower valley of the Mississippi.

Sail ho! The Tanana Chief cast anchor in midstream as a canoe came alongside. The solitary occupant greeted us with surprise but evident pleasure. His name is Butte Aitken and he tells he has hunted and trapped along the river near the Toclat all winter. His boat is filled with bales of furs gathered on his lonely expedition, which has now lasted for nearly a year. He quit his hunting and trapping camp and started down stream toward civilization.[55]

The Wickersham expedition arrived at the camp of Nachereah, the moose hunter, on May 19. "Fifty Athabascans and a hundred malamute dogs gazed at us inquiringly," he penned. "When our mules were put off the boat at midnight the natives gathered in open-mouthed wonder."[56] Almost immediately these strange animals were dubbed as "white man's moose." While every dog strained at the leash to chase them, the judge employed a guard while they slept that night.

After a bountiful spring hunt, the Athabascans were now on their way back to the fish camps at the Yukon–Tanana River junction. Everyone in the camp appeared well fed, including the dogs, and the judge could not help but notice their ingenuity:

These Apaches of the Yukon have learned the art of securing their dogs so they cannot chew off their leashings and return to distant camps or rob the tent and cache. They cut a hole in the flattened end of a small pole: a heavy thong of moose hide is tied around the dog's neck and through this hole so as to bring the pole close up to the neck; the other end of the pole, which is five feet or more in length, is securely tied to a tree, but with some freedom in movement so the dog can travel round the tree but cannot reach the leashing. Thus tied, the dog cannot cut the thong at his neck or at the tree, nor can he chew the pole itself. The Indian hunter is now assured he may not be abandoned in a distant forest camp with a heavily loaded sled and no cur to furnish motive power.[57]

Wickersham disdained the Indian dog, referring to it as "a vagabond and thief" and accusing it of stealing caches and cleverly prying its way into mining cabins with great ingenuity.

The adventurers watched the Athabascans with great interest as they built their birchbark canoes, using ribs of stout birch wood; these were shaped with knives and tied in place with spruce roots to longitudinal strips of split spruce, thus preparing the framework for the birchbark covering.

In this Tena shipyard, the ways were built on a sandy riverbank; posts were driven into the ground on the outer line of the frame, to which the ribs were fastened with thongs. The canoe's frame was leashed until the craft was ready for launching.

To obtain the bark, sheets were stripped from a living tree when the sap rose in the spring. The master hand then cut plates of bark to fit the canoe frame, allowing for overlaps in the sewing process—usually done by the squaws. Squatting on the ground, the women sewed sheets together and to the ribs with root threads, using a bone awl to open the way for insertion. Meanwhile, the master carved and shaped the bow and stern posts, ran spruce pitch into cracks and small holes, and painted the whole framework red. When completed, the canoe was a beautiful and graceful craft, used to reach the fish camps along Kantishna River in the summer season.

EXPLORATIONS IN ALASKA, 1903

The Kantishna River Route to MOUNT McKINLEY

MAP

Showing the Kantishna River Trail followed by the Wickersham party to the Hanna Glacier, thence on Mount McKinley and from the mountain down the McKinley Fork and the Kantishna River, in the summer of 1903; copied from the original map sent to the National Geographic Magazine with letter of October 15, 1903.

This historic map from the Honorable Judge James A. Wickersham shows his route from Fairbanks to the Peters Glacier in May, June, and July 1903.

The magistrate called the river valley "a happy home-spit in a hunter's paradise." Everywhere there were signs of moose, and on the high open slopes the party saw bands of white-fleeced Dall sheep. Wood for fires was everywhere abundant. So were snowshoe rabbits, mink, marten, and fox. On May 20 caribou steaks, purchased from a hunter, were garnished with crisp bacon and browned on an open fire. Webb's best coffee and biscuits were added to the fare.

Their progress was by mule on land and the small *Mudlark* on water propelled by poling and oars. When the judge's party arrived at another village, they called at a wigwam to pay their respects to the *sachem*.

> When we entered he rose and received us with a native modesty and simplicity that adorns and ennobles the primitive man. He is blind, slender and rather tall, though well-proportioned, and about fifty years of age. He enjoys the blessings and labor of two wives; the youngest is an active bright-eyed Tena Hebe, who keeps the chieftain's home cheerful and neat and his moccasins dry; the elder tans mephitic moose hides, and prepares odorous salmon for the drying rack, beneath which she keeps the fire asmudge that the fish may be dry and brittle for the well-worn teeth of her master, and keeps away fish-loving malemute dogs with a club and

a raucous voice. In civilized lands, or in a Circle City court, the old lady would have had the law on the co-respondent long ago, and possibly alimony of at least two of Koonah's best dogs and one moose hide per annum, but here in Tenaland she snares rabbits for the household and sleeps by the blaze under the fish rack.

Today we put Mark and Hannah across the Kantishna river, which is threateningly at high-water, much against their will. A mule loves the water as a cat does, but like that animal can swim if thrown into the stream. We first led Hannah gently to the high bank above the wide and rolling torrent and kindly invited her to enter and swim, as if it were an ordinary everyday matter, but she backed away, shaking her big ears in violent negation. Again and again we courteously led her to the jumping off place, begging and pleading with her to "be nice, old girl, it's all right," only to be denied in the most positive manner. Finally Webb made an unsportsmanlike kick, took a rough-mouth hitch over her head with a long, heavy rope, the other end of which lay coiled in the stern of the Mudlark, which was hanging to the bank.... Another rope was flung behind her with pressure where it would be most efficacious and with all hands on the hoisting rope we gave her a sudden rush over the bank, with a parting kick, and landed her broadside on the river current. The crew of the Mudlark hastily pushed off as they saw her strike the water and drawing her head rope taut, towed her ashore. We made short work of Mark and thus brought our quadrupedal companions into the village, whose inhabitants, biped and canine, lined the home bank and howled in happy unison at the first circus performance ever exhibited in Tenaland.[58]

The judge noted the maps of the region were incorrect in extending the headwaters of the Kuskokwim to the Chitsia Range. On May 26 the men climbed the nearby bluffs to study the landscape in company with the chief and another native. "These hunters ... pointed out the gaps in the hills through which we must go to reach the great glacier which they tell us comes down from its summit," wrote Wickersham.[59] These Athabascans were from Lake Minchumina—their summer home; currently, they were in the midst of their hunting grounds.

After consultation with the natives, the judge determined on May 27 to cache their small boat here. The men then rearranged and repacked their outfit for overland travel; the plan now was to cross the Chitsia hills toward Denali. This was to be the last of camping with the Athabascans.

Now traveling toward the junction of the Kantishna River and Moose (Chitsia) Creek with a native guide, on the 28th the party was enthralled by a lake in whose clear and limpid waters Denali was reflected like a great white cloud. Here they obtained their first view of "a symmetrical high peak to the west of Mount McKinley to which it is joined by a tremendous ridge."[60] At first Wickersham supposed he had discovered a new alpine giant, but the glacierized form proved to be Mount Foraker.

In addition to the views, wildlife was also abundant during their trek. From camp the next day, everyone "saw a monster bull moose spring from a willow thicket ... and run far across an old burn; he resembled a longlegged Kentucky mule with a big rocking chair set on his head."[61] At noon on May

31, camp at the toe of the Chitsia was made by a beautiful small lake, "out of which a stream of water cascaded over the graceful curve of a recently constructed beaver-dam."[62] Despite masses of winter ice still floating in the lake, McLeod's wilderness experience came into practical use.

> *He surprised us by walking quietly along the shore, gazing into the depths of the water as if seeking something. Suddenly he sighted his rifle and fired, the bullet striking the water about ten feet off shore. He immediately waded into the lake about that distance, knee deep, reached down into the water bringing up an eighteen inch pickerel which his shot had stunned but not struck, and threw it on the shore. The stunned fish turned their heads to the bottom and tails toward the surface, in which condition if seized and thrown on the bank, they were easily taken. In half-an-hour we had thus taken a dozen large pickerel ... each flashing with color and dewy with the crystal drops of ice water.... It was the first time I had ever witnessed fishing for pickerel with a .30-40 rifle.*[63]

From a higher elevation in the hills a few days later, a further view unfolded:

> *Minchumina Lake lies to the westward and glistens like silver in the sunlight. The view continues far south of Minchumina to the massive McKinley range. We can trace the course of the Kuskokwim into the Bull Moose hills and the portage from Minchumina lake to that river. The valley view from the Tebay's aerie is a widespread panorama of forest, lake, and river, stretching from the distant eastern horizon around by north and west, to the western flanks of Mount McKinley due south of us. This three-quarters of a circle is a wide, flat valley, carpeted with an evergreen forest, marked by rivers and dotted with lakes. The sun shone in glorious radiance over Yako's land, and we now understood and better appreciated the vivid description of it given to us by Koonah, the blind shaman of lowland Kantishna. We built a cairn on Tebay's hoof-worn rock, and turned our faces campward.*
>
> *June 3. Cloudy; showers from the west. Three of our party went over to prospect Chitsia creek for gold, while McLeod and I remained in camp and jerked caribou cutlets. They returned late in the evening reporting prospects of placer gold and ruby sand. We will remain here tomorrow and locate mining claims.*[64]

The adventurers-turned-gold seekers staked claims for each man and also for Captain Hendricks—the first mining claims to be located in the region. During the busy search for precious metal, they witnessed two black bears fighting while digging roots, but McLeod, who had an old Hudson's Bay Company gun, kept neutral in the fray. On June 8 the men found a small lake, which they named Lake Alma in honor of Stevens' sister (now Wonder Lake). Here the party camped for several days while leisurely hunting and prospecting.

From here, their route now took them over high meadows of caribou country on June 13, which the Minchumina chief told them was his band's hunting ground. These tundra meadows are located on a vast, high table-land (actually a piedmont slope) surrounded by mountains, and, as described by the judge, "The beautiful, rolling grass-lands and moss-covered hills make it a favorite feeding ground for caribou, and the sharp crags to the east are the home of Tebay, the white sheep."[65] Wickersham's party then came upon an old Athabascan lodge on a hillside, which had a skeleton pole rack for drying jerked caribou; the natives had camped here on their last annual hunt. The men saw many caribou antlers, dry and white with age, yet attached to the skull, thus proving entire herds had been slaughtered in years gone by.

Bull caribou shed their horns annually like the Alaska bull moose. Early in the spring the scar-like knobs on the bull caribou's head where the last year's horns grew, begin to swell and fill with a horny matter, from which the new horns grow rapidly, a yard in length. By mid-summer, and the beginning of the mating-season, the horns have reached maturity, are hard, sharp, and strong; ready for use in the fierce battles which the bulls wage for the favor of the young and handsomer females. After the mating-season in November is over, the horns, being no longer useful, begin to dry and grow weaker at the base and about mid-winter they drop off, leaving scar-like spots where they formerly stood, from which next year's pair will sprout and grow.[66]

Perhaps with their thoughts on caribou, the group unknowingly pitched their tent aside a grizzly trail. McLeod called out, "Look at these beartracks." The men investigated further: Each print was one foot in diameter, "marked deep in the hard, sandy ground about every five feet, as if grizzlies had set their feet on the same spot for ages past."[67]

Continuing toward their alpine goal, on June 18 the party followed a game trail to an old moraine close to Peters Glacier.[68]

The lateral moraine stands a hundred feet and more above the surface of the present glacier, thus showing without doubt, the former existence of an older glacier at that height. In its day it extended two miles or more farther out on the northwestern plain than the present glacier, as the great boulder-strewn field well attests.

While we rested for lunch on the big boulders Stevens examined those on the lower side with the field glasses and suddenly cried out, "A bear!" I snatched up the rifle and ran to the edge of the higher moraine upon which we stood, but could not see the bear. "There," he exclaimed, "by the big rock. Don't you see his big flat head by that rock?" I could not, but looking carefully I saw a wolverine. He excitedly called to me to shoot the bear and while I was looking for it the wolverine ran under the rocks. "There," he said, "It's gone under the rocks." We went down where he saw the bear and finally killed the wolverine. The field glasses had magnified ten diameters—and made a bear out of a wolverine. We saw two caribou on the moraine, and though we took a long shot at them, they ran towards the mountain wall where we saw them join four others. Jeffery had never shot a caribou, so we asked him and Stevens to go ahead and drive the animals as far towards the mountain as possible and then to kill one each for our camp. Slowly they followed the caribou to within a thousand feet of the perpendicular walls of Mount McKinley, then each killed one on the little meadow on the moraine,—and there we made our high camp.[69]

The Wickersham expedition had now reached an altitude of some 5,000 feet, north of where the geologist Alfred Brooks had ventured alone the previous summer. The skies were so clear on the following day, the judge was prompted to write, "When the sun is always shining, one loses one's sense of time." When he rousted Webb with a shout, "It's nine o'clock," the sleepy companion sat up, rubbed his eyes while blinking at the sky, and inquired, "Day or night?."[70] A breakfast of caribou ribs and coffee would awaken him soon.

While camped that night the adventurers were alarmed by the thundering sounds of an avalanche. "Great masses of snow and ice broke loose far up the mountain and with rapidly accelerating speed shot down its ice-encrusted slope now striking a jutting angle of mountain wall ... finally leaping ... like a great white cloud, upon the surface of the glacier. Its millions of tons of rock and ice, spread wide on the glacier below," wrote the judge.[71]

From their base camp, Wickersham, Webb, Stevens, and Jeffrey each filled a knapsack with bread, chocolate, and enough dried and jerked caribou to last three to four days and then set out up "Hanna" (Peters) Glacier.[72] Each man carried a 100-foot section of rope and an alpenstock "armed at one end with a sharp point of iron, and with pick and cutting edge on the other."[73] Wickersham also had a camera and binoculars.

Bearing southward between the great wall of Mount McKinley's north face and a frontal range on the right, the party followed a medial moraine on the ice, which the judge termed "a most remarkable causeway." In a sense, he said, it compared to a high railroad grade rising ten to forty feet above the glacier's surface. When a tributary glacier joins the main ice stream, two lateral moraines may join to form a medial formation—or a medial moraine may stretch away from a spur projecting into the glacier from above.

Although the judge had some alpine experience on Mount Rainier, certainly none of the party had encountered such a flow of granular, bubbly glacier ice. The complexly formed ice, which includes plastic deformation, was separated into surface rows of erosional debris slowly moving forward and downslope by gravity flow. Wickersham believed the glacier to exceed thirty miles in size, correctly stating that "its ice fields are constantly replenished by the winter's snowfall, formed from the moisture-laden clouds from the Pacific."[74] When snow accumulates in a basin, both from direct fall and from avalanches coming down from the surrounding slopes, it is compressed by the addition of successive layers and is gradually altered into a more compact form. Air is retained between individual snow particles, forming a mass of whitish granular ice. During surface melting, water percolates into the mass and refreezes at night. The mass, known as *firn*, accumulates and begins moving from the source basins, following the line of least resistance. Layers of clear-blue and whitish ice can alternate with the white granular ice derived from firn as a result of overlying layers.

The pressure within the ice mass, which produces a minor local fall in the melting point, liberates water molecules. These now form a lubricating film that helps ice grains move relative to each other. Thus, there is a gradual downhill movement within the ice mass.

Glaciers have been classified as both temperate and polar—the amount of surface melting being a factor in each category. The differences are not well defined on Mount McKinley, because glaciers are of the "cold" variety in their upper portions and "temperate" on the lower half of the mountain. To further complicate glacier flow analysis on the northern façade of the mountain, both the Peters and Muldrow glaciers have *surged* (advanced at an unusually rapid rate) in certain past years.

The would-be alpinists now chose to ascend a branch glacier from the left.[75] "Great séracs hovering far overhead, pushed forward by the slow-moving and constant pressure of rearward accumulations of ice," wrote Wickersham. They "threaten to leap into space"[76]

> *Snowslides of every size, and every form of glacial movement, are on exhibition in this great natural amphitheater, and we viewed these wonders in safety from our high, dry seats on the great moving, curving causeway along the glacier's backbone. And over all these manifestations of the force of nature, there is a riot of shades, shadows, and colors produced by the rays of the ever-circling, never-setting sun, acting on sky, mountain, ice, and snow; and the rainbow's perfect curve. Nor have we forgotten the fearful tales of the magic power of Yako over the mountain he created from a wave of the sea. It is easy, now, to understand how the mind of the gentle Tena lowlander is filled with fears of the supernatural forces that can so easily destroy him on Denali, for here Nature is ever ready to destroy.*
>
> *The left-hand glacier which we have chosen to follow, rapidly ascends the bench on the mountainside and climbs higher and higher towards the much desired ridge which may lead to the summit, and we toiled up its soft snow carpet during the long sunlit night. Where it bends downward over the roll of its bedrock, we were forced to cross several bad crevasses. We were careful at these bottomless pits not to loose the long, supple, and safe life lines. We walked fifty feet apart in Indian file. The leader kept sounding for crevasses with the long hickory handle of his alpenstock and when he found one, sought for the safest snow bridge which he crossed carefully on his hands and knees, those behind holding his life line loosely, but so nearly taut as to break the drop and catch his weight should [he] break through and fall into the depths of the mighty ice crack. The second man, fifty feet from the leader, and the same distance ahead of the third man, would follow in the same careful way, and thus each man was eased safely across several bad places where bottomless crevasses were exposed.*
>
> *About 7 o'clock this morning, after traveling for nine hours, without rest, we reached an arête or sharp ridge of bare rock at the extreme upper end of the bench glacier, and found, to our intense disappointment, that the glacier did not connect with the high ridge we were seeking to reach, which yet seemed as far above us as when we began the ascent. We are now about 10,000 feet above sea-level on a sharp ridge of rock. Here our bench glacier roadway ends, for over this arête which juts out from the mountain wall, the descent is almost perpendicular to the great bergs of the main*

*glacier, far below as they crowd over each other to enter the narrow gorge.
Here is a tremendous precipice beyond which we cannot go. Our only line
of further ascent would be to climb the vertical wall of the mountain at our
left, and that is impossible.*[77]

The pioneer climbers reluctantly turned away from Denali, speculating
about the certain destruction awaiting the unfortunate mountaineer caught
in the path of an avalanche. Recognizing their salvation lay downward, not
upward, the four Denali worshippers left their rocky perch at nine o'clock
in the evening of June 21 and reached their camp safely, having been gone
three days and nights.

When they returned to where McLeod had remained with the mules, "a
small band of caribou ran to meet us," wrote the judge. They had "the
curiosity of antelope, but since we were not in need of either food or
excitement, we threw rocks at them to scare them out of our path."[78]
Wickersham, indeed, had scruples about shooting unnecessary game.
McLeod, wishing at all costs to avoid an encounter with a grizzly, had slept
on a high platform he had built in a spruce tree.

Wickersham still had notions about climbing Mount McKinley, now
thinking about the northeast flank, which "seems to afford the road we
have been looking for,"[79] but any further attempt would have to wait
another season, for court was soon to open its term.

On June 22, as he began his descent along the Kantishna valley, the
judge recalled a heartfelt incident that had occurred during the prior week.
"The boys caught a young fox" and tied it to a tree, where it could hide under
a rock. "His beautiful glossy coat and brush, and his bright beady eyes were
a source of pleasure to us and he was well fed."[80] When the party headed
for Denali, they turned the fox loose, but the youngster came back hungry,
deciding to remain beneath the rock until fed again. On this day he was
large enough to catch mice. Bidding farewell, the party left enough caribou
meat under the rock for many delicious meals.

The travelers soon reached the McKinley and Minchumina river forks—
which form the main Kantishna. Here they were in the finest moose
country in the world. After building a raft large enough to carry their
mules, the men set off on a five-day float to the Tanana River. They could
now relax and dwell on the prohibitive slopes of Denali, and on the
naturalist's paradise they were within. When everyone celebrated on July
4 with a volley of firearms, the frightened mules jumped from the raft and
headed for the lush grass.

Not long afterward, the expedition disbanded and the judge filed his map
in the recorder's office at Rampart. It was quickly copied by prospectors,
and in 1904 many gold seekers arrived on the Kantishna trail. In *Old
Yukon Tales,* there were a few final words:

*Thus happily ended the first attempt of white men, or probably any
other men, to scale the mighty walls of Denali. The members of our party
returned to civilization in perfect health, the mules rolling fat. Not a
moment's sickness nor a crippling accident to man or beast had afflicted
us. We returned to our labors without any feeling of failure but with a glow
of satisfaction that we had done so much with so little. We acknowledge*

our unpreparedness, both through inexperience and want of equipment, but at least we blazed the trail to the great mountain's northern base, mapped its approaches, the trails and rivers, and bore back to waiting prospectors the hint of gold in Chitsia gravel bars. We had the unalloyed pleasure of a glorious summer's outing, in the finest big game country in America. We brought back maps and other data for prospectors who are now invading the Tanana wilderness and will surely prospect the Chitsia range for placers. We are pleased to have been advance scouts for them. We passed two happy months in entire subjection to that primitive urge which is so near the surface in every civilized man, wandering as freely and as happily as our brothers the Tena hunters do when blessed with an overflowing cache of moose, caribou, and fish.[81]

As could be expected, Wickersham was invited to every social affair of importance in the territory, gave numerous speeches, and frequently attended banquets. The first banquet in the Tanana valley in 1904 was tendered to members of the bar by the judge on the evening of April 28 at Tokio Restaurant. The bill of fare was extravagant:

Hiyu-Muck-a Muck
Hooch-Chena Cocktails
Consomme, a la Tawtilla
Olives
Chicken Mayonaise, Oyster Patties
Sauterne
Wine Jelly, Cream Sauce
Roast Moose, Prospector Style
Mashed Potatoes, Green Peas
Ice Cream—Yuma Canned
Jelly Cake
Nuts, Raisins, Cheese, Coffee
Cigars

After the feast, the guests were entertained with speaking until a late hour; Wickersham and others responded to toasts.

Between this first mountaineering expedition of 1903 and the first complete ascent in 1913, no fewer than eight assaults were made on Denali. The pioneer mountaineers soon learned that the immensity of the 120-square-mile massif is truly impossible to comprehend even after a sojourn to its glaciers.

In *Mt. McKinley,* Terris Moore summarized the early expeditions: "None equal the charm of this first narrative, for it took place in the spring of 1903, when the Alaskan world was young, and is described for us by the man destined to become Alaska's best loved and most versatile citizen of his generation."[82]

▲ ▲ ▲

CHAPTER 4

A Search for Fame Leads to a Great Hoax

Hidden in the heart of Alaska, far from the sea, far from all lines of travel, this newly crowned alpine rival pierced the frosty blue of the Arctic within reach of the midnight sun.
Frederick A. Cook
To the Top of the Continent, 1908

"Dr. Cook Expelled by the Explorers' Club," blared the *New York Times* on December 25, 1909, and then under the page's headline: "Directors in a Stinging Report, Declare Him Untrustworthy of Belief."

In a closed-door meeting of the Explorers Club directors on the previous day, Dr. Frederick A. Cook was dropped from the club's exclusive membership in a unanimous vote after being "adjudged guilty of a serious breach of faith in having failed to appear and prove his assertions that he scaled the peak of Mount McKinley." Not only did Dr. Cook allege that he conquered Mount McKinley in September 1906 but also, in headlines erupting around the world, claimed to have reached the geographic North Pole on April 21, 1908. Having to cope with exorcising the ghosts of his past, Cook's polar exploit was questioned the following year by Admiral Robert Peary, who disputed his account. This not only began The Great Polar Controversy but also set in motion a simmering debate that continued for decades. Phantom questions still linger in the parochial world of exploration and mountaineering: Did Dr. Cook actually reach the North Pole? Did he scale Mount McKinley?

Dr. Cook, after his lengthy 1903 expedition, which was noteworthy because it circled Mount McKinley by horseback, foot, raft, and riverboat, was elected president of the Explorers Club as well as given various honorary memberships. In 1909, however, the groups who honored Cook called for proof of both his alpine and polar claims, and by year end the American Alpine Club also cut him from membership.

Frederick Albert Cook, born in Hartonville, New York, in 1865, was the youngest of five children. His father was a German immigrant physician who changed the family name from Koch to Cook. Cold air and far reaches seduced this young medical student. After receiving his degree from New

York University in 1890, Dr. Cook almost immediately sought an alternative career—that of the professional explorer. Catching the polar wanderlust, Cook showed ambition and enormous energy, spurning a sporadic medical practice to offer himself as surgeon or leader of eight expeditions. In 1891, after the North Greenland Expedition, Cook earned Robert E. Peary's praise for unruffled patience and coolness in an emergency. In 1894 Cook navigated an open boat across ninety miles of polar sea to obtain a rescue. The Arctic Club of America was born from this voyage, Cook becoming its first president. As ship's doctor with Roald Amundsen's Belgian Antarctic Expedition of 1897, the leader applauded Cook's unfaltering courage and noted that he earned the respect of all after the expedition became unexpectedly caught in the sea ice.

By all accounts, Dr. Cook was a vivid personality. As explorer, wanderer, and sportsman, certainly the spirited and convivial Cook possessed a flair for self-promotion. He had an obsession with travel and the personal charm to obtain financing. By 1903 Cook was internationally known as an explorer, and his ambition to be the first to reach the North Pole was no secret, nor was his zeal to scale Mount McKinley. Proposing the coveted ascent of North America's highest mountain, Cook persuaded *Harper's Monthly Magazine* to finance a portion of the expedition planned for that summer.[83] In an unusual donation, the aunt of Robert Dunn, who was an expedition member, gave $1,000 with the stipulation that Cook's wife leave the expedition when the ship from Seattle reached its Alaska destination.

According to Dunn, who later exposed Cook's supposed lack of abilities in *The Shameless Diary of an Explorer,* Cook was not an alpinist but, rather, had polar experience. The largely inexperienced party also included Fred Printz, a short, valiant horse packer who was an expert at throwing the diamond hitch; assistant packer Jack Carroll; Ralph Shainwald of New York; and Walter Miller, who joined the expedition in Seattle as a photographer.

Dunn, then twenty-six, was chosen to serve as geologist and as reporter for the New York *Commercial Advertiser.* In 1898 he had been a gold rusher on the Klondike Trail and, in 1900, explored Alaska's Mount Wrangell. After the 1903 expedition with Cook, Dunn published a narrative that appeared both in issues of *Outing* and in book form, the copy featuring the party's squabbles in what Hudson Stuck called "brutal frankness."

The horses required for the approach to Mount McKinley were selected in eastern Washington from the Yakima Indians, but the outfitting was largely done in Seattle. Food was calculated to weigh eighty-six pounds per man per month. The staples were flour, bacon, beans, sugar, and tea. Because Cook counted on killing sheep, moose, and caribou on the northern flank of the Alaska Range, four guns were included in the considerable outfit. There was a canvas tent for four as well as a silk tent for mountaineering. For cooking, a primus stove was taken; kerosene was brought for foothill camping and wood alcohol for use above the snow line. For the attempt on Mount McKinley, the party brought along four eight-pound eiderdown quilt bags, arctic clothing, ice axes, and horsehair ropes.

On June 9 the assembled party boarded the Alaska coastal steamer *Santa Ana,* its decks filled with gold seekers, whose whistles must have awakened all of Seattle. Cook wrote, "Men were on the docks cheering for their parting comrades en route to the new Eldorado of gold and hope,"[84] all this accompanied by a chorus from the dogs, pigs, horses, cattle, and chickens aboard. While steaming northward the following day, the explorer turned thirty-eight, anxiously envisioning fame and a grand alpine challenge.

At Tyonek, then the only settlement on Cook Inlet, wolfish dogs were seen chasing each other as the local Native Americans awoke to the ship's whistle. The crew then let the horses overboard to swim ashore in the cold, strong tide. Exhausted, they were then routed into the forest by the dogs. Cook's plan was to follow the 1902 pioneering route of Alfred Brooks and to take advantage of forty miles of trail cut in the timber; here he was fortunate to have the resourceful Printz (who had packed for Brooks) along as a guide. On June 25 the outfit began along the tidewater beach, each horse loaded with 150 pounds.

On the following day the expedition was welcomed to Alaska's wilderness by witnessing a large brown bear of the grizzly species pitching salmon onto the beach. After reaching the Beluga River—which takes its name from schools of white whales ascending its waters—a Native American winter trail left for the tundra. Dunn reported that here they sank "ankle-deep into sick, yellow moss, and wobbly little ridges separate small ponds." The horses went down, groping helplessly in the mud as the men "struggled waist-deep in yellow muck, unsnarling slimy cinches, packing, repacking the shivering, exhausted beasts."[85] It was endless torture to advance eight miles in two days.

Cook and some of the party ascended the mosquito-plagued Susitna and Yentna-Skwentna rivers in boats so as to meet the pack train in one week. All the while, Cook reported in *To the Top of the Continent,* "these persistent pests followed us over the waters in clouds, with a buzz that drove us to the verge of madness."[86] Despite veils, repellant, gloves, and mosquito-proof tents, these insects could not be thwarted.

Drawing on his encounters with mosquitoes in various regions of the world, Cook professed, "The Susitna denizens are certainly in my experience by far the most desperate in their attack upon man and beast."[87] Furthermore, to make progress miserable, it rained almost incessantly, sometimes snow squalls adding to the misery. The taxing route in part followed the "Keechatna" (Kichatna) River and crossed the Alaska Range divide at Simpson Pass, used by Spurr and Herron five years earlier. In his book, Dunn jested about "The Professor's [Dr. Cook's] lack of horse-packing knowledge and apparently foolish questions concerning directions and distances." On July 17 the pack train was "going to the devil, and he doesn't pay the least attention. Still just packs and unpacks his instruments. I wonder if he can use a theodolite, after all."[88] Threats of mutiny arose. Dunn continued his tirade rather darkly, "He's a fearful combination of stubbornness and indecision."[89]

By August 3 when in the Kuskokwim River drainage, there were only four sacks of flour remaining, but fortunately a grizzly was soon shot. Like Stone Age man without fire, the party devoured strips of raw bear flesh. Moving rapidly across a "Nimrod's dreamland" for over 100 miles, Cook's party passed Mount Foraker on an open tundra slope. When near Herron Glacier, every hour was livened by caribou, sometimes up to thirty fawns gliding about the hills like distant specks. The men shot some for food, but Dunn felt guilty because "caribou are too human and gentle. Believe I'd only skin one if I were starving."[90]

On August 14 Printz led the party to an Alfred Brooks campsite, where Dunn estimated it was barely fourteen miles to the summit of Mount

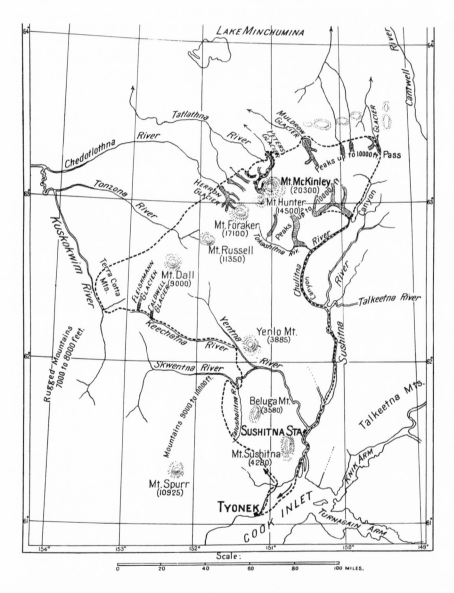

Robert Dunn's map traces Dr. Cook's 1903 expedition route. The expedition accomplished the first circumnavigation by land completely around Mount McKinley.

McKinley. After taking terrorized horses across glacier ice, where the animals sometimes had to jump open crevasses, the party made its first alpine camp, at an estimated 7,300 feet in altitude. But finding their route onto "Hanna" (Peters) Glacier blocked by cliffs and chasms, Cook now shifted the probe onto the mountain's slope some twenty-five miles eastward. Here, near the Peters Glacier tongue, the men stared in frustration as a grizzly ambled across a glacial stream toward a pleasantly vegetated island where they envisioned camping. Because they were without guns at the time, the bear's presence was alarming, but as Cook noted, "After eying each one separately, and then taking a side glance at the horses, he rose, sniffed the air, and turned into a great basin for the highlands, from which he watched the curl of the smoke of our camp-fires, while the aroma of caribou steaks kept his nose pointed."[91]

The men now packed loads into the upper glacier cirque, pinnacles of ice and crevasses replacing tedious moraine. While camping at night on the glacier, they devoured caribou steaks cooked on an alcohol lamp. On August 29 the intrepid but inexperienced party made a dedicated assault, putting their ice axes to good use, along what Cook termed the "south-west arête" (this distinctive feature is now known as the Northwest Buttress of the North Peak). Cook described the next portion of the ascent:

> We began ... in the track of a harmless avalanche of soft snow. This gave us a good slope for a few hundred feet, and then we were forced to cut steps up a slope ranging from forty to sixty degrees. Our greatest difficulty was not the work of chopping steps in the ice, but the effort of removing fourteen inches of soft snow before we found trustworthy ice upon which a safe footing could be made.[92]

Robert Dunn also remembered the frightening situation:

> Everything was ice, not an inch of névé. It seemed to take ten minutes to cut each step, which then held one toe, or one inch of a mushy, in-trod boot-sole. Nothing for mittened hands to grip.... But we kept on as before. "It's getting a little leveler," said the Professor. It was. And then I would ply him with questions about that leveling, laughingly fishing for more assurances. "Rocks ahead, the edge of a ridge, something, see them," he said. So there were. "Thank you, thank you," I said, as if that were all the Professor's doing. "God! I admire the way you take this slope," I'd exclaim. And by heaven, with all these mean pages behind, I still do.[93]

Finally, according to Cook, the setting sun forced them to seek a camping place. The camp, at an estimated 9,800 feet in altitude, gave them a starting point for the following day, with the "difficulty of cutting steps greater." Here they were "compelled to cut a camping floor to keep from rolling down three thousand feet."

> Camp was pitched in a hole cut out of the steep icy slopes; we nestled closely to get warm under eider-duck skins, and over hard blue ice. A frosty blast of wind was blowing hard crystals of snow against the silk walls of the tent, making a metallic noise. There were four of us as tightly pressed together as sardines in a box. From each there came a cone of breath which

rose in curious circles to the top of the tent, and there the moisture was frosted, falling in beautiful crystals only to add misery to our condition.[94]

Difficulties that appeared innocent from below now seemed to defeat Cook. He later acknowledged Mount McKinley as the most arctic of all great mountains.

Behind us were the awe-inspiring successive cliffs of Mt. McKinley, its glittering spurs piercing a dark purple sky nine thousand feet above us. The great mountain presented all the phases of the most terrible conflict of elements. Hundreds of avalanches were thundering down the sides of the giant peak, with trains of rock and ice followed by clouds of vapour and snow. Against this chaos of awful noise and lightning movement there drifted a steadily moving fleet of snow-charged clouds. Vapours were dragged down and set into violent agitation by the swift currents of the avalanches. At high altitudes we got only an occasional peep through a rift in the clouds, but this peep was full of gloomy mysteries.[95]

Dr. Cook's fantasy now took on the aura of optical illusion, similar to his claims of three years later. "Now we saw a mountain rise, move, explode, and vanish, then we would see a lake vague in outline, rich in colour."[96] This narrative was followed by the description of a great peak's upbuilding— one that appeared to rival Mount Foraker.

Although they were mountaineering amateurs, the men's attempt was commendable, with Printz usually leading with the axe. Even Dunn agreed that Cook was really making an effort "for all he's worth." On August 31 Dunn and Printz concluded that further progress was impossible.

"After a careful search we were compelled to acknowledge defeat, for there was no way around the succession of sheer granite cliffs," Dr. Cook later wrote, and his packer Fred Printz agreed, stating, "There ain't no way."[97] Summarizing his party's admirable effort on the great mountain's flanks, Cook related, "Though thwarted by an insurmountable wall, we had ascended Mt. McKinley far enough to get a good view of its entire western face.... Avalanche after avalanche rush down the steep cliffs and deposit their downpour of ice, rock, and snow on the [Peters] glacier."[98]

On the morning of September 4, wrote Cook in *Harper's,* "we started on our long, weary march along the western slope of the foot-hills above the tree-line.... The lunch was eaten with some relish.... It was the usual meal of boiled caribou ribs, cold and without salt." Cook continued his narrative:

As we descended from our second attempt to climb Mount McKinley, we were made to realize by frozen grass and increasing snow-storms that the season for mountaineering had closed; furthermore, the north wind convinced us that if we wished to get out of the country before the long winter and the night stilled the subarctic world about us, we must quickly reach the head waters of some big stream. We did not care to go to the Yukon, because in doing so we would cover explored territory. We could not return as we had come, because horse-feed along the western slope of the range was already frozen. We were not yet ready to leave Mount McKinley, provided we could only linger at some point where our retreat would not,

▲ *View to Eldridge Glacier from 4,700 feet on Kesugi Ridge in Denali State Park (photo by Dave Johnston)*

▼ *Wading McKinley River, with Mount McKinley in distance (photo by Brian Okonek)*

▲ Left: *Brown bears are often seen in the region. (photo by Randall D. Miller);* right: *Dall sheep in Denali National Park and Preserve (photo by Roger Robinson)*

▼ *Cow parsnip and delphinium in Denali State Park (photo by Dave Johnston)*

▲ *Mount Hunter* (left), *Mount McKinley, with Tokosha Mountains in foreground; note skater on frozen pond (photo by Dave Johnston)*

▼ *Moose eating pond lilies near Denali State Park (photo by Dave Johnston)*

◄ *Lower Ruth Glacier and mountain harebell (photo by Roger Robinson)*

▲ *Bearberry in Denali State Park, early September (photo by Dave Johnston)*

▼ *Willow ptarmigan with young, in summer plumage, in Peters Hills (photo by Dave Johnston)*

▲ *A telephoto view of the full moon and Mount Foraker from south (photo by Roger Robinson)*

▼ *Mount McKinley from near Denali State Park (photo by Dave Johnston)*

Overleaf: *Aerial view of Mount McKinley from south; Mount Hunter is on far right (photo by Jim Okonek, K2 Aviation)*

▲ *Glacier pilot flying over cloud-wrapped peaks of Alaska Range (photo by Jim Balog)*

▼ *Winter storm clouds stacked over Mount McKinley, with Tokosha Mountains in foreground (photo by Roger Robinson)*

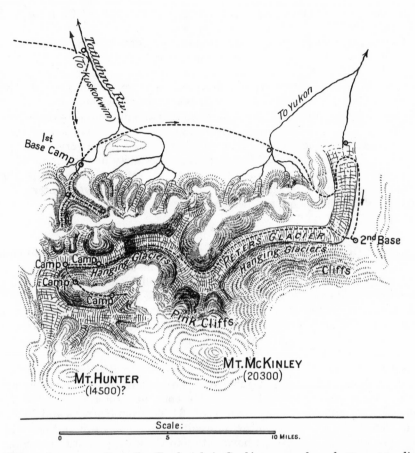

This early map outlines Dr. Frederick A. Cook's approach and attempt to climb Mount McKinley in the summer of 1903. His first base was near the Straightaway Glacier and his second, to the east of the lower Peters Glacier. The peak labeled "Mt. Hunter" is now Kahiltna Dome.

as was likely in our present position, be suddenly cut off. Altogether, our purposes would seem best served if we could cross the range and get into the Sushitna Valley; but the possibility of such an effort seemed doubtful, in the time at our disposal, unless we were fortunate enough to find a pass within a few days' traveling. Accordingly, we resolved to make a desperate attempt to cross to the eastern slope of this great range, and, in the event of failure in this, our alternative was to make the deep waters of the Toklat, and travel thence by raft to the Tanana River.[99]

Completing their "circumnavigation" of Mount McKinley, the party moved east some fifty miles, fortunately locating a pass that horses could use, and then made a most lucky and dangerous raft descent of the Chulitna and Susitna rivers.

One of Dunn's last bitter comments came on September 3, when all the men sought out their stray horses, except Cook, "who lazed in camp." Only six of the thirteen remaining horses were found by Dunn and Printz; the wolves would find the rest.While following Brooks' route, Cook crossed the Muldrow Glacier terminal moraine on September 5 without recognizing this ice valley as a feasible summit route. On the outbound route, which here lay near the present George Parks Highway, "Now and again we could see the summit," Cook wrote, "and from here it resembled very much the crown of a molar tooth."[100] The near-desperate party barely managed to reach the Chulitna River, where they built two rafts and abandoned the horses. After a truly reckless run down the churning canyon waters, the party finally hailed some prospectors.

▲▲▲

In 1906 Dr. Cook became an advocate of a southern approach to Mount McKinley, where he hoped to find a breach in the mountain's defenses. In *To the Top of the Continent,* his words rang a bell for alpinism during this period of worldwide discovery: "Mountaineering as we assume it in this venture is a department of exploration, and as such it is worthy of a higher appreciation than that usually accorded it. Among our British cousins there has long been an admirable spirit of mountain adventure which has developed into a well-defined sport."[101]

Bolstered with favor and reputation, Cook now had little problem obtaining the necessary financing, a publication agreement, and new participants for his second sojourn to Alaska. Backed by both the Explorers Club and the American Geographic Society, he received $1,000 from *Harper's* and $5,000 from Henry W. Disston (grandson of wealthy Henry A. Disston, the Philadelphia saw manufacturer), who was to join Cook in the autumn for big-game hunting.[102]

The more resourceful and experienced party now included Belmore Browne, wilderness explorer, hunter, and artist; Herschel C. Parker, a physics professor and mountaineer (who also contributed to expedition financing); topographer Russell W. Porter, recently with the Baldwin–Ziegler polar expedition; and again the photographer Miller and packers Printz and S. P. Beecher. There was also a new recruit, Edward Barrill, a tall forty-two-year-old Montana blacksmith who was destined to play a pivotal role in Cook's future.

A foreboding of wilderness problems struck the men as they landed at Tyonek on May 29, when their horses were stampeded by a large pack of dogs after swimming ashore from the ship; six of the twenty horses were never found. In a wise move, Cook had obtained a forty-foot shallow-draft boat (the *Bolshoy*) to ease the river travel on the Susitna and Yentna, while the pack train would take the overland route to the head of navigation. Anticipating a superior approach to Mount McKinley's southwest flank, the expedition followed the Yentna River, but in its upper canyon fords proved dangerous. A typical Alaskan mountain river, the Yentna is swift, turbid, and full of treacherous sandbars formed by silt—the result of glacier drainage.

Without benefit of today's maps and aerial photography, the expedition gambled on which upper western river forks to follow. They erred in not taking the best route and ended in narrow defiles. Yet on June 14 Browne wrote that it was possible to see the "rounded sheep mountains of the Kuskoquim!"[103] They had to get the pack train there, however, and in attempting this, regularly found themselves narrowly escaping death. On that same day Browne was nearly drowned during a glacial ford. As he was wading downstream to an island, he found that he could not return against the current. The hot sun had raised the river level, and the roar of water was loud. After being swept from his feet, Browne rolled over when he made an "all-out" effort to get back. Finally, he saved himself by reaching a sandbar and eventually the opposite side.

On June 15, Browne wrote in his diary, "The Doctor got in a serious position yesterday on an almost perpendicular snowbank that dropped away 1,000 feet below him. He got on it and couldn't turn back and finally succeeded in reaching the far side with the aid of a hatchet."[104] Two days later Browne was in the icy water and rolled three times, later recalling "don't know how I got out." Cook described the same incident: "We tried in vain for a good ford, and at last Browne in a desperate spirit plunged into the raging torrent, lost his footing, turned several somersaults, was carried downstream some distance, and saved himself only by landing on a submerged boulder."[105]

Four hours later the party climbed "wet to our hips with boots full of ice water" on steep slopes with underbrush "as dense as tropical verdure, and on hands and knees we climbed and crawled between branches."[106] The spiny and thorny devil's club shrubs (*Oplopanax horridus*) filled their clothes with needles. By day's end their trousers were torn in strips, and they were thoroughly exhausted. As Robert H. Bates wrote in *Mountain Man: The Story of Belmore Browne,* by now Cook "must have felt that he *deserved* the first ascent [of Mount McKinley]."[107] Finally the men made it back to camp, having gone seven days on three days' provisions. For four days there was one cup of tea and a partial slice of bacon.

On June 27 the plucky Browne wrote in his diary, "All of us have been in danger of drowning, and twice the Professor [Cook] has nearly lost his life."[108] In one of these instances, Parker and his horse Billy Buck lost their footing in midstream; Parker might have drowned without Barrill's quick reaction. The horse and pack swept around the cliffs and was feared lost, but later a scouting party found the animal serenely feeding in the grass.

Continuing to spend energy and valuable days in the frustrating search for a pass suitable for a pack train nearer their objective than that used in 1903, at one point the expedition was forced to ford a torrent just below a glacier terminus. Browne's diary for July 1 describes the desperate crossing:

The roar of the water made talking impossible and great blocks of green ice jammed the stream and threatened the horses.... Brill's [Barrill's] horse lost its footing and he and his mount were swept past me in a

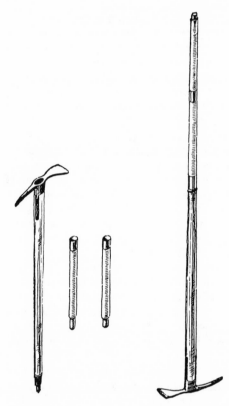

Sketch of ice axe and tent pole used on Dr. Frederick A. Cook's 1906 expedition (from Harper's Monthly Magazine, May 1907)

smother of spray. At times I could see nothing but the angry water as they were pulled under by the whirlpools. Then my horse was seized by the current and down we went with the choking, freezing flood, full of small pieces of ice, sweeping us past the rugged cliffs. [109]

At last they crawled ashore and lay shivering on the bank. No wonder Browne added, "There is something terrifying about savage glacial water."

Dr. Cook and Belmore Browne were the most obstinate members of an expedition that exhibited great courage and energy in a perplexing approach to the glaciers of Mount McKinley. The flawed probing amid the rugged peaks of the range failed to reveal a pass suitable for use by a pack train, and as each sortie entered disastrous topography, the summer advanced and overall energies diminished. Both Cook and Browne reasoned that it would be wisest to rearrange the plan and to bear toward the south and southeast flanks of the objective, where the Kahiltna and Ruth glaciers might provide a superior entry. On July 7 several industrious members of the party, including Porter, climbed Mount Kliskon to survey and hopefully determine a glacier entry to Mount McKinley from the southeast. Without much respite from bogs and bugs, Dr. Cook on July 8 adroitly observed, "It rained most of the night and in the morning we were pelted with hail. Good weather does come occasionally but like gold it is found in small bits." [110] Continuing toward Lake Chelatna and Kahiltna Glacier's gravel bars, the expedition struggled through the bogs—a "floating jungle"—between the East Fork of the Yentna River and the Kahiltna.

While passing through the gold prospects of the Dutch Hills, an entertaining Native American, Susitna Pete, joined them, providing local color but not much reliability as a guide. When they had reached Tokositna Glacier, Barrill wrote in his diary for July 17 that he and Cook, from a high peak north of camp, could see Mount McKinley about fifteen miles distant, but that it did not look as though they could climb it. Fearsome icy ridges and rocky amphitheaters barred continuation. Parker and Browne agreed with Barrill's appraisal, given the time of year, distance involved, and condition of the horses. Cook added, "The overwhelming bigness of the whole scheme [made continuing] a seemingly hopeless task."[111]

Four days later Cook, Browne, Parker, and Barrill decided to explore Ruth Glacier. Crossing the divide from the Tokositna, they regularly encountered bear trails. In one frightening episode a brown bear was discovered digging out a squirrel burrow in a ravine. The main group had no arms except their ice axes, which on the whole were not suited to bear-hunting, as Browne later jested. Because he had the only weapon, but was about 400 yards ahead, the rest of the party shouted and tried dancing to distract the bear's attention. "Their plan succeeded for he left his digging and stalked past me and sitting down about ten feet away began to study my companions, turning his head from side to side," recounted Browne. "At last the bear turned around and saw me, and as long as I live I never expect to receive such a disgusted look as that bear gave me." As the bear left, Browne took a shot, causing the confused bear to dash toward the party. Everyone scattered, and "for a few minutes there was a sound of shouting and a dizzy blend of figures on the mountainside, and then silence once more settled among the hills."[112]

In another grizzly encounter, when only Browne and Parker carried Luger pistols, a bear suddenly came at the four men with alarming speed as they were ascending a ridge between streams. According to Browne, the "beast" was making a beeline for them. When the bear finally faced Browne, not over twenty feet away, he fired a shot, prompting the bear to bolt away.

Adventures with dangerous grizzlies and rivers replaced challenges on Mount McKinley that season. With no reasonable prospect of a successful ascent, the expedition began its return on August 8 to Cook Inlet, where Cook and Browne expected to meet Disston for a hunting trip across the Alaska Range. Although it had rained 50 of 110 days, Porter had made good use of his topographic observation opportunities. Taking a mean from five stations, all thirty-two to seventy miles from the summit, he later computed the height of Mount McKinley at 20,310 feet—a remarkably close figure.

▲▲▲

Late in August, as it rained incessantly, Dr. Cook waited in Seldovia for Disston, who did not arrive on the steamer as expected. The resourceful doctor had a knack for adapting to changing circumstances. While Browne made alternate hunting plans, Cook had the temerity to telegram Herbert L. Bridgman of Brooklyn, "Am preparing for a last, desperate attack on Mount McKinley."[113] Almost immediately, giving the pretense that with Barrill he was planning to explore the Susitna River country, Cook left Tyonek with the *Bolshoy*. Upon his return Cook sent another telegram, announcing that the two of them had finally succeeded in reaching the summit of Mount McKinley!

Taking along prospector John Dokkin, Cook reached the Chulitna River canyon in just two days; soon thereafter they arrived at a locale where the prospector had decided to winter, two miles up the Tokositna River. From his cabin, about one mile from Ruth Glacier's snout (Cook had named the glacier for his stepdaughter, Ruth Hunt), Cook could see "forty miles away, far above the clouds, the summit of Mt. McKinley, the Top of the Continent, the Ultima Thule of our ambition."[114] Moose and bear tracks led to the glacier and then a game trail along its northern flank provided excellent traveling. Dr. Cook related continuing events in *To the Top of the Continent:*

> On the evening of the second day [September 9]—we took to the ice, crossed the first northerly tributary, and camped on a beautiful moss-covered point [Glacier Point] about fifteen miles from Mt. McKinley.
>
> As we crossed the glacier and jumped the crevasses Dokkin developed quite a fear of the bottomless pits and said that he would prefer not to trust his life to the security of his footing. Barrille [sic] and I had been on glaciers before and did not entertain the same fear. Indeed we regarded this glacier as one particularly free of danger and hardship. Its surface was unusually smooth. We had about determined that the limit of our effort would be the top of the north arête at 12,000 feet; from there we believed that we could thoroughly outline the glacier drainage and also a route up the mountain. For this purpose Dokkin was not needed, and since he wished to prospect for gold in the lowlands I sent him back with instructions to read the base barometer and to place emergency caches along the glacier.
>
> The snow on the glacier was hard and offered a splendid surface for a rapid march but the advantage of its hardness was offset by the treacherous manner in which it bridged dangerous crevasses. As we advanced these snow bridges increased and we held to our horsehair rope with more interest.[115]

On September 10 Cook and Barrill entered the crevassed Great Gorge of the Ruth (the first men to reach within this grand granitic cathedral of immense rock and ice walls); their farthest camp was near the gorge's end. Precisely what Cook did in the days that followed varies greatly with his later written claims. As reported in the *New York Times* on November 28, 1906, Cook stated,

> On the fourth day after leaving the boat we reached the top of the ridge. There we were confronted with a granite cliff 4,000 feet into the air on top of the ridge, which was 12,000 feet high. We found it difficult to pitch a tent, so built a snowhouse, and slept in that.
>
> On the fifth day we found a way around the cliff by cutting steps in cornices of ice.... Very early in the morning of the eighth day we made a dash for the peak.

To the Top of the Continent is a curiously anecdotal book that mixes animated personal reminiscences and reflection with indulgent accounts of events. Cook inclines to a mixture of fanciful prose, including a delight with the scenery and a venue of passages where he creates scenes of questionable truth. He strains for effect. Cook's pen name might be The Explorer, but there was nothing nostalgic or maudlin about his sense of himself. In his sometimes lyric account, in which he claims to have reached the true summit of Mount McKinley with Barrill on September 16, Cook describes

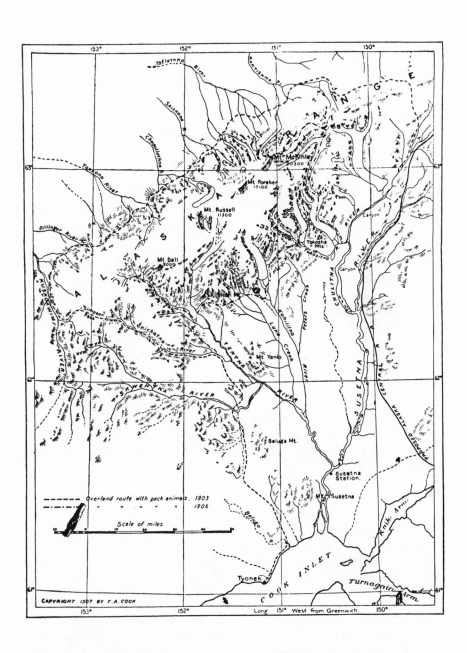

Dr. Cook's map that accompanied his Harper's Monthly Magazine *article of May 1907. This map includes Cook's exploratory route of 1903 and depicts his alleged route northward on the Ruth Glacier to the northeast flank of Mount McKinley in 1906. The course of the glacier's trend is quite fictitious, but is consistent with Cook's verbal description of his route to the summit from the northeast.*

the fearsome avalanches, a realistic threat on this arctic mountain:

> *The night was dark and we were restless like soldiers on the eve of a battle. Snugly wrapped in our bags we rested well, but slept little because of the violent thunder of avalanches and the angry rush of winds. Out of black clouds from the invisible upper world there rushed with the noise of a thousand cannons and the hiss of a burning volcano indescribable quantities of rock and ice mixed with snow and wind. The tumble from cliff to cliff, from glacier to glacier down the seemingly endless fall was soul-stirring to the verge of desperation. The glacier under us cracked, the whole earth about quivered as from an earthquake, and as we tossed about in our bags the snow squeaked with a metallic ring. That third night we felt as if we were at the gates of Hades.[116]*

Climbing from "ridge to ridge" and "from cornice to cornice," Cook claimed they reached "the divide, the wall between the Yukon and Susitna." This locality proved to be "in the firing line of clouds from the tropic and the arctic."

> *The winds came in gusts now from the east and then from the west; with each change there was a fall of snow and a rush of drift. This locality did not appeal to us as a camping ground. In seeking for a sheltered nook we found a place where the snow was hard enough to cut blocks with which to build a snow house. In less than two hours our dome-shaped Eskimo igloo was completed and thereby shelter and comfort were assured us for the time of our stay on the ridge.[117]*

At this point, Cook's published narrative includes the scenario of a "ceaseless warfare between the pale arctic clouds and the dark Pacific clouds." The claim that the two pushed on to a final 18,000-foot camp "with not enough energy left to talk or eat" is certainly a realistic experience for Mount McKinley climbers, but continuing his story of the alleged ascent, Cook gets carried away: "Our axes had been kept chopping steps all day…. We uttered a sigh of relief as we rose on the icy steps of our Jacob's ladder." Attaining the summit, Cook alleged, "The Arctic Circle was in sight; so was the Pacific Ocean."

> *It was ten o'clock in the morning, the sky was as black as that of midnight. At our feet the snow glittered with a ghastly light. As the eye ran down we saw the upper clouds drawn out in long strings, and still farther down the big cumulus forms, and through the gap far below, seemingly in the interior of the earth, bits of rugged landscape. The frightful uncanny aspect of the outlook made us dizzy. Fifty thousand square miles of our arctic wonderland was spread out under our enlarged horizon….*
>
> *We could see narrow silvery bands marking the course of the Yukon and the Tanana, while to the south, looking over nearby clouds, we had an unobstructed view. Mt. Susitna, one hundred miles away in a great green expanse, was but a step in the run of distance. The icy cones of the burning volcanoes Redoubt, Illiamna, and Chinabora, the last two hundred miles away, were clearly visible with their rising vapours. Still farther the point of Kenai Peninsula.[118]*

On the night of October 2, Bridgman (in Brooklyn) was rousted out of bed to receive a telegram (with $12.50 in charges due) from Cook, dated September 27 at Tyonek. It read, "We have reached the summit of Mount McKinley by a new route from the north."[119]

The report was immediately communicated to the newspapers, and New York soon read of Dr. Cook's success. The October 3d issue of the *New York Times* announced the ascent, running the subheadline "They Estimate Alaskan Peak's Height at 22,800 Feet," adding, "16 Deg. Below Zero at Top." The story disclosed that, because of unusually favorable weather in early September, Dr. Cook had decided to make another attempt on the mountain. The article added that the latest equipment, including a light silk tent, eiderdown sleeping bags covered with silk, and Swiss ice axes, helped the two men save weight and climb efficiently. Among those who read the news with more than passive interest was Professor Parker, now back at his teaching position. When delivering a lecture within the week, the stunned academic expressed his doubts, stating that he simply did not believe that Cook made the ascent of Mount McKinley.

When Cook heralded his triumph, his former associate Robert Dunn (who met Cook in Seldovia) believed the dispatch, but after the initial shock, the astute Browne was gradually swayed by disbelief, for he knew that the time the two men were absent was entirely unrealistic for a successful ascent. In *The Conquest of Mount McKinley,* Browne later stated his dilemma:

> I now found myself in an embarrassing position. I knew that Dr. Cook had not climbed Mount McKinley. Barrill had told me so and in addition I knew it in the same way that any New Yorker would know that no man could walk from the Brooklyn Bridge to Grant's tomb in ten minutes.
>
> This knowledge, however, did not constitute proof, and I knew that before I could make the public believe the truth I should have to collect some facts. I wrote immediately on my return to Professor Parker telling him my opinions and knowledge concerning the climb, and I received a reply from him saying that he believed me implicitly and that the climb, under the existing conditions, was impossible.[120]

Browne was not alone in his incredulity. A few months later the knowledgeable Alaskan missionary Hudson Stuck sent a letter to the geologist Alfred Brooks, blasting Cook not only for irreverence, but also for fraud:

> My dear Mr. Brooks:
> So you were taken in by that fake telegram about the ascent of Mt. McKinley! No sir! he never got on top: got no higher than he did before, and never will get up unless they build a railroad to the summit.... Dr. Cook is a prig: moreover I find it hard to contain within myself my vehement suspicion that he is an ass.[121]

But the small mountaineering community and explorers and prospectors who might question Cook's contradictions could not sway the media and public, including many members of the Explorers Club, who had faith in the explorer and who did not comprehend the magnitude of the mountain and its serious environment. By May the following year, Dr. Cook related his story in *Harper's,* complete with a route map and a suspicious and carefully cropped photograph allegedly depicting Barrill on the true summit holding an American flag lashed to his ice axe. "After a long siege, during which we were compelled to acknowledge several disheartening defeats, we have at last conquered the highest mountain of our continent," wrote Cook in *Harper's.* "For danger, hardship, and maddening torture this essay of the great mid-Alaskan peak has been my worst experience. For hellish conditions and physical discomfort the north-pole chase is, compared with Mount McKinley, tame adventure,"[122] he added.

Both Browne and Parker could not confront Dr. Cook before he left the United States on his arctic expedition, but after the appearance of *To the Top of the Continent* in 1908, their indignation seemed completely justified. The two men were now in possession of irrefutable proof that there were numerous falsities in Cook's route descriptions and about the equipment he used. Browne recalled, "We were influenced, however, by our own ideas of fair play as well as by the suggestions of our friends, and we refrained from publishing anything derogatory to the Doctor's character while he was absent, and unable to defend himself. During his absence in the North Professor Parker and I were planning another attempt to climb Mount McKinley."[123]

As experienced mountaineers, the two men were convinced the "summit" photograph shown in both *Harper's* and Cook's book was a complete fabrication; distant, higher peaks of Ruth Gorge appeared in the book's photograph, but they were cropped and retouched in *Harper's.*

The photograph in the magazine entitled "The view from 16,000 feet" appeared in the book with a different caption, and its background detail gave Cook away, for several granitic peaks fronting Ruth Gorge matched the detail of those along the right-hand edge of the supposed summit as shown in the book. Browne later stated that when the book was published, he and Parker could virtually locate Cook's "false peak" before even leaving for Alaska to prove it on the terrain.

Time elapsed. Dr. Cook's fame peaked after his North Pole expedition, when his claimed success was greeted as enthusiastically as the later news of Lindbergh crossing the Atlantic Ocean. He received the adulation of the world, first in Denmark, then in New York. Speeches lauded him, and he was given a gold medal by the Arctic Club. At a lavish dinner sponsored by the National Geographic Society, with a seething Peary in attendance, President Theodore Roosevelt hailed Cook as the conqueror of Mount McKinley and the first American to explore both polar regions.

In Copenhagen, Cook's claim of reaching the North Pole had been heralded with headlines. On September 1, 1909, the American minister read a cablegram to his guests at tea. A message from the Danish Foreign Office, dispatched in the Shetland Islands by a Danish vessel, read, "Dr. Cook reached the North Pole April 21, 1908. Arrived May 1909 at Upernivik from Cape York. The Cape Yorkers confirm to Rasmussen the voyage of Cook."[124] There was no reason to question the message, for the name of the eminent Knud Rassmussen was "gold."

While Europe cheered Cook, less friendly factions awaited him in New York. Robert E. Peary cabled from Labrador, "Cook's story should not be taken too seriously. The two Eskimos who accompanied him say he went no distance north and not out of sight of land."[125]

Although Peary's rebuttal set the tone for The Great Polar Controversy, as Terris Moore pointed out, the American authorities rejoiced in this, for they had "not one, but two, North Pole heroes, the second regrettably jealous of the first."[126] Newspapers taking a readership poll found that in 1909 the public believed Cook, not Peary. The *Times* of Watertown, New York, for example, made a straw vote: The results were three to one in favor of Cook.

In *Mt. McKinley,* Moore described the accolade the polar explorer received upon returning home:

> So when the Oscar II with Dr. Cook aboard dropped anchor off Quarantine in lower New York Bay, September 21, 1909, a score or more of boats, crowded with cheering passengers, soon surrounded her. One of them was a tug, carrying Dr. Cook's wife and two daughters. To this he was transferred and the four of them were then taken aboard the Grand Republic, an excursion steamer chartered by a Brooklyn welcoming committee. As they started up the bay for a tour of the harbor a band on the ship played "Hail to the Chief" to wild cheering. Summing up, the New York Herald the next day referred to Dr. Cook's tumultuous reception as "a demonstration of popular confidence and enthusiasm without parallel in the history of this city." Some days later, when the "freedom of the city" was officially bestowed upon him, that paper further noted: "Dr. Cook is the first American to whom the keys of the city have been given."[127]

The pendulum of belief, however, eventually began to swing against Cook. A discontented Barrill, who had initially conciliated Cook and then avoided public contact, now made an affidavit that he and Cook never climbed above 10,000 feet. Investigative stories in New York newspapers concerning the Mount McKinley ascent made the front page. In the New York *Globe and Commercial Advertiser,* lengthy accounts set the Cook controversy into almost tabloid reading. On October 14 the *Globe* published the entirety of Barrill's affidavit and the next day disclosed the details of his pocket diary. One subheadline captioned, "Entries of Sept. 9, 10, 11, and 12 Doctored and Changed at Dr. Cook's Direction, While the Explorer Himself Dictated to Barrill the Notes Which Appear for the Other Six Days." It appeared to the *Globe* that Barrill kept his diary faithfully until September 12, "when Dr. Cook directed him to stop writing in it and leave the pages blank."

The *Globe* editor noted that it was apparent from a cursory glance of the Barrill diary that numerous erasures had been made and new statements made. The diary entry on September 14 told of the building of a snow house (which was never done) and the next day's entry states, "Dr. Cook is getting jubilant over our success.... We have to tie our bandanna over our ears to keep them from freezing." Finally, "we had a grate [sic] time shaking hands

4 | THE NEW YORK TIMES, FRIDAY, NOVEMBER 11, 1910.

EXPLODES DR. COOK'S MT. M'KINLEY CLAIM

Prof. Parker of Columbia Proves His "Top of the Continent" Yarn Wholly False.

THE PHOTOGRAPHS FICTION

The Great North Pole Claimant Never Got Nearer Than Twenty Miles from the Peak.

Prof. Herschel C. Parker of Columbia University and his co-explorer, Belmore Browne, say they are now able to knock in the head for all time any claim Dr. Frederick A. Cook may still pretend to have of having reached the top of Mt. McKinley, often described by him as the "Top of the Continent."

Prof. Parker and Mr. Browne are back in town from their futile attempt last Summer to ascend Mt. McKinley over the route Dr. Cook says in his book he accomplished the feat. They bring with them photographs which they say stamp Dr. Cook's pretensions to having climbed the peak as false on their very face.

Chief of all in their collection is a photograph which is unmistakably a duplicate of that taken by Dr. Cook and published in his book, "To the Top of the Continent," as the summit of Mt. McKinley. It is not Mt. McKinley at all, but a rock in the Amphitheatre Glacier twenty miles southeast of the base of Mt. McKinley and only about 5,000 feet high, instead of 20,390 feet, as Dr. Cook graphically describes it to be.

Prof. Parker and Mr. Browne found this exactly where Edward Barrille, the guide, who turned against Dr. Cook, said in his affidavit it would be found. Dr. Cook had taken his famous photograph of the "Top of the Continent" with Barrille standing on the summit waving an American flag lashed to an axe handle. When Barrille returned with Dr. Cook he told many in the West that the explorer had done all he asserted, so when his affidavit was published denouncing Dr. Cook's story as a mere fabrication many of the latter's friends refused to believe him. Prof. Parker declares his photographs establish as correct every sworn statement made by Barrille.

A Double Mission.

Prof. Parker had a double mission in going to Mt. McKinley last Summer. He wanted to climb it, it is true, but as much as that, he wanted to prove the truth or falsity of Dr. Cook's story, already assailed by Barrille, the only man who was then with him, with a view that Capt. Peary might not suffer further from the effort of Dr. Cook to rob him of the credit of having discovered the North Pole. If Dr. Cook hadn't scaled Mt. McKinley when he said he had, no one would he expected to believe his North Pole yarn.

It was from this little peak, 5,000 feet high or less and hemmed in on all sides by towering peaks, that Dr. Cook said he could see the Pacific Ocean, 250 miles away, while Mount Susitna, 100 miles distant, seemed almost to lie at his feet. The frightful, uncanny outlook made him dizzy he writes in his book. He felt like shouting, but had no breath to spare after edging up along a steep, snowy ridge and over the heaven-scraped granite at the top. And then, after several long breaths, he naively remarks that the "ghastly unreality of his position" began to excite his frosted senses. "It was Sept. 16, [1906,] the temperature 15

Prof. Parker's Photograph of a Low Peak, Twenty Miles from Mt. McKinley, Identical with Dr. Cook's Pretended Photograph of the Top.

degrees below zero, the altitude 20,390 feet."

"And Mount McKinley twenty miles away and 15,000 feet above him," replies Prof. Parker, with photographs here to prove it.

Corroborating Barrille's sworn confession, Prof. Parker said yesterday:

"We left our boat on the Tokositna at about the same spot where Dr. Cook and Barrille took to the ice," said Prof. Parker, who was a member of Dr. Cook's expedition in 1906. "My idea was to follow as closely as possible the route taken by the doctor, and we had no difficulty in doing this with Barrille's map at hand. In a few days our party reached the spot noted on the map as the point where Barrille's picture was taken. This was in the Amphitheatre Glacier, in the foothills of Mount McKinley and twenty miles from its base.

Hunting a Rock.

"Having reached the place, the problem now confronting us was to pick out the rock on which Barrille stood when he was photographed with the flag in his hands. This, perhaps, was easier to do than one might imagine, in spite of the fact that there were innumerable rocky peaks on all sides of us.

"There will be noticed in the lower right-hand corner of Dr. Cook's photograph a peak in the distance, the snow formation on the top of which should make it easily distinguishable. It was therefore a comparatively simple matter to identify the peak as the second of the seven peaks of Ruth Glacier, only a few miles away from where we stood. Dr. Cook has said that there are twelve peaks, but he evidently did not carry his investigations far enough to discover that there are only seven. Then we soon found the rock we wanted in the snow saddle Barrille mentioned, and at last we were at the 'Top of the Continent.'

"You will remember that Barrille swore that the picture in Dr. Cook's book, captioned 'First Five of the Twelve New Peaks of Ruth Glacier,' was taken on the same day that Dr. Cook took the famous photograph of the guide. That this statement was true is readily noted. In another of the pictures, entitled, 'An Amphitheatre,' the rock which Barrille stood may be seen.

"On account of the formation of the snow cornice it was impossible to photograph the rock from the exact spot where Dr. Cook himself stood. These cornices are shaped according to the whims of the winds that blow, and the formation varies from year to year. It will also be noted that there is more snow in the photograph I took. This is due to the fact that I was there in July, while Dr. Cook's photograph was taken in September.

"A considerable amount of snow naturally would melt away in two Summer months. But you can readily see that the photographs are of one and the same

rock, and a very paltry rock it is at that. I duplicated a number of other photographs in Dr. Cook's book at totally different points from where the doctor says they were taken, and these, with a detailed account of my expedition, will be made public at a later date. But these photographs are of far less importance than that of the 'summit' itself.

Couldn't Scale the Peak.

"After getting all the material I wanted in this neighborhood we pushed on twenty miles further to the base of Mc-Kinley and made numerous attempts to cross to the northeast ridge of the mountain. But our passage was effectually cut off by a 12,000-foot range of ice peaks at the head of Ruth Glacier, which were impassable on account of pinnacles and crevices. Dr. Cook makes no mention of them in his book, never having been far enough to see them.

"Then, turning back, we went as far as possible on the southwest face of Mc-Kinley, and after reaching an elevation of 10,000 feet gave up any further attempts to scale the mountain. While I regret that we were unable to get to the top, still we had accomplished the object of my mission and felt well satisfied with the result of the expedition."

In the talk about future attempts to scale Mount McKinley it was evident that neither Prof. Parker nor Mr. Browne believe Tom Lloyd ever reached the top of the mountain, but Prof. Parker denied that he had ever said Lloyd's story was untrue.

"What I did say," he said, "was that although our party got within seven miles of it, none of us could see, even with the strongest of glasses, the flag or pole Lloyd says he planted there to stay. How ridiculous, therefore, the statements were that the flag had been seen from Fairbanks, 140 miles away!"

Mr. Browne said he didn't attach much importance to Lloyd's tale or to Lloyd himself, but that Taylor and McGonigle, the men with Lloyd, were first-class men. He added, however, that neither had come out of the mountain fastnesses, and the world so far had only Lloyd's yarn. He thought it more than probable that when Taylor and McGonigle did hear what Lloyd had said they would take the attitude that it was Lloyd's affair, not theirs, and let it go at that. Mr. Browne says the sporting element in the feat is entirely lacking in the ordinary Alaskan's viewpoint.

Mr. Browne added significantly that the world would not be kept waiting long on the Lloyd story, as he and Prof. Parker intended returning to Mount McKinley next Fall. They will make the attempt by the route Lloyd says his party took. He said he had heard while away that Lloyd and his party had a row when about 12,000 feet up the mountain and turned back from that point.

"False peak" claimed by Dr. Frederick A. Cook as the true summit of Mount McKinley. This "summit flag" picture appeared in Dr. Cook's article in Harper's Monthly Magazine *(May 1907) and was labeled by him "The Flag on the Summit of Mt. McKinley." In the image, the background peaks flanking the Great Gorge were purposely excluded, but they are plainly visible in Belmore Browne's photographic duplication efforts of 1910.*

on top." The diary, which was well worn but legible, included a route sketch map; the falsified period was from September 9 to 18, 1906.

On October 15, 1909, the *New York Times* fueled the doubts by disclosing "Cook Never on M'Kinley's Top," based on Barrill's sworn statement that "at no time did Dr. Cook and he get nearer than a point fourteen miles in an air line from the top of Mount McKinley." Barrill asserted Cook ordered him to alter his diary; Cook then retaliated by stating "Barrill Statement False."

In his affidavit of October 4, 1909, Barrill stated that his diary was altered between September 12 and 16. "In order to prove that this point [the false peak] was the top he stated to me as follows: 'That point would make a good top of Mt. McKinley.'" On September 12, "The doctor had taken a photograph of the point with me standing on the top thereof, with the American flag in my hand." In the affidavit, Barrill stated, "We gave up any further attempt towards ascending the mountain upon Sept. 15 and returned to the boat.... On the 16th, when at our first camp returning from the glacier, I doctored and changed the entries ... under the orders of Dr. Cook."

Barrill also stated that the drawing of the snow house "is entirely false, as we never built a snow house on the trip." Concerning the photograph of the false peak, "I made the remark that the eight peaks on the other side of this point where I had been photographed would probably show in the picture, and he said that he had taken the picture at such an angle that those peaks would not show."[128]

When the Explorers Club committee met on December 14, 1909, there was at first a disposition to sympathize with Cook. Witnesses at the meeting included Browne, Parker, and Charles Sheldon—all stating their convictions that Cook had falsified his contentions. Although Cook had earlier faulted his agreement with the remainder of the party that no further attempt would be made in the 1906 season, and though he had entered an agreement with *Harper's* for an exclusive story—this to embarrass his associates—the damning conclusions of the committee and directors were that Cook had deliberately set out with Barrill to take a false summit photograph. Just as creditors peck at the carcass of a fallen financial empire, Cook's former boosters began an abrasive inquest into the facts and myths concerning the McKinley allegations of September 1906. The committee concluded that it would have been impossible to ascend glaciers and frozen snow slopes wearing rubber shoepacs—certainly not in the time spent away from Cook Inlet. Other insufficient and improper equipment would not have allowed a successful ascent.

To the chagrin of the committee, Cook evaded his promise to appear and testify after he requested one month to report to the committee. When it seemed Cook had left for Europe, the committee prepared its final report. Browne later remembered,

> *I am still filled with astonishment at the incredible amount of vindictive and personal spite that was shown by the partisans of Doctor Cook. Men who had never seen an ice-axe or a sled-dog wrote us reams of warped exploring details and accused us of untold crimes because we had dared to question Cook's honesty.*

Mount McKinley as seen from minor peak (the "false peak") claimed by Dr. Frederick A. Cook in 1906 as the summit of Mount McKinley. Photograph taken during the Browne–Parker Expedition of 1910. (photo by Merl LaVoy; courtesy W. F. Erskine Photograph Collection, University of Alaska Archives, Fairbanks)

> *I was visiting Professor Parker at that time and scarcely a day went by when we did not receive abusive anonymous letters. In the face of this blind public partisanship, we realised that we would need more than documentary and circumstantial evidence to convict Doctor Cook irrevocably. The Polar controversy had put an entirely new light on our claims against Cook. Originally our claims against him were really more or less private and personal. While Mount McKinley was a splendid mountaineering prize, our attempt to climb it had been in the nature of a sporting proposition.[129]*

Spurred by the desire to prove what peak Cook had actually climbed in September 1906 and to locate a route to the summit of Mount McKinley from the southeast, in 1910 Browne and Parker led a party on behalf of the Explorers Club, hoping in the process to review the doctor's claims. While proceeding up the Susitna River to Talkeetna, where there was now a trading post, they met a four-man Mazama Club group of Portland, led by Claude E. Rusk, a man of high standing in his community who had similar plans. Both expeditions had cordial relations; the Browne–Parker expedition welcomed the Mazama group, for it seemed their party would provide a competent and impartial investigation, free of any personal feelings and past relationships. In time, Browne and Parker located the false peak and asserted that the contrived summit photograph was taken on a very minor rock peak north of the lower Ruth Glacier—some 15,000 feet below the top of Mount McKinley.

Browne's approach plan for the 1910 season was to omit horses and, instead, use a shallow-draft motor boat (*The Explorer*) with an eighteen-horsepower, two-cylinder engine and a propellor in a tunnel to reduce the damage from silt. By taking the boat some thirty miles past Talkeetna to the head of navigation on the Chulitna River, the expedition could bring nearly one ton of equipment and food to within thirty-five miles of the base of Mount McKinley. Then the men would carry heavy packs along the moraines and on Ruth Glacier's surface. In addition to Browne and Parker, the party included Herman Tucker of the U.S. Forest Service, Valdemar Grassi, Merl LaVoy of Seattle, Professor Cuntz of Stevens Institute (along to map the confusing region south of Mount McKinley), Arthur Aten of Valdez, and J. W. Thompson, the boat engineer.

First on the scene, and with careful detective work, Browne and Parker studiously compared Cook's photographs of the region and were able to "trace him peak by peak and snowfield by snowfield" to where he had exposed each picture. On June 22 Parker shouted in exaltation, "We've got it!" A minor rock point at about 5,300 feet above sea level matched Cook's false peak photograph taken on September 16, 1906. The background peaks of Ruth Glacier's Great Gorge are plainly visible in Browne's own images, with his own party members holding a flag as Barrill had.[130]

The Mazama party at first was convinced that Dr. Cook did indeed climb Mount McKinley, and they hoped to prove this. In the end, though, they fully agreed with Browne and Parker that Cook had falsified the record. This party found serious discrepancies between Cook's map and the terrain, and they also found all possible climbing routes too formidable to continue. Their leader, Claude Rusk, in the January 1911 *Pacific Monthly*, wrote,

> *[Cook] had many admirers who would have rejoiced to see his claims vindicated.... But as we gazed upon the forbidding crags of the great mountain from far up Ruth Glacier ... we realized how utterly impossible and absurd was the story of this man who, carrying a single pack, claims to have started from the Tokositna on the eighth of September and to have stood on the highest point of McKinley on the sixteenth of the same month.*

Belmore Browne, whose passion for exploring was infectious, still had summit ambitions, so with his companions he continued toward the savage eastern flank of the mountain. As Browne's struggling party was only able to advance camps one mile per day, they understood why Cook could not have succeeded in climbing McKinley and returning to the Tokositna River with merely a forty-pound pack. Near-disasters accentuated the dangers and difficulties of even reaching the true foot of the mountain. In the Great Gorge of the Ruth, in early July, LaVoy fell into a hidden crevasse full of water, "almost helpless in the tangle of his pack and snowshoes." Because his pack load consisted of dry beans, it became buoyant and he surfaced—a close escape.

Not all the problems were glacier and mountaineering dangers. During one stormy day the men lay in sleeping bags, the tent frozen to the snow. Browne felt weak, and his mind filled with illusions. Finally he staggered to his feet and went outdoors, unable to stand upright. Then Parker came out and fell headlong into the snow. Another member of the party brought tea, reviving both of them from severe nausea and spasms of shivering. The cause of the unpleasant incident was oxygen deprivation because of the alcohol stoves burning in the airtight tent!

Advancing on McKinley, the party found that the sun's heat wet their clothes with perspiration, and "yet to [their] surprise the temperature in the sun was only 48°!" Meanwhile, "avalanches breaking from the walls struck the cliffs with a noise like artillery."[131] Even under a temperature of fifty degrees the glaciers became blinding sheets of white light and the sun burned like fire. Following the West Fork of the Ruth (past the Rooster Comb and Mount Huntington), Browne and Tucker found themselves hemmed in. "Stupendous rock walls rose on either side. I have never seen cliffs of more grim and savage beauty," Browne later reported.[132] At a little over 10,000 feet, they were confronted by a bergschrund stretching across the ice slope. The attempt ended here.

▲▲▲

In *Arctic Profiles,* December 1983, there is the editorial comment that Dr. Cook "spent half of his life surrounded by such controversy that his real field work has been largely overlooked." Browne and others pointed out that his genuine achievements, now almost forgotten, became obscured when his Mount McKinley summit claim was discredited. His North Pole assertion was seriously questioned, even though his documentation was as solid as Peary's. Hudson Stuck commented that the indignation of Cook's falsehood is "swallowed up in pity when one thinks upon the really excellent pioneering and exploring work done by this man, and realizes that the immediate success of the imposition about the ascent of Denali doubtless led to the more audacious imposition about the discovery of the North Pole—and that to his discredit and downfall."[133] Yet today there remain Cook supporters who believe his claims despite the overwhelming evidence against his Mount McKinley adventure. The greatest irony is that Cook died dogmatically claiming he had reached the summit.

Dr. Cook, championed more in Europe than in the United States, has had his arctic claims revived since the appearance of new literature on the North Pole question since 1960. At least three arctic experts have elevated Cook's claim to "probable and possible" attainment. Dr. Frederick Albert Cook was a controversial and enigmatic figure in the history of exploration.

▲▲▲

CHAPTER 5

The Sourdough Expedition

... to Pete Anderson and Billy Taylor, two of the strongest men, physically, in all the North, and to none other, belongs the honor of the first ascent of the North Peak and the planting of what must assuredly be the highest flagstaff in the world.

Hudson Stuck
The Ascent of Denali, 1914

The legendary Sourdough party of Alaskan gold miners who made the first ascent of Mount McKinley's 19,470-foot North Peak in 1910 gave birth to a frontier story that became world news.[134] Before proof of the ascent was barely rescued three years later, the ascent gradually faded into public disbelief, because of its contradictions, as another tale of the Far North.

Most Alaskan mountaineering experts fully agree that this courageous exploit was simply phenomenal, one of the most noteworthy expeditions of all time. The Sourdoughs stood as a symbol of intrepid pioneering spirit, men who believed in themselves, and their only reward was a defiant pride in their own courage and endurance. Carrying a heavy spruce pole, not acclimatized to altitude, and with only rudimentary technical equipment, two of the party succeeded in scaling Mount McKinley's second highest summit.

Billy Taylor and Pete "Swede" Anderson, in an astonishing episode, made the final push by climbing over 8,000 feet and descending—all in just eighteen hours. W. F. Thompson, who related the Sourdough ascent in the *New York Times* on June 5, 1910, wrote, "They took with them no historian, no photographer, and no topographer, although they had been deluged with requests from professional men who desired to accompany them. They wanted no publicity and they cared not if the world never heard of their trip." The feat, he added, "was undertaken not for the enlightenment of the world, but to prove the pluck and endurance of the members of the party." The entire cost of the exploit was $1,500, the expenses being mainly polar survival and travel equipment and but little of the "junk" that "mountain climbers generally carry," according to Thompson's editorial. To document the climb, the party trusted an ordinary Kodak camera worth only $5.00.

Members of Sourdough Expedition of 1910, which pioneered the ascent of Mount McKinley's North Peak. Left to right (standing): Charles McGonagall, Peter Anderson, William Taylor; (seated): Thomas Lloyd. (courtesy Historical Photograph Collection, University of Alaska Archives, Fairbanks)

In Alaska, even when his claim was first generally believed, some pioneers were skeptical of Dr. Cook's supposed ascent of Mount McKinley. Especially in the mining village of Kantishna, from where the great Icy Crown could be dramatically seen, men openly questioned his brash claim. Partly to disprove Cook's controversial assertions, the brazen Sourdough party carried with them not only the pole but also a six-by-twelve-foot American flag, which they hoped could be sighted from Fairbanks.

Local boosterism, in fact, was the prime spark that set the expedition in motion. In the fall of 1909, Tom Lloyd, a Welshman who had followed the Klondike gold rush to the Kantishna hills, was in a Fairbanks saloon when the discussion turned to Dr. Cook's supposed 1906 ascent. According to Lloyd, bar owner Bill McPhee, a Yukon pioneer who became an Alaskan, did not believe "any living man could make the ascent." Lloyd, with some braggadocio and likely anticipating certain fame, disagreed, stating he would prove that the mountain could be climbed. Further talk resulted in McPhee offering $500 for Lloyd's expenses to undertake the ascent, and soon two other Fairbanks and nearby Chena businessmen each added $500 to the original stake, one of them offering to furnish a large flag.

Lloyd, over fifty and somewhat stout, was not considered by his backers to be an obvious mountaineering candidate, but he knew the hardy and loyal Kantishna miners intimately. "I am not going to coax anyone else to go into it, but I know some of my boys will go with me if I say the word," Lloyd reportedly stated. Although without alpine experience, Lloyd had listened to Charles Sheldon and Harry Karstens in 1908, who both speculated about what appeared to be an ideal approach to Mount McKinley by way of the great Muldrow Glacier. The snout of this great ice causeway was passed by Brooks, Cook, and Muldrow, none of them apparently realizing its access potential. From Kantishna, only thirty miles north of the mountain's summit, the entire potential route, except from 9,000 to 12,000 feet, was visible.[135]

After Lloyd organized a seven-man party during the winter, the proposed assault inspired Fairbanks newspaper headlines: one editorial promised not only that the Alaskans would succeed, but also that they would show up Dr. Cook and other expeditions. As publicity emanated from Fairbanks, the *New York Times* requested that Thompson's newspaper, the *Fairbanks Daily News-Miner,* make arrangements to have a correspondent join the prospectors on the proposed expedition.

Lloyd's chosen group of miners and dog-team mushers were a hardy set. William ("Billy") Taylor, a mining partner of Lloyd, who he described "as strong as a horse"; Pete "Swede" Anderson; and Charles McGonagall, a pioneer who carried mail by dogsled, formed the nucleus. Taylor was twenty-seven, Anderson forty-three, and McGonagall forty. The surveyor-topographer C. E. Davidson and another man had planned on participating but left after a disagreement with Lloyd.

For the winter-season approach, Lloyd used his dogs and sleds, while the men trudged along on snowshoes. For footgear, the winterwise Sourdoughs used high waterproof shoepacs made of insulated rubber with a leather top; their homemade crampons (*creepers*), however, would later be strapped onto Native American moccasins of caribou-skin uppers and moosehide soles.

Clothing consisted of heavy long underwear, a shirt, bib overalls, a "duck" parka, and mitts, and for bedding the party included caribou hides, wolf-skin robes, and down sleeping bags. To cut firewood and long poles to safeguard crevasse crossings, the party had poles and double-bitted axes. While Lloyd planned to bridge the larger crevasses with timbers, all took long alpenstocks with a hook at one end and a sharp steel point at the other. The party purposely did not bring climbing ropes, and Lloyd later remarked that they did not need them. Besides the one camera, the party brought a watch, a thermometer, and Lloyd's small memorandum book. Each man took a thermos bottle.

The usual bacon and beans of the pioneers would be cooked on a coal-oil stove. Other foodstocks included flour, caribou meat, butter, coffee, chocolate, sugar, dried fruit, and doughnuts. In addition, Lloyd made quantities of bread and froze it. While in the forest region, Lloyd's party planned to live off the land, killing moose and caribou for steaks and stews.

Before the Sourdoughs left Fairbanks, boosters gave them a rousing goodbye, mindful that this "all-Alaskan effort" whould prove men from the Far North could do what Dr. Cook had only envisioned. On December 3, 1909, with three horses, a mule, and the dog team, the expedition departed for final outfitting in Chena.

▲▲▲

Lloyd and McGonagall left Kantishna on February 11 to search out the best approach, breaking trail and hauling supplies to a location between the two forks of the McKinley River. In two days they found the old Alfred Brooks camp of August 21, 1902, at timberline on the river, below Muldrow Glacier. In eight more days Lloyd and Anderson had forged into the high tundra, about ten miles southward in the direction of Mount McKinley; here they found some willows where a good camp could be made. This location (about 2,900 feet in altitude) on Clearwater Creek became known as Willow Camp. As nature's reminder that it was still northern winter, a blizzard blew so hard from February 23 to 25 that the dog teams were completely stalled.

After shooting two badly needed caribou on the 28th, Anderson and McGonagall scouted the foothills along Cache Creek and then reached the key pass, which McGonagall had discovered during a search for gold and one that provided easy access to the Muldrow.[136] In honor of their first backer, the Sourdoughs named this important defile McPhee Pass (later McGonagall Pass), and what later became the Muldrow was called Wall Street Glacier, Lloyd choosing this name because it was "inclosed by exceedingly high walls on each side."[137]

The second camp, some four miles up the Muldrow from the pass, took the name Potholes Camp. Since Lloyd had lost their only aneroid barometer, they could only estimate their altitudes—which turned out to always well exceed later measurements. Although Lloyd intended to rely on coal-oil stoves for the glacier camps, the party decided to pack wood blocks cut from the timber region along with a good but heavy wood stove. Without the dogs and sleds, this frontier tactic would not have been practical.

Lloyd's story of continuing progress was transcribed from his diary later by a court reporter and then edited by W. F. Thompson for the *New York Times*, appearing under the headline "First Account of Conquering Mt. McKinley."

> *March 5—Charley, Pete and myself started up the glacier. After we were up a ways, it was such a grand sight I returned to the camp for the Kodak and took six pictures: the first of the camp, the second, third, fourth, and fifth of Mount McKinley. All the while I was thinking, "There's only 10,000 feet more to climb!" The sixth picture was looking back down the glacier over the trail we had just traveled.*
>
> *The upper part of the glacier is full of crevasses. We looked down some of them, and in some we could not see the bottom. We will start to climb from right here over this glacier.*
>
> *Started back to the Willows Camp at 3:20, arriving about dark: 26 below zero, but a fine day.*
>
> *March 6—Pete returned to McKinley Fork today for a saw with which to saw wood. He mushed downhill ten miles to find the saw, and then climbed back. McGonagall looked for the aneroid, but could not find it, so tonight we made a rake and will hunt tomorrow for it. At 7 p.m. it is 20 below, and we have had fine weather all day. I spent the day baking for the trip.*
>
> *March 7—We hunted all day for the aneroid without being able to find it, so must give it up. Saw a band of caribou today. Pete spent the day on a trip to Clearwater with the dogs for wood and poles....*
>
> *March 9—The boys are still hauling wood. I spent the day cutting stakes to stake the trail over the glacier, so that we can find our way up and back in the storms. I have 750 stakes cut. The weather is fine.*
>
> *Taylor had 50 miles to go for fish when he left on March 2, a week ago today, and he has not returned yet. I am becoming anxious about him. We have only two dogs here, and can't do much about hauling wood. It is only 10 below tonight.*
>
> *March 10—Pete and Charley took a load of firewood and poles out on the glacier to the pass....*
>
> *March 12—The trouble we have now is fog. It is cloudy this morning. We took two dog team loads of wood to the Glacier Pass, the round trip being about fifteen miles. If the weather permits we will move camp to Wall Street Glacier tomorrow, but will leave one tent here at Willow Camp for protection.*
>
> *March 13—Took stove, tent, and bedding to Wall Street Glacier.... I would not like to estimate the height of the walls, but in places it honestly looked to me to reach 10,000 feet straight up. Of course, it cannot be anything like that distance or height, but it looked to be—stretching straight up in the air. It is the grandest thing I ever saw in my life— that long stretch of glacier.*
>
> *Going across the glacier toward McKinley for the first four or five miles there are no crevasses in sight, as they have been blown full of snow, but the next eight miles are terrible for crevasses. You can look down in them for distances stretching from 100 feet to Hades or China. Look down one of them, and you will never forget it. Some of them you*

*can see the bottom of, but most of them appear to be bottomless. These
are not good things to look at.*

*Over the upper eight miles of that glacier you cannot move a foot in
safety unless you have snowshoes on....*

*Arrived at the Pothole Camp. We sank straight down in the snow,
(about four feet and a half into the glacier and snow in a kind of a
pothole,) where we pitched our tent. The weather is fine. Had no
aneroid to determine elevation, but estimate it to be about 9,000 or
10,000 feet.*

*We have seen some great ice slides down the sides of Wall Street
Glacier today. The weather (thermometer) about zero the warmth
causes the ice to break away from its anchorage, and it comes tearing
down the sides of the almost perpendicular walls with a most awful
noise, grinding and tearing its way.*

*A slide seemed to be taking the glacier under the tent away, and
startled by the sound, like the report of a great gun, (I had never heard
anything like it.) I jumped up. It didn't seem to affect the other boys, and
the Swede, who had crossed many glaciers, paid no attention at all. He
simply looked at me and smiled, and said: "It's just rippling a little
below; it is safe here." We had hauled timber here to put the stove up on,
and to put rock under the stove for a base we had to go half or three-
quarters of a mile to an old moraine for some volcanic rock. The rock
is black slate; it looks like volcanic slate. I could not classify it, but have
sent some of it to Geologist Brooks, and he can say what it is.*

*We put some of this rock under the bottom of the stove, but the stove
would sink, naturally, from the heat, and we had to keep digging down
and lowering our beds to keep on the level, with the stove. Around the
tent we piled snow, so that the storm could not move it. We were finally
down four or five feet in this hole, and we tied our tent down and filled
it all around with snow, and it was all right then. This tent we had was
the balloon-silk tent. If the four of us were in this tent, which is about
8 by 10 feet ... there was plenty of room.*

*We had two caribou hides for beds and mattresses for four of us.
They are the clear quill to put on the ice or snow.*

*Pete had a mountain sheep skin sleeping bag as well, and besides
that we had three robes in all for the four of us ... and a piece of canvas
to throw under all. You want to be sure and keep the snow and ice from
thawing underneath you.*

*March 14—We arose at 5 (never on the trip did we arise later than 5 in the
morning; we were always up, so as to be ready to start out just at
daylight). By 8 it was blowing a gale, when Pete and Charley went over
the glacier to locate a trail forward. Taylor went back for wood.*

Certainly with their acknowledged awareness of the crevasse risks to
both the men and dogs, only the Sourdoughs' deft mastery of winter survival and steely courage against the elements kept them going forward.
Lloyd's diary continues:

*March 15—I was born Feb. 4, Taylor March 15, Pete in April, and Charley
in May. The prospects seem good for all of us spending our birthdays*

on Mount McKinley this year. It blowed pretty much all night.

We had one magazine in the party—all the reading matter we had—and we read it from one end to the other. As in our conversation we always referred to Mount McKinley as "Mac," so we called the magazine the "mag."

I don't remember the name of the magazine, but in our estimation it is the best magazine published in the world, whatever its name may be. I remember among other things that it had pictures in it of Morgan and some of them guys, but I can't remember the name.

It is still there on Mount McKinley, within a few miles of the summit, unless a slide has carried it away, and maybe some of those Cheechaco climbers will find it there some day and make the find an advertisement for the magazine.

March 16—It started to snow at 9:30 a.m., and at 2 p.m. it was snowing heavy and hard, but we concluded to move—or try to. Charley and Pete went ahead on the trail, but it became too thick or foggy for them, and they returned to camp about 4:15. It is clearing up a little this evening, and we hope for a clear day tomorrow.

I passed part of the day on the glacier and found the crevasses to be very numerous, and some of them seemed to be miles in depth. I dropped rocks down some of them, but couldn't hear them strike bottom. This is no "jolly." It can be demonstrated to any person on earth.

March 17—St. Patrick's Day. We are setting stakes across the glacier to mark the trail to the "saddle" that we may find our way back to camp by them from now on, as the next camp will be our last sleeping camp on the climb. The trail is eight miles long, and we are staking all of it.

We would push on each day as far as we could and drop back at night to the Pothole Camp until we had finally established our last camp at what we judged to be the 15,000-foot level, although we had no aneroid to measure height.

It has been very soft in places and very dangerous on the trail, but we can travel it now with the assistance of our poles and with roughlocks on our snowshoes, because there is more or less snow filling in the trail, making the going easier over the glacier. You couldn't walk it without snowshoes.

We believe that on account of the crevasses, this is the only time of the year that any man can go over this glacier unless they build bridges across the crevasses—bridges of lumber—or have something to throw over the crevasses on which they may be crossed, because the crevasses are so numerous and are from a foot to fifty feet wide, and on some of them there is perhaps but one spot where it is possible to cross them.

In many places we had to put long poles across them, as they were too wide to jump over. We would throw the poles across the crevasse, throw snow on the poles until it "stood up," and fill in until we could snowshoe across. The pole would go through them any place, but a snowshoe would keep us up.

The snow we threw on the pole bridges would freeze and make a bridge across which we could travel on snowshoes, but when it thaws in the Spring it would be impossible to cross those bridges.

That was the theory upon which we attempted to climb Mount McKinley at the time we did, and upon that theory we made the ascent.

I would not think of starting to do it at any other time of the year, nor attempt to pass over the glacier at any other time: nor does Pete think it can be done at any other time, because he says if you tried it any other time, you would be threatened with destruction by ice slides and avalanches from above, and by the danger of falling into the crevasses below or under foot.

It has been a fine day. Taylor went back to Willow Camp this evening with the dog team. Charley and Pete returned to camp at 4:15. It is a little colder, but fine.

The formation along the Wall Street Glacier where it is uncovered by slides (on the side facing south) seems to be slate and feldspar, with numerous fissures showing. We have samples of the rock to take back with us, and Brooks will know.

March 18—This morning took the blue tent up to our last camp (at the Saddle) and approximate the elevation at not less than 15,000 feet. We drove a tunnel into the snow on the left-hand ridge to make a place to pitch the tent in. The tunnel seems now to be built of solid ice. Then we dropped back to the Pothole Camp.

It has been a fine day on the glacier, but it is a little cloudy this evening. Taylor returns from Willow Camp with dog feed and some provisions, but unfortunately he brought a "wrong" quarter of caribou, from an old bull we had killed, and it is not fit for dog feed. Consequently we have no "eating" meat. It is blowing a little and looks like a storm for tonight.

The Sourdoughs' final camp, a snow cave named Tunnel Camp, was located on the adjacent ridge flank (to be named Karstens Ridge) probably at about 11,000 feet near the head of the Muldrow. Lloyd remarked, "This camping in a tunnel in the ice is no summer picnic." A great storm blew all night, and on the 19th the men could not "move out of camp all day."

While Taylor made a final return to Willow Camp with dogs for wood, flour, and fresh meat, McGonagall and Anderson industriously climbed upward along the narrow ridge, "cutting steps and staking the way," according to the diary account. By March 25 Lloyd was concerned about Taylor, who had not yet appeared: "Opposite our camp a great slide came tearing down the rise, and I tell you she was a pretty sight. She came half way across the glacier, and it looked as if it was coming all the way, but it filled up the crevasses as it came and stopped when it had covered about half the distance across." Some of the slide "chunks" were "bigger than any house."

By March 26 Lloyd's diary included statements that can only be interpreted as fictitious. What is evident is that McGonagall and one or both of the other men had been cutting steps with a coal shovel as far as the ridgetop (at 14,600 feet).[138] By preparing the route in this manner and keeping this staircase clear until the summit push, the climbers were able to move quickly.

Lloyd did not climb higher than Tunnel Camp, and in his entry for

March 29 he reported returning to the pass, where he saw six buck sheep. Yet his diary entry for April 1 states, "I started this morning for the summit to join the other boys for the final climb." Lloyd appears to have remained at Willow Camp, waiting during the period when Taylor, Anderson, and McGonagall were climbing toward the North Peak on April 3. Since Lloyd was the only Sourdough who kept a written record, the exact details must be pieced together. What seems certain is that the three others climbed 3,600-foot Karstens Ridge, crossed the upper Harper Glacier, and ascended a steep gully to upper Pioneer Ridge, hauling and packing along the fourteen-foot spruce sapling. Anderson apparently led for most of the gully, cutting steps when necessary. The instep creepers buckled onto rubber-soled shoepacs barely held. Given such equipment, today's Mount McKinley veterans are amazed that these inexperienced men could ascend and descend this relentless gully without mishap. Yet they did!

McGonagall apparently halted a few hundred feet short of the summit, perhaps because of altitude sickness; here the pole and flag were set up on the final exposed rocks below the summit. In a later interview, Taylor stated that he and Anderson spent over two hours atop the North Peak. "It was colder than hell,"[139] he related, and their mitts became frozen. They must all have been hungry, for each man took along only a hot thermos bottle of cocoa and six doughnuts.

By nightfall the three adventurers were back at Tunnel Camp, and on the following day they descended to where Lloyd was waiting. Immediately, Lloyd took several dogs and within a week managed to reach Fairbanks, where he brashly announced that *all four* had reached both Mount McKinley peaks. This evoked a hero's welcome. On April 12 the *Fairbanks Daily Times* headlined "M'Kinley Is Conquered," and the *Fairbanks Daily News-Miner* bannered the ascent, adding, "Tom Lloyd and Party Reached the Summit of Mount McKinley on April 3.—Claim Cook Did Not Reach the Top." News of the success quickly reached the national press, prompting president William H. Taft to send a congratulatory telegram.

Lloyd's exaggerated accounts to the press, however, soon created a skepticism concerning the Sourdoughs' efforts, although Lloyd's Fairbanks backers believed him. Doubts about the authenticity of the ascent grew stronger when Charles Sheldon, who knew Lloyd and his shortcomings, advised the public to await a report from the other party members. None of the Sourdough party, however, disputed Lloyd's part-fictitious account—largely because in Kantishna the "summiters" did not realize the extent of the questioning, and in any event they would not contradict Lloyd.

Finally, when the ascent was openly called a hoax by some, supported by the facts that the pole and flag could not be seen and no photographs were taken above 11,000 feet, Lloyd persuaded Taylor, Anderson, and McGonagall to repeat the ascent quickly and secure photographs. What actually occurred on this second effort on Mount McKinley remains a mystery. The three may have climbed as high as Denali Pass, but photographs were never published, nor located later. When Lloyd's firsthand story was prepared by W. F. Thompson, it appeared with photographs in the *New York Times* on June 5, the account then immediately appearing in London's *Daily Telegraph*. Thompson, the experienced frontier editor who was pro-

The New York Times.

SUNDAY, JUNE 5, 1910.

FIRST ACCOUNT OF CONQUERING MT. McKINLEY

Thomas Lloyd, Leader of the Successful Expedition, Tells How He and His Comrades Planted the Stars and Stripes on the Heretofore Baffling Peak, the Highest Point on the American Continent.

DRAMATIC STORY OF THOMAS LLOYD

He Reinforces His Simple Narrative of the Remarkable Climb with His Diary of Each Day's Journey.

Alaska and rejoiced in the failure of "numerous Easterners" (who he termed "highbrows"), was a close friend of Bill McPhee and the other Sourdough sponsors. Thompson introduced Lloyd's story:

> *These four men have performed a feat that has set the world talking— a presumably impossible feat—during which they risked their lives a dozen times. They have stood upon the highest peak of the American continent, have seen sights that thousands of people would give much of their time and money to see, and have passed those sights up without particular interest or attention.*

Exulting at the Alaskans' feat, Thompson stated, "The Lloyd party traveled every step of the way across the vast glaciers on snowshoes, and declare that they can be traveled in no other way. Dr. Cook makes no reference to the use of snowshoes, nor is it a matter of record that he would know how to travel a foot upon snowshoes." Thompson claimed that the Sourdoughs reached "the summit from its base," and that this proved there were "two summits of equal height."[140]

> *Their only desire was to prove to their three backers and to the pioneers of the North that they personally were just as "husky" as they ever were and could still reach any place they started for—that and the desire to give to the Cheechacos "the laugh" by proving that what the Easterner brags about and writes about in magazines and which to the Easterner is impossible, the sourdough Alaskan performs as a part of "the day's work."*

Yet as the summer of 1910 ended, conflicting beliefs about the actual ascent tended to categorize Lloyd's sullied story as another frontier tale. Meanwhile, Lloyd held to his claims, stating that for $50,000 he would guarantee to make a permanent trail from the base of Mount McKinley, with lumber bridges across the crevasses, miles of continuous rope handrails, and shelter camps built of lumber, containing beds and stoves, "so that Mount McKinley may be ascended in safety and comfort by future Cook tourists."

As historian Francis P. Farquhar pointed out in a story on the early exploration of Mount McKinley,

> *It is unfortunate that Lloyd's boasting and the hasty acceptance of his exuberant report by his backers in Fairbanks and by the newspapers should have had the result of discrediting the truly remarkable achievements of the men who actually made the climb. Taylor and McGonagall, mining partners with Lloyd, were reluctant to talk. They had agreed to let Tom do all the talking and they stayed with it. Anderson was an employee of the partners, and in any case was not much concerned about what he appeared to consider as something all in the day's work.*[141]

Norman Bright, in describing his interview with Billy Taylor many years later, summarized the proof of the flagpole:

> *Had Lloyd, on returning to Fairbanks, told the simple truth, instead of padding his story so that all would get credit for the first ascent, there would have been no question concerning the validity of their claims. As it*

was, not until three years later was any credence given to the Sourdoughs'
just claim to the North Peak. Credit for the verification of their climb
should go to the eagle-eyed Walter Harper, halfbreed native boy, who,
climbing toward the S. summit with Archdeacon Stuck in 1913, de-
scribed, on the apex of the North Peak, the flagpole put there three years
before by Billy Taylor and Pete Anderson. Save for the splendid eyesight
of this Indian lad, and for the fact that the pole had withstood the storms
of three years, their climb would remain today merely as a mountaineer-
ing legend instead of as mountaineering history, and Billy Taylor's
recollections of the expedition would be regarded as pleasant fiction. For
the flagpole has disappeared long since.[142]

Bright concluded that Lloyd was searching for fame. "He conflicted his
stories by telling his intimate friends he didn't climb it and told others [and
the press] he was at the top."

Questions still linger about the Sourdough Expedition of 1910 and its
obvious heroic proportions, an almost unbelievable epic on a dangerous
polar mountain by men without alpine experience and with mostly primitive equipment. Yet, the fortunate flagpole sighting saved the event from
oblivion, confirming Hudson Stuck's belief in the basic story, unique "in all
the annals of mountaineering."[143] Certainly it was an intrepid feat by brave
and hardy men, who unfortunately climbed the lower North Peak rather
than the true summit of Mount McKinley.

▲ ▲ ▲

CHAPTER 6

The Greatest Heartbreak in Mountaineering History

*Only those who have experienced bad weather at great heights can
understand how impossible it is to proceed in the face of it. The strongest,
the hardiest, the most resolute must yield.*

Hudson Stuck
The Ascent of Denali, 1914

Belmore Browne was one of North America's leading expert outdoorsmen
in the early twentieth century. Descendent of a prominent Eastern family,
he matured in Europe and the Pacific Northwest, ingesting the liberal arts
during a mildly bookish education. Eventually Browne found in the Far
North the wilderness he so loved. He tarried for a year as a logger and then
undertook his sketching and painting apprenticeship. When he became a
renowned artist, Browne's superb paintings of Alaskan and Canadian
wilderness scenes, some featuring the great mammals, were exhibited in
prestigious museums. More than a mere witness to the northern environment, Browne became politically active when he and naturalist Charles
Sheldon became the prime movers to establish Mount McKinley National
Park. In 1916 both men were deeply involved in Senate hearings for the
Park's establishment.

By 1902 Browne's credentials were such that he was asked to join an
American Museum of Natural History expedition to Canada to collect
mammals. Under the famous Andrew Jackson Stone, he secured moose and
caribou in the nearly unknown Cassiar and Stikine regions of British
Columbia. Not large, but strongly built, Browne energetically stalked mountain game, securing some of the earliest specimens of Stone and Dall sheep.

As hunter-artist for Stone's 1903 expedition to Alaska's south coast and
the Alaska Peninsula, Browne killed some of the largest brown bears ever
taken, sometimes at great risk—as Robert H. Bates wrote in *Mountain
Man: The Story of Belmore Browne,* at times following "a wounded bear into
dense cover."[144] Three years later Browne solidified his lifelong wilderness

*Mount McKinley, showing Pioneer Ridge, the North Peak, and Wickersham Wall;
caribou herd feeding on tundra. Painting by Belmore Browne, 1915, oil on canvas.
(courtesy Glenbow Museum Collection, Calgary, Alberta)*

association with Professor Herschel Parker. Both staked their lives on
horseback in the fording of turbid torrents and a decade later on dangerous
glaciers where a crevasse fall could well be fatal. Browne most of all loved
the mountain environment and its mystic nature. As Bates has written, he
epitomized a breed of men who were more arctic explorers than alpinists.

In 1912 the thirty-two-year-old Browne was already a Mount McKinley
veteran. Certainly he had the ardor and organizing talent for a successful
ascent, especially given a three-month allowance for the approach. Browne
again teamed with his mountaineering partner Parker (whom he had met
on a Canadian Pacific train in 1905), and they were joined by a new
associate, photographer Merl LaVoy of Seattle. Parker, thirteen years older
than Browne, was head of the Physics Department at Columbia University
and had climbed both Mont Blanc and the Matterhorn before focusing on
the Canadian Rockies, where he made some first ascents.

Because Browne was satisfied that the Sourdough Expedition had pioneered the way to the South Peak of Mount McKinley via Karstens Ridge,
and because he was convinced that the southern and eastern façades were
impossible, he planned for the Muldrow Glacier approach and a wintertime

dog-team trek to reach the mountain's northern flank. He did not wish to risk being thwarted in reaching Denali from the lowlands in summer. Since sea ice had choked off Cook Inlet, Browne, Parker, LaVoy, and Arthur Aten of Valdez landed at Seward on February 1, 1912. With Aten mushing the dogs along the wintry trail to Cook Inlet, the adventurers plied northward where the Alaska Railroad now transports supplies and tourists. The men traveled on snowshoes, while the dog team pulled rawhide-lashed basket sleds made in Nome.

Along the frozen waterway of the Chulitna River, after they had passed the last settlement, the party had an unexpected surprise when it discovered a clever wolverine had climbed a thirty-foot cottonwood tree, stolen a food cache, and chewed up a camera case. Dismayed at this thievery, Browne reviewed his arms, which consisted of a .30-40 Winchester rifle, a carbine, and a Smith and Wesson .38 revolver, but the wily wolverine had long vanished, and Browne had to console himself among his books, which included works by Omar Khayyam, Shakespeare, Emerson, Stevenson, and Browning and a copy of *Reveries of a Bachelor*.

The evening of their last day in crossing a new pass in the Alaska Range well east of Mount McKinley, a route that saved many miles, ended with the only entertainment. This Browne later described in *The Conquest of Mount McKinley:*

> Four men and a pack of wolf-dogs, in a storm battered tent, slung on two sleds 6000 feet up on an icy ridge! The red hot stove cast a crimson glow on the strange gathering. Our party progressed splendidly, until "Laddie," Aten's "leader," backed into the red hot stove! In an instant the tent was filled with a choking, blinding cloud of smoke from the burned hair. A deep growl of disapproval came from the pack of dogs, and Professor Parker went head first through the tent door, and showed good judgment by refusing to come back.[145]

At their first camp on the north side of the range, Muldrow Glacier acted as a huge wind funnel. To save their tent the party was forced to build windbreaks out of their freight. As they began to push camps forward, they crossed a big-game paradise. Many caribou trotted across their route; ptarmigans and rabbits scattered about the party in seeming millions, and the snow was punched with moose tracks. Browne noted that the caribou ranged as high as the Alaskan bighorn sheep. From the sheep they shot, the men used the best ones for their climb—later they found that the fat on the skins did not absorb moisture when lying on the snow.

To avoid traveling up the convoluted lower glacier, the men searched for the best pass to reach Muldrow Glacier's middle section. Browne chose the central of three passes—5,720-foot Glacier Pass, now called McGonagall Pass—and during this reconnaissance was overjoyed at the promise of the proposed route on McKinley. On April 28 they began their advance on the mountain with a 600-pound outfit sledded by the dog team. Their equipment included one mountain tent, rope, ice axes, crampons, alcohol lamps, stoves, and fifteen gallons of alcohol. By modern standards the equipment was heavy. Their food consisted of 102 pounds of pemmican (a mixture of dried meat and melted fat that was popular in the Far North), with 75 pounds

"Summit of Alaska Range," 1912 (Merl LaVoy; courtesy Belmore Browne Collection, Dartmouth College Library)

more for the dogs, 100 pounds of hardtack, sugar, raisins, and chocolate.

Soon the party crossed the tracks of grizzly bears that were wintering among the icefalls of the glacier. To secure the firmest surface, the party traveled at night, but they were plagued by dangerous crevasses, the rope saving them from plunges into deep holes. Browne usually led, for he was the lightest and was accustomed to the treachery of crevasses, but nobody was immune—even two of the dogs fell into a crevasse and had to be rescued. One morning LaVoy did not probe while leading, and the snow suddenly broke. "I will never forget the few seconds that followed while La Voy's weight was pulling me towards the crevasse," Browne remembered.[146] Browne repeatedly jabbed his ice axe into the hard crust until he finally stopped only six feet from the edge of the chasm. Luckily LaVoy landed on a ledge of ice. Browne added, "I examined the crevasse as soon as he joined us; it was about six feet wide and as far as I could tell it extended to China."[147] This section of the Muldrow was so dangerous that the men had to probe the surface every foot of the way for over six miles. Then a new problem arose—bitter cold and snow squalls. The men took the dogs to 11,000 feet, where they left a 300-pound cache, and then descended to await improved weather.

The interlude at base camp allowed everyone to delight in the wilderness splendor. Browne wrote in his diary, "The northern lights were beautiful beyond words. The sun sank only a short distance below the horizon, leaving a blue twilight that threw a veil of mystery over the valleys and mountains; the cool smell of the snows crept down from the grim ice-barriers of the main range, and the lowlands rolled away to the Yukon like a great blue sea."[148]

On June 5 the final attack began, with Aten taking the dog team to the base of the first sérac. The constant crevasse dangers did not stifle Browne's precocious passion for scaling McKinley. There was also concern about avalanches; one was sighted falling some 3,000 feet from high on the northeast ridge. On June 8 the men heard unusual sounds, which they later discovered were from the Katmai eruption, 380 miles away. Because Harper Icefall topples over a great rock cliff, the party chose to detour to the northeast (Karstens) ridge between 11,000 and 14,000 feet, as did the earlier Sourdough party. After digging in at a col and fending off a blizzard with a snow-block wall, the men followed a sensational route along a great white knife-edge crest. Sometimes the party cut steps on the steep icy ridge, and sometimes the snow was soft, making step-kicking laborious. Finally, on June 24, they took their loads to the shelter of some rocks, placing a camp in the lee of granite slabs (later the location was called Browne Tower). Browne called this locale "the wildest and most desolate spot imaginable. We are on the very edge of the Big Basin that divides the two summits of Mount McKinley."[149] Here at 15,000 feet—higher and much farther north than the Matterhorn—the party became stormbound: the wind shrieked and avalanches boomed. Browne could finally rest his eyes, which had become so affected from light glare that he wore sunglasses inside the tent.

On the 26th the men established a camp 1,000 feet higher, where everyone suffered from the intense cold and the altitude. All had difficulty digesting pemmican—their staff of life. Each man wore all his clothing in a seventeen-pound sleeping bag. Browne had on three pairs of wool socks, two pairs of heavy wool underwear, woolen trousers, two heavy wool shirts, a sweater, a parka, a wolverine fur shield, and a muskrat fur cap to combat the minus nineteen degrees Fahrenheit temperature. Parker was dressed even more warmly, wearing a complete llama wool suit in addition to his mountain clothing. It is now believed that their diet contributed to their chilly state.

When the party carried loads to the "second sérac" at an estimated 16,615 feet, Browne described the savage cold after the sun had set: "On the south frozen snow-fields swept gently ... in an easy grade to the final or southern summit of the great mountain.... Our feet and hands were beginning to stiffen as we pitched the tent ... and we were seriously worried for fear Professor Parker would freeze."[150] Yet the prospect seemed optimistic for the next day: The final route appeared easy, with the summit only some 3,500 feet higher, and at night the temperature held at minus eight degrees. An early start on June 29 increased the mood, particularly when a firm surface crust permitted an ascending progress of 400 feet an hour. When the three men reached 18,500 feet, they were joyfully aware that they had surpassed the Duke of the Abruzzi's altitude record for Alaska, set on Mount Saint Elias in 1897. After continuing farther on the northeast ridge, everyone noticed a sea of clouds rolling like a surf against the main range to the south, but the summit cone—perfectly clear—looked innocent. Browne recited an optimistic note: "We *knew* the peak was ours!"[151]

But the southern sky rapidly darkened as they proceeded, and with little warning the hardy group faced a snow-laden gale. Browne's epic book describes how his companions "loomed dimly through the clouds of ice-dust and the bitter wind stabbed through 'my parka.'" Five minutes after he began chopping steps, Browne's hands began to freeze. "La Voy's gloves and mine became coated with ice in the chopping of steps. The storm was so severe that I was actually afraid to get new, dry mittens out of my rucksack for I knew my hands would be frozen in the process."[152] At last, Parker's barometer indicated they had arrived at the 20,000-foot mark. Browne was still determined to continue, although LaVoy's face mirrored the dangerous situation. As Parker passed them, his face showed white from cold through his parka hood.

"The last period of our climb on Mount McKinley is like the memory of an evil dream," Browne recalled in *The Conquest of Mount McKinley*. LaVoy was completely lost in the ice mist and Parker's form was a blur. Browne was forced several times to stop and fight with desperate energy the deadly cold that was creeping up his hands and feet.

The snow was hissing—an inferno of mist and blowing snow. Browne, who kept a detailed journal from which he wrote detailed accounts of his explorations, told of the ordeal: "As I brushed the frost from my glasses and squinted upward through the stinging snow I saw a sight that will haunt me to my dying day. *The slope above me was no longer steep!*"[153] The three men were midway between Farthing Horn (20,125 feet)—a small snow shoulder—and the true summit.

Browne kept moving onward a short distance and kept seeing the summit just ahead through momentary breaks in the tempest. He crawled along on hands and knees for about ten minutes but then gave up.

Bradford Washburn once concluded that this was one of the greatest heartbreaks in mountaineering history. "Exactly thirty years later [in 1942]," he recently wrote, "a U.S. Army party *strolled* to the top from that same spot in twenty easy minutes."[154]

The three climbers huddled for a brief rest but began to freeze. It would be suicide to continue. This prophecy seemed correct, for as the men retreated not a trace of footsteps remained. "We reached camp at 7:35 P.M. after as cruel and heart-breaking a day as I trust we will ever experience," Browne concluded.[155]

Their timing was unfortunate. On the following day, with clothing filled with frost particles and iced boots so that they simply could not climb, the storm subsided. Had they held up one day, likely Browne and his two stalwart companions would have been etched into history for the first ascent of the great Denali. A final effort on July 1 was halted at 19,300 feet when wind-driven sheets of snow forced them back again. Because the party's chocolate was now gone, and the ten-day stockpile of useless pemmican could not be digested, they simply could not remain at their high camp for another effort.

Certainly these mountaineers possessed the tenacity so necessary to endure the persistent discomforts of a sustained "polar" expedition at a high altitude. It has been stated that climbing and expeditions provide a sense of purpose and companionship seldom encountered in civilization. If this statement is ever true, it certainly applies to the heroic 1912 attempt on Mount McKinley.

The turnaround so near victory was an example of the sort of violent, cold wind that killed numerous climbers in later years. Browne's expedition deserved success but was foiled from further waiting because their fatty pemmican proved inedible at the high altitude. Although the party's camp was the highest yet in North America, it was low by today's standards, and a somewhat higher position should have assured success during the ideal weather on June 30. Hindsight makes this evident. Furthermore, as Mount McKinley veterans Robert Bates and Bradford Washburn both have pointed out, the frequent step-cutting that was necessary in 1912 because of the use of "ice creepers," which gripped poorly on the frozen surfaces in comparison to modern crampons, considerably delayed the party's pace and contributed to fatigue on the foiled summit attempt.

There is a sequel: A great earthquake struck the mountain on July 6, shortly after the party had descended, loosening great blocks of ice. The northeast (Karstens) Ridge was so shattered that Hudson Stuck's party, which made the successful climb to the South Peak the next year, had to spend three weeks hewing out a three-mile-long staircase in the shattered ice. Stuck once stated that even if Browne's party could have escaped the avalanching icebergs they could never have descended that ridge after the earthquake.

Browne's party made a providential escape, working their way back safely to base camp, where abundant rations and plentiful game awaited them. With renewed energy, the intrepid trio could face the 250-mile wilderness trek to Cook Inlet.

In our times, no expedition endures the explorations and risky wilderness approaches that the 1912 climbers did. As Mount McKinley expert Bradford Washburn wrote in a foreword to Robert Bates' *Mountain Man,* "Today's Alaskan mountaineers, equipped with down jackets, nylon rope, freeze-dried food and feather-light boots, look back on the mountain explorers of eighty years ago with both astonishment and respect. New equipment, techniques, and ski-equipped aircraft have revolutionized the game."[156]

▲▲▲

CHAPTER 7

A Missionary Leads the First Complete Ascent

I remember no day in my life so full of toil, distress, and exhaustion, and yet so full of happiness and keen gratification.
Hudson Stuck
The Ascent of Denali, 1914

An Episcopal missionary, Hudson Stuck, then Archdeacon of the Yukon, had carefully followed the mountaineering assertions and attempts on Mount McKinley. After the near-success of Browne's party in 1912, English-born Stuck, then forty-nine, decided to make his bid. By 1913 the Sourdough ascent of the North Peak was largely relegated to a frontier falsehood, yet Dr. Cook, though expelled from the Explorers Club, still maintained he had reached the true summit. Stuck, who had a boundless admiration for the Sourdoughs, whom he knew through his missionary rounds, fully believed their story and intended to follow their pioneering route.

As a traveling man of the faith, Stuck visited native settlements in winter with a dogsled, therefore becoming accustomed to hardship and the cold Alaskan winter.[157] Although by 1913 Stuck had lived in Alaska for nine years, he was an "unknown" to the press and in mountaineering circles, where the names Wickersham, Cook, Lloyd, Parker, and Browne had become familiar. Yet the missionary had done some climbing, notably in Great Britain as a boy (Scawfell and Skiddaw); later he had holidayed in Colorado and the Canadian Rockies and had climbed glaciated Mount Rainier.

Denali, as Stuck preferred to call the great Icy Crown, clearly cast a spell with its shimmering beauty. Of the glorious, broad, massive uplift, he asserted, "I would rather climb that mountain than discover the richest gold-mine in Alaska."[158] As the magic of Mount McKinley continued to grip Stuck, he methodically set out to recruit participants for his proposed expedition, the project now approved by his superior, the bishop. Stuck's principal choice was Harry P. Karstens, then thirty-five years of age, who carried a reputation as an expert wilderness explorer. An ex-Klondiker,

Hudson Stuck, the missionary who organized and led the successful 1913 ascent of Mount McKinley's South Peak (courtesy Charles E. Bunnell Collection, University of Alaska Archives, Fairbanks)

Karstens had freighted dog teams from the Yukon, had worked as a gold miner, and had guided the naturalist Charles Sheldon. In 1906 the two men appraised a potential summit route from the foothills via Muldrow Glacier.

For his other colleagues, Stuck chose youngsters Robert G. Tatum and Walter Harper. Both were twenty-one. Tatum, stationed at the Nenana mission, undertook to be the expedition cook. The half-breed Harper, a wise choice as it turned out, had been a dog-team driver in winter and a boat engineer in summer. None of Stuck's team had mountaineering experience, but all were tough and accustomed to the wiles of winter travel and survival. Of all the early expeditions to Mount McKinley, Stuck's appears to have been the most carefully planned and organized, unquestionably a vital factor in the final success.

For the standard footwear, Stuck chose a rubber "snowpack" boot that had leather soles fastened and nailed underneath; however, the party found that moccasins with up to five pairs of socks proved superior on the frigid upper slopes. The missionary had crampons and ice axes made in Fairbanks—the axes being "ridiculous goldpainted toys with detachable heads and broomstick handles."[159] For bedding, Stuck chose down quilts and camel's hair blankets, and Karstens purchased a twenty-five-pound wolf robe. The addition of four silk tents brought the costs of equipment and food to roughly $1,000, a mere fraction of the cost of previous expeditions. For cooking at the glacier camps, the leader wisely chose a Yukon wood-burning stove, this to be replaced by a primus stove high on the mountain.

With fourteen dogs and two sleds, the entire company, increased to six with the addition of Native American teenagers Johnny and Esaias, who

Left to right: Robert Tatum, Esaias, Harry Karstens, Johnny, and Walter Harper at Clearwater Creek camp in spring 1913 (photo by Hudson Stuck)

were to assist with base camp and the driving of a dog team back to Fairbanks, set out from Nenana on St. Patrick's Day. First following the beaten trail to the Kantishna gold camp, there was well over one ton of weight to be hauled to the mountain's base, including a generous amount of meat, milk chocolate, rice, figs, almonds, and tea tablets.

Their dogsled journey passed through a region that had changed greatly during the decade since Judge Wickersham in 1903 had found a virtually undisturbed wilderness. In 1906 there was a wild stampede to this region. Two or three thousand people went in, chiefly from the Fairbanks district. Small towns came into existence—Diamond City, Glacier City, Bearpaw City, Roosevelt, McKinley City—all with elaborate saloons and gambling places, at least one of which was equipped with electric lights.[160]

Following the Sourdough route, the expedition moved to Kantishna's Clearwater fork and then to the pass leading to Muldrow Glacier discovered by McGonagall. Below the 2,000-foot timberline of the Clearwater, caribou and mountain sheep were killed and the meat made into pemmican. Several hundred balls of minced meat were buttered, spiced, and then frozen. The animal hides were also used, carried as far as high camp for extra bedding.

The seemingly countless crevasses on the glacier made for dangerous travel. Wisely, the advance climbers on snowshoes probed with a long pole and remained roped. "The whole glacier," wrote Stuck later, "was crisscrossed by crevasses completely covered by snow.... Some of the gaps were narrow," he recalled, "and some wide, yawning chasms. Some of them were mere surface cracks and some gave hundreds of feet of deep blue blue ice with no bottom visible at all."[161]

The dogs struggled to pull the heavy supplies, now increased in weight by wood cut in the forest. Once, the favorite dog, Snowball, fell through a crevasse to a ledge. Karstens lowered Harper on a rope to pull the dog out. On May 1, when the party was near 8,000 feet, it was so hot that the men were "sweating, through four or five inches of new-fallen snow, while the glare of the sun was terrific."[162]

A near-disaster occurred when a cache at the base of the Great Icefall caught fire from a carelessly thrown match. Fortunately the high-altitude food was saved, but Stuck lamented the loss of sugar and baking powder. About this time it was discovered that the germ in the sourdough was killed by the cold; therefore, the dough failed to sour and rise. These events contributed to low energy and a craving for sweets and bread.

From just past Stuck's 11,500-foot camp, where the Muldrow ended in its immense icefall, on May 9 Johnny guided the dogs back to base camp. From here, however, Stuck found, to his complete dismay, that the northeast ridge showed no resemblance to the written description or photographs of the Browne–Parker Expedition of the previous year. Below a sharp cleavage on the crest was "a jumbled mass of blocks of ice and rock in all manner of positions, with here a pinnacle and there a great gap."[163] The glacier floor was strewn with "enormous icebergs," some the size of houses. Stuck was first perplexed at this situation, and then it occurred to him that this chaos must be the result of the earthquake that shook the mountain just after the 1912 party descended with their providential escape.

On a portion of the route that the Sourdoughs had climbed in only one day, the Stuck party spent three weeks hewing "a staircase three miles long in the shattered ice."[164] Every few yards presented a separate problem: once it took an hour to pass a thin ice block that needed to have steps chopped along its face.

Occasionally the men glimpsed animal life in this austere, icy wilderness. A rabbit had followed them nearly to the ridge, gnawing at the bark of willow shoots used as route markers, and ptarmigan were seen both on the Muldrow and at 16,000 feet. During poor weather the men spent time reading package labels, Stuck being amused by "the meagre English of the merchandisers."[165] Vacuum bottle labels informed them that a "glass product" could not be guaranteed against breakage. And Harper learned that by gathering 1,200 zwieback end-seals, he would be entitled to a free "rolled gold" watch (the zwieback had been the entire stock of a Yukon grocer). The sugar destroyed in the fire was a keenly felt loss, especially when an attempt at pudding without it became a failure.

Day by day the party advanced slightly farther on the ridge, always returning to camp. One day they were driven off by a threatening high wind that almost swept them from their footholds, but by May 25 it was feasible to occupy a new camp, one close to 13,000 feet. Here the sun struck the tent at 4:30 A.M., but the capricious weather changed rapidly. Clouds often swept about, producing snow squalls. "Sometimes everything below was visible and nothing above, and a few minutes later everything below would be obscured and everything above revealed," wrote Stuck in *The Ascent of Denali*.[166]

Karstens and Harper usually did the route-finding on the ridge, while Tatum and Stuck relayed supplies to caches. By May 27 the lead pair reached the ridgecrest above the earthquake cleavage, immensely raising everyone's spirit. Now traversing into what the men called the Grand Basin, a campsite was placed near 16,000 feet. This region of upper Harper Glacier was bitterly cold, with gusts blasting the men when they moved about. One night the temperature fell to minus twenty-one degrees Fahrenheit. Toes and fingers became very cold, even with their large moccasins and thick gloves with fur mittens. Despite the bitter morning cold, it could be insufferably hot at noon, with faces burning "as brown as Indians." Lips and noses split and peeled in spite of continual applications of lanolin. Thanks to new amber snowglasses, there were no eye problems.

While at the expedition's 16,600-foot camp, Walter Harper made a pivotal discovery: with his sharp eyesight, he sighted the Sourdough's flagpole on the ridge below the summit of the North Peak. Quick to share the profound excitement, all others of Stuck's party confirmed the existence of the pole with binoculars. This fortunate event rescued the claim made in 1910—for the pole was never seen or found again.

At this stage of the ascent, Stuck and his methodical group could barely go wrong: with fuel and food for some two weeks still at hand, they moved leisurely to a final camp on upper Harper Glacier near 17,500 feet. All of the party had been sleeping well, with sheep and caribou skins in the tent for insulation, down quilts, blankets, and the wolf robe for bedding. In fact, when the primus stove was operating, it was downright toasty in the crowded tent. With the boiling point thermometer registering 180.5 degrees Fahrenheit, rice required one hour to boil. Time was not a problem. Keeping warm, conservative progress, and maintaining everyone's health was the steadfast policy.

Now that it had been proven the North Peak had indeed been conquered, it remained for the missionary's party to tread onto the highest snowdrift of the North American continent. During the final, almost monotonous ascent on June 7, the four stalwarts circled eastward to gain the final northeast ridge, as Browne had the previous year. Clad in full winter outfits—"more gear than had sufficed at 50° below zero on the Yukon trail"[167]—they managed the summit rather easily, except for headaches, panting for breath, and the chill from the cruel north wind. As the wind drove the vapor from the peak, Stuck recalled, "So soon as wind was recovered we shook hands all round and a brief prayer of thanksgiving to Almighty God was said, that He had granted us our hearts' desire and brought us safely to the top of His great mountain."[168]

To the reverent Tatum, their unique position was like "peering out of the windows of heaven." Their chief impression, Stuck noted, was not of their connection to the flat earth far below, "but rather of detachment from it. We seemed alone upon a dead world."[169] Almost mystically, all could see the lingering snow "glittering with streams" above the horizon beyond the North Peak. In the opposite realm stood an infinite tangle of mountain ranges. To the now-fulfilled leader, "The snow-covered tops of the remoter peaks, dwindling and fading, rose to our view as though floating in thin air when their bases were hidden by the haze, and the beautiful crescent curve of the whole Alaskan range exhibited itself from Denali to the sea."[170]

The devout party made a few scientific efforts, erecting a small instrument tent. A mercurial barometer was set upon its tripod, and the men read angles with a prismatic compass. The alcohol minimum thermometer read seven degrees Fahrenheit. Stuck planted a six-foot birch pole with flag in the almost optimum conditions, yet he dared not withdraw fingers from his mittens to change camera film.

The descent was uneventful, safe, and methodical, a lesson for future mountaineers. At their old base camp, the leader related how the dogs gave "a most jubilant welcome.... What a change had come over the place! All the snow was gone from the hills; the stream that gathered its three forks at this point roared over its rocks; the stunted willows were in full leaf; the thick, soft moss of every dark shade of green and yellow and red made a foil for innumerable brilliant flowers."[171] There were packsaddles to make for the dogs, guns to clean and oil, bread to bake, coffee to drink, and biscuits that Johnny had ready. The ptarmigan had now begun their change to summer brown. In great numbers, their cries reminded Stuck of the Frogs' Chorus in the comedy of Aristophanes. Taking advantage of water not available on the glaciers, "we all took at least a partial bath in the creek, cold as it was."[172]

Crossing the broken terrain to the McKinley fork was toilsome: the thick elastic moss gave way three to four inches at each step, a feature of tundra hiking that numerous mountaineers and hikers have experienced since. The drainage of a previous night's rainstorm had swollen the McKinley fork's channels. When the main one was reached, Stuck recalled how its waters swept by Karstens up to his waist while he probed for solid footing.

The dogs did not like the look of it and with their packs, still wet from yesterday, were hampered in swimming. Two that Tatum was leading suddenly turned back when half-way across, and the chains, entangling his legs, pulled him over face foremost into the deepest of the water. His pack impeded his efforts to rise, and the water swept over him. Karstens hurried back to his rescue, and he was extricated from his predicament, half drowned and his clothes filled with mud and sand. There was no real danger of drowning, but it was a particularly noxious ducking in icy filth.[173]

Fortunately a warm sun enabled the victorious but now-wet party to bask on nearby rocks. Tatum, with no dry change, had to wring out his clothing and, to his regret, lost his ice axe, a well-earned anticipated souvenir.

While the Stuck party did not possess the remarkable endurance of the Sourdoughs, they wisely kept in good health and set a precedent for future mountaineers with their good judgement and careful procedures. Stuck began another precedent, this being a powerful opposition to the use of Mount McKinley as a name; he continued to plea for Denali, a sentiment shared today by a large majority of Alaskans.

▲▲▲

CHAPTER 8

The Hidden Crevasse and the First Tragedy

Allen Carpé and Theodore Koven were the first in a long and ever growing list [of fatalities]. Two beautiful snow peaks that tower above the scene of the accident have been named in their memory.
                         David Roberts
                         Mount McKinley: The Conquest of Denali, 1991

After the success of Hudson Stuck's almost uneventful expedition, another nineteen years would pass before man would again venture onto Muldrow Glacier. Unknown to each other before 1932, two separate expeditions had Mount McKinley plans that year. One would become the first scientific expedition, a high-altitude cosmic ray study sponsored by the University of Chicago and led by mountaineer Allen Carpé, and the other a proposed ski ascent and descent.

Alfred D. Lindley of Minnesota and Erling Strom, a Norwegian ski instructor, planned to use the mean between winter cold and summer storms, choosing an April 1 arrival. Upon reaching Mount McKinley National Park headquarters, however, they learned that mountaineering approval was now required and that, regardless of their experience, a two-man team was considered insufficient. Fortunately for them, Harry J. Liek and Grant Pearson joined them, abetted by an arrangement with dogsled teams to haul supplies.[174]

The Lindley–Liek Expedition used ski skins of seal fur for upward progress on Muldrow Glacier. The fur lies flat when the ski is slid forward but "acts like a brake," according to Strom, when the ski slides backward. Of the four men, Pearson was the only novice. Later he related how he felt "awkward as a duck in mud" when learning to use this specialized sports equipment. On a practice run Pearson fell face-forward into snow "so deep I figured I wouldn't get out till summer" (many a skiing beginner will be quite familiar with this experience). Fortunately he had the expert Strom as instructor.

The dog teams, which took supplies to 11,000 feet, had a much more difficult experience than the skiers while crossing crevasses. Pearson related how, once, part of a team dropped out of sight—two dogs dangling helplessly until the handler could pull them out. While the Lindley–Liek Expedition was progressing up the Muldrow, a ski-equipped Fairchild monoplane piloted by the veteran Joe Crosson landed well below them, to bring the scientific party members closer to the summit. This was the first such landing on the mountain's slopes. As Edward P. Beckwith, the scientific consultant to the expedition, later wrote,

> *Crosson turned the plane sharply toward the mountain and flew over a ridge, bringing the Muldrow glacier just below us, that is, the upper part, as it is some forty miles long. We flew back and forth about eight hundred feet above it, examining the surface carefully. It looked smooth for several miles. After considerable conversation with Carpe, which I could not hear above the noise of the motor, Crosson made his decision, apparently quickly, and dropped the plane toward the surface, landing with no difficulty whatever on about the middle of the glacier. The altitude measured slightly over six thousand feet, which was about the best we had hoped for. Carpe was delighted and shook hands with Crosson, who took it much as a matter of course and lit a cigar before leaving the plane.*
>
> *The mountain above was partly covered with clouds but the air was clear at the time we landed. The glacier was perhaps a mile wide with a high ridge on one side and a low one on the other.*
>
> *We immediately began to unload the plane. The time required was short, but it was enough to effect a complete change in weather conditions. Clouds descended from the mountain and a wind came up across the glacier which sent some of our lighter equipment on a journey. With it came blinding, drifting snow, not dry and powdery, but just at the point of freezing. It clung to every part of*

Northern slopes of Mount McKinley; E. P. Beckwith sketch shows route taken and accident scene in 1932. (courtesy American Alpine Journal)

our baggage and melted on it as the baggage was warm from the plane. It seemed to get into every part of the equipment, cameras, duffle bags slightly open, and where there was no opening the wind made one.

Crosson was seated in the empty plane and at his direction we wound up the starter. With no good-byes he disappeared in the whirling snow up the glacier. It seemed a long time before he left the ice, which was not remarkable since the required speed at this altitude was seventy miles an hour, but we saw that he did get into the air. We waited to hear him overhead as he would naturally circle and fly back. There was no sound but the blowing wind and we concluded he had probably crashed.[175]

Carpé and Theodore Koven skied several miles to find the aircraft stuck in the snow and, walking their way, Crosson, who made an emergency landing when the plane would not clear a ridge.

On the following day the ground party skied to the aircraft to assist another takeoff. Beckwith continued his narrative:

I was trying to take a photograph and at the same time respond to Crosson's yell to pull the tail around as he wanted to get off as quickly as possible. I left the camera open on the ice and as Koven and I swung the tail around a blast from the propellor caught the camera and I saw it disappearing down the glacier.[176]

The men now rocked the craft by its wings while Crosson drove the propellor at full speed. Beckwith jumped in at the last moment, experiencing a long, rough ride before getting airborne for Nenana. On the following few days, Crosson continued to shuttle team members and equipment between the glacier and Nenana without incident.

Meanwhile, along narrow Karstens Ridge, the Lindley–Liek Expedition packed along their skis with some difficulty. At one point they anchored

Allen Carpé pulling sled at first icefall on Muldrow Glacier, April 1932 (photo by Theodore Koven; courtesy American Alpine Journal*)*

their rope during a traverse around an ice corner "just above an almost sheer drop down to the Muldrow." While at their 15,000-foot camp, the four ski-mountaineers were surprised to see "a red airplane come up the glacier, circle near the head of the Muldrow, and drop bundle after bundle," a prearranged airdrop by Crosson for Carpé, who with Koven had now moved forward to an 11,000-foot campsite.

May 7 on upper Harper Glacier proved calm and clear. Because of the crusty, firm snow conditions, the Lindley–Liek party found their skis to be of no use, so they left them at the high camp. Although it was intensely cold, the party was fortunate to have four consecutive perfect days to climb both the South and North peaks—almost routine ascents. Heading down the Harper at one location, there was almost a serious accident. Pearson's crampon point caught on his overpants, causing a sliding fall on the frozen surface. In attempting to use his ice-axe point to arrest himself, the tool flew out of control to badly gash one of his wrists. Fortunately Pearson was able to halt, but he was an "awful sight," according to Strom. He was covered with frozen blood from the gash and other cuts received from the battering fall; luckily he had only lost his stocking cap, not his gloves.

Making a nighttime descent of Karstens Ridge, the party arrived at the Carpé camp early the morning of May 11, finding no occupants but two packs and sleeping bags. In *My Life of High Adventure,* Pearson recalled that it looked strange, because evidence within the tent suggested the occupants had not intended to be gone long.

Erling Strom's narration of the sequence of unfolding events appeared in a yearbook of the Norsk Tinde Klub (Norwegian Climbing Club); a translation from *Mt. McKinley* follows:

> *It is impossible for me to describe the impression it made on us to find the tents empty. Worn out as we now were after eighteen hours of constant toil and nervous tension, I must admit that everything whirled around in our heads for a few minutes. All kinds of possible thoughts flew through our heads. That something wrong had happened we at once understood. A thick layer of fresh snow covered all tracks around the tents. Everything showed that no one had been there for several days. Our first thought was of the Ridge, where we ourselves had just spent fourteen hours in intense excitement. Had these men also wanted to try to get up, perhaps used a rope, and then slipped and pulled each other down? Could we then have passed by where that had happened without detecting it? It astonished us to find only two sleeping bags. We had expected to find four or five men. Then we soon found the two men's diaries. One belonged to Allen Carpé, the leader, the other belonged to Theodore Koven. From these it appeared that the two men were brought to Muldrow Glacier by airplane from Fairbanks more than a week earlier, that they had followed our trail up along the Glacier, found the depot, and started to take their observations. On the 7th they had written in their diaries for the last time, but their cosmic ray observations continued until the 9th. They were then worried about the three other members of the expedition, who had not been able to start at the same time, and had not yet appeared. From the diaries we might conclude that the two men had gone down the glacier to meet their three friends.*

By this we became a bit relieved. We could hope that they had found the others further down the glacier, and that they were still alive, although we did think it peculiar that they had not taken with them their sleeping bags. Other things in the tents also indicated that they had expected to return the same day, but had not returned.

Having no peace of mind we did not consider the good rest we had hoped for. Neither did we take time for a meal, other than some rye crisp with butter and jam, before we started down the glacier. Our trail was not easy to follow. It was practically obliterated by 8 to 10 inches of new snow. Fortunately we had spent ten days on this glacier on the way up, and covered each section many times so we knew the route well. From time to time we saw some ski tracks in the new snow, made a few days earlier. Also these were more or less covered by the very last snowfalls. We noticed that they did not follow our trail very accurately. This frightened us again. If the men had not been able to follow the original trail they were bound to get into trouble. We should soon realize that this had been the case. Three miles or so below the camp we discovered a black spot to the left of us, well off the trail. We stopped dead. None of us said a word. None of us were in doubt.

Being in the lead on the rope I turned slowly out to the left. As we arrived close by, we stopped again. There in front of us with his face turned down was the body of a man lying in the snow. It was Theodore Koven. He was partly covered with snow, and appeared to have been lying

Upper Muldrow Glacier and Karstens Ridge (right), looking north from 12,500 feet. The 1932 accident occurred in the crevassed area in upper center of view. (photo by Allen Carpé; courtesy American Alpine Journal)

there for several days. A wound in the head and a bad wound in the leg, showed that he had fallen into a crevasse. He was not wearing skiis. We concluded that these were broken when he fell, that he then had been able to climb out, but on account of loss of blood and exhaustion had not survived very long. We could only partly follow his tracks, but saw that they led from a very dangerous part of the glacier.

In case we might possibly discover the fate of Carpé, we followed the tracks between a maze of big crevasses. Here and there we also detected some ski tracks. All of them were almost obliterated after the snowfall of the last days, so what actually had happened, it was impossible for us to understand. Wherever Carpé might be, we knew that he was not alive. Probably he was lying in one of the twenty or thirty crevasses in our immediate neighborhood. They were all extremely deep, some of such dimensions that a whole railway train might disappear into them. After an hour's careful search of the glacier at this spot, we gave up all hopes of finding him.

Our next thought was to bring back Koven's body with us to that part of the Glacier where an airplane might land. While Liek and Pearson sat down waiting for us, Lindley and I went back for the sled. It was a long hour to wait. As we came down again, we wrapped Koven in the tent we still had with us, and tied him onto the sled with our own rope, as there was no other. One end of the rope I pulled the sled with, Lindley holding back the sled with the other. We were both on skiis, while Pearson and Liek now followed on snowshoes. They did not dare use skiis, as we now could not wear a rope. The whole maneuver was risky, but something had to be done. We scarcely advanced 200 meters before Pearson, the third in the row, suddenly disap-

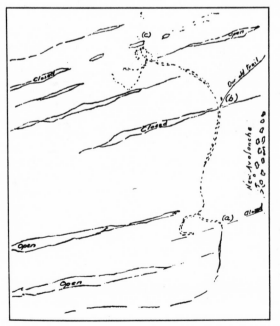

peared. A round hole in the snow between us and Liek was all we could see. We at once started to call, but at first got no answer. With a firm grip on the rope, Lindley went to the edge of the crevasse and called again. From the bowels of the glacier

Sketch from memory by Erling Strom of crevasses and footprints at the accident scene in 1932: A, position on route where Koven's body was discovered; B, position where body was left and Pearson fell into crevasse; C, fatal crevasse.

we heard a voice which answered "All right! But I need a rope!" Still another hour was spent, first to get the sack and then the man up again. He had fallen 40 feet right down, but into a small crevasse, where the knapsack was so wide that it touched the sides and slacked the speed. He broke his snow-shoes to bits, but was otherwise not hurt.

It became now quite clear that under these circumstances we had to leave Koven where he was. We needed the rope for ourselves and did not dare take any more risks. The sled we put up on end as a mark where we left him. We still had ten kilometers left of the glacier, with more than a hundred cre-vasses which we got to know about on our trip up, and at least as many which we had not yet discovered. Then also a sinister certainty that it was worth our lives to follow a trail which we could absolutely not see.

At 3 a.m. (the third day) we reached McGonagall Pass, at the spot where we might leave the Glacier. Here we found the second part of Carpé's expedition. One man (Beckwith) was ill. This was the reason for the delay. Another man (Olton) was there to nurse the sick one. The third (Spadavecchia) was wandering through the wilderness to find a hut with a telephone, so that he might call for an airplane from Fairbanks for the sick man. He had been gone for four days, and probably lost his way, but not yet in much danger, as he was in the lowlands, where ptarmigan abounded, and plenty of wood. Even without a gun we counted on his being able to kill enough for his own use.

If we now had had a tent with us, and not used it in another way (to wrap Koven's body), we would certainly have camped here. As it was, we continued to our original base camp, one Norwegian mile (10 kilometers) further down, where we already had a tent, plenty of provisions, chopped wood, and everything prepared.

This camp we reached at 5 a.m. on the third day. We had then kept going for 41 hours, each with 60 pounds on our back, and only eaten one small meal. In spite of it all I believe the psychic strain had been worse than the physical. Liek and Lindley just dropped on the floor of the tent and fell asleep, Liek with his knapsack only half off. Pearson, however, who felt better after getting off the glacier, had other things in mind. In starting to build a fire in our small tin stove he turned and said: "Well, there ain't no heroes without food, let's eat." I used my last bit of energy to open some tin cans. Having kept up with Pearson on this entire trip I could not let him get ahead of me this 42nd hour.[177]

Allen Carpé, then thirty-eight, was a research engineer widely respected for his Northland first ascents of Mount Logan, Mount Bona, and Mount Fairweather—an accomplishment in Alaskan–Yukon mountaineering that no other climber would equal in his time. He more than qualified for a seri-ous Mount McKinley ascent, but in an interlude of nonchalance, he and Koven became the first and needless fatalities on Denali. As Grant Pearson ex-pounded, "The story was plainly written in the snow—a stark tragedy of two men, supposedly experienced mountaineers.... They had gone down the gla-cier unroped, over a trail they thought they knew."[178] Two peaks in Denali National Park, Mount Carpé and Mount Koven, are named for them.

▲▲▲

PART II

THE LAST HALF CENTURY: A SURGE OF POPULARITY AND TRAGEDY

Climbing party below Windy Corner on West Buttress of Mount McKinley (photo by Olaf Sööt)

CHAPTER 9

The Western Route and the Ski-Wheel Airplane

With his usual determination, Washburn led the party up the West Buttress. He was, in effect, following his own dotted line—the one he had drawn on the photo published four years earlier.
David Roberts
Mount McKinley: The Conquest of Denali, 1991

Mountaineers continued to attempt and ascend the confirmed Muldrow Glacier route, perhaps recollecting Hudson Stuck's belief that the west side was sheer precipice and that, regarding a southern route, it did not appear from the top that such an approach existed. The first six ascents of the South Peak and three of the North Peak were made in virtually the same way. Robert Dunn, a Dr. Cook party member in 1903, was the first to suggest that the western barriers might be breached, but Belmore Browne was less hopeful, stating that he could not see one promising route. The prevailing attitude was "why risk failure?" when to reach Mount McKinley from the south and west was more difficult, more expensive, and a seemingly unacceptable length to undertake.

Ever since his photographic and mapping flights over Mount McKinley for the National Geographic Society in 1936, scientist, cartographer, and explorer Bradford Washburn had become intimately associated with the mountain. He had climbed the Muldrow Glacier route in both 1942 and 1947 and was the logical person to seek an alternative. Acting as his own visionary, he prophesized the West Buttress route and predicted that, with aerial support, it would prove to be the easiest and safest way to the summit. His aerial reconnaissance showed this buttress to be a long ascent route but technically relatively simple and virtually safe from objective danger.

By midcentury, Washburn had become a renowned explorer of the mountain ranges of the Yukon Territory and Alaska, and he was *the* Mount McKinley expert. As Ansel Adams wrote in the preface to Washburn's coauthored *Mount McKinley: The Conquest of Denali,* "You recognize the explorer in Bradford Washburn at first sight.... [He] is one of the very few

Operation White Tower research expedition's camp on Muldrow Glacier below Mount Carpé, April 1947 (photo by Bradford Washburn, Museum of Science, Boston)

Igloo-building near 18,000 feet on Harper Glacier during 1947 Operation White Tower research expedition. Jim Gale, left, and Hugo Victoreen are the designer-builders. (photo by Bradford Washburn, Museum of Science, Boston)

people who have combined spectacular experience in the wilderness with equally spectacular achievements in the world of civilization."[179] Preparatory to making his own climbing plans for the western route on North America's highest mountain, forty-one-year-old Washburn agreed to join a Colorado group that planned to set forth on this route in 1951.

With his customary careful planning and securing of support services, Washburn arranged with the Alaska Air Command of the U.S. Air Force for a drop of the majority of the expedition gear near Kahiltna Pass—west of the summit near the 10,000-foot level. The goals of Washburn and his seven teammates were to make surveys for a detailed map, discover a new and feasible route to the summit, and study geologic structures along the way.[180] The joint expedition was sponsored by Boston's Museum of Science, the University of Alaska, and the University of Denver.

The 1951 expedition, in a sense, was a continuation of the surveying program that Washburn undertook in 1947—Operation White Tower—during which an extensive field testing of cold weather outdoor and mountaineering equipment had been carried out and a cosmic ray research station was set up at Denali Pass. Captain William D. Hackett, stationed at Fort Richardson in Alaska, had taken part in the 1947 expedition.

Because of its size, the team was initially divided into two groups. On June 20 and 21, 1951, Terris Moore, an academic New England bush pilot who was then the University of Alaska's president, landed Washburn, Hackett, Jim Gale, and Henry Buchtel at 7,600 feet near the base of Mount Crosson on the previously unvisited Kahiltna Glacier. Moore used his 150-horsepower

Super Cub on hydraulically operated ski-wheels and found the landmark glacier landings on aluminum skis relatively smooth and routine. This high landing gave the expedition a tremendous advantage over one that required a long approach from the coastal lowlands—such air support would forever change the nature and tactics of most Mount McKinley ascents.

On June 22, upon reaching a 10,100-foot base camp near Kahiltna Pass, Washburn's party received a series of airdrops by C-47 transport planes of the Tenth Rescue Squadron. In all, there were thirty-nine free-fall units and five parachute loads of breakables among the one ton of supplies. All the drops landed within 200 yards of camp, and one bundle even fell within six feet of the mess tent. Among the air-dropped food were ample quantities of frozen chicken and strawberries from Birdseye—an arrangement that Washburn had thoughtfully made long before heading to Alaska from his New England base.

On the day of the airdrops, the four mountaineers dragged in the bundles, tramped out an 800-foot landing strip for Moore, dried the parachutes, and set up tents. On the next few days, the men climbed Kahiltna Dome, where they read many angles with a theodolite. Standing somewhat isolated at 12,550 feet, this summit was climbed more than once for photography and surveying. On June 25 Moore skilfully landed again with a small load, Hackett noting in his diary, "He landed perfectly."[181]

The remainder of the team made a long overland approach by horse pack

Bradford Washburn sighting through a theodolite on "Peak Z" (Kahiltna Dome) during West Buttress expedition of July 1951; Bill Hackett is recording. (photo by Bradford Washburn, Museum of Science, Boston)

Terris Moore's Super Cub on Kahiltna Glacier with Mount Hunter in left background, June 25, 1951. Katrina and Terris Moore on left; Barry Bishop on right. (photo by Bradford Washburn, Museum of Science, Boston)

from Wonder Lake and then traveled on foot to Peters Pass before continuing on to Kahiltna Pass. As this group progressed, they mapped, studied the geology, and climbed Peters Dome. Meanwhile, the air support intensified on July 2, when Moore landed with more supplies and the air force made additional drops.

Base camp now featured an igloo, three Logan tents (seven-by-seven-by-seven feet), and a five-foot wall tent. On June 29 the four climbers spent the inclement weather making up food packs for eight men for two weeks. Considering that the expedition had purchased forty-nine varieties of food items in Anchorage, this became a detailed task. Certainly the men were eating bountifully, given the airdrops of frozen fryers, potatoes, corn, peas, strawberries, and sliced bacon. That evening they served themselves fricasseed chicken well seasoned with salt and paprika.

When the mountaineers set off for the next camp at 13,100 feet at the head of Kahiltna Glacier, they were burdened with monstrous packs—a symbol of Mount McKinley climbing tactics. The next camp was placed near Windy Corner (which Hackett named during a morning blizzard that blasted the party's igloo and cook tent). To make the location more secure, a second igloo was constructed. The highest wind recorded at this camp by the anemometer was eighty-one miles per hour. During the snows that accompanied this wind, several feet drifted over tentage and equipment, requiring continuous digging. Meanwhile, on June 30 the overland party of

Barry Bishop, John Ambler, Melvin Griffiths, and Jerry More arrived at base camp.

Beyond the altitude of 14,000 feet, the expedition's real toil began. It was necessary to plow almost 1,000 feet directly upslope on snowshoes until a breakable windblown crust and loose snow beneath made further progress almost hopeless. Without snowshoes, a man would sink waist-deep.

For three hours Washburn and Gale shoveled and tramped a deep trench for some 200 yards, finally coming to a steeper and firmer slope. In a short distance this slope became hard ice, "each step requiring 20 or 30 hard whacks,"[182] as Washburn remembered it. Near the top of the slope, the laminated ice became so treacherous that the two climbers took to the adjacent rock—but found the climbing hardly better. To speed and secure forthcoming relays, they left a thin, fixed rope trailing on the ice slope during the descent.

Near the bergschrund below the ice slope, the two men built a small igloo (future Camp II) and slept well while a sixty-mile-per-hour wind roared through the night. The next day the weather quickly changed for the better, and the route soon eased with intermittent shattered granite and well-packed gradual snow slopes. On a shoulder of the buttress at about 17,200 feet, Washburn, Gale, and Hackett built an igloo at what became the expedition's high camp.

On the night of July 9, the temperature stood at three degrees above zero, "a tropical reading for that altitude on McKinley," as Washburn later wrote. "A brilliant half-moon rode in the sky just above the icy dome of Foraker."[183]

July 10 was "summit day." Heading for Denali Pass, the three men climbed half-hardened sastrugi altered with patches of loose powder and breakable crust—all lying atop ice. Amid the choppy snow at the pass, they sighted the old cosmic ray cache, now a solid, immovable, cemented mass. In his *American Alpine Journal* account, Washburn related, "The cache of food and equipment left neatly by Gale, Victoreen and Lange at the end of their cosmic ray work in 1947 was an incredible mess. The 1948 expedition [of Walter Gonnason] ... had removed the covering from the cache ... abandoned it to the elements ... as wanton an exhibition of vandalism as could be seen in the mountains." Washburn added with disdain, "The day is sure to come when this tragic thoughtlessness may be seriously felt by another party equally in need of food and tentage."[184] Indeed, this came true in 1967, when the first winter ascent party barely found enough survival food from this same cache. At the pass the thermometer left by the 1947 party registered minus fifty-nine degrees Fahrenheit.

Given the ideal weather, the South Peak's summit was easily attained. In *National Geographic*, Washburn extolled on the vista, "a cloudless panorama stretching nearly 400 miles from horizon to horizon ... in a single sweeping glance!" It was possible to identify many great peaks, including Mount Hayes and Marcus Baker, and Lake Minchumina, which shone "like a jewel on the plains."[185]

This was the seventh ascent of Mount McKinley; the conditions were ideal, for the clouds had dissipated and it was no colder than zero.

On the 11th, Washburn, Gale, and Hackett descended all the way to base

West Buttress expedition of 1951 during the first ascent of route. Climbers Bill Hackett (ahead) and Jim Gale approaching summit of South Peak, July 10, 1951. (photo by Bradford Washburn, Museum of Science, Boston)

camp, while the others methodically moved into higher camps, the last of them reaching the summit in good form by the 14th.

The Washburn Expedition proved that airplane landings were feasible on Kahiltna Glacier and that the West Buttress was the ideal summit route. The Kahiltna had fewer crevasses than the Muldrow, and the route was relatively safe but for the onslaught of storms. In addition, the western exposure made it warmer than the Muldrow, with the prevailing westerlies behind one's back rather than "cutting squarely into your face."

Before many more years passed, bush pilots appeared, mountain guides set up business, and the era of the adventure traveler–mountaineer began. As a consequence of the loosening of National Park restrictions and the dramatic increase in the number of climbers, however, there was a rise in injuries, frostbite, mountain sickness, and death. The West Buttress route has become the standard, but it never will be a trade route for the unfit. Since 1951, when eight mountaineers carefully and successfully climbed to the summit of the South Peak, the mountain has become increasingly social: in 1970 more than 100 climbers appeared, in 1976 more than 500, and today over 1,000 set foot on the great Icy Crown every year.

▲▲▲

CHAPTER 10

A Buttress to Each McKinley Peak

Washburn has often said that the joy he gets vicariously from seeing others succeed on difficult new routes he'd discovered ... was almost as great as if he'd done the climbs himself.
David Roberts
Mount McKinley, The Conquest of Denali, 1991

Judge James Wickersham, who led a small Fairbanks party to about 8,000 feet onto the immense northern flank of Mount McKinley in 1903, concluded, "Our only line of further ascent would be to climb the vertical wall of the mountain at our left, and that is impossible."[186] Under the appointment of President William McKinley, Wickersham served as U.S. District Judge in the territory of Alaska from 1900 to 1908, but the good magistrate was a mere adventurer, not an alpinist. He knew the Far North and understood its frontier society and its politics, but he had no training in deciphering the complex variables concerning one of the world's greatest mountains. Furthermore, given the crude mountaineering equipment of the day, there was little chance that his would be anything more than a mere sightseeing trip. It is well that Wickersham halted there, for he was far more valuable as a territorial leader than a heroic victim of avalanche, a fall on steep ice, or destruction by the fierce elements.

Fifty years later, Alaskan mountaineers were far more experienced, had climbed in other ranges, and possessed equipment barely resembling that which the honorable judge carried. The word *impossible,* a curse that still applies to some mountaineering challenges, was gradually becoming a pedantic term. The grand 17,000-foot wall that Wickersham described and was eventually named for him—the greatest sweep of topography in North America—was not a place for 1903 mountain dabblers. Wickersham Wall was eventually climbed by two routes, but not until sixty years later. And it has never become popular with the human ants that now crawl along the favored West Buttress as if it were a honey pot.

Not long after midcentury, the Alaska Alpine Club, while small in membership, had grand ideas concerning challenging new routes on the mountain that Wickersham called Denali. During the club's series of informal meetings at the University of Alaska in Fairbanks, students and faculty were considering two unclimbed routes during the 1954 season. Both objectives were massive buttress formations—one leading to the South Peak from the south and the other trending to the North Peak from the northwest. Dr. Donald McLean, recently graduated from medical school, and Charles R. ("Bucky") Wilson, a physics researcher who enjoyed speculating about the origins of the northern lights, conceived a plan to forge a route near where the judge had probed decades earlier. Another faction, inspired by Elton Thayer, made plans to traverse the great ice mountain from south to north. Both notions, however, were not original ideas but, rather, were inspired by Bradford Washburn's illustrated proposals—which gave the three-time McKinley summit veteran a vicarious pleasure. Having accomplished a careful mapping of the convoluted terrain, Washburn was pleased to suggest new lines of attack to prospective alpine heroes.

Two other climbers were soon added to the Northwest Buttress expedition plans: Captain William D. Hackett, who learned of the proposed expedition through Washburn, and Henry Meybohm, a German skier who had emigrated to the United States in 1951. Engaged for ski patrol near Fairbanks during the winters at the local ski hill (the area claimed to be the nearest one to the North Pole), Meybohm soon met the local mountaineering fraternity. When McLean invited him along for a ski tour to test his stamina for an expedition, it was Meybohm who broke trail and set the pace.

Hackett, thirty-five at the time, was chief of training at the Mountain and Cold Weather Training Command at Fort Carson, Colorado. Carefully managing both military and mountaineering careers, the enterprising Hackett had already climbed Mount McKinley twice and, during World War II, led a platoon of the U.S. Army's Tenth Mountain Division in Italy's Appenine Mountains, for which he received a Silver Star for Gallantry in Action. He was now on a quest to climb the highest summits on each of the world's continents. With his military connections, Hackett arranged to test "walking penguin" down sleeping robes and vapor-barrier sleeping pads for the air force. The white felt army boots were so oversized that one could wear four pairs of woolen socks; while the boots proved warm, they hampered foot control with crampons. Four members of the party carried two pairs of these boots, one pair to be kept dry for use above 15,000 feet.

The expedition had three mountain tents: one was a four-man Logan tent with centerpole, and one was a prism-style French tent for two persons. The remainder of the equipment was the standard of the times: flexible crampons, gold line climbing ropes (prusik slings were carried for crevasse rescue), long ice axes with wooden shafts, aluminum-frame packs, and snowshoes.

McLean and Wilson had long ago decided to undertake the ascent in May, anticipating better weather even though it would be colder than in summer. As Fairbanks climbers, the cold was less of a threat than the possible wet snowstorms of July. Food had been prepacked for a ski-plane landing on Peters Glacier by bush pilot Dick Collins. The packing effort assumed that the food would be landed, and not air-dropped, as eventually was done by the army.

Less than one month before the planned May 2 departure from Fairbanks, Hackett suggested that I join the already-formulated team. Wishing to add to my experience of three previous Alaskan expeditions (none in the Alaska Range), and not being involved with a serious romance at the time, I decided affirmatively rather quickly. While not purposely avoiding the months of planning, procuring supplies, and packing, the opportunity to join a "ready-made" expedition was hard to resist.

When I arrived at Fairbanks on the flight from Seattle, my first reaction was to shiver. There was still snow in the black spruce forest, and the chill bit through my springtime traveling clothes when I stepped outside the airport building. But with a warm greeting from the remainder of the party—all new acquaintances except for Hackett—the environment seemed more hospitable. That same day I shopped about the city for warm clothing and had a wolverine fur "ruff" sewn onto my army parka hood.

Fairbanks seemed like a wintry Oklahoma plain, with its frontier culture, clapboard buildings, the birches and willows appearing barren on the hill behind the several bustling principal streets. Only the boreal forest along the Chena River floodplain reminded me of the evergreen Pacific Northwest. But beyond the still-frozen river, far to the southwest, rose Denali, the route of the Sourdoughs almost directly facing the city. The fierce pioneer pride that had given birth to the valiant ascent of the North Peak in 1910 was still evident among the citizenry—a legacy of the mining heyday.

Fairbanks, once a tent city after the discovery of gold in 1902, was preceded in Far North fame only by Nome and the Klondike, whose reputations were established by frenzied stampedes. At one time "gold fever" kept Alaska prices as well known as the abundance of the yellow metal, but even in 1954 living costs were very high (stated to be 116 percent higher than those in Washington, D.C.). When I purchased aspirin at the local drug store, I found the cost to be twice that of a bottle in Seattle. Residents tended to blame the Alaska Railroad and steamship companies for high freight rates—which have some validity considering the distance and separation from the "lower states."

The former gold-mining camp was located on a bench of the Chena River, the northern terminus of both the Alaska Railroad and Richardson Highway. We visited prospecting outfitters in the business district along First and Second avenues, where log houses of pioneer construction still stood nearby—the city obviously still close to its frontier past. There was even a Finnish bathhouse (which we did not visit) and the North Pole Bakery, which freezes thousands of loaves of bread to be thawed later in outlying camps.

"Bucky" Wilson, a physicist at the Geophysical Institute, briefly showed us the campus of the University of Alaska, perched on a hilltop above the river valley and which specializeed in arctic studies. Here is a concentration of serious polar scientists and many of the world's best students of auroral activity and of the earth's magnetic field. Talk turned to the nearby Nenana Ice Sweepstakes, a famed Alaskan institution that was reaching its annual frenzy. Each year officials rig up a tripod on the frozen Tanana River and connect it to a clock on shore. As the ice cracks and shudders during movement, the wire from the tripod snaps, halting the timepiece.

The lottery, which was begun in 1917 by residents who hoped to relieve the long winter boredom, now draws thousands of Alaskans (and the world press), who attempt to wager the day, hour, and even minute of the ice breakup. More often those who trust astrology to determine the exact time of this unreliable event come closer than the scientific engineers of Fairbanks, who once spent much time taking daily measurements of ice in numerous rivers and then averaged the ice melting and its final destruction. In 1932 an Anchorage resident was told by an astrologer that the ice would break on May 11, but because the stars failed to inform the astrologer as to the exact hour that the ice would move, the resident covered every minute of the day at $1.00 per minute—altogether betting $1,440. That year, however, the ice broke on May 12, and a Fairbanks bus driver collected $70,000 on a $1.00 wager.

We would miss the excitement of the sweepstakes, due to soon occur. After assembling the many boxes and canvas bags of equipment and food that our Fairbanks contingent had put together, we took it by truck to the airport. From here we flew to frozen Lake Minchumina on May 2—a distance of some 150 miles—in a twin-engined Beechcraft. It was a grand, bright day, with the sun reflecting the snow-covered tundra and muskeg and, to our left, the magnificent bulk of Mount McKinley, getting ever larger in our personal windows. At this frontier hub we transferred to a

Mount McKinley Northwest Buttress party at frozen lake near Straightaway Glacier, May 1954. Left to right: Captain Bill Hackett, Charles ("Bucky") Wilson, Donald McLean, Fred Beckey, Henry Meybohm (photo by Charles R. Wilson)

smaller craft, a Piper Pacer on skis, owned and piloted by Dick Collins of the local Civil Aeronautics Administration.

In several trips Collins flew us some sixty miles to a frozen lake where a ski-landing was readily made. Here, at the foot of Straightaway Glacier, we could see the entirety of our proposed route. On May 2 Wilson recorded in his diary, "This is about the most beautiful scenic spot I think that I will ever see. McKinley is about 15 miles away and is 18,000 feet higher than this lake. I am sitting here in some soft moss and heather slopes ripe with red berries with my shoes off and no shirt enjoying the view and solitude. A ptarmigan bird is rattling at me from a distant mound."[187]

Wilson, who took the first flight, could scan the proposed route from 12,000 feet to the summit of the North Peak. "It looks truly difficult," he noted in his diary. McLean later commented in his account for the *American Alpine Journal* that a major drawback to the northwest route was the late daily arrival of the sun—all but the peak would be shadowed until 11:00 A.M. Wilson, meanwhile, felt good about the party he had helped organize and, at the same time, recognized that we all would have the "charm and warmth of the heather country without the plague of mosquitoes that will reign in a few weeks."[188] In this peaceful, remote, and quiet part of the world only a small bird made a "peep."

The first chore was to walk four miles with snowshoes, carrying nine days' supplies and five additional packets of food to cache at the glacier terminus for the return hike. By the time we slogged two more miles over snow-covered tundra to a bench campsite at 3,400 feet, we were tired. On May 3 we "webfooted" along grassy benches and snowpatches, once following a moat some distance. We placed our outbound cache on the moraine, high on an eight-foot boulder that we hoped the bears and rodents could not reach.

The reflected sun made the moat hot, and we were glad to arrive at a cooler position just above the corner of Crosson Glacier. After supper, while some of us repaired snowshoe bindings, Wilson wandered up a talus slope in the hope of getting echoes. "They answered 4 times!" he jotted in his diary. By the next evening we had climbed from 5,800 feet into 8,200-foot Peters Pass and descended the sastrugi-covered slopes of Peters Glacier. In his account, McLean wrote, "Here we were shocked to find the sun shimmering on the glare ice of the glacial basin, where we had anticipated deep snow to cushion our air drop!" Not far ahead lay "Cook's Shoulder," its white mass studded with ice patches in pastel shades of green and blue. "It was broken by fields of séracs and icefalls, by a headwall and great yawning crevasses, couloirs streaked with avalanche debris and topped off by a huge pyramid of rock,"[189] he added.

We established base camp well out of reach of avalanches on a patch of flat sastrugi that had survived the blasts of the wind. Surrounding us in the great basin was the dirty tone of névé (old snow from the previous year). Casting a glance sideways at the overwhelming Wickersham Wall, which rose to the summit of the North Peak in an unbroken and dangerous sweep, we were relieved that the Northwest Buttress did not seem to present a particular ice avalanche hazard. Before retiring for the night, Wilson jotted down some thoughts: "This climb is going to take a lot of work.... I feel that Bill Hackett will be a steadying influence on Fred" (referring to my possibly favoring a more technical route-line than the others desired).

The expedition now divided into teams to carry loads toward the lower buttress. On May 5 Hackett and I explored a route to the southwest, climbing to almost 10,000 feet, but found poor rock amid the ice pitches. Wilson and McLean encountered soft snow atop hard ice on their probe; the climbing was awkward and a traverse over an avalanche chute caused brief concern.

As the snowfall thickened during the day, and with increasing wind, we decided to split our food rations in the event that our expected supplies became delayed; in the morning we tramped out an airstrip on the bumpy surface. When back in the tents to cook breakfast, we heard the roar of an airplane engine: Collins had passed low over the glacier. We had expected him to land or make a drop, but he never returned. Although there seemed little point in searching, we went out onto the glacier in two ropes toward the pass, but in the poor visibility saw nothing. Then, at exactly 10:15 A.M., Dick and Jeanne Collins strolled unexpectedly into camp. Wilson recorded, "I was so surprised that I knocked over the tea in the tent." Crowding into our shelters, they explained that a downdraft had forced the plane onto the glacier perhaps one-half mile away. Although it overturned, they were unhurt. Wilson, like all of us, was amazed that they had survived not only the crash but had walked unroped, safely, into camp. "It was a miracle that one of them didn't go into a hole!" he wrote in his diary. Several of us had already punched through into large crevasses without wearing snowshoes, but we had always been roped.

A check on the airplane during the blowing snow had determined that the radio did not function. The entire right side of the craft was mangled, including the wing, ski, and elevator. The food inside was brought back to camp during high winds, when the tents were taking a blasting. Not long after, the turbulence again threw the aircraft over on its back to essentially destroy it.

In the evening McLean, Meybohm, and Collins returned to the crash site and confirmed that the plane was now a relic on the glacier. In the meantime "the wind was up to 100 m.p.h. and Fred and I had a hard time holding the tent down," Wilson noted in his diary. We turned the French tent around and prepared for a violent, crowded night, one that promised no sleep. Rather quickly, thoughts turned from the Buttress to survival. With the high wind sweeping the glacier cleaner than ever, it seemed safer to crawl than walk when outside the tent. "Chunks of ice & snow were being blown horizontally," Hackett wrote in his diary.[190] I was glad that we were at 7,000 feet, in the lee of the main tempest, rather than on the exposed 18,000-foot summit plateau. We avoided answering the "call of nature" except when absolutely necessary.

After the storm conditions subsided partially on May 8, Wilson and McLean decided to escort the Collinses to the frozen lake, where they hoped a rescue would be made. A last stop at the airplane disclosed that it had flipped over again and lost a wing. Near the pass they sighted an SA-16 reconnaissance airplane searching the valley below, but the pilot did not see their mirror signal.

Climber on Cook's Shoulder, near 9,000 feet on Northwest Buttress during the first ascent, May 1954 (photo by Charles R. Wilson)

It was a hard hike for the fliers, especially with the additional trauma of losing a $7,000 uninsured aircraft. To aid in the search, the party had cut some trees to spell LAKE in six-foot letters with a large arrow beneath; at the lake a pile of dry spruce was lit as a signal fire. Wilson later observed in his diary, "The most unusual thing about this whole rescue business is that the 'kopter didn't see us when he flew within 100 yds. of our signal five times. The SA-16 was over us three times and didn't see us." The reason given later was that the search pilots did not expect the ground party to have walked out so quickly and were concentrating nearer Peters Glacier. On the evening of the 10th, the Collinses were found and taken to Lake Minchumina.

Meanwhile, Hackett, Meybohm, and I solved the route to the top of Cook's Shoulder by cutting a glassy staircase that began on the left flank of the slope. We made a cache at 10,500 feet. Beyond was a cornice that fell steeply to the north, probably just beyond Dr. Cook's high point in 1903. It was here that a member of that party, the packer Printz, remarked, "It's not that we couldn't have done it if there was a way; there ain't no way."[191]

Not long after the Collinses were rescued, "Ginny" Wood flew past, scattering expedition equipment and food over the glacier. When we retrieved the airdrop, we found that the food bags had exploded, the duffel

Northwest Buttress party on ice slope of Cook's Shoulder, near 10,500 feet (photo by Donald McLean)

bags had torn, the spare ice axe was broken, and one of two fuel gallons leaked; the supplies and food had not been packed in anticipation of an airdrop. There were still more expedition supplies at Lake Minchumina, and concern grew that we would need them on the mountain. Wilson recently wrote to me that "the army was talked into parachuting our food and equipment into us at Peters Basin by 'Ginny.' If it were not for her help in this matter, we would have had to abandon our attempt."[192]

On the following day an Albatross of the 74th Air Rescue Service made a merciful appearance, setting loose a bundle and two cargo parachutes near Peters Pass—this ending the aerial bombardment. That evening Wilson and McLean appeared in sight near the pass, returning from their escort tour.

On packing a load to the Shoulder on May 12, Wilson recorded in his diary, "The route has about five spots where a slip would be fatal for the whole party. It is mostly hard snow in which steps have been chopped, but there are some spots of blue ice." Because the knife-edge ridge cornice at 11,000 feet proved to be a "balance act," McLean and I first cut some steps to facilitate the crossing with packs—"an extremely exposed spot," agreed Wilson when it came his turn. He added, "It is about one foot wide and drops 3,000 feet on the south and 2,000 feet on the north." McLean added his version:

Sitting astraddle this knife ridge during delays was like riding a horse! Camp I was established beyond this tricky crest, at the "windless oasis," perhaps 300 feet below and to the left of the ridge at 10,500 feet for reason of protection from possible high winds. Beside the Logan and French tents Fred dug a snow cave which we fortunately never were obliged to use for anything except storage.[193]

During a final relay on the 14th, coming back across the ridge with loads to the 11,300-foot cache was very bad. Wilson noted in his diary, "The wind was blowing the wet snow and we made very poor time up to the rocks." From the cache they could see McLean and me at the base of the rock pyramid at 12,000 feet and, surprisingly, could hear us talking 1,300 feet higher than their position.

We were now beyond Dr. Cook's last probe and nearing the pink granite cliffs laced with black schist, which he had accurately described. On May 13 McLean and I climbed gradual windblown slopes and then frozen schist that was loose and unpleasant to the crest of a large rock pyramid. This prominent formation, which Hackett referred to as Abruzzi Ridge, was composed of reddish brown schist that McLean described as cracked in all directions but with a favorable dip for climbing:

The slope began at about 20° but steepened as we reached the pyramid where there was actually an overhang in places. We climbed unroped because of the severe exposure and treacherous nature of this loose rock, some-

Party digging out Camp I on Northwest Buttress. Left to right: Beckey, Wilson, and Hackett (photo by Donald McLean)

times frozen, sometimes not. By placing fixed ropes on a few of the rock tow-ers leading to the pyramid, we were able to make it reasonably safe for travel with packs weighing about 40 pounds. On the following day we all reached the top of the pyramid, utilizing more fixed rope but not as much as we would have liked. Here at 12,500 feet we placed another cache and, on the following day, Wilson and I set up the French tent at this elevation.[194] We reconnoitered above this, leaving camp in the late afternoon because earlier the scud had prohibited higher travel. It felt good to be once again not only on crampons, but roped as well. At 13,100 feet we were blocked by another escarpment of rock, Pyramid II. Not knowing what lay above or beyond this rock cliff, we traversed around it to the left, across a great sloping cirque. We could see above us the long serrated ridge which we had just skirted, while the steepest portion of the Wickersham Wall, looking very very bad, lay in profile to our left. A broad snow-filled couloir led from the cirque back up to the northwest ridge, well beyond Pyramid II and the cathedral spires that surmounted it. After six hours of continuous step chopping up this couloir, we reached the northwest ridge again at approximately 14,200 feet. The ice

Lenticular cloud during ascent beyond Abruzzi Ridge on Northwest Buttress (photo by Donald McLean)

chips here would skip and slide down to the Tuluna Icefall, 6,000 feet below us. The rock on the ridge had changed to black schist, especially dark in contrast to the overall whiteness of the snow. Here, well above the clouds which obscured everything below 13,000 feet, stood only Denali and Denali's wife, McKinley and Foraker, alone and serene. The clouds, like a greater Niagara, poured down from central Alaska eastward between these two peaks, reaching as far as the Kenai Peninsula, where they simply evaporated upon reaching the sea. From here it would be an easy go on crampons to the base of the last real obstacle, the rock pitches at 14,800 feet and an ideal site for Camp III.[195]

Fortunately we were able to use the last of a three-day fair-weather spell to climb onto the solid granite rock blockade—a section of the route that appeared to be the technical crux. Hackett, Meybohm, and I put in about 400 feet of fixed rope here, someone joking that I had placed the first of several rock pitons on McKinley. To end a long and hard May 19, we cached loads at over 15,000 feet at the ridgecrest.

To subdue our elation, the following day at our second camp proved to be a poor one. According to Wilson's diary, we spent the hours "talking about our past experiences with women and enjoyed it thoroughly." At the time Hackett was reading *The Sex Habits of American Women*, which Meybohm urged him to finish. According to the others, I was deeply immersed in Edith Hamilton's *The Greek Way to Western Civilization*.

Camp atop Abruzzi Ridge on Northwest Buttress (photo by Charles R. Wilson)

It snowed for much of the 21st, and in camp the dialogue ran from our reading to logistical plans. When we went to sleep, the temperature had dropped to a very polar minus twenty-two degrees—it was too cold to even play Hearts. But the sun shone the next morning: we dug out and laid our sleeping bags out to dry. Because Wilson and McLean were ready first, they drew trailbreaking duty. After entering the couloir they had to kick steps in soft snow for four hours before reaching the 14,200-foot saddle. All the old steps had been filled in with sixteen inches of new snow, which gave everyone extremely cold feet. I dallied at a rest stop and took my boots off, attempting to warm toes under my down jacket. McLean and Hackett that day established our third camp by setting up a tent at 14,800 feet under the massive rock cliffs.

The cadence of weather turned good again on May 23, enabling further load-carrying on the rock buttress, where six inches of new snow made the progress difficult and cold. Wilson observed in his diary that the rock climbing was the most serious he had ever encountered. The last pitch from 15,400 to 15,600 feet, which required three hours, "was a bitch—ice between the rocks under the snow made it extremely difficult. I was in the middle of the rope. Fred was belaying me from above and Bill was belaying me through a piton and carabiner and I fell. My foot slipped on the snow and down I went. I fell about six feet before the rope tightened." Wilson grabbed a handhold and pulled. "If it weren't for the good belay we all would have gone down about 4,500 feet." Wilson was not really shaken, but "winded from the effort of lifting [his] body and pack with one hand at an elevation of 15,500."

After the exertion of bringing heavy packs up the ropes, which now draped the buttress, a natural dip on the buttress was welcome. It was a logical and pretty spot for Camp IV. The temperature was frigid, but we were optimistic about our chances for the summit. Although it snowed that night, the morning was again clear. Meybohm, Hackett, and Wilson carried loads to 17,400 feet on a route-finding mission. For a time during this five-hour "easy walk," it was actually hot, making the tour hard going. In the meantime McLean and I hauled the remaining equipment on ropes from the 15,400-foot belay spot and then carried on to a 16,600-foot snowfield point on the ridge—and our first view of the South Peak.

In the morning it was so cold that it took 3½ hours to get moving. McLean recalled,

We all reached the new cache at 17,000 feet the next day, deciding to place Camp V there early in the evening because the weather had closed in. We purposely had carried only the Logan tent above Camp IV. To set up camp here at 17,400 feet on a moderate slope, we were obliged to cut a six-foot platform, the inner wall of which was four feet high. In a way, it was unfortunate that we had had such excellent weather because we had climbed so fast that we had not become acclimatized. Three of us suffered headache, nausea, and vomiting. I administered to each an intramuscular injection of Acth-Ar-Gel, a pituitary hormone which stimulates secretion of the adrenal cortex and is known to be of exceptional value in stress conditions.[196]

"Today was a bitch!" Wilson wrote in his diary. "Fred was very sick and yet he managed to climb to 18,000 with a light pack and then to 18,600 with no pack." Wilson recalled that I collapsed a number of times and vomited six times "on all fours." "He is really ill. But made a valiant effort."

Carrying fifty-pound packs to the 18,500-foot camp was grueling. Wilson noted, "I took 6 deep breaths to every step." We were suffering from the effects of the altitude; our camp would be the highest yet pitched on Mount McKinley.

On the morning of May 27, Wilson paid for the previous day's effort with dizziness and vomiting. Some hot tea was comforting and helped combat the bitter cold outside the tent. All of us had spent poor nights because of the cramped space. Donning all the clothes we could muster, we laced boots, tied into the ropes, and started for the North Peak, but then the weather closed in. After a long rest in the tent, we began again, this time making an easy two-hour ascent to reach the top at 6:45 P.M. The hoped-for view was murky, and a planned descent by Wilson and McLean to look for the Sourdoughs' flagpole was scuttled because of approaching weather. The temperature stood at twenty-five degrees below zero, but there was hardly a breath of wind.

The next three days "were miserable and difficult." The cold "made life horrible," wrote Wilson. Each morning our sleeping bags were covered with a half inch of frost, which soaked us and "made sleeping with the wind battering the tent almost impossible." Hackett wrote in his diary for the 30th, "We all pray that good weather will release us from this existence by morning."

May 31 dawned cold and clear with a forty-mile wind. We arose at 3:00 A.M. and began drying boots and clothes for an attempt on the South Peak, beyond Denali Pass. But we had to turn back in one hour because of the hostile elements. Wilson's diary read, "The hair on our faces was covered with ice and frost." We did make another start on the first day of June but soon saw the situation again degenerating into a high-altitude storm. McLean, now quite sick, wrote, "When the fuel ran out and we were forced to descend, we left without regret."[197] Descending was awkward because all the old tracks were lost; sometimes our boots would strike a mixture of fresh snow and ice. At the ridge of Point 18,000 feet, "Don was so unbalanced that we were afraid he would fall off," wrote Wilson in his diary. We halted at 15,600 feet, where we could now sleep in two tents again.

The storms of the past few days had scoured off the upper plateau and McKinley's summits but loaded the buttress and Wickersham Wall with deep, dangerous new snow. Descending the granite cliff was not only dangerous but also difficult with packs. The great blocks of speckled-orange granite were blurry white ghosts of strange configuration—reminiscent of a Patagonia nightmare. Finding anchors required probing and digging. In the end we made five 200-foot rappels to reach the 14,700-foot level, with Meybohm finding this technique a new experience. He "did extremely well," jotted Wilson in his diary. Meybohm then led the way from the schist ridge to the 13,100-foot camp through snow that was often hip-deep. We tied all the ropes together, descending 440 feet in one sequence. The progress, wallowing forward with much exertion, made for "a really difficult day."

Bill Hackett rappelling from rock step on Northwest Buttress (photo by Donald McLean)

Finally we reached the campsite, totally exhausted, at midnight.

After drying out sleeping bags during a fine morning, McLean, now feeling well after the descent, forced a path through more hip-deep snow for two hours. At Abruzzi Ridge the steep slope on its west seemed dangerous, so we took to the rock and made a series of ten rappels. In his account for the *American Alpine Journal,* McLean had this comment, "The great cirque over which we had strolled in our ascent was now covered with six feet of new snow. Fortunately, we had a small aluminum shovel which could be attached to an ice-axe, so we were able to dig a path until we finally came to the ridge where the winds had blown much of the snow away."[198] What should have taken us three hours of simple descent required eight hours of taxing effort. That night at the 11,000-foot camp, Wilson complimented me in his diary, "Fred did a terrific job of setting up the rappels," adding, "Henry continued to be the best tempered person on the trip."

During the slow descent, while each man waited for his turn to rappel, we had time to study the changes brought on by the advancing season. To our east, the grand Wickersham Wall was more laden with new snow than it had been during our ascent, and warmer temperatures combined to set off cascades of avalanches. To the far west, the great tundra and gravel plains of the Alaska Range's slope seemed dark in tone, now shed of their winter cover. And, as Wilson penned in his diary, "Lake Minchumina was fire orange in the distance."

Curiously, we spotted an aircraft flying near Straightaway Glacier far beneath us—this the third one we had seen or heard in the past week. "I wonder if they are checking on us?" noted Wilson. On our final day on the Northwest Buttress, there were only scattered cumulus against the dark blue sky. Exertion reached a high level, because the sticky snow constantly balled-up on our crampons. We were nervous about the "gumbo" conditions, which required that we knock off the snow from our boots with an ice axe at each step, fearing that the surface might begin to slide in the sun's warmth. At only one place under the snow did we strike ice, where we set up a rappel.

By the time we had bid farewell to Mount McKinley and crossed Peters Pass (where we had left our snowshoes on the moraine), it was time for head nets and mosquito repellant. Because we had filmed the ascent and now had to carry out a heavy movie camera and numerous sixteen-millimeter film rolls, our packs were both heavy and cumbersome. Wonder Lake—some fifty miles distant—seemed as far as the moon.

Wilson's diary entry for June 5 began, "We left Crosson Corner camp at 10:30 with Bill & Henry off like race horses." By the time we arrived at our old food cache, we sighted our first caribou. Camp that night on the soft tundra became a "greeting party" for the seemingly thousands of bugs. Because our tents had no netting, sleep was impossible in this tundra region.

The next day my feet, somewhat frostbitten from the cold on the mountain, were beginning to pain and I fell far behind the others among the sedge tussocks of the tundra. Fortunately, when Wilson exchanged his shoepacs for my U.S. Royal boots at Slippery River, my pace improved. While the others were waiting for me on a moraine ridge with a clear view in all directions, the next episode occurred, described here by Wilson. "We sat to wait for you and looking back saw a large brown bear following you. We shouted at you to turn around to see the bear and the bear, hearing our noise, stood up on his hind legs just as you turned around. The bear was huge—both you and the bear ran off—but in different directions."[199]

Muddy River crossing between Peters Glacier and Wonder Lake, with the Wickersham Wall in the background, May 1954 (photo by Charles R. Wilson)

Just before reaching the Muddy River (which drains Peters Glacier and flows into the McKinley fork of the Kantishna), McLean and I became separated from the others because we wanted to take a swim in a small lake. The bugs were so relentless that the others put up the Logan tent immediately on reaching the river. Not knowing where they had struck the river, McLean and I could not find the camp. In the morning of the 7th, Wilson, Hackett, and Meybohm went out to search for us before breakfast, thinking that the bears might have done us in, but in fifteen minutes we met.

The river, turbid to its name, delivered its icy waters from Wickersham Wall. As we looked for a crossing, we saw a maze of gravel bars and channels that constantly altered its course. Since it was common knowledge that Wilson was the best swimmer of the party, he stripped and swam the frigid, rushing brown torrent with a rope tied to his waist and, in doing so, hit his knee on a rock. "I remember feeling that I was not going to make it just as my hand got a root," he jotted in his diary. He made it up to a small tree, to be greeted "in my nakedness by the mosquitoes." He later recalled that the others were more interested in laughing at his predicament than "throwing my pants over to me." Wilson recalled that on a previous attempt on the mountain (in 1952), he had to swim the Muddy River in the same spot "because all other eight people claimed they could not swim!"[200]

To get the rest of us and the packs to the opposite bank, Wilson carefully set up a belay rope from the tree and a tight handline—the crossing procedure took until nearly noon. Now we followed the Muddy's torrent for some five miles, Wilson limping from a sore knee, and then bore east several miles to Clearwater Creek. We finally arrived at its confluence with the McKinley River. The fording of its thigh-deep braided channels (all coming from Muldrow Glacier) had its dangers, but they were mild in comparison to those of the Muddy. After wading some one dozen channels, it seemed that my painful feet would never be normal again.

McLean and Wilson continued that day to Bar Cabin in three more hours. Here they sighted the signatures of Morton Wood and Les Viereck in the cabin register and wondered about the statement "in memory of Elton Thayer." McLean later wrote, "It was grim news to receive after our own thoroughly enjoyable trip."[201]

On our final day Meybohm and Hackett left for Wonder Lake to arrange for a ride to the McKinley Park hotel. A Mr. Hardy appeared with a car, agreeing to drive us for $25.00, and in the process we learned the details of the Thayer tragedy. We could now forget about the overweight packs, sore feet, and tired backs while taking one last glance at Wickersham Wall glistening in the sunshine and, near its right perimeter, the Northwest Buttress. In the years since, it has never become a popular route, but as Jonathan Waterman wrote in *High Alaska,* "it offers the full spectrum of climbing snow and ice cornices, a knife-edge ridge, couloirs, frost-fractured schist towers and pink-speckled granite."[202]

▲▲▲

Even before the expedition to the Northwest Buttress had left Fairbanks for Peters Glacier, the four-man party organized by Elton Thayer to climb the South Buttress had already reached Ruth Glacier. Thayer, who had worked as a ranger in Mount McKinley National Park, had made first ascents of Mount Hess in Alaska and King Peak in Yukon Territory—both major summits in their respective ranges. His teammates, all Alaskans, were Morton Wood, George Argus, and Les Viereck. Each had considerable wilderness experience but little in the way of technical mountaineering skills. For all of them, an ascent of Mount McKinley by a new route would be a significant accomplishment. In the tradition of the early pioneers, the men decided on a long overland approach without any aerial support except for a supply drop.

The exploit, which began on April 17, 1954, at Curry on the Alaska Railroad, involved carrying top-heavy seventy-pound loads with the danger of grizzly bears and river crossings and the exasperation of struggling through tangled alder growth. Wood described one of the approach problems in the *American Alpine Journal:* "We had been obliged to use our snowshoes during the entire trip, and in the heat of the day one could never take more than two steps without knocking off the heavy mass of wet snow that adhered to them. This condition continued for the 50 miles to our base camp."[203]

On the seventh day the four expeditioners had snowshoed past the gargantuan granitic monoliths of Ruth Glacier's Great Gorge—today considered one of the mountain world's most spectacular topographic features and the scene of extremely difficult modern alpine rock ascents. By prearrangement, the expedition received an aerial supply drop from Wood's pilot wife Ginny.

Wearing their long and heavy trail snowshoes past Mooses Tooth, Rooster Comb, and Mount Huntington (none of which had even been attempted), the Thayer party reached the head of the glacier's western fork, as had Belmore Browne in 1910. The South Buttress, a massive feature of Mount McKinley that separates Ruth and Kahiltna glaciers, had not yet seen the footprint of a human, although Browne and his partner had come to perhaps 600 feet of its high glacier col. The route's principal problem was conjectured to be its length and average height: Eight miles of the buttress are located above 15,000 feet. Because the Thayer party was planning on traversing the mountain, all supplies had to be carried forward in relays, coming back to camps as necessary for additional loads. Wood continued his story:

We began to realize that this route would be too dangerous in any adverse snow conditions, as the height of the steep walls on each side of the glacier exceeded its width. To find safe campsites would then be impossible.

Elton and George, tied into one rope, explored to the south as far as they dared and found nothing but impassable séracs. Les and I went to the right along the rim of the crevasse to the edge of the glacier and found one possibility which would involve climbing down to the wide bottom of the crevasse, then cutting steps up the other side. If this could be done, I could see that we should be able to reach the other side by digging a short tunnel up through the ice and snow of the overhanging lip. This we did and, upon emerging into the daylight again, called for Elton and George to climb down and tie their packs onto the rope which Les and I lowered to them.

Getting ourselves and all our gear up through the tunnel consumed considerable time, but by 10:00 we had arrived at what appeared to us the least dangerous spot for our base camp. Before us rose the sheer walls of the head of the canyon. Blue ice slopes of 50° to 70° pitch, icefalls, and rock cliffs led us to dismiss the possibility of this originally proposed route. Our previous study of the aerial photos had given us no idea at all of the fantastic height of this canyon's sides. We had seriously underestimated not only heights but also the steepness of the route.[204]

The four climbers now realized that farther right there was a forty-five-degree slope that offered their only possibility. Although the slope was broken by several icefalls, there were smooth areas that appeared to be safe. That afternoon Thayer and Wood still found time to make a short examination of the slope.

On May 3 the climbers cut steps for hours on the crux of this 1,200-foot slope, and then the cold and fatigue forced a return to camp. "One of our greatest difficulties," wrote Wood, "was in trying to keep out of the way of falling ice chips dislodged by the lead man cutting steps."[205] On the following day, the men chopped some 100 yards of steps in five hours of steady work. Then, they installed three ropes to make the load-carrying safe.

On the night of the 5th, following a day of intense cold and little progress, a three-day storm arrived, coinciding with that striking the Northwest Buttress party, and "made it scarcely possible to move outside." The home-made tents (surrounded by snow blocks) withstood the battering of the blizzard, although it "seemed no fabric could possibly resist such stress as the storm inflicted." On May 9 the party dug out the drifted camp to find the skies clear again. The Thayer party now made continuous progress along the high buttress, except at the first peak on the crest, where they were forced into almost boyhood antics. Here they were blocked by an immense cornice, not of snow, but of ice—"an overhanging glacier if such a thing exists!"[206] This obstacle fortunately formed a strange ice cave through which the party walked and crawled for a long distance. In some places, each man had to remove his pack and push it along.

When they attained the long buttress crest at 15,700 feet, the four men could scan the northern flank of Mount McKinley and the still-white tundra stretching toward the Tanana River. The men had now been at or near 15,000 feet for so long that they were well acclimatized. As anticipated from Washburn's photographs and a route outline that he had carefully prepared, the climbers marched across the wide glacier basin below and east of the South Peak (now Thayer Basin). At just over 17,000 feet, the route they had pioneered merged with Karstens Ridge—now a familiar feature to five decades of Mount McKinley mountaineers.

Here Thayer's party left packs, climbing in good conditions to the summit on May 15, accomplishing the third route on the vast mountain. With the victory attained, they now faced the next, and seemingly easier, objective—completing the first traverse.

On the following day the weather was sunny, but snow conditions were too soft for a good descent. When reaching Karstens Ridge just below 13,000 feet, the surface was very hard for an ice-axe shaft belay, whose security in any case was flawed because both Argus's and Wood's tools had been broken earlier and now were repaired with tape. Descending one at a time on a single rope with their heavy packs, the loose surface and drifted snow underlain by ice, the party came to an old fixed rope fastened to wooded wickets. While Argus led, with Wood next, Thayer was last. As the four men skirted north of the crest, where it was less steep, but with a 2,000-foot drop to Muldrow Glacier, "Elton slipped and started sliding," Wood reported later to the National Park Service.[207] Because Thayer was last on the rope, he developed speed and all belays pulled out. In his article, Wood described the almost-instantaneous action:

> When I saw Elton slide past, I braced myself to be able to hold the point and pay out rope gradually in case Les should be dislodged from his position. In seconds he was pulled loose and my belay was not strong enough to hold two men. This all happened in a flash. After that, I only remember tumbling end over end in the loose snow, now and then being pulled by the rope and always unable, because of the heavy packs, to roll over on my stomach and dig in my axe to check.... It was like a bad spill while skiing in powder snow except that it seemed to last for an eternity. I remember once falling ... and then landing on my pack in deep snow. It was not at all an abrupt jolt but rather a ... glancing blow. More sliding, rolling, and another long free fall—then suddenly silence except for the gentle hiss of the snow that was still in motion all around me.[208]

Wood recalled almost suffocating, his chest constricted by the rope's strong pull. The force barely permitted him to breathe, then with a struggle, he managed to loosen the strain. His pack's magnesium frame was smashed to pieces. Then he saw Argus, sitting in the snow and asking, "Where are the others?" Wood recalled, "I looked up for the first time and saw that Elton had fallen over a vertical outcropping of ice about 15 feet high and was hanging from the rope." After Wood and Viereck lowered Thayer and determined that he had died, a feeling of nausea and weakness swept over everyone. "I felt like giving up,"[209] wrote Wood, who believed that the impact of the rope from the free-fall's force broke Thayer's back.[210] Scanning the slope above, the men concluded that they had all slid out of control from 800 to 1,000 feet, when the fall was arrested by Viereck, who had landed in a crevasse.

By now the sun had set behind the North Peak, making the air bitterly frigid. Wood and Viereck, still badly shaken, erected a tent and got Argus—whose legs pained badly and whose teeth had been pushed in—inside and into a sleeping bag. He was only half-conscious; later it was learned that he had broken a hip.

The stricken mountaineers now remained in their tent for six days, fervently hoping someone would fly by and read their emergency messages stamped in the snow. On May 22, when the party was already overdue, Wood and Viereck wrapped Argus inside a tent, placed him atop two air mattresses, and then tied rope loops around him to get him downslope. With one man ahead and one behind, they ventured down the exposed slope, one no climber would consider under ordinary circumstances. While still in avalanche danger, the two men finally cut troughs in the ice to slide Argus to the Muldrow.

On the next day Ginny Wood flew by in her Cessna 170, her altitude limit of 11,000 feet keeping her from getting abreast of Karstens Ridge, where she suspected they might be. With the party below her in the shadow, where she did not expect them, she failed to sight them.

Discouraged by this turn of events, and now nearly out of food and with only one quart of fuel remaining, the desperate men decided to descend the dangerous Muldrow Glacier for a rescue. Fortunately Argus was able to cook, read, and even use an improvised bedpan made from a gallon gasoline tin. When they finally reached the Park road near Wonder Lake in record time, Wood and Viereck saw no tire marks. The road entry was still closed!

"The prospect of walking another 85 miles to the railroad was at this point almost too much for us to bear,"[211] wrote Wood. Despite being "dog-tired" from the lack of sleep, the two men trudged on to Kantishna. While resting at a cabin, they heard a voice across the river. Soon it was evident that the chief ranger and Grant Pearson had shoveled through drifts and made the first trip of the season in a station wagon.

Soon a rescue team reached Argus by helicopter, finding he had survived the lonely vigil surprisingly well. In a tribute to their lost leader, Wood later wrote these fitting words: "Of Elton Thayer it could be said that climbing to him was a deep spiritual experience rather than a mere struggle to accumulate as many ascents [as possible] or impress others with his feats. He climbed because he loved the mountains."[212]

▲▲▲

CHAPTER 11

Denali's Child—1954

*It is the steepest and most spectacular of the three great peaks in the
Alaska Range.*
                    Jonathan Waterman
                    High Alaska, 1988

To honor expedition sponsorships by his aunt in 1903, Robert Dunn had
applied the name *Mount Hunter* to a minor uplift on Mount McKinley's
western buttress—now Kahiltna Dome—but when maps appeared after
the turn of the century, the name mysteriously appeared for the third
highest peak in the Alaska Range, on the opposite flank of Kahiltna
Glacier. Through a government surveyor's error, a spectacular unnamed,
14,570-foot colossus of rock and ice nine miles south of Mount McKinley
became Mount Hunter. As generally was the case, the earlier native name
did not survive: the appellation of the natives was *Begguya* (Denali's child).
Dr. Cook, who often saw the strategically located mountain, called it Little
McKinley, and more than one prospector referred to it as Mount Roosevelt.
   Not remotely resembling Mount McKinley or Mount Foraker (Denali's
wife), Mount Hunter is a massive, complex bulk with three summits, seamed
with cliffs 4,000 to 7,000 feet high—a three-mile-wide high plateau with
numerous icy ridges that on a map resemble the tentacles of a spiny octopus.
   Now considered the most difficult 14,000-foot peak in North America by
knowledgeable mountaineers, little was known about the present Mount
Hunter until Bradford Washburn made a photographic study flight and in
1953 published a detailed proposal for a probable route via its five-mile-
long west ridge.[213] Unlike Mount McKinley, Hunter's highest peak is the
northern one, but like McKinley, the western ridge has become the most
popular (although not the easiest) route to the elusive summit.
   In late spring of 1954, after the expedition to Mount McKinley's Northwest Buttress, Henry Meybohm and I decided to extend our mountaineering forays to Mount Deborah and Mount Hunter, fortunately enlisting the
most capable companionship of the famous Austrian mountaineer Heinrich
Harrer. The renowned alpinist, who took part in the Eiger's first ascent in

Mount McKinley (top left) and Mount Hunter from southwest. Note West Ridge of Mount Hunter above clouds (September 6, 1966). (photo by Austin Post, U.S. Geological Survey)

1938, was visiting Alaska for the first time. Harrer drove from New York City in a "beautiful" green Packard and on the graveled Alcan Highway "had countless blowouts and flat tires."[214] Originally, Harrer just wanted to travel about the United States, but he changed his plans when he saw a *National Geographic* article illustrated with mountain photography, including Mount Hunter and captions indicating the peak was unclimbed. "I tore out these two pages and went to Alaska, where I found you by chance," Harrer recalled recently.

While I was on Mount McKinley, Harrer had climbed Mount Drum in the Wrangell Mountains and was now ready for a more serious challenge. After we met through common friends in Fairbanks, the three of us readied for an attempt on the imposing Mount Deborah—its unclimbed, corniced summit striking a spire into the sky southward. The Austrian's best recalled anecdote related to expedition preparation: "I told you and Henry to buy food for 20 days—one kilo a person a day. I also said, buy what you enjoy to eat, I don't care. After we landed on the glacier and Sheldon had left we sorted out all you had bought: it was the greatest amount of weight with the smallest amount of calories. I learned for the first time the way of American institution."

After the ascent of Mount Deborah, Don Sheldon, who had not yet gained fame as a skilled glacier pilot, flew us directly to Talkeetna. Inspired by Terris Moore's glacier landings, Sheldon had recently converted his green Piper Super Cub to have ski-wheel capability. Still elated by our quick success on Deborah, the three of us spent an impatient week under cloudy skies in the little town, where we were likely considered bizarre mountain tourists. In the early 1950s the town was merely a boat landing on the Susitna River and a way-stop on the Alaska Railroad. Tourism had not yet made its mark (there was an inn and a trading post), and anyone appearing in alpine attire was probably marked as a bewitched personality who was preparing early for Halloween.

To add to our abnormal appearance, instead of staying at the inn or tenting out, we set up headquarters in Don Sheldon's hangar. Alaskan hospitality reached out quickly. During our first saunter through Talkeetna, we met an outdoorsman who, upon learning our plans, offered to let us stay in his hunting cabin in the Dutch Hills (which we later did). Another resident set us up with the opportunity to fish the river. While waiting for the cloudy weather to move out, we caught three great salmon—the largest weighing fifty-four pounds. Relaxing in Talkeetna turned into a generally good time.

One day Sheldon came over to our corner in the hangar and asked, "Do you get any money for climbing?" Not quite satisfied with our philosophic ramblings on our "inner needs" for alpine challenges, he returned in an hour and asked if we would like to make some money. With Harrer skeptically quizzing the adventurous bush pilot, Sheldon explained that an aircraft had crashed on a mountain (he did not disclose where) and that he needed alpine climbers to get the payroll in the crash and bring it down the mountain. The tentative plan was that Sheldon would purchase an old airplane and land it in the very confined crash area. Because the airplane would never be able to fly out, Sheldon would descend with the mountaineers after retrieving the payroll. We never heard more about the potentially lucrative plan.

In my account in 1955 in the *American Alpine Journal,* our departure from the Talkeetna dirt airstrip is described:

> *Finally, on June 29th, the clouds seemed to break up to the west, and on flying toward Mt. Hunter we saw the entire Alaska Range basking in broken sunshine. Our air course took us over the Tokositna country and*

then over some rugged peaks to the upper Kahiltna Glacier. Again there were busy moments as we attempted to study the route and at the same time locate an area for a safe landing. We landed about 1 1/2 miles west of Hunter, in the level area (alt. 6700 ft.) between it and the bulk of Foraker. It is best to make these summer glacier landings very early in the morning, while the crust is still hard. Unfortunately, we were delayed, and by the time the craft was ready to leave, the crust had softened to an extent that it required twenty minutes of taxiing on the glacier before the plane gained sufficient momentum for the take-off. For a while, we were certain we would have to feed another man![215]

With complete confidence in Washburn's proposal, we pitched our single Logan tent on the glacier, "stacked up our food supply, and set out to explore the lower section of the ridge with light packs."[216] Midday in the hot sun is not the optimum time to move along on clumsy snowshoes, but despite the wet "goo" clinging to the webbing, progress would have been slower without them.

There were several potential ways to the ridgecrest at 9,100 feet, none of which were in ideal condition under the blaring early-summer sun. On our first probe to the West Ridge, we chose a minor glacier trough that formed a depression between two granitic rock walls. Although the trough was exposed to some falling ice debris, it seemed generally safe but for one jumbled area. According to my account, "It was necessary to clamber about for a half-hour on some steep slopes to bypass a great bergschrund, but then the glacier sloped back again."[217] We climbed a 200-foot snow wall to where a rock pinnacle blocked progress on the crest; here we made some explorations before finding a way through blocks to the ridge and then made three rappels to a narrow col. Here we left a cache, feeling secure that we had mastered the uncertainties of the first third of the West Ridge.

The morning of July 1 greeted us with a quick storm, which brought a sparkle onto the otherwise dull tone of the glacier. Leaving only some food marked with a pole for the planned outbound trek, we carried clumsy loads along our tracks and then again rappelled to the cache at the col. Adding the additional load to our packs, we continued along the narrow, corniced ridge. Because of our awkward packs, we were barely able to scale a short, vertical snow wall at the peak of a 9,550-foot ridge hump.

The route now traversed the crest to a steep "drop-off" where we had to cut steps in the ice to descend. Our first camp was located at a minor col adjacent to a large rock step. Finding some flat stones here, we laid down a level tent platform. My account continues:

One of the chief problems of the ridge is the granitic rock wedge that rises for the next 500 feet. We explored it that afternoon in a flurry of snow, leaving a cache at the highest point and putting in three fixed ropes. Generally, we found it best to keep a hundred feet south of the crest, but at the middle section, we had to climb some difficult cracks and a chimney, including some overhang. When it came time to bring up our packs, it was necessary to haul them up a 50-foot chimney, a key point on the climb of this ridge. Needless to say, belays were in order the entire distance. On the final push to the highest camp at 10,600 feet we were fearful of the snow

Climbing Mount Hunter's corniced West Ridge during the first ascent, looking west, down-ridge, July 1954 (photo by Heinrich Harrer)

surface atop the glare ice of the steep ridge slopes, so waited until the sun left them in the evening before beginning the ascent. There is ample light to travel all night, for at this latitude the rose-pink sun poises below the rim of the horizon for only a few hours and the sky remains suffused with light. As we had hoped, the steep wall at 10,000 feet was well crusted; we were able to crampon up it with but a few steps, though the points bit into hard glare ice. Even more exposed was the great ridge sweeping to a point at 10,600 feet. Here we had to cut away a swath of drifted snow on a very steep slope, hew out many steps, and place an ice piton for safety. This slope ranges from 45° to 70° for several hundred feet and is best overcome with a fixed rope.

As if to remind us of the cornice danger, a large section of drooping ice broke off almost adjacent to us as we plowed along a level stretch of knee-deep snow on the ridge. Secure in the knowledge that there was no further danger at this exact spot, we decided to place our final camp here. It was midnight and our feet were becoming cold; so the tent was put up, and then without loads we reconnoitered a route over the next ridge hump and along the dangerous cornices to the saddle beneath the final ridge of Hunter. Several tension rifts cracked as we broke the tracks along the ridge; we carefully stayed as low off the ridge as we possibly could, always keeping on the alert for a break and the necessity of a lightning-quick belay.[218]

Once back at camp, we had a near-catastrophe when my stove blew up just as I was crawling out of the tent. If the blast had occurred just seconds earlier, I might have been engulfed in flames. Fortunately I was not burned and my companions were safely outside. Though it was very small and intended only for bivouac, our spare Borde stove carried through with snow melting and cooking.

In high spirits and with promise of another perfect day, we went to sleep. Our climbing plan was to rest through the day and start late in order to climb on the steep and dangerous slopes after the sun had left them. Accordingly, we packed and dressed for the final ascent—taking down jackets and large lunches—and left the tent at 4:30 P.M.

The long and quite exposed ice slope, which extended from 10,700 to 11,500 feet, turned out to be the most taxing on the ascent. Although the front points of our crampons bit well into the ice, so eliminating the need to cut steps, the surface was often unstable and insecure. We deemed it wise to chop bucket-sized belay stances and to place ice pitons between the thirteen belays.

The route continued much like Washburn had predicted: more cornices, steep and short ice pitches, then more cornices. As the sun dropped behind bulky peaks south of Foraker, the temperature plummeted; the wet rope became stiffly frozen, retaining its kinks and curls.

As we gazed toward Mount Hunter's 13,200-foot upper plateau, all that could be seen was a menacing icewall barrier that capped the ridge. Below "tumbled an array of crevasses in every direction."[219] We were concerned that the ice barrier could end our venture rather soon, for no feasible bypass was apparent.

We approached hopefully and kept looking at a large longitudinal crevasse entering the wall directly above the ridge. As we reached its height, we saw that it afforded a route on its sloping side; the "Golden Gate," as we named it, proved a godsend, for it was an avenue to the upper plateau. Any other route to the summit would have been next to impossible; this one worked out readily.

Crossing the half-mile of level névè was tedious because we kept breaking through to the knees. Never had we seen snow conditions such as these. Even on wind-blown ridges one would break through, and only on the steepest slopes was there hard ice. Between midnight and four we plodded across the slope, attempted the corner of the summit ridge, turned back for the west face of the summit pyramid, and climbed a very steep loose snow slope to the final crest. On the last stretch we came into the glorious radiance of the full morning sunshine. Hunter had been climbed! It would be difficult to imagine a more beautiful view than that afforded by the summit. It was warm enough to take off gloves and jackets, and for an hour we rested and photographed. The glittering surrounding summits provided a fascinating study, and of course McKinley and Foraker were resplendent. We agreed that the entire region was one with a great mountaineering future.[220]

Ice pitons and chopped bollards (small pedestals cut out of ice) enabled us to rappel the long, relentless slope, and in twenty hours after leaving the tent we returned for a much-needed rest. We were fatigued. On the 6th we resumed our way back along the long ridge with lighter packs. To reduce error on the steepest rock and ice sections, we resorted to rappels. Descending with packs proved awkward. Below 8,000 feet the snow surface sometimes slid; several times we even found it prudent to begin minor slides in order to make the descent safer. All this required vigilance and patience—always difficult to maintain when nearing the base of a mountain.

Once below the threatening sérac wall, we were out of danger. Fortunately our old steps still appeared, permitting us to take the correct route through and around crevasses to reach the base cache without incident.

After looking in vain for a buried bundle of fresh salmon we had brought on the ski-plane from Talkeetna, we then speculated about the unproven route down Kahiltna Glacier. To get the best possible surface conditions, we began at night, taking nine hours for the first six of the thirty glacier miles. Soft snow reinforced the imminent danger of crevasses: wearing snowshoes, we always kept the rope tight. Pushing hard we continued for nine more hours to reach the "great bend"—some eighteen miles from the cache. Our camp that night was leveled from rocks and ice of a medial moraine. On July 9 we continued on ice ribbons near the glacier's central area. In five miles we were forced to the east by a zone of crevasses, and to exit from the ice we had to ford a deep stream. Meybohm, the lightest man, was swept off his feet and forced to crawl into a thick alder jungle on the far bank.

After ascending the embankment, we followed the stream valley upslope, heading for the hunting cabin near the Dutch Hills. By the time we reached the cabin, we were truly starved. Our last taste of food (cornmeal and an upland bird) had been at breakfast on the glacier. On our last day we struggled along the bushy upland tundra near Dutch Creek (aware that this was grizzly bear habitat), somewhere crossing the Browne–Dr. Cook route of 1906. A last crossing of the Dutch Hills brought us to a placer mine and a crude roadway. The cordial owners welcomed us to a hearty supper and, to enliven the setting, one of the miners poured more gold nuggets onto the table than any of us had ever seen. Harrer could not resist buying a few for souvenirs—they certainly would get some attention in Austria.

As the three of us, sometimes mixing the German and English tongue, chatted about our good fortune with the weather and the ascent of Mount Hunter, the time now went quickly. This was fortunate, for our feet were blistery and sore, and our backs ached from the tiresome tundra hiking. We reflected on how we had planned the ascent (and descent) of much of the West Ridge so that the dangerous passages were undertaken when they were in the shade or during the short Alaska night. Later I wrote,

> On Mt. Hunter the cornices were so huge that it was necessary to remain far below the crest in certain places. At point 10,800 feet we kept two rope lengths from the edge, but received a great scare from surface settling— possibly a slab formation on the prevailing windward slope. Three times we heard, and once saw, a cornice loudly crack, but not collapse, almost at our knee level. One fracture crack ran right above the steps of a previous reconnaissance. At one place there was a crest cornice atop a flattened, wide ridge which collapsed almost at our feet, despite the fact the cornice rose only some 15 feet atop a flat ridge. At Point 10,600 feet, where one has to climb a great wall and overcome a lateral cornice-wall, one is exposed to the danger of a general collapse of the entire edge of the slope, which acts as a cornice of its own; a small portion of it broke as we maneuvered to belay atop the point.[221]

Since our ascent, skilled mountaineers have sought out numerous other challenging routes on Mount Hunter. There have been some remarkable ascents made on this colossus of rock and ice. Vin Hoeman, who was a member of the peak's second-ascent party, prophesized the future when in the 1960s he compiled a guidebook to Alaska's mountains. In this unpublished work he termed Mount Hunter the "most steep and spectacular of the Alaska Ranges' three great giants, with a multitude of difficult and dangerous routes awaiting those who would attempt them."

▲▲▲

CHAPTER 12

The Parachute Brigade Expedition

The expedition split up with phenomenal speed at Waterloo, its compo-
nent members vanishing into the depths of London.
James Mills
Airborne to the Mountains, 1961

In the mid-1950s, Captain James Mills, a regular soldier in the Royal
Army Service Corps, convinced the War Office to support the first British
attempt on Mount McKinley. In hopes of receiving free air passage to Alaska,
Mills limited the group to four members, all trained parachutists and members of the Brigade Mountaineering Club. They were Captains Donald
Kinloch and Warwick Deacon and Lieutenant Derek Pritchard. Not only was
the Brigade Expedition, which remained in the field six weeks, supported by
the British army but also by the Royal Canadian and U.S. air forces.

All equipment was purchased from London shops, except the snowshoes
and ice axes (which later proved of inferior quality). The rubber "snow"
boots, although without Vibram soles, proved warm and adequate. One
man's fiancée had included a box of Fortnum and Mason's crystallized
fruits. This loving gesture "sealed irrevocably his bachelor fate,"[222] the
parachutist marrying less than a half year after returning to England.

Upon arriving in Alaska in May 1956, much supported in their transport, the four climbers organized their food and supplies, making final local
additions. Flying close to the great mountain on a sightseeing mission,
Mills later described this flight in *Airborne to the Mountains:*

> *We sped up the Traleika, with moraines seaming its face, and then*
> *around the western buttresses of McKinley. A shout from Bob and below*
> *us I saw Derek's plane flashing past, minute against the enormous wall.*
> *There came to me the sudden realization of the majestic, forbidding*
> *vastness of these mountains. The starkness of their challenge burst in*
> *upon me, violating the security and warmth of my transparent cocoon....*
> *We banked to the right and gradually hauled our way round the*
> *enormous bulk of the mountain. On the other side was the terrifying*
> *downward plunge of the Wickersham Wall; its 13,000 feet entirely dwarfed*

our speed and we seemed only to drift past it. The avalanche-torn slopes and ice-fluted faces swept by in a frighteningly beautiful panorama. We dropped down fast, turned over the lower glaciers, and raced up the fretted knife-edge of Pioneer Ridge, then pulled up in an effortless curve over the summit.

Our speed was too great to note any one detail and it was too dangerous to fly low in the glacier canyons, for fear of the sudden pull of a downdraft....

The earth swung and tilted, rushed towards me, the detail of its surface becoming clearer with alarming speed, then dissolved, in a flash of a silver wing, into the blue, cloud-wisped sky. My limbs felt weightless and then lead-heavy by turns and in the circling kaleidoscope of heaven and earth I lost all sense of the plane's forward motion. So we mocked the mountains, scorning their challenge with airy flight.[223]

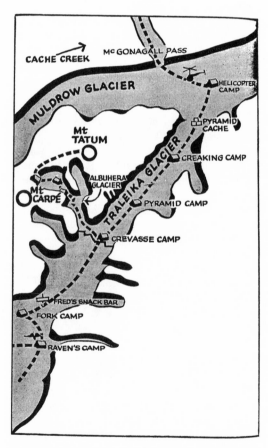

This sketch map from James Mills's Airborne to the Mountains *shows part of the route taken from McGonagall Pass to the upper Traleika Glacier by the British Parachute Brigade Expedition in 1956.*

Using a U.S. Air Force helicopter to set down the expedition members, along with 450 kilograms of supplies and equipment, the Brigade Expedition made the transition from Fairbanks to a camp on Muldrow Glacier near its junction with Traleika Glacier in just under twelve hours. This arrangement saved immense labor of heavy backpacking or the use of dog teams across McGonagall Pass. Later the air force parachuted more supplies, including mail, to expedition camps.

In hauling loads up the heavily crevassed Traleika for some twenty miles, a plastic sledge proved barely suitable, the party reflecting that a longer Nansen sledge would have been ideal. Snowshoes were used to move from camp to camp, five of these sites being made on the glacier beyond Helicopter Camp. Early morning with cool temperatures provided the best marching and sledge-hauling conditions and was also the safest time for crossing crevasse bridges.

The Brigade Expedition climbed four virgin peaks, including Mount Tatum, but icefalls and route difficulties at the Traleika's head barred a successful bid on Mount McKinley. The men found the advantage of climbing in Alaska to be its continuous daylight in May and June, enabling one to chance the best weather and snow conditions. Yet during an attempt on Anniversary Peak, between Traleika and Ruth glaciers, the men had to undertake serious ice climbing with poor snow conditions brought on by previous heavy snowfalls. The principal excitement that occurred on the ascent to Waggoner's Col near the head of the Traleika was Deacon's crevasse fall:

> There was no good axe belay and Warwick was already probing some yards ahead. Some protection was necessary, and I took the rope round my body in a standing belay. By this time he was almost at the full extent of the rope and had stopped, probing carefully. For a moment he ceased his investigation and turned his head to call over one shoulder, "I think I'm on a snow bridge."
>
> I braced myself; the others—interested spectators—had not moved. He made another thrust with his axe and then abruptly and in complete silence he dropped from view. I had the impression of his body, bolt upright, going down as I imagined an executed man falls through a trap door. The rope began to run out across my shoulders. I felt the heat of its friction. I began to check it, but as it slowed, the pull became too much and I was impelled forward, in a few staggering steps, until jerked, face downwards, into the snow. By now I had stopped the runout but was towed forward by the weight of Warwick's falling body, towards the hole. I dug in my elbows and snowshoes, forcing my body into the snow, trying desperately to stop myself. Through my brain two thoughts hammered. I must stay on top or he's done for. If he dies the expedition's finished.
>
> My ploughlike progress began to slow. I felt the pull from behind and stopped. Then the strain came fully upon my right arm, with which I was holding Warwick. I thought it was coming out of its socket. I could not hold the rope much longer. Twisting slightly, with my other hand I managed to unclip the rope from the waist karabiner. I yelled for Donald to take in the slack and anchor the rope and Warwick. The strain came off and I staggered to my feet, then with my own axe anchored the rope through a loop. I crawled forward to the hole and was surprised to find that it was so large.[224]

The others sent down a second rope with a loop, planning to use the stirrup (Bilgeri) method to raise him. In this manner, Deacon could put one foot in a loop of the climbing rope, so taking the strain off his chest. Into the second rope he placed his other foot. To act as a buffer, Mills placed an ice axe crossways near the overhanging crevasse edge.

> Inch by inch we raised him, hoping that he could fight off the cold and shock, and retain enough strength to help himself. Then Derek lowered a loop and in a moment Warwick's face appeared above the snow. He looked grey and exhausted. He gave a crooked grin and said "Hulloo" in a Fred

Eccles Goon voice before he was hauled over the edge. Derek supported him as he walked forward and an enormous relief took the tautness from me. I felt drained and tired. Donald pushed a thermometer into Warwick's mouth (for the cause of science, it registered 95.8°F) and diagnosed shock. We put Warwick into his sleeping bag and, at Donald's suggestion, put up the tent on the island of stones to camp there until that night.

While we ate supper Warwick told this story. "I didn't feel the bridge go. There was that feeling you get parachuting from a balloon, when your stomach floats upwards."[225]

After completing their climbing of peaks bordering the Traleika, the expedition descended to near its junction with the Muldrow, here experiencing the beginning of exceptional glacier motion, which displaced surface features as much as four miles downvalley and lowered the ice surface of the upper portions of both glaciers as much as several hundred feet. In a symbolic farewell to the Traleika, during a dismal wet mist on a moraine, Mills related that after breakfast Kinloch ceremoniously burned his shattered snowshoes and fed the flames with the cardboard boxes and meta tablets from the cache.

We descended into the trough which lay like a ditch along the line of séracs. It was dotted with small glacial lakes on which a few frozen-looking ducks huddled. Skirting these we cramponed down the steep incline and came to the first defenses of the séracs, which marked the junction of the Traleika and Muldrow glaciers. This, we thought, was the last barrier before the clear run across the ice to the McGonagall Pass.

Crowding close upon one another, with their steep sides and tottering masses of ice, the séracs posed a difficult problem. We cut steps, made short vertical ascents, trotted along sharp knife-edges, and leapt more fearsome chasms like humpbacked, claw-footed demons. As we surmounted the last row of these giant dragon's teeth we saw, beyond another strip of smooth ice, a chain of vast moraine heaps.[226]

Here the climbers spent hours clambering up steep ice faces, "crampons clashing with the rocks. Again, and again, we thought that the end was in sight, only to see another wave of filthy mounds barring the way. Underneath, torrents of water ran gushing like a glacial sewer. Eaten up with frustration we cursed all glaciers, *séracs,* and moraines."[227]

Mills later learned the scientific explanation; the glacier surge was the result of unstable dynamic conditions in the particular glacier systems. The mechanism indicated is that of an ice "reservoir" forming in the middle portion of each glacier and being filled over a period of years with ice which flows in from tributaries while the stagnant lower terminal portion of the glacier is being reduced by ablation. When certain critical conditions are reached the glacier becomes unstable and a sudden brief movement of the ice takes place.

While the Brigade Expedition is a relatively unknown adventure on Mount McKinley, it is significant because of its pioneering Traleika Glacier exploration. Although the expedition members did not scale their objective, they conducted a worthy venture, made solid friendships in North America, and carried on safely and in good style.

Upon the expedition's return by ship to England, the War Office had them make a television appearance. Remarkably quickly came the anticlimax and letdown. Mills wrote how the depression "reached its nadir as the four of us sat in a cafe in Hyde Park dejectedly drinking tea from cracked cups. Around us the shabby green tables and chairs, sticky with spilled tea, and with their paint peeling, offended and disgusted me." The "faceless crowds which hurried and eddied" about them in the city did not fathom the alpine world. To Mills, only the "mountains seemed real."[228]

▲ ▲ ▲

CHAPTER 13

The Italian Climb of the South Face

This mountain is truly infernal.
Riccardo Cassin
"McKinley, versant Sud," 1962

Much has been written about Cassin Ridge, climbed by the first Italian party to visit Mount McKinley while making the twenty-third ascent of the South Peak. At the time of their intrepid climb in 1961, the mountain's highest summit had only seen four routes, and none on the gargantuan main southern flanks.

Standing forward like a rock prow some 9,000 feet high, nearly in the center of the south face, the ridge is unmistakable and elegant from the climber's standpoint. It was bound to be the subject of modern alpinism. Bradford Washburn had already written that the ridge presented an almost unbroken succession of precipitous pitches of granite and ice. His words in *The Mountain World*—such as "probably the most difficult and dramatic of all potential new routes on Mount McKinley"[229]—inspired serious alpinists.

Riccardo Cassin, then fifty-three and noted in alpine circles for his daring routes on the Piz Badile, the Grandes Jorasses, and Cima Ovest di Lavaredo, in 1961 assembled a team of expert Italian Alpine Club climbers for the audacious plan of scaling the spectacular ridge. Cassin's party, which took fourteen tortuous days to make the first ascent of this spectacular ridge, was composed of Annibale Zucchi, Gigi Alippi, Giancarlo ("Jack") Canali, Luigino Airoldi, and Romano Perego—all members of the Spider Climbing Club of Lecco who had made notable and difficult climbs in the Alps. Carlo Mauri, who accompanied Cassin on Gasherbrum IV in 1958, had planned to be on the expedition but was recovering from a ski accident.

Technically, the Italian expedition was well equipped with ice- and rock-climbing equipment and had brought enough perlon rope to fix some sections of the route. They appear, however, to have quite underestimated the severity of the cold and wind in relation to their past mountaineering, despite Washburn's caveats concerning the climate's hostility. Certainly their clothing and footgear (single leather boots with no insulation) were minimal. Although the Italians consulted with Washburn when they arrived in the United States and listened to his warnings about frigid temperatures, it was likely too late to exchange their boots for warmer models.

In mid-June veteran pilot Don Sheldon landed the Cassin party at 7,700 feet on Kahiltna Glacier. Stifled in progress by snowfall and the labors of load-carrying, the base camp was made on the glacier's east fork at 11,300 feet. On July 6 the party climbed and fixed ropes up a couloir to the crest of the impressive granitic rock of the lower ridge. This couloir, however, was not the one that Washburn had marked on photographs (the Kahiltna Notch couloir) but, rather, an adjacent one that began 200 yards farther up the glacier—this error resulted in more rock climbing and route-finding than later parties experienced.

On July 9 and 10 the Italians learned how violent Mount McKinley weather could be, when gale-force winds threatened to blow them all off the ridge. The situation would have been much worse had they been high on the route during this storm.

When on the technical portions of the ridge, the Cassin party used expedition tactics: An advance team of three would climb first with light loads, locate the route, and then leave fixed ropes for the second team to climb with packs of equipment and food. Camps would be set up at the best sites and then left for the descent.

The first difficult climbing took place on the spectacular rock prow above Kahiltna Notch. The seriousness of the prow forced them to the west flank, near what is now called the Japanese Couloir. Here the Italians climbed steep, powder-drifted granite beside the couloir.

Cassin, in an account in the *American Alpine Journal*, described the logistics of July 13:

> With heavy loads, Annibale, Luigino, and I arrive at Camp I around three and are just about to leave when Jack, Gigi, and Romano return from reconnaissance above. They have seen the ridge. It is almost a kilometer long and of dry, unstable snow, lying on a base of hard ice. They have pitched a "Nepal" tent at the site of Camp II. We others return to Base Camp, while Jack and Gigi will carry loads to Camp II and then reconnoiter a route through the initial icefall of the hanging glacier. Annibale and Romano will ascend fully equipped from Base Camp to Camp I. Luigino and I will go to the landing area to collect mail.[230]

In time, the challenging route was fixed with ropes across a corniced arête, a hanging glacier, on a chimney at 15,000 feet, and at a final icy corner.

From their third camp on the long ridge, at 17,000 feet, on July 19 the six climbers set out for the summit. Cassin and Canali were roped together, moving to the entrance of a couloir. Cassin stated that it was no longer snowing, "but strong winds attack us from the west without respite and make every forward step a torture. Icicles bristle from the rocks on either side and cut our faces."[231]

Exhausted and numb from the cold, which was estimated to be thirty to forty degrees below zero, Cassin wrote, "Our crampons and boots are frozen together." Canali's feet were now dangerously cold when Zucchi took the lead, struggling "desperately nothing can stand in his way." The six Italians reached the summit at 11:00 P.M., almost in darkness. The incomparable

Mount McKinley from camp on Northeast Fork of Kahiltna Glacier (southwesterly view). Note the prominence of the West Rib, Cassin Ridge, and the south face. (photo by Olaf Sööt)

Cassin had a brief recollection: "Filled with emotion, we throw our arms about each other. The icy wind prevents us from opening our mouths to speak, even for a moment."[232] When they finally struggled back to their high camp, twenty-three hours had elapsed.

On the descent Canali's feet were so swollen that he had to wear Alippi's boots, while the latter climbed only in his overboots stuffed with extra socks. The fixed ropes left in key places were now covered with snow and ice from the storms, but they saved the party—certainly Canali, who had to reach base camp immediately. Cassin and Zucchi descended from the second camp to the first with Canali, while the others rested.

On the following day a furious storm arrived when they were descending through the rock towers on the fixed ropes. At the final couloir, a mass of snow slid as Cassin was holding onto the rope: "In all desperation I clutch the rope in my hands and succeed in maintaining my position, but for some time afterward I can do no more than hang there, too stunned to either speak or move."[233] When the second group descended the next day, Alippi often slipped, because he could not wear crampons on the flexible overboots. Fortunately, no avalanche fell to make a "sweep" of the route.

Finally reaching base camp, the climbers were almost too tired to appreciate their good fortune. They could now quench their thirst, but Canali was "suffering unabatedly." An efficient evacuation by sled to the landing area, where Sheldon could fly Canali promptly to Anchorage, permitted him to recover without losing his feet. The competent Italians managed the difficult climb without accident and despite terrible weather. Washburn's final comment was that this ascent, without question, was the greatest climb in North American mountaineering history.

Both the Cassin party, who used six-, nine-, and eleven-millimeter perlon ropes for climbing and fixing pitches, and the Japanese second-ascent party left a total of some 1,000 feet of rope on Cassin Ridge. Boyd Everett, who undertook the next ascent, mentioned that the Japanese rope (not a nylon type) was about ¼ inch in diameter, and it was easily cut although only one month old; its use led to a fall by one member of his party.

▲ ▲ ▲

A Canadian team recently gave an interesting account of the Cassin Ridge climb, which they wisely prepared for by spending three weeks acclimatizing on the West Buttress. During their ascent the party left caches at 14,300 and 17,200 feet and a second pair of skis at 11,000 feet (to ski back to base camp).

> *May 22: A long long day of slogging up the east fork of the Kahiltna—14 hours from Base Camp to the base of Kahiltna notch at 10900'.*
>
> *(The usual approach to the Japanese Couloir is up the N.E. fork of the Kahiltna, but this way is extremely threatened by snow and serac avalanches. The east fork is quite safe to 10900', but to reach the Couloir we will have to climb to Kahiltna Notch, follow the ridge to the top of the Cassin Couloir [original line climbed by Cassin on the first ascent], then rappel 300'. At this point we will be in the bergschrund at the head of the N.E. fork, about 600' right of the Japanese Couloir. The climb to Kahiltna notch is up an avalanche bowl and will be very dangerous after recent snowfall.)*
>
> *May 23: Leave camp at 11:00. 4 pitches to a 50 foot rock band broken by a 65 degree narrow ice chute. Recent snow has started sluffing from above and it is still snowing. We are standing to one side of the chute when we are engulfed by the powder of a huge sluff. The only choice is to descend and wait.*
>
> *May 24: Leave camp at 10:00. Quickly up through the chute before any big sluffs come down. Paul is belaying in a protected corner in the gully above the chute. J.A. has just exited the gully above when a good sized sluff flies by, about 3 feet from Paul's stance. J.A. puts Paul on belay and he climbs out of the gully at lightning speed. "Who says you can't climb fast with a 50 pound pack?" The obvious line goes for about 6 pitches straight up 45 degree snow and ice slopes to Kahiltna Notch. But we turn right and gain a safe snow ridge, then follow this to cliffs at the top of the dangerous snow slopes. One more pitch along the base of the cliffs (our 11th) and we find a terrific platform under an overhang. We set up camp as sluffs from a small slope directly above*

us shoot out past the overhang and land about 20 feet from our tent.
May 25: 2 pitches to Kahiltna Notch, then about 6 pitches along the ridge
to the top of the Cassin Couloir. The final 300' is a scary knife-edge
snow ridge. By about noon it has warmed up from –15° to about –1°.
The soft snow becomes very wet. Our crampons ball up as we traverse
the final knife-edge ridge. Our boots get damp and the rope is soaked....

When it is too late we realize that we should have traversed above the
bergschrund. We finally make it to the camp. That evening we check out
the couloir and get psyched for the climb.
May 26: Up at 3:00, climbing by 6:00. Crossing the bergschrund is easy,
then 5 straightforward pitches on 50 degree ice and snow. The 6th pitch
starts with a short vertical step. Looks easy but turns out to be pretty
serious, and longer than expected....

At the top of the gully Paul looks over to the campsite. He cannot
believe that he is looking in the right spot. Up comes J.A. to check it out.
It's small but if you look hard you can see it (once you are standing on
it that is). We take advantage of a warm afternoon sun to dry the ropes,
which have been a constant hassle of kinks and wirelike sections all
day, and other gear.
May 27: Up at 3:00 again. We cache the haul rope and bag....

4 pitches of mixed climbing and we make the Tent Ridge. Moving
together we arrive at the glacier camp (14000') at 13:00....
May 28: Away at 5:30. We climb together passing another good campsite
at about 14300'. Another 200' and we come to a huge crevasse that
spans the entire glacier. It is about 10 feet wide and the top edge towers
about 40' above. We follow a track to the left and find a fixed line
anchored by a good icescrew. We rappel the line down vertical ice for
75' and find ourselves on 50 degree slopes at the left extremity of the
glacier. Up again, this time in a wide gully with good ice. After 4 pitches
we regain the glacier and follow partially filled tracks in deep snow to
the bergschrund at 15000'.

It is now noon. The bergschrund offers a good campsite for one tent
but we elect to push on. The mixed climbing is just ahead. 4 leads later
we pass 3 Koreans descending the route. They had attempted the
Cassin with only 8 days food and no period for acclimatization. They
had run out of food and were heading back to basecamp. Another group
of two Koreans were ahead of them, camped at about 18600'. A sixth
member of their group was picked off the route earlier today by
helicopter, complaining of headaches. We wish them good luck and
push on. Pitch after pitch of straightforward mixed climbing: snowing
but warm and calm. The rib pitch (supposedly the crux) is easy: a short
10' vertical rock step led without a pack. One more pitch to the snow
ridge. Winds on the ridge are strong but we can see nowhere to camp
below the ridge. Paul is bagged but J.A., ever strong, breaks trail
through the calf deep snow. Finally we see the tent platform vacated by
the Koreans this morning. We quickly set up the tent and dive in. It is
21:30. The usual 2 hours of cooking, then sleep.
May 29: Luckily the winds are still strong so we can use the weather as an
excuse for a rest day....

*Evening view northward over cloud cover, taken from high on West Buttress
(photo by Olaf Sööt)*

*May 30: Wind gusts up to 40 mph during the night. Morning temperature
is –17°. By mid morning the winds subside and we break camp. We do
5 pitches to the top of the "chimney" pitch at about 16500' and the end
of technical mixed climbing. We find the "chimney" to be actually a
gully: easy mixed climbing led with our packs on. We see fixed lines up
and right in the rocks above but elect to go straight right (even down a
hair) for 4 rope lengths to gain a snow field, then climb steep snow to
17000'. We are relieved that the technical climbing is behind us....*

*May 31: The morning shows clearing trends. It is –20°. We traverse about
1000' to the right, climb a short snow gully, then drop down a few feet
to the glacier above Big Bertha. The snow seems to get deeper with every
step.... It looks like easy going to a good camp at the base of a snowfield
at 18200' so we press on. J.A. breaks trail through waist deep snow. We*

cannot follow the easy snow slopes but have to stay on the rocky ridge. Even there the snow is knee deep. Eight hours of slogging and we have gained 1200'. We set up camp and build a wind wall under a pointed boulder at 18200'. Paul is exhausted, is coughing badly and has a nose bleed. J.A. is tired but otherwise fine.

June 1: A beautiful morning. Cold but clear and calm. We leave camp and climb over easy snow to 18600'. Here we find the two Koreans. One of them has lost his sense of balance (later we learned that he had had a stroke) and they can not possibly get off the mountain by themselves. They knew of our ascent through radio contact and had waited for us 4 days hoping we would "rescue them." We do not understand why they did not lower themselves down the easy snow slopes to the good camp at 17000'. The rangers contact us and urge us to help them to the summit ridge, but they do not realize we have at least 1000' to climb. The winds on the summit ridge are constant and in excess of 50 mph. We discuss options. Paul feels morally obliged to stay and help the Koreans but fears for his own health. His cough continues to worsen. The Rangers attempt an air drop but the weather has deteriorated and visibility is poor. We feel angry that the Koreans did not do more to help themselves. One of them was rescued from this route 2 years ago. What are they doing here anyway? J.A. feels fine so the final decision rests with Paul. We have lots of food and gas so with the Ranger's encouragement we give the Koreans 3 days supplies and head for the top. We have been delayed for 6 hours and it is 15:30. Slog, slog, slog.

Going to the actual summit is out of the question now and we try to pick the line that will bring us to the summit ridge at the lowest point possible. A tricky section around a rocky buttress, more thigh deep snow, some more rocky steps. We look up and see snow plumes streaming from the ridge. We are very close now but have one more ridge to cross: will it go?

J.A. continues to forge ahead, slowly but steadily. The route is good and J.A. soon stands, elated, on the summit ridge at about 19800'....

We can see the well worn West Buttress trail and charge towards it.... The Rangers await with hot drinks. We find a vacated wind shelter to erect our tent. At last: rest and warmth.[234]

▲ ▲ ▲

CHAPTER 14

The Southeast Spur

The South Buttress was a forbidding place, windswept and arctic in character.

Boyd N. Everett, Jr.
American Alpine Journal, 1963

After Bradford Washburn proved in 1951 there was a feasible route to the summit of Mount McKinley other than the traditional Muldrow Glacier, mountaineers from both Europe and North America began planning for new and more inventive technical ascents. Certainly the pioneering of a memorable route on North America's highest peak would gain a certain amount of fame in alpine annals. When Washburn published some of his outstanding photographs depicting the virtually unknown details of the immense mountain, enterprising climbers studied them and his route proposals.

Both the Northwest and South buttresses were climbed in 1954, the West Rib of the south face in 1959, and both Cassin and Pioneer ridges in 1961, and two routes on the dangerous Wickersham Wall would evolve in 1963.

When a group of New York climbing friends, organized by the methodical twenty-eight-year-old Boyd Everett, Jr., after the 1961 season, studied the photography, they decided to tackle the great mountain by a very long, indirect, and somewhat corniced route, now known as the Southeast Spur. Topographically this five-mile bulwark of snow and ice rises from 7,700 feet on the Northwest Fork of Ruth Glacier to intersect the even longer South Buttress at 15,500 feet. It did not take a great deal of scrutiny of Washburn's images to realize this route was climbable but would present intermittent difficulties involving steep ice sections and hazardous cornices. Any rock outcropping on the Spur could be circumvented, but the overhanging cornices, always risky in high mountains of the world—certainly in Alaska, Peru, and the Himalaya—would have to be chanced to conquer the Spur. It was known that a six-man party, including some Mount McKinley veterans, ascended to about 10,000 feet on the projected route in 1958 before turning back because of difficulties and dissension.

The Mooses Tooth, its eastern faces, and the Buckskin Glacier; Mount McKinley in background. The Southeast Spur and South Buttress are left and below the summit of the South Peak. (photo by Austin Post, U.S. Geological Survey)

Boyd Everett, although he had not climbed Mount McKinley, had considerable alpine experience in other ranges, and he possessed the capacity to carefully organize the expedition logistics and select a closely knit team. He often climbed in the Shawangunks (in New York State) and undertook several trips each winter to climb the ice gullies on Mount Washington; in this way he had occasion to meet a number of regional climbers. Considered rather proper and always well dressed, Everett, a successful Wall Street securities analyst, suggested the idea of this route on Mount McKinley at a party.

Everett's passions in a simple life were mountaineering, expedition planning, bridge, classical music, and attending the movies. He occasionally sought out publicity for his climbs, which some of his contemporaries thought was pretentious. On Mount Logan Everett played the highest bridge hand and attempted to sell the story to *Sports Illustrated*'s bridge column, but it was rejected because the hand itself was insufficiently interesting. He appeared on the TV game show *What's My Line?* as being the first man to climb the four highest summits in North America. Everett was a natural for this show, because he did not look like most people's conception of a mountaineer.

Everett had the reputation of not caring for the hard climbs at the Shawangunks, but Yukon expedition member Dennis Eberl contended that he was always in on the toughest leads of the ascents. Eberl also noted that "some people may have thought that he wasn't cool because he was a businessman who worried about whether or not his shoes were polished when he met his boss in the elevator, at a time when climbing mythology favored vulgarians and homeless 'hippie-type' climbers."[235] As a mountaineer, however, Eberl felt that Everett may have had one fatal flaw—a tendency toward hasty generalization. For example, after several Yukon expeditions, Everett firmly believed that it never rained there and that avalanches were uncommon (both conditions were later experienced on Mount Saint Elias).

The final makeup of the Mount McKinley expedition would be Samuel Cochrane, a twenty-nine-year-old New Jersey telephone repairman who was the latest of the party to take up climbing. It was said that Cochrane appeared at a New York climbing area with an old hemp rope borrowed from his job; the local experts told him to go away and return when he knew how to climb. On his next vacation, Cochrane flew to Great Britain, where he practiced the rock-climbing arts in Wales under private tutelage; later he climbed in the Alps and Andes. Twenty-five-year-old Sam Silverstein was a student at New York's Albert Einstein College of Medicine; on the expedition he regularly checked each man for oxygen deficiency. Christopher Wren, a twenty-six-year-old New Hampshire native, had climbed nine years; he would later write an illustrated story about the Southeast Spur for *Look* magazine. Charles Hollister, also twenty-six, was a marine geologist from Santa Barbara. Henry Abrons, the youngest at twenty-one, was a Harvard undergraduate who was asked to join almost at the last moment when another man became seriously ill before departure. Caught on short notice, Abrons borrowed boots and a sleeping bag from friends and made his own pack to attach to a Kelty aluminum frame.

Basing tactics on his successful 1961 Mount Logan expedition, Everett's philosophy leaned toward security and safety: he preferred to lay siege to a long, technical mountain route instead of focus on speed and lightweight equipment. Planning the details of the projected expedition for some six months, the members agreed that survival was the single most important goal. They were most aware that frostbite had crippled three of five Mount McKinley expeditions in 1961 (including the Italians on Cassin Ridge). "We believed no mountain was worth that price,"[236] wrote Wren in *Look* three months after everyone returned to their business and student life. All agreed to take well-insulated double boots and that these would be stuffed into sleeping bags at night to retain warmth.

Everett knew that success on Mount McKinley was related to how well the men, regardless of their past background, could withstand the cold and fatigue associated with serious Alaskan mountaineering. The best equipment available was chosen, sometimes mail-ordered from Europe regardless of cost or weight. The food rations were planned for $2^{1}/_{2}$ pounds per man per day. The $^{1}/_{2}$ pound above the normal for such a route added an estimated 100 pounds to the total "but was well justified as the improved stamina resulting from improved nutrition contributed appreciably to the expedition's success and safety,"[237] Everett later wrote.

Packs would be limited to fifty pounds to avoid fatigue and to provide mobility on the difficult sections. The plan was to establish ample camps: in this way the team could remain together and also make any return trips—or relays—to bring additional supplies on the same day as the leading rope team, often a tiring repetition. When the ascent was complete, ten sites had been used—an unusually high number. Wren, after the expedition, made the adroit comment, "We can claim that we literally climbed Mt. McKinley two or three times."

When the New York–based party arrived in Talkeetna on the first week of June 1962, they were forced to wait nearly one week because of inclement weather, a common delay. After landing on Ruth Glacier's Northwest Fork about one mile from the Spur,[238] the climbers could study the situation above with their own eyes. Regardless of the quality of an aerial photograph, the personal scrutiny of a mountain route provides a different perspective. The surface conditions and angle of the difficult sections, even though foreshortened, provide an on-site analysis.

The first 3,500 feet of the Spur ended at a large "bump" at 11,280 feet. This section of the route was a series of small ice walls, crevasses, and cornices, not to mention avalanche areas. While this sector of the Spur posed significant problems, the first true concern was a long line of immense cornices that hung like an oversized oriental roof above a seventy-degree slope of insidious bluish ice.

To avoid saturation snowslides, the procedure on the first portion of the Spur was to climb at night—a long-established Alaskan mountaineering tactic to make safer and faster progress. Being only three degrees south of the Arctic Circle, Mount McKinley mountaineers find it quite possible to see adequately during the night hours in late spring and early summer; however, the colder temperatures at higher altitude sometimes make this policy unwise when high on the mountain.

After placing a camp at 9,200 feet, a violent storm so immobilized the expedition that two weeks after Sheldon's glacier landing they were still based at this relatively low site. During this seventy-one-hour tempest, a four-man rented tent "blew out" as the high winds lashed at a weak spot in the fabric. As the shelter ripped apart, "we scrambled from our sleeping bags across to the other tent and threw ourselves in on top of its dozing occupants," wrote Wren.[239] With a spare two-man tent (thanks to Everett's planning) and by digging occasional snow caves, the men were later still able to set up adequate camps.

With no notice other than the silent movement in a barometer, six perfect days without appreciable wind followed the disturbance. Everett recounted the next events of the ascent:

> On the evening of June 14 Sam Cochrane and I laboriously reconnoitered the route to the Arrow in deep snow. We bypassed the ice wall at 9,700 feet on the far right over a thin snow-bridge; fortunately it extended 30 feet along the length of the crevasse so that we were later able to find new places to cross whenever our heavier members fell through! Higher up, the windslab covering the 45° slope below the Arrow settled ominously under Sam three times in quick succession, each time accompanied by an audible crunch; luckily it did not avalanche.[240]

Abrons later described the fifty-to-sixty-degree slope as consisting of a mixture of unstable corn snow, with crystals as large as popcorn. Under the thin crust, the "corn" would shift rather than compact: the climbing was very delicate, and forming steps that would hold a man's weight was laborious. Ultimately, to safeguard repeated ascents of this section of the Spur, 600 feet of fixed rope was anchored to belay devices driven into the surface.

On the following night Cochrane and Abrons located a route through the problemsome Arrow formation. The technique used in overcoming this obstacle involved several hours of step-cutting and then boring a snow tunnel through the cornice to its opposite slope with an ice saw. The solution was an uneasy triumph, because the two climbers had to undermine the overhanging structure when cutting through. If Cochrane "dislodged too much snow," wrote Wren, "the cornice itself would collapse, sweeping him off the mountain."[241] Later as the climbers relayed packs beneath the cornice, the ice crumbled away, and icicles from the rooflike formation snagged the loads and pushed the men off balance.

The next obstacle was not as intimidating as the Arrow but probably just as dangerous. At a corniced ridge that rose to an ice wall at 10,700 feet, four vertically oriented crevasses trended along the fall-line. Bridged by snow, they were not even seen until one man fell through a weak spot. The surest method of climbing here was to follow the narrow space between treacherous snow and the blue ice below. In testing this section, Everett pushed off a deceptive cornice, which surprised everyone by collapsing without warning (his steps were only two feet below the fracture line). Everett described the problems: "The ice above overhung and 10-foot icicles extended down to waist level in front of us. Climbing to the first belay spot was tricky because our packs caught in the icicles. It was a spectacular place that no one trusted, even though we used two ice pitons in addition to the rappel picket to protect the belayer."[242]

What was considered the crux pitch on the Spur, a section that became known as The Corner, was encountered after completing the traverse around and above the ice wall.

> *Twenty feet beyond the belay spot the ledge ended. We rappelled off a picket for 20 feet down to a bit of rotten snow over the 65° ice, which was wet enough to pack fairly well. By scraping this snow off the ice and catching it with our feet, we could build up a solid snow step on the ice. The resulting steps plastered against the ice were weird but effective. After 50 feet of this we tunneled through the slightly corniced ridge corner beyond which we hoped the going would be easier. Almost immediately, however, we came upon something completely unexpected, a Swiss cheese type of ice, two-thirds of which was air! It broke easily under the impact of an ice axe or heavily placed foot. One 10-foot section of this ice acted as the roof of a giant cavern. Had the bars of this "Jungle-Gym" collapsed, it would have meant a mean fall into the hole. A rappel picket placed loosely between a few spurs of ice provided doubtful security. For another 50 feet the surface was poor but by clearing away four feet of rubble, we got down to firmer ice. Solid snow was reached just at the end of the 150-foot rope. It took an entire day to lead and carry loads over the Corner.*[243]

Above Camp III, which was pitched at 10,800 feet, a broad plateau of about a half mile led to Peak 11,280 feet. Here the Spur dipped to a saddle, a logical spot for the next site. There was one final technical problem, a knife-edge ridge of about 1,000 feet in length—a dangerous locality the climbers named The Fluting. Wren described the feature as "a row of fluted ice cornices that did not look as if they could withstand a man's weight."[244]

Here Abrons and Silverstein spent most of a night forcing a route along the crest, finally deciding to traverse the north face under the cornice to avoid the danger of one breaking off. Wren described the action: "Hank, a brilliant young climber, swung off the north side of the ridge. He crossed under the ice flutings and climbed back up on the other side. It was hazardous, because the vertical wall avalanched during all but the darkest hours."[245] Near the end of the obstacle, he made a spectacular direct-aid lead to mount a twenty-foot overhanging ice step to reach a dip on the corniced crest.

The next six pitches were all fixed with ropes by the party. Here a fifty-degree snow slope was threatened by cornices and séracs from above—and when a sérac did fall, it caused an avalanche some 400 feet wide and 4 feet deep, big enough to destroy a battalion. Then came the labor of carrying loads across the difficulties; even with fixed ropes this required exhausting hours.

The Spur required perseverance. Now that the serious difficulties were behind, it would seem that the summit should be soon attained. But for the next eight days it snowed, causing regular avalanching of the steeper slopes and putting the expedition behind schedule.

Alaskan alpine conditions can be so unpredictable that a climbing team must be prepared for almost anything. Given firm, windblown snow, climbers can sometimes move rapidly. A solid crust can offer marvelous progress, but if the surface is breakable under a person's weight, the effort becomes incomparably greater. Blue glacier ice in the polar environment is the hardest ice on any mountain on earth—a fact that European alpinists learned, to their dismay, when climbing both Mount Huntington and Mount McKinley. To mountaineers of the early decades of the century, climbing ice even on gradual slopes meant endless, tiring step-cutting, for the blacksmith-contrived "ice creepers" were essentially only short-pointed, strap-on crampons, really of no comparison to today's high-tech devices made by professional companies.

Because of Mount McKinley's frigid temperatures, when snow settles on its upper slopes without being blown off, moving upward can be exhausting beyond belief. The Everett party encountered three feet of new snow deposited in two days when reaching the Spur's crest at 13,100 feet. Fortunately the surface slides were not hazardous, but, on the 25th, a one-mile traverse that should have been a simple maneuver proved to be an exhausting procedure because the wind had consolidated the new powder and formed a breakable crust. The first man on the rope, therefore, was forced to punch steps thigh- and waist-deep! Sometimes it was simply easier to crawl. As Everett explained, "The leader has to break a trench, sometimes with the ice axe, sometimes with a knee."[246]

Wren described the exhausting "trail-breaking," which was made at a pace of three rope-lengths per hour, "as wading in cold oatmeal."[247] At the same time, climbers can never know when a man's weight will find a hidden crevasse. Even during this exhausting progress, two of the expedition fell neck-deep into such disguised and dangerous holes. And to make the expedition's progress more difficult, the strong and continual wind blew snow into the tracks that had been carved; on the next relay much of the labor had to be repeated.

When the expedition members reached a locale where there was ice, it was a welcome relief after the wading in deep powder. Because of the past two storms and often slow forward progress, the mountaineers were reduced to only nine days' food and nearing the end of their vacation time. To ensure success by at least someone from the expedition, it was decided that all six would carry light loads rapidly so that two men could strike quickly for the South Peak's summit.

Where the Southeast Spur met the South Buttress, the difficulties of the ascent ended. Still, the wading in cold, deep snow continued. On June 27 the entire party established a 15,600-foot camp on the crest of the buttress. On the following day Everett and Cochrane followed the 1954 party's route and then struck off for the upper southeast face. Here they encountered a mixture of rock outcrops and snow couloirs, which they were able to skirt without any technical problems. And, as if to receive a reward for overcoming the awful conditions lower, the snow was now fully firm. When moving across a plateau at 19,000 feet, the two climbers were battered for five hours by high winds, which regularly knocked them down. At times they were forced to crawl like infants in sand, but they remained confident of success. "On the windswept summit," wrote Wren, "Boyd and Sam deposited a medicine bottle with our names on a piece of paper and a handful of dirt Sam Silverstein had scooped from New York's Central Park."[248] In the incessant wind, both men were afflicted with the "exhaustion shakes" and, to bolster their strength and acumen, took Dexadrine and empirin pills.

The four men in support were to try for the summit on the following day, but the mountaineers awoke surrounded by storm clouds. Because Everett needed to return to New York, everyone reluctantly prepared to descend, a long, tiring, and sometimes dangerous undertaking. As most experienced alpinists well know, the descent can be the most hazardous of times, one reason being the "letdown" experienced after a victory. It parallels team sports—the upset of the top-ranking club by an inferior team can be the result of lack of concentration and overconfidence.

But during rest stops, the mountaineers would occasionally turn their thoughts to The Big Apple and its hot, humid summer months, crowded streets and sidewalks, rude taxicab drivers, sophisticated art museums, skyscrapers of steel and glass, the well-dressed women in swanky and trendy attire, and, of course, Greenwich Village. Only a minute percentage of Gotham's residents would be able to comprehend why six stalwart and intelligent men from their city would choose to undertake risky and frozen slopes of a polar mountain instead of spending a leisurely vacation on the beach in the Caribbean or at the cultured capitals of Europe. The publication press, which always keeps a keen eye for the curious public, evidently decided that such a climb was a sensational adventure, for *Look* soon accepted a story and color photography featuring the dazzling white cornices of North America's Icy Crown.

▲ ▲ ▲

CHAPTER 15

The Winter Ascent:
The Most Desperate of Odds

We solved none of life's problems, but I believe all of us returned with a new awareness of some of its realities.
Art Davidson
Minus 148°, 1969

As new routes on Mount McKinley were being climbed in the fifth and sixth decades of the 1900s, thoughts turned to another type of unknown challenge—a winter ascent. Just exactly when this notion first took a serious vent is uncertain, but when Art Davidson of Alaska and Shiro Nishimae of Japan were on a South Buttress expedition in 1965, they conjured a vision of what a winter ascent on this polar mountain might involve. Despite the West Buttress being the route of choice, they wondered about the uncertainties: could men survive the temperatures, likely to be at least minus 100 degrees Fahrenheit at times, and the brutal and unforgiving winds, which could knock a man down and sometimes likely exceed 100 miles per hour? Perhaps the psychological aspect was the most frightening, for as Davidson later wrote in *Minus 148°: The Winter Ascent of Mt. McKinley*, "We shuddered to imagine McKinley's most eerie winter aspect—the darkness."[249] In February mountaineers could expect only seven hours of continuous daylight.

At best, the two climbers mused, mere existence high on the mountain would be brutal. Making camp and cooking in the darkness, carrying the extra clothing that would be needed, and the heavy packs were all sobering thoughts. The unknown factors seemed to have no ending; the one certainty was that such a project would be a high-risk adventure. Yet there was a certain magnetism to this idea that compelled them.

Not all climbers would wish to join such a gambler's plan, one with more than money to lose. During the next year the idea fermented, with the cast of possible participants both growing and shrinking simultaneously. At one time Davidson was the only confirmed member, but as Nishimae and Dr. George Wichman (an orthopedic surgeon originally from Germany) agreed

Winter expedition of 1967 party members at Talkeetna. Left to right (standing): Shiro Nishimae, Jacques Batkin, John Edwards; (seated): Don Sheldon, Dave Johnston, Gregg Blomberg, Dr. George Wichman, Ray Genet. (photo by Dr. George Wichman)

to join an attempt early in 1967, Gregg Blomberg, who had been indecisive about assuming the strain and toil of leadership, finally agreed to come if at least one more experienced climber could be confirmed. Apparently Davidson and Nishimae had confidence that Blomberg, a Colorado manufacturer of mountaineering equipment, would be better suited to lead and fuse the undertaking than either of them.

Fortunately for the vital continuation of the undertaking, a most experienced and obsessed Alaska climbing vagabond, Dave Johnston, agreed to join. Tall and strong and ever optimistic, Johnston offered seasoning from an epic Mount McKinley–Mount Hunter traverse that was reassuring. Because he had worked outside near Fairbanks that winter, his hands and body were accustomed to frigid temperatures. While Johnston felt the proposed winter group was strong, it would not be similar to keeping up with Vin Hoeman on the epic traverse, which he compared to hanging on to a ski-tow rope.

Despite the addition of Johnston, the winter expedition's personnel was hardly hand-picked. Climbers joined sometimes by invitation and at other times by just appearing at an appropriate time. The participation took another tangent when Dr. John Edwards, a New Zealand biologist (with a reputation as a comedian) who Davidson met at the Arctic Institute of Biology, wanted to climb Mount McKinley. By now the membership came to six and the project was assured. Davidson related how the group took an even more international turn in December:

> *Gregg in Colorado and I in Fairbanks, Alaska, began receiving long-distance phone calls from a man with a thick Swiss accent. His name was*

*Ray Genet. Genet asked if he and his French friend Jacques "Farine"
Batkin could become expedition members. Batkin we had heard about. He
was said to be an incredibly powerful climber, noted for having pioneered
long, difficult winter ascents of steep ice and rock walls in the Alps. Three
years earlier he had climbed what many judged to be the most difficult
route ever put up in Alaska; on this expedition with Lionel Terray to Mt.
Huntington he was considered the best-liked party member and was
chosen by the leader, Terray, for the first summit attempt. Farine appeared perfect for McKinley in the winter. It was true that we might have
some problems communicating with him, since he had mastered only a
few dozen words of English, but we were anxious to have him with us
nevertheless [Edwards spoke French and could chat with Batkin]. Genet,
however, was a different matter. His mountaineering background wasn't
particularly impressive. He cited his youth in Switzerland's Alps, cross-
country skiing, and winter hunting trips as his experience. His most
notable ascent was of a squat, roundish peak only forty-five hundred feet
high. I considered his main qualifications for this climb to be his limitless
enthusiasm and a determination to be included. Certainly enthusiasm
and determination were important qualities for a winter McKinley climber,
but would they compensate for a lack of experience? It wasn't until much
later that we learned how Genet had helped Gregg and me decide to let
him join us. On the phone he had told Gregg I wasn't opposed to his
coming. Then he called me to say Gregg approved his coming if I agreed.
Before we realized it, Genet was a member of the expedition.*[250]

In time, Genet's natural physical strength became an asset, although
once on Kahiltna Glacier, Johnston needed to demonstrate knot-tying and
show him how to rope-up and belay.

During the food and equipment organizing phase, Blomberg solved equipment and clothing problems with his innovative arrangement with Alp
Sport for special down sleeping bags and other items that made it possible
to withstand polar conditions. In addition to the best winter clothing
available, the expedition members wore warm vapor-barrier "bunny" boots.
Davidson, ever the promoter, found a partial sponsor in the form of the
Institute of Arctic Biology in Fairbanks, who organized the scientific studies of human performance during the ascent and afterward in Fairbanks.
In January the party members gathered at the institute for a series of
physiological tests, one of them a treadmill "run," which the thirty-six-year-
old Batkin easily won "with an astonishing score." Certainly his former
career as a flour-sack carrier in France enhanced his stamina.

Near the end of the month, veteran pilot Don Sheldon began ferrying the
climbers two at a time to Kahiltna Glacier near the 7,000-foot level. Blomberg
and Johnston, who arrived first, roped together and snowshoed forward
about one mile to find the best crevasse-free route. Upon their return to the
landing area, they were alarmed to see Batkin romping about, alone and
nonchalant about the concealed glacier dangers. Davidson later had this
comment: "Even though Gregg and Dave were disturbed by Farine's apparent carelessness, they chose to say nothing about the incident since Farine
spoke no English and they spoke no French, they figured it would be nearly

impossible to caution him without insulting him. After all, Farine had more experience on glaciers than either of them had."[251]

Perhaps because of their impatience to "get the show going" and their long winter waiting period, the climbers packed loads during the first night on the glacier. Procedures were not uniform, however, because Genet and Batkin traveled unroped, while the others remained tied together—some on snowshoes and with Genet on skis for one day. Some questioned moving unroped, especially when Genet plummeted twenty feet into a hidden crevasse in the blackness. Fortunately the crevasse had a sloping bottom, which he used to walk out; Genet then roped with Davidson and Nishimae.

On the second day the party carried packs to a cache, marking the route with wands to the next planned campsite. There appeared to be no crevasses. On the third day everyone carried loads, unroped, along the wind-packed route. Along this stretch, Davidson had fallen up to his shoulders into a hidden, wind-drifted crevasse—a short way from the wanded route. Barely supported by a snow fill, with all his strength he managed to pull himself out of the death trap and roll away to one side. He later wrote, "My lungs heaved wildly to catch their breath. I was shivering. My head was roaring."[252] Davidson was still in panic, fully aware of how close he came to tragedy.

Here was proof that some crevasses simply could not be detected. Davidson planned to insist that ropes should be used on the glacier (at this stage of progress, Blomberg was still the nominal leader). When Davidson arrived at the new site, where three of the party were shoveling a place for the tents, the men looked backward along the tracks, noting there were two others on their way. But when they looked again, there was only one person. Sensing something was wrong, they quickly descended. Batkin, who was following Johnston, had fallen into the same crevasse that almost engulfed Davidson!

> In the distance a figure was coming toward us. For a moment we thought it might be Farine, but it was Gregg. When he suddenly stopped and bent down to the snow there could be no more doubt that something was wrong.
>
> We ran up to Gregg out of breath. His eyes were glazed and frantic. He was yelling into a hole in the glacier. "Thank God you guys are here!" he cried.
>
> Bending over the hole again, he screamed "Dave, Dave, Dave, can you hear me? ... Dave!" Though Dave was standing beside him, getting a rope ready, Gregg didn't yet realize that it was Farine and not Dave who had fallen into the crevasse.
>
> Both Dave and Pirate [Genet] declared that they were going down into the crevasse to rescue Farine. Gregg insisted that only one should descend; he knew that two people down the hole would create confusion. Without hesitation, Gregg decided Dave was the one we'd lower down; he had more rescue experience than any of us. Pirate accepted the decision without saying a word; I noticed that his hands were knotted into tight fists.
>
> Edging his way carefully to the lip of the crevasse, Gregg shouted again into the dark hole. "Farine! Farine!" His voice was cracking. "Farine! ..." There was no answer.

Gregg turned to us with a frantic sigh. "Oh God, I don't know if I can face a body."

Gregg and Pirate anchored themselves thirty feet from the crevasse. Two ropes ran from them into the hole. Dave fastened Jumar ascendars, small clamps that grip a fixed line, to the rope he would descend on. He tied into the other rope for protection. Flicking on his headlamp, he disappeared down the hole.[253]

Batkin died a completely needless death, as have numerous others before him and since on these dangerous glaciers. Had Batkin been wearing snowshoes, as had Johnston just before him, he probably would have crossed safely. In a sense, his strength was his undoing: Batkin carried the heaviest load—the added weight perhaps being the reason he broke through the snow.

The climbers then tied into a single rope and, guided by headlamps, silently marched to the camp, pondering on this ill-fated turn of events. They were too numb to think straight, to feel the horror. Everyone accused himself of carelessness: Blomberg, as leader, knew he should have enforced traditional safety techniques; Davidson, in particular, agonized over the fact that Batkin had perished near the crevasse into which he had just fallen.

That night in the tent, the burdened party gloomily discussed the tragedy. Blomberg wanted to discontinue the ascent. Others were undecided, but Davidson, Genet, and Johnston proposed to continue, solidified in the spirit of their French companion. As total shock and a sense of despair prevailed, the men reviewed the events that led to the tragedy, but nothing could now change the situation: Batkin had died. The night was like a nightmare as the climbers wept or silently pondered their ill fate. They wrote thoughts in diaries and said but little.

Batkin had been a man who was content with little, happy in his freedom to be unroped and to wander in his own peaceful, satisfying manner.

On February 4 (only four days after the crevasse death), glacier pilot Jim Cassidy happened to fly by and sight a distress message on the glacier. He landed and then contacted Don Sheldon, who soon landed to take Genet out with the body. Blomberg had written a message for the public: "Jacques Batkin died in the pursuit of a winter ascent, in which he truly believed. We will continue the attempt with his spirit and presence."[254] Ice crystals high in the atmosphere over Mount Foraker, a sun dog, caught the sunshine to refract it to rainbow colors. The climbing party interpreted this as a welcome sign, a beckoning to dedicate themselves to the ascent. Yet they were fully aware that some others would scorn their tactics, no matter what they did from then onward.

The following day, the expedition would have lost another man, except this time they had resolved to stay roped. Without any sign of a crevasse, Edwards broke through the surface and fell some forty-five feet while en route from the base camp igloos to the cache where Sheldon had landed the party (this was not ineptitude, for everyone wore snowshoes on an ostensibly safe portion of Kahiltna Glacier). The ordeal of getting out took three hours; for Edwards, it was a bruising and freezing experience, one he had never encountered during his climbs in the Alps and Great Britain. Discouraged by the trauma, and the hidden dangers, Davidson became concerned that the party was struggling in a kind of quicksand, the efforts only bringing frustration.

When Genet, who had flown out with Sheldon to inform the authorities and the press about the tragedy, returned on February 9, he seemed to revive morale. Fresh food and supplies and a CB radio that functioned stirred enthusiasm. The next step was to locate a camp near Kahiltna Pass. Here the party built a complex of igloos with passages and even a dining area—all sheltered by blocks of ice. Despite the wind protection here, the temperature was so frigid that the climbers wore face masks and curled their toes and fingers. They "marched" in place just to keep shivering to some control.

On February 14, the party left the igloos, hoping to set up a new camp in the bowl above 14,000 feet, but the slow progress and short daylight hindered everyone. At a supply cache at an estimated 12,500 feet, it was decided to halt and spend the night. A thermometer reading gave minus forty-two degrees Fahrenheit; Davidson noted "What an event to celebrate on St. Valentine's Day."[255] Continuing in the morning, the extreme cold "burned" lungs as each man breathed the dry, frigid air.

Camp at 14,400 feet was barely set up when a lenticular cloud appeared over Mount Foraker, and by morning snow was falling. For the next three days "the blizzard pelted [their] basin with so much snow that visibility was restricted to less than fifty feet most of the time."[256] But when they could start again, it felt invigorating. Seemingly, the blizzard was a force that they could pit themselves against, while on the Kahiltna, as Davidson wrote, "the strain of the hidden crevasses, the accident, and even the uncertainty of whether we'd go on had confused us, and had made us turn against each other."[257]

Although a cloudcap obscured the summit and the route to 17,200 feet, the men began to be infected with "summit fever." The end of the climb seemed to be within reach, and on the 17th Blomberg wrote in his journal, "We are all optimistic that if we can carry a load up to 17,200 feet tomorrow we can all move up the next day.... We could be through by the twenty-fifth and I could be home by the first. Man, that would be nice!"[258] In just two days this prophecy seemed fulfilled, for the skies cleared sufficiently to permit an ascent of the steep ice slope leading to the upper ridgecrest.

Having the CB radio enabled the party to hear an Anchorage forecast—and just as the prediction indicated, February 22 began clear, cold, and calm. Blomberg, Genet, Wichman, and Edwards carried a tent, their sleeping bags, food, stoves, and shovels to the high camp location. Meanwhile, the three others made a carry from below and then moved up to the new snow cave on the next day. Despite the discouraging frostbite and fatigue, chances for the summit now appeared favorable. The expedition had experienced bitter cold, some minor altitude sickness, but no long, drawn-out storms. No 100-mile-per-hour winds had come to flatten them.

When on February 27 a summit attempt was inaugurated, the windchill was so intense that each person had to shield his face. At least twenty minutes were required to lace crampon straps because of numb, cramped fingers. Stomping about in tight circles barely seemed to improve foot circulation. Again, the environment kept the party from a planned early start. As the men ascended beyond Denali Pass, rests became more frequent; the altitude was certainly affecting progress. Davidson remembered that he was not quite dizzy, "but my ears were ringing slightly and my head felt light. I laughed to myself at the thought of my red-bearded, begoggled, down-hooded head floating off over the Alaska Range like a circus balloon."[259] As headaches and fatigue took their toll, dense clouds enveloped the upper mountain: the tardy start allowed the men little chance of reaching and returning from the summit before nightfall.

On February's last day, a howling and violent wind spelled danger. Davidson stated that all were aware that "up high in winter even a 50-mph wind could destroy a climbing party, because at −50° a 50-mph wind creates an equivalent wind-chill temperature well below −100°. None of us had ever experienced conditions like that, but we expected that if the wind caught us above this camp there could be no retreat except to dig in under the ice and sit it out."[260]

Quixotically, after breakfast the wind lessened. Wichman and Edwards were still exhausted from the previous day's attempt, Blomberg was pained with frostbite, and Nishimae opted to wait for him. But Davidson, Johnston, and Genet decided to make the attempt, the first serious bid for the summit. Slowly and methodically forging ahead, they used the rest-step technique, making deep breathing a conscious effort. Quite concerned about the bitter chill and oncoming darkness, it was almost night by the time they moved slowly along the final ridgecrest to the summit's marking pole. Normally an ideal time without a wind in summer, a 7:00 P.M. arrival could be critical in the darkness, which allowed the lights of Anchorage to appear dimly in the distance.

Wisely, the three mountaineers had left their sleeping bags at the Denali Pass supply cache; Nishimae and Blomberg had arrived at the pass during this interlude but were too exhausted to continue.

Most fortunately the victors had the strength and balance to safely descend to the supply cache, but here an important decision was forced upon them, for the upcoming icy traverse below Denali Pass in the darkness, an area where numerous falls and tragedies have occurred, was an invitation to disaster. Johnston wanted to descend, Genet wished to rest until daylight, and Davidson saw the advantage of each choice. Finally, the men decided to remain at the cache, huddling in sleeping bags beneath a parachute left from a supply drop by an earlier expedition.

As March 1 dawned, the parachute flapped wildly and a bitter blast of wind finally tore the fabric away from the mountaineers. Now the men were critically unprotected in the far-subzero temperatures, fully exposed to the biting wind. During some time that day, the men estimated that the wind-chill temperature dropped to minus 148 degrees Fahrenheit.

The expedition was now split between Denali Pass and the 17,300-foot camp, with no means of communication. Isolation and the terrific wind caused the greatest of strain within each group, who could not know the fate and location of the other one. Edwards recalled that the wind sounded like the continual roar of jet engines. Davidson recalled their first day at the frigid pass:

For more than an hour I had clung to the ledge on the ice, feeling the frostbite blisters swell on my hands and watching helplessly while Dave dug a cave in the ice. Just before he had completed it, Dave had collapsed from exhaustion; by then Pirate had pulled himself together, and despite his hands and feet, which were beginning to swell with frostbite blisters, he had somehow made it over the crest to finish hollowing out the cave. Dave had recovered enough strength to help me through the small hole in the ice which was the entrance to our new home.[261]

During this survival epic, Nishimae and Blomberg again attempted to reach Denali Pass, but the gale-force blast turned them back. Through the blowing snow, they may have seen a sleeping bag, perhaps with Genet, but they never reached it to find out.

In retrospect the three men at the pass indeed had a genius for survival. Most fortunately Johnston had found some food—ham, bacon, and peas— left from a previous expedition. Inside their cave he managed to cook, his hands being the only ones flexible enough to manipulate the stove. While the tiny cave proved cramped, too short to stretch out fully and barely high enough to lie on one side, it unquestionably saved them.

The tempest continued as if it would never halt. Due to some spoilage because of punctured cans, the remaining food was adequate for less than one day's requirement. Then, to augment this crisis, the stove failed to light because fuel had run out. Again, the gods of fortune prevailed. Johnston had cached fuel nearby in 1964, and in a desperate search managed to find it. Once more, the party was able to start the stove and melt snow for acutely needed hydration. Davidson at the time remarked that one advantage of being dehydrated was that he rarely had to urinate into the can inside his sleeping bag.

While the support party descended the ridge to the West Buttress' fixed ropes, the intense wind repeatedly blew the members over. Blomberg was twisted around by the wind force with his crampons fixed and sprained his ankle; he suffered intense pain during the remainder of the descent. Two members from the concerned support party struggled to base camp, finding that the deep new snow had covered almost all of the route-marking wands. After navigating in a whiteout to the igloos, they called Anchorage by radio. This dispatch began a major rescue effort. On March 6 the three weakened and nearly frozen mountaineers planned to descend: the wind had calmed, but now a whiteout made movement impossible. In desperation, Johnston, Davidson, and Genet searched the supply cache found earlier and, with much chopping away of the ice cover, found one more unopened box. This one contained dried potatoes, ham, and raisins "packaged in a wrapper that had gone out of style at least fifteen years ago."[262] This discovery may have saved the three, for one more night in the tiny cave without food could have been fatal. Luckily, they could now eat and brew drinks.

Somewhat fortified in the morning, the mountaineers were able to leave the cave—the worst part being to don frozen boots and thereby suffer the pain of severe frostbite. Somehow the men managed to straighten out the frozen rope and tie into it with their almost immobile hands. Progress was intensely painful, and in their weakened state, a minor slip would likely have been the end of them. Somehow, the almost-anticipated mishap did not occur, and the three reached the now-abandoned snow cave at high camp. Soon pilot Sheldon, who had been searching for them, flew by and dropped some oranges—a reminder that supermarket shoppers could obtain fresh fruit, while the winter mountaineers were just subsisting on discarded food scraps left by past expeditions.

Revived after eating food left at the snow cave, the three now took a new lease on existence and managed to stagger down to the next lower camp— in the 14,000-foot basin above Windy Corner. The support party had by now descended, having given the winter climbers up as certain fatalities.

Sheldon's sighting of the three men precipitated a rescue, and on the following day a plane flew by, parachuting food and a radio. Then, as the mountaineers were painfully hobbling nearer Windy Corner, a certain confusion arose when two helicopters quickly appeared above them. Radio contact with a circling C-130 aircraft indicated that a major front was anticipated, with winds in excess of 100 miles per hour. It was deemed best to get the mountaineers off the mountain immediately. With increasing gusts, which created a howling snow plume nearby, one helicopter was barely able to land, just long enough for the men to clamber through the doorway. Soon there was warmth, comfort, and a rousing welcome from other expedition members and assorted friends at Talkeetna. More traumatic and painful would be the hospital recovery from this coldest of winter epics.

The National Park Service's written report detailed some of the rescue plans and events.[263] The Alaska Rescue Group on March 5 stated that a private aircraft flying over Kahiltna Glacier had spotted two men of the winter expedition at their 10,200-foot camp, where an international distress signal was stamped out. Search and rescue efforts proceeded, including overflights: mountaineers with their full winter garb were brought to Talkeetna from Alaska locations and Seattle. By radio Blomberg reported that six days previously all seven climbers had been at a high-camp snow cave and three had set out for the summit. Meanwhile, the weather had turned unbelievably bad, with winds in excess of 100 miles per hour. Two men had attempted to reach the summit plateau to assist those above but were "blown off the mountain." Blomberg at the time believed Davidson, Genet, and Johnston were indeed in serious trouble, if not dead due to dehydration (he had no knowledge of the gasoline cache). Meanwhile, there was a ray of hope that the three had been able to find some food in Washburn's old cache at Denali Pass. Around noon on March 7, a C-118 aircraft reported via radio to the Federal Aviation Administration station that it had sighted three climbers moving down-mountain toward the 17,300-foot snow cave.

Meanwhile, Wichman and Nishimae could not be located (by now they had given up any hope for the summit party). The search for them continued the next day, and they were found by helicopters at 10,200 feet. Certain that three summit climbers had perished, their first words were, "Did you find the bodies?"

▲▲▲

CHAPTER 16

Two Contrasting Expeditions: Success and Tragedy in July 1967

The ascent of McKinley is a curious paradox. Under certain conditions it can be surprisingly easy, while under others it can be almost fiendishly difficult.

Bradford Washburn
The Mountain World, 1956–1957, 1957

A mountaineer with a consuming interest in expedition climbing, Boyd Everett was the ultimate logistical planner. The complex organization and attention to food, equipment, and myriad details that he made for his Yukon and Alaska expeditions to Mount Logan, Mount Saint Elias, and then to Mount McKinley in the summer of 1967 had no equal. Before he met death on Dhaulagiri in the Nepal Himalaya in a massive avalanche two years later, some contemporaries believed that investment analyst Everett spent entire winters carefully refining projected plans and writing detailed expedition reports. Certainly his treatise *The Organization of an Alaskan Expedition* was a primer unequalled in its field. In *High Alaska* Jonathan Waterman summarized Everett's private goals: "Few of his Wall Street associates would suspect that this precise man who dressed in conservative business suits, was quietly initiating huge climbing expeditions. He would become a peerless organizer of climbers and equipment, a Chris Bonington of Alaskan expeditions."[264] Drawing on his comfortable income, Everett built a cadre of competent mountaineers who regularly took part in his expeditions to the great ice peaks of the Far North.

The 1967 expedition that Everett so diligently organized was composed of fifteen young mountaineers, to be separated into three climbing teams all starting from a common base on Kahiltna Glacier. The threefold objective was the second ascent[265] of Cassin Ridge, the second ascent of the South Buttress via its northwest ramp, and the first climb of the direct south face—later to be named Centennial Wall. Although thirty-three-year-old Everett had been cited for being overequipped and abnormally methodical, all of the party members returned safely from successful ascents with only minor injury, and no cases of frostbite or serious altitude illness occurred (one climber on Cassin Ridge did break an ankle when an old fixed rope broke, but was able to descend on his own).

To undertake the contemplated ascents during the Alaska Centennial year, Everett drew his climbers, including seven Dartmouth College men, from various parts of the United States. One of the students, Anthony Horan, served as expedition doctor. Later writing an account in *Dartmouth Alumni Magazine,* he explained the nature of the professional supplies:

> *The drug companies, particularly Rexall, were prompt in their dona-*
> *tions of antibiotics, skin salves, and nostrums. We carried a half hour of*
> *oxygen for pulmonary edema in aluminum bottles kindly donated by the*
> *manufacturer, Lif-O-Gen. (After the summit, in our camp at 18,000 feet we*
> *sucked from these bottles in lieu of cocktails.) The most valuable items in*
> *our kit proved to be aspirin, which was effective against high-altitude*
> *headache, and Seconal, a short acting barbituate effective in the induction*
> *of sleep under the peculiar daytime conditions of the glacier. Climbers who*
> *had slept well could be spotted by their cheerfulness.*[266]

Although Everett was not the grand scientific and military-assistance promoter that Bradford Washburn became on his Alaskan expeditions, he inspired Art Davidson to sell the idea of footing the massive expedition's food expenses to the Alaska Centennial Committee, which as someone later quipped might be a wise plan to pursue again in the year 2067. As part of the Centennial connection, Everett's party conducted some physiological testing under the Institute of Arctic Biology (which had received a grant to study the effects of altitude on mountaineers) and carried out a rappeling and prusiking demonstration at the Fairbanks fairgrounds; only a handful of spectators, however, were curious enough to pay a visit.

At Talkeetna, preparatory to flying the mountaineers and their ponderous supplies to Kahiltna Glacier, bush pilot Don Sheldon had the men clearing rocks off the runway, for he anticipated heavily loaded takeoffs. By June 22 most of the expedition and its supplies had been landed at 7,400 feet on the glacier's southeast fork. The first logistical chore was to separate out specialized technical equipment and food for each of the three climbing groups, prior to the sledding and carrying of loads to the foot of the objectives. The equipment to sort out, aside from the base camp tents and radio, included the following:

    10 gold line climbing ropes
    18,000 feet of fixed rope
    52 ice pitons
    167 rock pitons
    60 snow pickets
    10 piton hammers
    6 ladders
    5 snow shovels
    100 rolls of toilet paper
    3 spare ice axes and crampons
    4 "walkie talkie" radios
    30 gallons of white gasoline
    6 stoves
    alpine tents

The Gerry Logan tents (nine by nine feet), which stood erect with a high centerpole, received a high rating for base camp usage; the smaller two-man tents were used higher on the mountain. Ropes of $5/16$-inch diameter proved the most useful of several sizes taken. The favored stove was the Optimus 111-B, which burned for three hours on a single filling. A great advantage in cold temperatures and the close tent confines was that the stove's pressure pump would permit lighting without pouring inflammable gasoline on the burner.

On all three Mount McKinley routes climbed, the men wore high-altitude double boots with protecting overboots. Each man had a Kelty frame pack as well as a smaller rucksack. Both Grivel and Simond crampons were worn, and Jumar ascenders were used to attach to fixed ropes. Because modern climbing harnesses were not yet available, nylon waist loops were used to tie the climbing rope to each man. All members had long-handled, straight-picked ice axes (nobody used two ice tools). Attire focused on down duvets of several types. Everyone wore wool sweaters, wool trousers, nylon wind pants, and parkas.

Adequate nourishing food was not overlooked in the planning process. Base camp food included copious amounts of fresh meat, canned fruit, and pound cake. Fresh bread with jam, peanut butter, and honey was a staple. For the three south face routes, Everett had worked out a 700–man-day food list. To begin with, there were forty loaves of Logan bread—a most popular item—baked in advance. In his account, Anthony Horan dwelled on the chore of buying and packing food at Fairbanks when the party first arrived in Alaska.

> *One thinker calculated that it would take one man between four and six months to do the job thirteen men did in three days. Breakfast was oatmeal or cream of wheat followed by cocoa. Strange to say, cold cereal proved an exceedingly popular change of pace. I suppose its crispness accounts for this. After weeks of mush, one developed a ravenous appetite for crackers and cookies. Lunch was nuts, three candy bars, half a can of kippers, sardines or tuna, and flavored water, usually Wyler's. Supper consisted of a dried soup followed by canned meat and rice or potato. We always drank jello or pudding hot, a beverage New Englanders might try on a bitter January day. In short, ours was standard expedition fare; we could not buy the more sophisticated dried foods because purchasing was done in Fairbanks, not exactly a world-trade center.*[267]

Yet, for an Alaskan expedition the fare was extravagant. Freeze-dried Crab Newburg appeared among the dinners, and there was an ample supply of canned meats. Chicken and beef gravy mixes and onion flakes were helpful in preparing a regular meat "glop" dinner. Chicken spread and deviled ham were always popular with crackers.

Food was packed into various man-day rations for four, six, and eight men, each box being wrapped with fiberglass tape; in all, there were 2,000 plastic bags and 90 soft-drink food boxes available for packing (each box held six to eight man-days of food). To clean pots and dishes, there were 100 brillo pads and 100 rolls of paper towels. In retrospect, it is doubtful that any of the climbers lost weight on the extended expedition, although food rationing sometimes had to be enforced because of the high percentage of stormy days in the summer of 1967. Perhaps anticipating plentiful and tasty meals, a wolf was spotted somewhere below the south face, leading to a concern the beast would raid caches placed on the glacier.

▲ ▲ ▲

"The expedition was in full swing when the glacier pilot, Don Sheldon, flew me to base camp a week late," wrote Horan. "The shock of being lifted from a virtual rain forest to 7,000 feet on McKinley was great. Nothing grows there. No living thing. Immense masses of snow and ice are heaped on all but the steepest pitches. There are no sounds except the wind on the tents and the intermittent thunder of avalanches falling somewhere. I was dressed for ice fishing in Antarctica. These clothes were quickly discarded in the twenty-degree, windless weather. I was soon surrounded by men who had lived in that forbidding landscape for a week, a fact which in itself I found reassuring."[268]

After he became involved with packing toward the beginning of the South Buttress route, Horan recalled how "trudging along in the semi-darkness, one's thoughts focused inwardly. Revery was possible when a rhythm was established." Every night the men carried fifty pounds for five miles and 1,500 vertical feet on snowshoes. "This labor cannot be duplicated in ordinary life. Perhaps the only time men push themselves this hard is in combat," Horan reminded his readers. But there is an appeal, perhaps difficult to define. "One source of appeal is the simplification of the task," he wrote. "How many times in life does an adult have just one purpose to pursue without interruption for five weeks? No telephone rings to tell you of a dozen conflicting obligations. When confined to the tent by storm only three objects command your attention: book, cup, and spoon. The greatest material loss imaginable is the loss of one's cup. Life is, for a time, simplified." Another source of appeal, of course, is the stunning beauty of the surroundings on such an expedition. But the hazards are numerous. Horan had the comment, "It would appear from what little information is available, that the seven members of the Wilcox expedition who ... died on the North side, while we were climbing the South side, took unnecessary risks in reaching the summit."[269]

The three Dartmouth undergraduates planning to attempt the South Buttress—James Janney, Paul Kruger, and Michel Zalewski—along with Anthony Horan found their route to the 12,000-foot camp "a bit too close to a hanging glacier, but we had no choice." The ascent went well until they first became conscious of the altitude at 15,000 feet, where the four men experienced headaches and breathlessness. Then "a curious cloud cap, like a beret" signaled a weather change, forcing the party into tents for five of the following six days.[270]

What one does for five days in a tent was explained by Horan:

The problem is by no means acute ... [because] one's mentality is blunted. Time passes quickly, if you are able to sleep 14 hours a day.... For expeditions I favor French novels because they yield more reading time per pound, if you read French as slowly as I do. The Dartmouth students all read The Rise and Fall of the Third Reich simultaneously by chopping it in thirds.[271]

At one time visibility above the party's 16,000-foot camp was so poor that it was possible to see only ten feet. Once two of the group lost their way in a whiteout and "wandered in a complete circle finally intercepting [their] own tracks."[272] Fortunately, green wands left by their companions led them to a campsite placed behind an immense snow wall.

July 27 proved to be the first of three sunny, windless days. Moving as slow as an invalid, "four breaths to a step," Horan was slowed by nausea. But on the summit, the temperature stood at a reasonable minus eight degrees Fahrenheit, "without a breath of wind." A jubilation set in as the four men returned to their high camp.

On their third perfect day, the descent commenced:

The afternoon was unforgettably beautiful. The sun gilded incredible cloud formations far below us. We stopped to photograph snow cornices etched by indigo shadows. I was on the second rope of two. We were about to negotiate the second icefall near the hanging glacier mentioned at the start of the actual climb, when we heard a sound like a rifle shot. A mile above us and to the left of the track we had just descended, an enormous avalanche had started.

For a moment, it seemed a distant event, scarcely disturbing the evening calm, but we were in its path. I looked around, but there was no shelter. A huge, boiling snow cloud thundered towards us. At the second I could at last perceive that we would certainly be hit, we were in fact hit by titanic wind and snow. I was rolled over and over for two hundred feet, like a child at the beach caught in a great comber. I thought I was dying. Then the turmoil ceased—I was weightless, suspended in air.

The wind whistling past me told me I was falling. This is death itself, I thought. An image of a painting depicting one of the first deaths on the Matterhorn flashed into my mind. There was plenty of time to think because I fell 130 feet, or thirteen stories, into a cavernous crevasse. Then imperceptibly, slowly, I stopped falling, I knew not why. Cascading snow formed an opaque curtain around me as I hung upside down unable to interpret what had happened. When, after many minutes, the avalanche ceased, I could see I was hanging by the climbing rope which must be attached to my climbing partner, Paul Kruger, whom I thought buried beneath tons of snow.

At first, efforts to extricate myself seemed futile, since I was surely marked for death. Gradually, I came to perceive that my situation was not hopeless. I was only twenty feet above the bottom of the crevasse, which had been filled in with ice and snow. Moreover, the crevasse seemed to open out into the glacier at one end. This flicker of hope increased my anguish because I was rapidly losing strength. The waist loop constricted breathing so much that unconsciousness seemed near. The pack turned me upside down.

My first efforts were pointless. I tried to fix myself to the wall of the crevasse, a maneuver of no value at all. After many minutes, I remembered the

▲ *Mount Huntington, showing northwest ridge and west face from air (photo by Jim Okonek, K2 Aviation)*

▼ *Lenticular cloud over Mount Foraker (photo by Brian Okonek)*

◄ Glacier pilot flying over immense crevasses of Kahiltna Glacier (photo by Jim Balog)

Parapenting at 14,300 feet, ▶ with upper West Buttress in background; note snow walls in camp area (photo by Mark Bebie)

Windstorm at sunset on ▼ Muldrow Glacier (photo by Brian Okonek)

◄ *Camp at 16,200 feet on West Buttress, with Mount Foraker in the distance some thirteen miles (photo by Brian Okonek)*

▲ *Climbers at 17,200 feet on West Buttress (photo by Roger Robinson)*

▼ *Avalanche pouring off Rooster Comb in Ruth Amphitheatre (photo by Scott Fisher, Mountain Madness)*

▲ *Climbing party on West Buttress route. Note the long shadows effect. (photo by Jim Balog)*

▲ *Army Chinook helicopter rescuing injured Korean climber on Cassin Ridge at 18,200 feet in summer 1988 (photo by Jim Balog)*

▼ *A fortified high camp at 17,200 feet on West Buttress (photo by Brian Okonek)*

▲ Left: *Climbing snow dome on West Rib, near 13,000 feet (photo by Charles Sassara);* right: *climbing party on traverse to Denali Pass, high on West Buttress route, with Mount Foraker in distance (photo by Brian Okonek)*

▼ *A peaceful evening at 17,200 feet on the West Buttress of Mount McKinley, with Mount Hunter below (photo by Brian Okonek)*

◄ *Gray Thompson climbing above Camp II on south face of Mount McKinley during the first ascent in July 1967 (photo by Dennis Eberl)*

▼ *Sunrise over Mount McKinley's North Peak at 3:00 A.M. from 19,000 feet on South Peak (photo by Brian Okonek)*

proper sequence of actions. Drop the pack so that it hangs from the end of the climbing rope, I told myself. This allowed me to work rightside up. I took off my one remaining snowshoe and so was able to step up into the stirrups we always fix to the rope for this eventuality. Now I was relieved of the terrible constriction of the waistloop. About this point in my efforts at self-help, Paul called my name. Never a sound more welcome, relief more profound. Paul had a wonderful stoic calm on the trail. He was lucid now.

"What do you want me to do?" he asked.

"Lower me," I replied.

Magically it seemed, I was lowered from the gallows. We discussed my plight. The usual method of climbing out of crevasses seemed impossible because the rope had cut into an immense cornice. Moreover, it appeared an easy scramble out onto the glacier. I elected to unrope and climb out of the ice-fall alone. In retrospect, I think I should have tried to climb the rope, but the memory of the cornice has faded and that of the icefall is all too vivid.

After picking my way for an hour in the deep snow and ice blocks, sensing that each step would drop me into a dark tomb of ice, there to die slowly over the course of days, I could see that the crevasse did lead to the glacier, but that a 150-foot cliff of ice was interposed. Panic was close to the surface now. I saw another opening in the gathering darkness. Without crampons, I slipped and fell continually on my way towards it. The opening proved fruitful. A snow cone from the smooth surface of the main glacier pointed towards me, with a short ice cliff intervening. In the darkness (it was now midnight) I could not be certain whether it was fifteen or fifty feet high; it looked like fifteen. I knew I would fall on the pitch and did, but I merely spilled out on the glacier in a gentle snow slide. Only at this moment did life seem certain.[273]

Kruger stated that the route down the icefall was unrecognizable. Séracs had toppled. The normal six-foot snow cover had been swept away, leaving polished ice where the men had snowshoed. Kruger had been swept about 100 feet into a shallow crevasse, which sheltered him from the avalanche. He gloomily sensed that the two others on the first rope must have been buried. Horan related how they limped through the semidarkness of midnight toward the advanced base camp and food cache.

There we saw a tent, pitched rather limply.... Our companions were there. We spoke in low tones like shell-shocked veterans of combat. They had been rolled two hundred feet as we had, but in addition had been pelted by blocks of ice so that each looked and felt as though he had been destroyed in a fist fight. One appeared to have a broken rib. Neither was sure he could walk in the morning.[274]

When in a dehydrated state they reached a cache (all stoves had been lost), they happily found canned fruit and each man ate three meals in succession. With a restored source of strength, the party came to a melt pond on the main Kahiltna Glacier. All felt immense relief with the certainty of survival— and as a blessing, it was no longer necessary to eat snow.

▲▲▲

On the ascent of Cassin Ridge, Boyd Everett's five-man party climbed carefully, even cutting many steps in the hard ice sections. While Everett was not a technical specialist, he had solid mountaineering skills, stamina, and vision. His *modus operandi* included the fixing of ropes, a practice of the 1950s and 1960s (he had used 2,400 feet of rope on the Southeast Spur in 1962). On Cassin Ridge, the 1967 party used 7,800 feet of fixed rope, 56 rock pitons, 10 ice pitons, and 16 rappel pickets. The climbers were sometimes forced by the wind and ice conditions to clip into the ropes to just leave the front entrance of their tents. "Holes began to appear in the tent floors revealing the cold rocks below,"[275] wrote Del Langbauer in the *American Alpine Journal*. After completing the classic ascent, they saw Sheldon's small aircraft search Denali Pass below them. Puzzled, they had no way of knowing that he was searching for the missing members of another expedition (the Wilcox party).

The four climbers meanwhile engaged on the Centennial Wall route (the direct south face) were focused for an even more technical alpine climb. Three of them, Dennis Eberl, Graham ("Gray") Thompson, and David Seidman, were attending Dartmouth College, while Roman Laba was a Fordham University student and informally associated with the "Vulgarian" climbing club. Eberl and Thompson had accomplished serious alpine ascents in the Saint Elias Mountains of Yukon Territory, while Seidman would later participate in a landmark route in these mountains.

The four-man team discussed attempting the south face alpine style: at the time no one had done a climb of this magnitude without resorting to expedition tactics. The Centennial Wall party finally compromised between alpine and expedition techniques by pulling most of their fixed rope with them, "thereby cutting our safety cord to the ground,"[276] as Eberl concluded. Given the atrocious weather of that summer (it snowed sixty of sixty-five days during the expedition), the men agreed that it was wise that they did not attempt the route alpine style.

In reviewing the Centennial Wall ascent, Laba complained of "the monotonous brutality of load carrying and all the other ponderous movement of a large and long expedition."[277] Yet he admitted that a well-organized movement plan, with considerable fixed rope and hardware, was to prove the deciding factor in success. The south face route began with 3,000 feet of avalanche face; next came 1,000 feet of low-angle rock and snow, and then three pink-granite buttresses barred the way, topped with a great façade of cornices from 16,800 to 18,800 feet. The route was so continuous that there were only four places where it was safe to untie from the rope—all of these high on the mountain. At all camps except the sixth, it was vital to be tied-in while sleeping.

Dennis Eberl later recalled the terror of speeding snow and ice on a great mountain wall:

> *A couple of times on this expedition I became aware of the power of winds that accompany avalanches. Once when Gray and I were carrying loads at the foot of the face, a large avalanche started near the top.... I turned to Gray and asked, "Should we run?" but Gray was already*

running perpendicular to the face and I then took the lead. I looked behind to see Gray disappear in a white cloud. I crouched down behind my Kelty and waited to be killed too, but was hit only by a wind blast full of powder. We had outrun the ice chunks which completely buried our former trail.[278]

The lower third of the face was moderately angled, hard Alaskan ice but did not hold snow. In discussing the route, Thompson's assessment was that the slope was scoured clean before much snow accumulated. "We cut many steps in this section to facilitate load-carrying before we gave up and front-pointed even as we ferried loads."[279]

The procedure on the face began with Laba and Seidman acting as a team; they climbed first, working out the route and sometimes placing fixed ropes, while Eberl and Thompson followed behind. About midway on the route, the teams switched roles. At their second camp, Laba and Seidman hacked out a flat in the ice where the person "sleeping on the outside had to hang his right buttock over a 1,500-foot ice slope. Debates over sleeping positions somewhat strained our friendship,"[280] Laba recalled. Pinned down at this camp by an intense thirteen-day storm, a huge rock avalanche, with boulders as big as a tent, "ricocheted down the main avalanche chutes 100 yards to the west." Eberl remembered that when their teammates were perched below them in the great storm, "Gray was outside tied into the safety lines performing one of the five essential biological functions when a baby avalanche gaily skipped over the projecting rock and filled his pants with powder snow, thus allowing us to come back saying this climb had hit us with avalanches on the run, asleep, and with our pants down!"[281]

The middle third of the route consisted of a leftward-leaning series of couloirs, gullies, and funnels leading through and around steep granite walls and buttresses. Here, the climbing was steeper than on the lower third, but belays and anchors from solid rock were possible because of the narrowness of the ice passages.

Eberl and Thompson had a giant fight in this section, just before the thirteen-day storm hit. They had reached the top of what was called the Two-Lead Avalanche Funnel, a point nearly halfway up the face—where Camp III (Spiral Camp) was later placed. Thompson recently recalled,

The funnel terrified me. It was built like a bobsled run, too narrow and steep to escape anything coming down it, with an immense area of the face above draining directly into it: a trap. We had carried our tent, sleeping bags, a stove, and food with us, thinking to set camp somewhere in the area if we could find a sheltered spot. The place wasn't well-protected, but I did not want to go back down the funnel, and argued for making a camp here.

We could see a big storm coming from our position on the face, and Denny argued that the place wasn't adequately sheltered, and that it would get smashed by slides if the storm brought snow. He wanted to retreat back to Camp I—the Lunch Rock [six pitches above the bergschrund], where we had dug out a platform below a small but pretty good over-hang.... The alternatives were either to retreat down the funnel, exposing ourselves to its dangers, or to dig in there and hope that the storm didn't bring much snow. Neither seemed like a good choice, and we were too tired to go further up the face with no certainty that we would find a better spot.

The argument degenerated into a shouting match, and culminated with both of us raging at each other, getting our 300-foot twin rope impossibly tangled, and finally cooperating in balling it up and throwing it down the face. We never saw it again.

Denny won, and we got ready to toss the ¹/₄-inch line that we were going to rappel down the funnel on. Just as we were about to throw it, with one end tied off this time, a patch of boulders the size of a bus detached from the top of the funnel and scoured it from wall to wall. We "rapped" with the smell of sulphur and rock dust heavy in the gully.

The weather that we saw coming was the onset of the thirteen-day storm that immobilized us at Camp I, and killed the Wilcox party. When we returned to the top of the funnel after the storm, the place was unrecognizable.[282]

"Later we found that the upper campsite where Gray wanted to stay had been creamed by avalanches," Eberl remembered. "So it turned out that we both had been right, about the danger of the avalanche gully and about the danger of the storm. The time spent arguing, however, probably had saved our lives."[283]

In his account in *Summit,* Thompson described being trapped at what was facetiously termed "Lunch Rock," while the other two mountaineers were in an even worse spot some twelve pitches higher.

For seven days we'd been cooped in the too-small two-man tent perched on our chopped-out platform on the 55–65 degree ice slope. The platform, which we had hacked out of blue water ice under the only overhanging rock on the ice face, wasn't even as wide as our Alp-Sport expedition tent. Denny, who had won the toss, slept on the inside gunched up against the rock; I, on the outside, wrested with the loser's alternative.[284]

Avalanches shot by both sides and over the top of the rock; the climbers dared not move up or down. Thompson continued,

Sometimes they came every thirty seconds, sounding like speeding freight trains at close range. The big ones sucked the air out of the tent, and from our lungs. The first big one ripped the fly from the tent, and we were sure that the tent wouldn't survive the night; in fact, we weren't sure that we would. Initially, the avalanches frightened us, but after a few days they became a regular part of the fabric of living in the weird little place.

During a short lull in the seemingly endless storm, Eberl and Thompson ascended to the higher camp, reclimbing the blue-ice traverse and then following the fixed ropes put in by the lead team—sometimes digging them out of the ice. The higher campsite had even less space than theirs. Eberl remembered, "To give you an idea about how bad their site was, part way through the storm Gray, who was getting sick of my company, suggested that we trade climbing partners. I said okay, but only if he were willing to move into the upper camp. Gray never complained again."[285]

Eberl suggested that it was unfortunate they did not swap partners, because on most of the expedition they were separated from the others and therefore did not get to know them well.

Roman and Dave also had a sanitation problem at their site. Gray and I always got our snow for cooking from one end of the tent, and used the other end for the latrine. However, our visit to the upper camp featured toilet paper in my soup. When I complained about it, Roman merely took his glove off and fished the paper out of my bowl. There was nothing else to do but keep eating.[286]

But cold temperatures (and cold feet) forced a return to the lower camp bivouac. Another storm hit them with a fury—this quick renewal was perhaps the principal factor in causing the worst single tragedy of Mount McKinley, Thompson believed. Meanwhile, the Centennial Wall climbers were unaware of the simultaneous grim events higher and beyond the summit.

"In the tent ennui reigned. For several days Den and I watched some tiny bugs crawling among the squares of the rip-stop roof of the tent," added Thompson. The bugs remained there for another three days. Meanwhile, "Denny worried that he was going to become a schizoid because he had read of an experiment which produced schizophrenic symptoms in subjects by depriving them of all external stimuli."[287] The two survivalists could eat but little of the bountiful foodstocks Everett had brought on the expedition because the storm had trimmed their rations. Eberl later wrote,

Looking back, the two weeks that Gray and I spent under the Lunch Rock were a turning point for me. To be so immobilized for so long in the mountains! To be bored to death on the South Face of McKinley! I think this experience later contributed to an interest I developed in sitting meditation (zazen). Part way through our stay at Lunch Rock, Gray allowed as though he might have something to ease the long hours, and pulled out a joint. I had never tried it before. After smoking some of it, I thought that it had no effect. I went out of the tent in my underwear to pee, not tying in, balanced on the ice slope in down booties, a thousand feet of space between me and the glacier below, supremely confident of my abilities. Gray was yelling, "No! Be careful! Tie in! Oh, this is so bad!" and I was laughing like crazy because Gray was so afraid for me when I had such exquisite balance. Gray said later that he was absolutely sure that I would fall, and that he planned to throw my sleeping bag down after me.[288]

Finally the avalanches became more of an annoyance than a danger, and they resolved never to come back to Lunch Rock. Climbing to the camp of the higher pair, their packs weighed at least seventy pounds because they picked up all the equipment and food they could tote. Much concerned about the higher team, they gained confidence as "a sign of great joy descended upon us, in the form of a piece of toilet paper tumbling down the slopes from above. The message was cryptic, but we knew that they were all right because nobody can be in too bad shape if he is still using toilet paper."[289]

During a high-camp "summit meeting," Laba began to question the sanity of the route, so the teams changed the leading. Thompson and Eberl pushed ahead with much determination when the weather finally cleared—climbing steep ice slopes, crossing avalanche gullies, and at times floundering in deep powder snow. Finally reaching the base of a steep granite outcrop, they were joined by Laba and Seidman, where all of them spent two hours chopping a miserably tiny tent platform.

The final third of the south face consisted of three attractive but challenging granite buttresses. The first was some 800 feet high and split by a broad, open chimney from 40 to 200 feet wide. The climbing here was the steepest and most difficult rockwork on the route, following icy holds up steep steps. Eberl recalled,

> Gray and I led the first buttress up grooves in the rock at night, when it was about 20° below zero. The climbing was perhaps 5.8 max, but challenging enough for us in crampons, in the cold, at altitude. While on this buttress we saw "End the War in Vietnam Now Pinnacle," so named by us because our contemporaries were dying in Vietnam rather than having fun climbing a mountain.[290]

Thompson and Eberl even had to engage in some pitoning and use direct-aid techniques at times, climbing the awkward rock with crampons for hours. They then left fixed ropes for the other team, who now had taken the following role.

Reaching a level "football field" at 18,000 feet, for the first time the climbers felt the high altitude, but, fortunately, little shoveling was needed for the two "nylon hovels." The top of the south face was overhung with cornices, and at first they tried to climb the sheer ice wall directly above them ("feeling very cocky"). But they compromised for an easier route through the cornices. However, on the summit plateau, the icy wind blew at an estimated seventy miles per hour, making for a miserable long walk to the mountain's highest point. Eberl remembered that the summit "was a mess of flags and other paraphernalia. I added to it by leaving a Dartmouth Outing Club trail marker."[291]

On the descent, the willow wands left by the South Buttress party were hard to follow, but Seidman took the lead and confidently led the team to a generous food cache. That night all of them gorged on candy bars from the cache, but they were forced to spend half the night digging out the tents from the blowing snow.

On Cassin Ridge, Bill Phillips had broken his ankle when a Japanese rope broke under his weight on the descent. Having fallen 100 feet and injured, he was alone on the ridge with Everett—who came down to meet the Centennial Wall party and ask if they could help. "The last thing we wanted to do was return to the dangers of the mountain," Eberl related. "We were utterly beat.... In the meantime, Boyd single handedly, heroically, helped Bill down the ridge to camp. Bill showed me his hard hat, which had a large indentation where he had hit his head on a rock during the fall."[292]

On returning to base camp on Kahiltna Glacier—some twenty miles distant—Seidman, who was once a hut boy in the Adirondack Trail system and used to carrying immense loads, carried a pack that weighed 125 pounds through the soft snow—they weighed it on a scale at base camp.

The expedition members went to Anchorage after waiting one week in poor weather for Don Sheldon to pick them up. Here, Eberl recalled, "We were picked up by a guy in a cowboy hat who took us to a strip joint, which he thought we would like because we had not seen women, or even taken a bath, in two months."[293]

In retrospect, Thompson, recently assessing the route, feels it is only moderately difficult in comparison to the new standards, yet it is very long, and there is a constant objective exposure to ice cliffs and avalanches. Every portion of the wall either slid or was hit by big avalanches while the 1967 party was on the face, most of them occurring during a very long storm; only tiny areas on the route were protected by rock overlays. These few localities were where camps were placed. The ideal and probably safest method to carry out this climb is to wait for a good weather forecast and then climb light and rapidly in alpine style, spending only some three days on the route. This, however, poses the problem of proper acclimatization, unless the party has already been high on the mountain.

▲ ▲ ▲

A little neglect may breed great mischief ... for want of a nail the shoe was lost; for want of a shoe the horse was lost; for want of a horse the rider was lost.
Benjamin Franklin

The immense tragedy on upper Harper Glacier in July 1967, when seven climbers died in a most violent storm, emphasizes a lesson to all McKinley aspirants. Quite in contrast to the Boyd Everett expedition's careful logistical planning and discipline, the tragedy is a case study in inadequate leadership, inexperience, ineptitude, impatience, tactical errors, and lack of human consideration.

The combination of twelve men from two separate parties climbing the Muldrow Glacier route perhaps led to the belief that there was safety in numbers. In a setup for disaster, seven members of the ill-fated Joseph F. Wilcox party died as a consequence of a severe multiday storm, mountain sickness, and colossal judgement errors. The accident became the single most tragic event to ever occur on Mount McKinley. The book by Howard H. Snyder, *The Hall of the Mountain King,* not published until six years after the events, portrays the tragedy as a consequence of his party and that of Wilcox merging without cohesiveness and provides a useful analogy of men in stressful situations. Snyder, who was quite critical in his assessment of Wilcox's procedures, believed that poor judgement and inexperience was the contributing factor to the disaster. Wilcox, who even later wrote *White Winds* in a defensive vein, displayed another perspective, claiming the participants were unlucky to be struck without warning by the most severe and prolonged summer storm ever encountered on Mount McKinley.

The Wilcox party, with one exception, was a "mail-order" assemblage, a young party (all were between twenty-two and thirty-one) recruited by letter. The leader, in fact, only knew one of his recruits, none of whom had high-altitude or winter mountaineering training. Wilcox had climbed Mount

Rainier (14,410 feet) six times, but little else. Clearly, four of the nine members were mountaineering novices.

Snyder originally had organized a party of four Colorado climbers with the intention of following the Muldrow Glacier route; when one participant had to drop out, he had to cancel plans or join another group because of the minimum-number requirements of the National Park Service at the time. The nine-member Wilcox expedition, which had similar plans, was the only one that appeared to offer a potential combination.

Snyder, who at twenty-one was three years junior to Wilcox, had ascended eleven peaks in the Alps and numerous high peaks in Colorado. Paul Schlichter, an air force cadet, had trained for altitude in December 1966 by climbing the three highest Mexican volcanoes. Jerry Lewis, the third companion, was a thirty-year-old student who had ascended numerous Colorado summits. In correspondence between the two leaders during the spring of 1967, Snyder felt Wilcox had formed some unconventional plans. It appeared he desired publicity and wished to accomplish a "first" by placing simultaneous camps on both the South and North Peak summits. The leaders and some members of both parties met at Mount Rainier, but the event was largely a brusque cordiality.

With Wilcox becoming the designated expedition leader, the two parties began their Alaska adventure from Wonder Lake in the month of June. With aerial support no longer permitted within the Park, a packer was hired to take the food and equipment to McGonagall Pass. Although the merged parties started as well as could be expected under the circumstances, misgivings arose early. The two groups remained socially fractured, tending to isolate themselves while in camp and traveling separately. As author Bill Sherwonit correctly perceived in *To the Top of Denali*, "from the start it was an unhappy alliance."[294]

Originally Wilcox had planned to keep his four novices below Karstens Ridge as a support party, but he later revised his plans to give them a summit opportunity. Most members of the combined expeditions required twenty-seven days to reach a high camp at 17,900 feet on July 14, the slow pace actually being beneficial for some of the climbers due to their lack of conditioning. Yet the leaders displayed impatience because of the continuing fine weather and pushed the men too fast, with heavy loads, between lower Karstens Ridge and the first Harper Glacier campsite.

The only serious mishap that occurred on the ascent to this point was the burning of a Logan tent at the expedition's 15,000-foot camp, when fumes from a stove's open and empty fuel tank were carelessly ignited by a second stove. Snyder later wrote, "The tent disappeared as though it had evaporated, leaving only the zippers and the neoprene coated floor."[295] The loss of this shelter would later affect vital movement decisions.

Without waiting for all members of both parties to arrive at the high camp, on July 15 the three Colorado climbers and Wilcox climbed to the summit of the South Peak without incident. One reason later given to make the ascent immediately was that a radio contact with the National Park Service at Eielson Visitor Center had indicated that a storm was imminent. This strategy is unclear, though, because the forthcoming isolation of the remaining men reduced overall strength and unity and, in effect, left the

Wilcox team without its leadership. Late that night, after the four returned from the summit, the predicted storm arrived, lashing the high camp with strong wind and snow.

On July 17, the "summit" unit with one other man chose to descend to the 15,000-foot camp. Both team leaders, Snyder and Wilcox, were included in the descent, leaving a very inexperienced group at the high camp. While descending, they presumed the others would set out for the summit because the conditions then were calm and sunny. But when glancing upslope the following morning, they sighted climbers still at the camp; apparently two of the seven were plagued by mountain sickness from the quick climb to a higher altitude, and the consensus was that it would be prudent to wait for those arriving from below.

Jerry Clark, the most mature person of the group and the one who had climbed with other Wilcox party members, provided a friendly and cohesive factor. He was designated to be the summit climbing leader; the others were Mark McLaughlin, Henry Janes, Walt Taylor, John Russell, and Dennis Luchterhand. These six (without Steve Taylor, who remained in camp) set out some time that day, taking sleeping bags in addition to the usual mountaineering equipment for the final 2,400-foot ascent. At 8:00 that evening while ascending, Clark spoke to the National Park Service through radio contact, but soon the weak batteries would no longer function for transmittal. Apparently the scarcity of wands placed on the route by the other team (most had been left at 15,000 feet) and a partial whiteout in the darkening twilight confused the Clark party as to their location. Given this orientation problem, it did not seem prudent to continue. Realizing a descent to high camp might mean abandoning the summit, the group foolishly decided to bivouac in the open at about 19,500 feet. It is doubtful that they carried shovels to dig in.

July 18 dawned clear, with all but John Russell (who remained behind or returned to high camp) reaching the summit. Apparently the party had now found the correct route, but cloud and mist enveloped the South Peak by midmorning. Clark was able to radio out a message stating that the view at the summit was completely whited out. An agreed next radio call for 8:00 P.M. never came. A major storm, with near-impossible visibility, set in during the party's descent and continued into the following day.

When the evening radio transmission from Clark did not occur on the 19th, Wilcox at the lower camp became apprehensive. He later wrote, "The situation had all the aspects of an emerging emergency. There were no options to consider; our only course of action was to climb back immediately to the high camp."[296] Much concerned about Clark's silence and the intensity of the tempest, Wilcox, Snyder, and Schlichter began ascending early the following morning, carrying clothing, sleeping bags, four gallons of fuel, and a stove. Soon a light snowfall turned into an intense ground blizzard, and in the deep powder the men could not find their previously placed wands. Sometimes the wind knocked them to the surface and obliterated their tracks. Although fearing the worst for those above, the conditions became so exhausting that they were forced to turn back, quite concerned that they might not find the route back to camp. That evening, Wilcox, in radio contact with the National Park Service, expressed his concern, fearing the climbers above might be very weak and out of fuel. He also requested that expert bush pilot Don Sheldon be called out to make a reconnaissance of the situation when conditions allowed.

On July 21 the storm intensified at the 15,000-foot position. Estimated to be 60 miles per hour, with gusts to perhaps 100, winds virtually tore the camp apart. When standing outside the tent, Wilcox was lifted completely off his feet, went airborne, and barely managed to grasp a line. He later related, "The snow was drifting faster than I could shovel and the tent was going under." Conditions became so desperate that anyone outside could barely breathe in the blizzard. As the camp became a disaster scene, his tent became so snow-drifted that all five men were forced to crowd into the remaining one, which became so packed that it was not possible to light a stove. Without water and hot food, morale sank. To judge by later versions of the epic, there was considerable tension and disunity between Snyder and Wilcox. During the nightly radio call, the stricken group affirmed that they were now too weak to investigate the situation at the high camp. Snyder reported that three men (including Wilcox) were sick; Wilcox believed the problem was mental. Years later in his account, he provided these words:

> I was astounded by Howard's desperation to justify the desertion of the high party. He had fumbled with the radio and battery pack in the cold for more than five minutes, critically draining our weak batteries to tell Eielson something that was not only incorrect but impertinent to the rescue situation.[297]

When Wilcox awoke on July 23 with painfully numb hands, Snyder had already decided to move the party down because of the chaos left by the blizzard. Wilcox thought that Snyder and Schlichter (now the only ones fit) were deserters; apparently they even packed Wilcox's gear as he lingered dejectedly in the tent. While making the downward traverse of Harper Glacier, everyone peered upward. There were no tents or climbers.

On Karstens Ridge, the group met a Mountaineering Club of Alaska party, who interrupted their ascent and escorted the weakened group to their 12,100-foot camp. Here they gave them food and medical care. The Alaska party understood a full-scale rescue was required as soon as conditions allowed. On July 24 five members of the Alaska party, led by Bill Babcock, prepared to ascend to the 17,900-foot high camp, taking along the radio and some emergency supplies for a potential rescue.

Rather than becoming united by the distress above them, the discontented members of the Snyder and Wilcox groups descended separately. In gusting winds, poor visibility, and deep snow, the groups bypassed each other and did not even camp together. The fordings of Clearwater Creek and McKinley River, swollen by rainstorms, almost finished Wilcox. After nearly drowning in the Clearwater, he decided to go on alone and obtain a helicopter rescue for the others. When the frigid river current swept Wilcox off his feet, he would have drowned in the glacial torrent except that it stranded him on a gravel bar. He was just barely able to continue to Wonder Lake and arrange to have an aerial pickup of the others.

When the returning climbers reached Wonder Lake, they were so dis-united that it appeared to others that a few of them barely cared about the fate of the men high on the mountain. At Park headquarters there was a conversation with the superintendent, who apparently held out hope that the climbers had dug in and were not in distress because of their group size; he even suggested that perhaps they had descended via the West Buttress. A continuing discussion about the situation on the mountain's upper slopes resulted in some unpleasant words with the Park staff. Wilcox and Snyder did not remain to wait out the results.

On the morning of July 27, Don Sheldon flew from Talkeetna to upper Harper Glacier, where he sighted the Alaska party but detected no other human activity. What had happened to the climbers of the Clark group?

The Alaska party would soon uncover evidence on the following day. While ascending to the high camp, they found relics along the route, among them a bamboo pole apparently carried by Russell; a sleeping bag was wrapped around the pole and an ice axe was nearby. At 17,900 feet they found two tents—one totally destroyed and one snow-filled and nearly buried. Inside the shredded tent they saw a man's body frozen to the fabric. He had apparently died inside the tent and was now in a grisly state of decomposition. There was some food remaining, but no fuel or sleeping bags. The Alaska party saw no sign of the other six climbers.

With the help of Sheldon's aerial guidance and radio communication, two more men were found frozen on a steep, crevassed slope between the high camp and Archdeacon's Tower—one partially wrapped in a sleeping bag. Despite additional searching by Sheldon and a later expedition led by Vin Hoeman to determine the mystery of the missing climbers, no new evidence was found.

▲▲▲

Snyder and Wilcox differed to a certain extent in their analysis of what occurred on July 18, but they both later agreed that snow caves should have been dug at 15,000 and 17,900 feet; such shelter would have probably saved Russell and Steve Taylor. At the two highest camps, tents were pitched at angles to the prevailing wind. It is not clear whether or not the party built fortifying snow walls to prevent snowdrift and tent collapse. It is clear, however, that insufficient fuel and food was brought to the high camp and there were too few wands for the first summit party to mark the route carefully.

Both party leaders affirmed that the National Park Service weather forecasting was unreliable throughout the duration of the expedition and believed the Clark group was not aware that a severe storm was rapidly approaching. At the time the Park Service did not have a direct radio communication with the weather services at Anchorage and Fairbanks, so forecasts were not timely; the forecasts that the expedition obtained related to the Anchorage area, not Mount McKinley.

Snyder, in his review of the mishap, believed that Clark's group reached Archdeacon's Tower during the descent from the summit but, instead of taking the usual route to Denali Pass in the "zero" visibility, they descended the steeper slope directly above their high camp. Near 19,400 feet the fierce wind and steep slope made further progress for the exhausted group impossible. The blizzard, in effect, cut off the retreat, and the group probably chose to bivouac again, despite the fact they had no tent, shovel, or stove. Although the men apparently still had sleeping bags, they may not have all survived the terrible violence and cold of the night. When it partially cleared on July 20, some of the group may have attempted to descend again. Two who were found frozen later did manage a small distance—one to 19,100 feet and the other to 18,800 feet. Perhaps the others slid into crevasses.

Wilcox, in rebutting the Snyder account years later, was defensive of the Clark group's efforts, which he felt were made with better preparation for the summit climb than the typical expedition. He believed the group brought not only sleeping bags but also shovels and extra food—and perhaps a stove. However, given a late start, slow progress, and increasingly poor visibility, the decision not to turn back was the crucial one in their eventual demise. The Clark group took its chances over retreat. Wilcox, somewhat like his counterpart, believed the group avoided the ridgeline descent to Denali Pass because of high-wind exposure and perhaps became separated. They huddled in sleeping bags afterward in the frightful elements, which pinned them down without shelter. Perhaps the group had dug a snow cave on the ascent and reached it again. But hypothermia set in during this second bivouac and the gale blew their equipment away. Meanwhile, at high camp Steve Taylor and John Russell attempted to keep the tent intact, a failing proposition. One of them remained gripping the tentpole and perished, while the other appears to have descended for the lower camp and vanished; possibly blowing snow drifted him over.

Wilcox was later critical that the five survivors became deserters, yet he was one of them. He was also critical that the group in the 15,000-foot camp could not and did not make a more concerted second rescue effort (after the one of July 20) and that they were self-serving in leaving companions higher on the mountain. Having fresh radio batteries would have secured communication, but in the wild elements that destroyed the Clark group, a timely rescue, certainly by others not on the mountain, would not have been possible.

Boyd Everett, who had three expeditions on the southern faces at the same time as the Wilcox expedition, recorded the weather from June 20 to August 18. Of 1,440 hours, there were 799 hours of precipitation; during 50 of 62 days his groups experienced precipitation, with prevailing winds from the south. In one July storm, sufficient snow fell to completely cover a cache four feet high at 8,100 feet.

July 18, the day the Wilcox party reported by radio that they had reached the summit, was the first of five days that were almost continuously stormy; winds were estimated to be at least sixty miles per hour. For the 19th, Everett recorded in a typed report "heavy snow and strong winds all day." These conditions continued until July 22 and then continued with alternately clear and snowy weather until July 31, when two feet of snow accumulated. Everett believed that on the summit plateau, winds from 80 to 100 miles per hour could easily have occurred. "The duration and violence of this storm seemed to be unusual even for Mount McKinley,"[298] he added.

Certainly the great storm of July 1967 was severe—as Wilcox wrote, "in a class by itself." He estimated that for 8½ days the winds averaged 80 to 110 miles per hour and were continuously extreme everyday. Guide Vern Tejas suggested that winds are higher at Denali Pass and upper northern slopes than on the southern flanks of Mount McKinley. For example, when Dave Staehli climbed the West Rib in winter, he was relatively protected while three more exposed Japanese climbers died from the elements.

Other expert opinions, including that of Bradford Washburn, hold that while the extended storm was indeed very violent, the winter tempests high on the mountain are much colder and far more intense. Washburn admits that the 1967 expedition had a degree of "bad luck," but they failed to heed the "mare's tail" cirrus signs of an approaching storm and the heavy clouds racing from the west. And they did climb into a sinister cloudcap and zero visibility, never a wise move. Certainly the disaster of 1967 is a grim reminder of Mount McKinley's ferocious climate.

The loss of these seven men was very personal, as it was a poignant statement to the leaders that they had overlooked some of the basic tenets of mountaineering wisdom.

▲ ▲ ▲

CHAPTER 17

Alone Among the Elements

One of mountaineering's extreme challenges is to solo: to climb alone, without the security and support—both physical and emotional—of teammates.

Bill Sherwonit
To the Top of Denali, 1990

Although the personal rewards of freedom, solitude, and perhaps acclaim can be positive, solo ascents in high mountains and in dangerous environments are often an extreme challenge. Climbing alone in these situations is emotional, risky, and very focused. There is virtually no allowance for error; even minor miscalculations, sickness, or injury may prove fatal. This is certainly true in the Himalaya, where rescue is unlikely, and it is valid on Mount McKinley during stormy or very cold weather.

In the present era of late-spring and early-summer rescue support on the popular West Buttress route, most solo climbers do not face an extreme challenge, for in a sense they rely on rescue capability and the moral conscience of nearby parties. In fact, solo climbers tend to annoy other groups during the seasonal peak, when it is difficult to be totally independent. In their attempts to have solo climbers recognize risks, the National Park Service often tries to convince them to join others—at least on the lower glacier areas where there is danger from crevasse falls.

After the successful winter climb of 1967, the logical new challenge for mountaineers was to make an unassisted solo ascent. In 1970 the National Park Service loosened its restrictions for such a plan, such as the requirement of arranging a standby rescue party. The first solo arrival was the Japanese adventure-climber Naomi Uemura, who at twenty-nine years of age had already soloed numerous high peaks, including Mount Everest. Uemura's plan on Mount McKinley in August 1970 was a wise one—to travel light, with a pack barely over fifty pounds. But his diet of bread, salmon, and salmon eggs might not have sufficed for the typical Western mountaineer, who would have preferred more energy-producing carbohydrates. Relying on his previous high-altitude experience and knowing his capabilities, Uemura ascended the West Buttress in eight routine days—a rapid but not unusual pace.

Other solo climbs seem to have gone unnoticed, especially the remarkable and quiet achievement of Charles Porter, who climbed the difficult Cassin Ridge on his own. But in 1981 John M. Waterman died from unknown causes while alone in the month of April on the Northwest Fork of Ruth Glacier. Waterman was not only a paragon of technical climbing but also one of the most bizarre personalities of the times: sometimes he would train for serious Alaska Range ascents by running on icy roads in crampons and, to condition himself for the frigid weather, by lying in a bathtub of icy water. In 1978 Waterman had accomplished an incredible, seemingly purposeful 145-day solo ascent on Mount Hunter, which his former climbing partner Glenn Randall called "the most difficult and dangerous solo ascent ever made in the Alaska Range."[299]

But Waterman was considered by some to be foolhardy, erratic and eccentric, and emotionally tempered to be alone. He seemed to be driven to life "in the fast lane." Glenn Randall penned his opinion in the *Anchorage Daily News:* "He so craved life on the brink that he was almost willing to die for it. In his twenty-ninth year, he apparently did."[300] Randall, who wrote *Breaking Point,* acknowledged elsewhere that "all of his close friends, those who had taught him to climb and accompanied him on his greatest adventures, had died, often in senseless accidents."[301]

Of Waterman's climbing partners, eight had died. As if on a vendetta with tragedy, he sometimes told close friends that he expected to die in the mountains, although this fatalistic outlook appeared to be balanced by wishing to "triumph in a way the world would notice." In fact, after his long Mount Hunter adventure, the enigmatic Waterman told Randall that he had hoped for a hero's welcome at Talkeetna. Instead, the only position anyone gave him was one as a dishwasher, this hardly improving his financial insolvency.

Waterman's problem was not related to physical conditioning. In 1979 he went into a frenzy when a cabin fire destroyed his climbing equipment: in winter he began for Mount McKinley from the shore of Cook Inlet, a purposeful handicap that ended at Ruth Glacier. On his final expedition, Waterman left Talkeetna on April 1, 1981, his stated plan being to climb the East Buttress of Mount McKinley and then descend via the Harper and Muldrow glaciers. He took only fourteen days of food and no radio, tent, or sleeping bag. The contemplated solo glacier approach route up Ruth Glacier's Northwest Fork was dangerously crevassed. In fact, a concerted National Park Service and overflight search effort later disclosed only an abandoned campsite amid a maze of crevasses.

▲▲▲

In 1984 Naomi Uemura returned to Mount McKinley for a winter solo climb, hoping to later ascend Vinson Massif in Antarctica during a solo trek across the southern continent. His energies were focused on such adventures, which included a 7,500-mile dogsled expedition from Greenland to Alaska. In 1978, mushing a dog team, Uemura became the first to reach the North Pole alone—the friendly, modest adventurer by now had become a folk hero in Japan.

Uemura began his winter bid via the West Buttress on February 1, 1984, wearing a forty-pound pack and hauling a sled. He took only the bare essentials, planning to sleep in snow caves and subsist on raw caribou meat, whale blubber, and seal oil. To protect himself from crevasse falls, he carried two long bamboo poles across his shoulders. On his forty-third birthday, Uemura safely reached the South Peak's summit (where his summit flag was later found). Pilot Lowell Thomas, Jr., with two Japanese photographers, flew nearby on February 13 and made radio contact but could not detect where he was located because of interfering clouds. Three days later pilot Doug Geeting, during a search for Uemura, reported seeing him near 16,000 feet, waving from an ice cave.

Then clouds covered the mountain; nobody could contact Uemura by radio. A search continued during intermittent weather and, during a break in the clouds, various pilots on February 20 failed to sight him. Bob Gerhard, the chief mountaineering ranger at Denali National Park and Preserve, announced to the press, "We believe the odds are extremely slim that Mr. Uemura has survived. We are continuing the search.... There are many things that could have happened."[302] Later a Japanese search party located much of Uemura's gear in a snow cave at the 17,200-foot level—leading to the speculation that he had died between the summit and that camp. But he may have bypassed this cave and not retrieved his equipment.

Conclusions regarding Uemura included his becoming lost in a whiteout and then falling over a steep headwall between 16,200 and 14,000 feet, or being blown off by high winds. His diary found in a snow cave he had dug at 14,000 feet revealed something of his gripping winter combat with the dangerous elements. Once Uemura fell into a crevasse, but his poles held him. As he approached Windy Corner on the third day, the gale was so strong that his face was numbed by the bitter cold; he could barely keep afoot. Higher, he was apparently able to find a filled-in crevasse for a dig-in, but one so small he could barely crawl in to escape the wind. Trapped at this cave, he nearly lost both his pack and ice axe. Once, Uemura thought he would die in the savage elements when he could not find this bivouac pit after coming out to retrieve his pack.

The solo climber continued on February 6 in minus forty degrees Fahrenheit temperatures, then he dug a snow cave. His diary tells of stress and hardship: "My face skin got peeled off because of the frostbite," the later translation into English read. "The weather is very mean to me." The winter climber used his stove to melt water and heat tea but probably ate his meat raw and frozen. His sleeping bag had moisture frozen into it, reducing its insulating capability. But he remained determined: "I am going to climb McKinley" were the final words.[303]

▲ ▲ ▲

In the winter of 1986, Dave Johnston made plans to climb Mount McKinley alone. Tall, strong, and usually reddish bearded, he was a legend of energy, generally being credited with keeping alive the three-man team that made the first winter ascent on February 28, 1967, and then survived Denali Pass in a week's ordeal. Although Johnston froze both feet on this desperate episode and lost portions of his toes during a long hospital recovery, he continued to undertake winter ascents.

Being an Alaskan, Johnston kept in condition with ski tours and endurance climbs. In 1984, when he was forty-one, he made an arduous solo ascent of Mount Sanford in the Wrangell Mountains near the Yukon border. In mid-February 1986 Johnston left his backwoods cabin near Talkeetna and skied some eighty miles to the West Buttress of Mount McKinley. Prepared to stay nearly two months, he carried a full pack and pulled two sleds, although he had arranged for a food cache to be dropped off by a pilot on Kahiltna Glacier.

After reaching his base camp in a week over unbroken snow, Johnston made two trips up the crevassed glacier, wearing a special ladder of twenty-foot-long aluminum tubing to ward off potential falls. Near the 11,000-foot level, he built a snow cave as a blockade against the worst of the cold and wind.

While violent, icy blasts scored the mountain's slopes, Johnston remained in his cave, reading and listening to his radio for weather forecasts from Anchorage. On the 28th he carried a load to Windy Corner and then returned to the cave. On the following day he found its tunnel drifted with snow; because his shovel was outside, he had to dig out with his cooking pot. Meanwhile, his toes were numbing in the intense cold and pain returned to his injured feet—despite holding a hot water bottle to them. When Johnston discovered the black color of frostbite on one of his big toes, he wisely gave up and skied back to his homestead.

▲▲▲

Wishing to repeat Uemura's winter exploit but return alive, guide Vern Tejas prepared for a climb alone in the winter of 1988. By this time Tejas had made over a dozen expeditions as guide, and his climbs on Mount McKinley included the difficult Cassin Ridge. He took part in the first winter ascent of Mount Hunter in 1981, led a winter exploit to Mount Logan in 1986, and also that year helped save two Koreans in a dangerous rescue mission.

In January 1988 Tejas was able to train for high altitude by first climbing Aconcagua in South America. Almost feeling Uemura's spirit when on the West Buttress in mid-February, he carried a Japanese flag. It certainly helped that he intimately knew the upper slopes of the buttress—sometimes finding wands and familiar rock outcroppings in storms and poor visibility. Also the timing was right—he missed a great storm such as the one that caught the Japanese climber.

Tejas wore "bunny" boots, nylon overboots, down pants and parka, and a wind-shell oversuit with a fur-ruffed hood. For sleeping he used a down bag inside a fiberfill one, with a Gore-Tex bivouac sack as an outer layer. Wearing skis on the lower glacier, he split his 150-pound load between his pack and a plastic sled and wore a sixteen-foot aluminum ladder attached to his waist. He did not bring a tent but constructed snow fences and trenches, covering them with a tarpaulin. After reaching the summit safely on March 7, he returned to disclose his adventure.

▲▲▲

PART III

ROUTES, ACCIDENTS, AND LOGISTICS

Climbing party on Kahiltna Glacier en route to West Buttress, with portion of Mount Hunter in background (photo by Olaf Sööt)

CHAPTER 18

Four Route Descriptions

THE WEST BUTTRESS

The preferred period for the West Buttress route, the standard on Mount McKinley, is from May through July. As done today, climbers are flown by ski-wheel aircraft to a landing area (and base camp) on the Southeast Fork of Kahiltna Glacier at 7,200 feet (2,100 meters). The normal procedure is to make camp near the landing area, leaving marked supplies for the return. Snowshoes or skis should be used for the ascent to 14,300 feet. The route bears north, climbing gradually, with some crevasse danger, for eight miles to near Kahiltna Pass (10,320 feet). The first camp is generally made at about 7,800 feet (2,400 meters) to the west of the Northeast Fork—close to where the route steepens (about three miles south of Kahiltna Pass). The second camp is often placed at the base of the ridge leading toward the pass, at about 10,000 feet (3,000 meters).

Hardly a rhumb line, the route now veers eastward, climbing 2½ miles toward Windy Corner; however, at 11,000 feet, a short, steep slope to the north rises some 500 feet. Because this is on the route, some parties make an intermediate cache here, because dealing with sleds and skis on this slope can be troublesome. Above this slope, traverse to a small bowl. As the toe of the West Buttress looms above, begin the straightforward 1½-mile pull to the 14,300-foot (4,300-meter) campsite. The buttress toe is easily passed on the right (south) via Windy Corner (13,200 feet) and leads to the large, sheltered basin and the standard expedition campsite. Surface conditions at and near Windy Corner may vary considerably and, of course, the wind factor may be anything from nil to extreme.

While there are always igloos at 14,300 feet, they may be occupied; if tents are placed, they should be well blocked by snow walls. Each year dozens of Mount McKinley aspirants take up residence behind the massive snow-block walls, which tends to give this camp with its tents in bunkers an artillery unit's appearance. The bombardment here will not come from the enemy's shells, though, but from the wind molecules. It is scarcely a campsite of solitude. A portion of the time at this camp will probably be spent waiting out the weather and becoming acclimatized. There is a ranger patrol camp at this site.

To continue the ascent, a steep ice slope, the technical crux of the route

Aerial view of Mount McKinley from southwest; West Buttress, West Rib, and Cassin Ridge routes are marked. (courtesy AeroMap U.S., Inc.)

(sometimes a fixed rope is in place), climbs directly to the buttress crest at 16,000 feet. A camp position at 16,200 feet on the buttress crest is an exposed and potentially windy position. The way can now hardly be missed, as it trends along the crest about one mile to a plateau below the ice slope rising directly to the 18,200-foot (5,500-meter) Denali Pass. Generally, a high camp is made at 17,200 feet, and then a moderately steep and ascending traverse is made to the pass. It is advised to use caves or an igloo at the latter camp, not tents. The National Park Service maintains a minimum-recording thermometer at this campsite. In the winter of 1988–89, the lowest recording was minus seventy-seven degrees Fahrenheit. Most likely this temperature was associated with an extremely cold arctic front that dominated Alaska's weather. Infrequently a party places a final camp (cave or igloo) at or near Denali Pass. Camping above 17,200 feet on the West Buttress route is strongly discouraged by medical experts. It is during sleep that hypoxic stress is greatest; therefore, sleeping altitude is critical in acclimatization. Because winds will likely be encountered on the mountain's

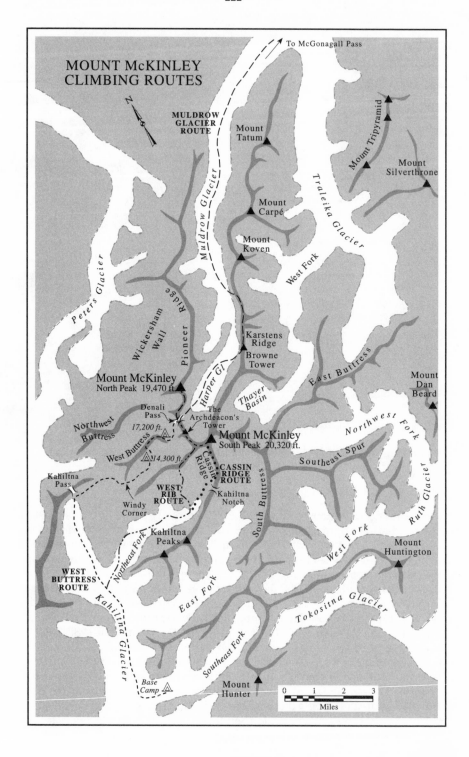

MOUNT McKINLEY
CLIMBING ROUTES

N

To McGonagall Pass

MULDROW
GLACIER
ROUTE

Mount Tatum

Mount Tripyramid

Mount Silverthrone

Muldrow Glacier

Peters Glacier

Mount Carpé

Mount Koven

Traleika Glacier

West Fork

Wickersham Wall

Pioneer Ridge

Karstens Ridge

Browne Tower

East Buttress

Mount Dan Beard

Mount McKinley
North Peak 19,470 ft.

Harper Gl.

Thayer Basin

Northwest Buttress

Denali Pass

17,200 ft.

The Archdeacon's Tower

Mount McKinley
South Peak 20,320 ft.

Northwest Fork

West Buttress

14,300 ft.

Cassir Ridge

CASSIN RIDGE ROUTE

Southeast Spur

Ruth Glacier

Kahiltna Pass

WEST RIB ROUTE

Kahiltna Notch

South Buttress

Windy Corner

Northeast Fork

Kahiltna Peaks

Mount Huntington

West Fork

WEST BUTTRESS ROUTE

Kahiltna Glacier

East Fork

South Buttress

Tokositna Glacier

Southeast Fork

Base Camp

Mount Hunter

0   1   2   3
Miles

summit terrain, put on extra clothing at a sheltered spot rather than waiting until it is too late.

It is two miles from Denali Pass to the summit of the South Peak. First climb steeper slopes to a 19,000-foot plateau. Here cross a half mile of near-level windblown snow to the final summit ridge. The sastrugi here can be especially tiring.

On the descent from the South Peak, parties should beware of fatigue and carelessness on the descending traverse below Denali Pass, where numerous accidents have occurred from slipping. An ice axe should always be used on Mount McKinley's upper slopes— never ski poles.

There is a total of sixteen miles (twenty-six kilometers) distance from base camp to the summit of the South Peak, with a vertical gain of 13,320 feet. To reach the North Peak from Denali Pass, cross two miles north and east to the base of the peak's summit uplift. The ascent is only moderately difficult.

Climbers descending upper West Buttress (photo by Olaf Sööt)

THE WEST RIB

Although the West Rib is a far more serious route than the West Buttress, most competent parties in good condition will make the ascent within two weeks. The preferred time to go is from May through July. The route's directness (eleven miles from the landing on the Southeast Fork of Kahiltna Glacier to the summit), moderate difficulty, and relative safety have made it the second most popular on Mount McKinley.

First, ascend the glacier's Northeast Fork; there is a sérac fall danger from hanging ice on both flanks of the glacier (choose a route away from this hazard). This passage is not recommended during twenty-four hours after snow- and windstorms. There is a relatively protected cache site at 9,000 feet, between rock buttresses of West Kahiltna Peak and Peak 13,710 of the West Rim. Proceed up midglacier to a camp at 9,450 feet on a knoll at the

Camp at 17,000 feet on West Rib of Mount McKinley during 1983 winter ascent (photo by Charles Sassara)

foot of a rib leading to the West Rim. Be alert for avalanches from East Kahiltna Peak. Make a note of calving patterns of the hanging glacier capping the prominent rock buttress that guards the eastern flank of the icefall at the 10,000-foot level.

The upper icefall changes seasonally and may require several right-hand detours around large crevasses. Keep a tight rope and negotiate several snow bridges through the crevasse field between 10,400 and 10,900 feet. Make camp at 11,000 feet. Between this campsite and 13,200 feet, the West Rib angles upward at forty to fifty degrees—the conditions usually are snow atop ice in the access couloir.

Cross the bergschrund and ascend the left margin of the couloir, using snow, ice, and rock protection placements. After a heavy snowfall, this couloir could be avalanche-prone. Climb to the top of the final rocks and merge with the first ice dome. Climb directly on the ridgecrest to avoid the hard ice of the face, and reach the "Apex" campsite at 12,900 feet (safe and protected).

Continue on to the second ice dome. Ascend this exposed dome, keeping back from the ridgecrest because a massive cornice forms and extends to 14,000 feet. Atop this dome (13,300 feet), the route levels to 14,000 feet (watch for slots). There are level areas at both 13,300 and 14,000 feet, but camps should be avoided due to high-wind exposure.

At 14,800 feet a bergschrund below a rock toe that extends down from the upper West Rib provides a small, well-protected campsite. Place tents well under the lip to protect from ice, rockfall, and snow sloughs; spindrift can be a problem during snow- and windstorms. For larger groups, use ski poles and rope to construct a "boxing ring" safety rail around camp.

Climb a small couloir that rises directly above, or traverse right and around the last prominent rock toe extending from the ridge higher. The former option will finish through easy, mixed terrain; both variations merge with a level snow bench at 15,300 feet (exposed and not a good campsite). Continue up snow slopes and back into mixed terrain. At 15,700 feet a prominent boulder marks the descent to the 14,200-foot camp of the West Buttress (a cache can be left here).

Ascend and carefully cross the snow ridge at 16,100 feet. The best camp is at 16,300 feet, immediately behind a rock thumb. A rope railing or solid downslope walls are again recommended. From here the route ascends the obvious gully into mixed terrain to the "Balcony" at 17,000 feet. This site is quite exposed, yet flat; good snow for block cutting may be hard to find. Take time to solidly reinforce this camp, for numerous tents have been destroyed here. There are no recommended camps above the 17,000-foot level.

The climb to the summit begins on mixed terrain to 18,000 feet and then assumes a leftward ascent of the Orient Express gully to join the West Buttress at 19,500 feet. Before topping out on the West Rib, find a sheltered spot to don extra clothing, for wind will likely be encountered on the summit plateau. It is imperative to carefully wand the top of the route to help locate the descent.

Note: The Orient Express has gained a deadly reputation during descent. Take care to place running belays or "leapfrog" anchored pitches on this and other exposed terrain. Most parties prefer to descend the West Buttress route from 15,700 feet.

Parties that plan to use fixed lines and "double carry" will need to bring 1,350 feet of rope, primarily to use on the access couloir and on the domes and gullies of the upper route. Bring two snow anchors and ice screws per person, eight to ten short runners with carabiners, four pitons, and four wired stopper chocks. Bring ski poles up the route, especially useful for descent of the middle and lower West Buttress, which can have soft and breakable snow.

THE MULDROW GLACIER ROUTE

Because air support is not permitted within Denali National Park and Preserve, the Muldrow Glacier, once the standard overland route, still promises an arduous approach. Its some thirty miles (forty-eight kilometers) requires more packing and camps than the West Buttress route. The vertical gain from Muldrow Glacier is 14,600 feet. An expedition should allow four weeks, preferably from April to July. Both the South and North peaks can be accessed.

Harper and Muldrow glaciers are part of the same glacier system that begins at Denali Pass (the col between the South and North peaks). The snow-covered upper glacier drops gradually from 18,200 to 15,000 feet and then cascades in a grand 3,500-foot icefall chaos to form the lower (Muldrow) glacier system. Crevasse dangers are extreme on both of these glaciers.

Climbing on The Coxcomb between 13,000 and 14,000 feet on Karstens Ridge, with Muldrow Glacier below (photo by Brian Okonek)

From Denali National Park road at Wonder Lake (2,100 feet at the trailhead), or from as far as one can drive in early season, hike to the McKinley River at 2,000 feet. Because the road is not usually open until June, early-season expeditions must fly to Kantishna. It is possible to have supplies taken to Muldrow Glacier from Kantishna in March by dog sled and then cached.

Fording the river is a potentially dangerous undertaking during high water; one must also ford the East Fork of Clearwater Creek. The route follows Cache Creek to McGonagall Pass (5,720 feet and 19 miles from the trailhead). Because of the area's fragility, camping is not permitted at the pass.

Most expeditions take the right (west) flank of the Muldrow for the first mile, travel up the center to the base of the lower icefall at 6,650 feet, and then bear west to skirt the lower icefall on avalanche cones. Try to avoid passing directly under the hanging glacier between 6,800 and 6,900 feet. At about 7,400 feet once again move to the center. Between 7,700 and 8,050 feet, expeditions encounter the "Hill of Cracks," which can be turned on the east, but this route is very exposed to ice avalanches from Mount Carpé, and it is safer to keep to the glacier's center and find a route through the crevasses. Typically, the great icefall (8,700 to 9,600 feet) is surmounted by first ascending the center and then working around the west side.

Now, ascend to the notch of Karstens Ridge at 10,900 feet (3,331 meters), or gain the ridge higher at 11,500 feet. Karstens Ridge, the technical crux of the route, is a steep and narrow crestline separating the Muldrow and Traleika Glacier's west fork. The ridge features snow and ice slopes from thirty to forty degrees. Ascend to Browne Tower at 14,600 feet (4,451 meters), and then bear rightward gradually onto Harper Glacier. This slope, known as Parker Pass, must be evaluated carefully for avalanche conditions.

There are two icefalls on Harper Glacier, one at about 16,000 feet (4,900 meters) and the other at 17,000 feet (5,200 meters); both can be turned on the right (north) side. Beware of falling ice from the slopes descending from the North Peak. From the upper glacier basin at about 18,000 feet (5,500 meters), bear south and ascend the south flank of Denali Pass. Here, complete the route per the West Buttress route, climbing to the 19,550-foot plateau and then to the summit.

Glacier camps are usually made at the base of the lower icefall (6,500 feet), about one mile above (7,500 feet), opposite Pioneer Ridge (9,700 feet), at the base of Karstens Notch (10,800 feet), on Karstens Ridge (12,100 feet), just after Browne Tower (15,000 feet), on Harper Glacier between 16,000 and 17,000 feet, and again below or near Denali Pass (17,700 feet).

CASSIN RIDGE

The elegant Cassin Ridge, whose history is discussed earlier, is no longer climbed expedition-style. Mountaineers must recognize its length, continual severity, and the difficulties of retreat in the event of heavy snowfall, wind, and altitude-related sickness. While an expedition should allow from one to three weeks for this route (May or June are the best months to climb here), it is a prudent procedure to first climb the West Buttress, or at least acclimatize on the mountain's higher slopes.

While the Italian party in 1961 took a direct beginning, the preferred start today is the Japanese Couloir. From the West Buttress landing area nine miles away, make the approach via Kahiltna Glacier's Northeast Fork as far as the West Rib route. Be aware that this tributary is threatened by snow and sérac avalanches. Alternately, the East Fork—used by earlier parties—is safe to 9,600 feet, but to reach the Japanese Couloir one needs to climb the prominent couloir with a narrow ice funnel to Kahiltna Notch (11,960 feet).

Beyond the West Rib's base, cross an icefall, then ascend through crevasses to the head of the glacier. Move left around a large bergschrund, then climb to the start of the Japanese Couloir; there is a small bergschrund to cross here.

The couloir rises from 11,700 to 13,200 feet; there is usually a web of old fixed lines in the steep couloir, which should not be fully trusted (the couloir may have considerable ice). After the fifth of the nine pitches, either climb Grade III water ice to the right or rock to the left. At the top of the couloir, proceed left and continue to Cassin Ledge (13,400 feet).

From the ledge, two pitches of mixed climbing lead to a 1,200-foot ice rib.

Climbers on Cassin Ridge at 13,400 feet, with Kahiltna Peaks and Mount Foraker in background, 1979 (photo by Mark Bebie)

First traverse right and up to the base of steep rock; then traverse farther right on rock to an obvious break (some class 5.5 on this pitch). The ice rib is nine rope-lengths of exposed, rising traverse on variable rotten snow and bullet-proof ice (depending on conditions) that leads to the small but prominent hanging glacier. Here is a good campsite, nestled on a flat area of the ridge at 14,000 feet (4,200 meters).

An active bergschrund and calving ice now make the route choice a challenge. Parties must either ascend into the bergschrund and either climb steeply (some direct aid) up the overhanging sixty-foot wall to the moderately angled glacier, or traverse west, rappel to a steep ice wall, and then make an exposed traverse pitch beneath the hanging glacier to gain a fifty-five-degree ice snout.

From the camp level, it may also be quite feasible to follow the contour below the bergschrund and hanging glacier, then ascend an ice runnel system, and higher, work back onto the easy glacier.

From the far right side of a small bergschrund at the top of the glacier (a protected campsite), ascend the first rock band on steep, mixed, high-quality granite for approximately 800 feet to a steep snow slope below the second rock band (here is an exposed bivouac site). When beginning this section of the route, traverse right two gully systems; look for an M-shaped rock at the base of the band, then ascend a mixed-terrain couloir.

At the second rock band, move left over large boulders toward a wide rock-and-ice S-shaped couloir that progressively steepens. The route then turns rightward over some steep, short rock steps, leading to one last long mixed pitch to moderate terrain near 16,700 feet.

From here, make a rising traverse right to a prominent snowfield just left of the hanging glacier, and then angle back left toward the obvious col near 17,300 feet (5,700 meters); here is an exposed campsite.

From the ridgecrest now follow snow couloirs to complete the route on the "Football Field" to the left (at 19,400 feet) on the West Buttress route. The alternative is to make a direct finish to the 20,000-foot plateau.

Base camp for Cassin Ridge can be made at about 11,000 feet on Kahiltna Glacier's Northeast Fork. Other campsites are at 13,300 feet (Cassin Ledge); 14,000 feet; 15,700 feet (5,150 meters), just below the second rock band; 17,000 feet; and about 18,100 feet. There is a bivouac site at 18,500 feet.

The most technical climbing on the route is on ice. Boyd Everett, during the third ascent, found many of the Italian "Cassin" pitons still solid and in place. Everett noted that the route holds pitons well because of good cracks; rock pitons can usually be placed in large boulders or on walls adjacent to the route.

It should be noted that the Cassin Ridge route has nearly 9,000 feet of vertical gain, much of it sustained ice and rock (particularly the first 5,000 feet) and all of this in a harsh environment. Parties should include a few pickets, about five ice screws, and a selection of eight chocks and possibly several pitons (baby angles to 1½ inches).

Most parties ascend over the summit and descend to the 17,200-foot camp on the West Buttress.

▲▲▲

CHAPTER 19

Lucky Escapes and Terrible Accidents

All is quiet today.... I am at elevation of about 5800 meters. Suddenly, I see above me a person sitting in the snow. I recognize a man in a blue down coverall who doesn't react when I say, "How are you?" He just stares at me. I noticed that he doesn't wear any gloves despite the cold.... He is sitting there completely apathetic. Only then, when I scream, he points in the direction of the summit.... I realized there was an accident. I tried to motivate him to descend.

Peter Habeler

A part of the mountaineering challenge involves risk and the participants' willingness to accept this. Those who venture to the Alaskan mountains must keep aware of certain risks and carry out a philosophy that is based on self-reliance. Accidents, even tragedies, have occurred to some quite self-reliant parties in the ninety-year history of human activity on Mount McKinley. Yet other groups, particularly in recent decades, have relied on the rescue factor. This irresponsible attitude may impose unacceptable risk on rescuers. Subsequent injury, illness, or death to those providing assistance has resulted because some mountaineers have defaulted in their self-sufficiency and tactics.

In the first six decades of mountaineering in the Alaska Range, the few expeditions were largely well planned, well outfitted, and with ample food. The participants knew that a serious accident would probably result in a fatality, for a quick rescue was unlikely—only the scientific mountaineering expeditions (1942, 1947, 1951) to Mount McKinley had reliable radio communications and an aircraft monitoring program. Tragedies did occur, notably in 1932 and 1954, but they were not associated with dependency on rescuers. As the Icy Crown magnetized an increasing number of climbers, however, there came a dispersal in attitudes.

1960 ACCIDENTS

Although the year 1960 had a record-setting twenty-three successful summit climbers, it also became known as the year of Mount McKinley's great rescue. Perhaps it was an omen for the new decade—when one in ten climbers was evacuated from the mountain, and 3.1 percent were killed.

In a sense, the decade ushered in a new popularity on the Icy Crown and marked the end of an era when most of the logical new routes had been done. The emphasis swung to bolder and more competitive, more rapid and alpine-style climbs. Technical advances in clothing and equipment made it possible to climb lighter and faster; fixed-rope techniques on steep slopes were largely discarded. Some mountaineers were lulled into a false sense of security because of the new advances, and the new knowledge and psychology probably caused the mountain to lose some of its mystery.

As Jonathan Waterman wrote in *Surviving Denali,* in the 1960s, "self sufficiency was superceded by radios, helicopters and dependence on other climbers. All of these factors had an adverse effect, causing caution to be thrown to the winds; such behavior would have been foolhardy for the radioless, isolated pioneer climbers."[304]

In May 1960 the most complex rescue to ever take place on Mount McKinley was set in motion when the four-man John Day party fell on an icy slope at 18,000 feet on the West Buttress route. The accident eventually involved a massive evacuation team from Alaska, Washington, and Oregon. Heroic ski-wheel and helicopter landings were made to save lives, indirectly leading to the death of a pilot and passenger. The rescue cost a fortune and risked lives.

When Don Sheldon flew John Day, Pete Schoening, and Jim and Lou Whittaker to Kahiltna Glacier on May 14, it was not the usual base camp landing but one at about 10,200 feet because of a special permission that was granted. Making rapid progress the party was able to follow a beaten, wand-marked path of three other expeditions, and on the 15th they were already in position to receive a Sheldon airdrop at 14,400 feet. Given good weather and a support not usually allowed, the Day party moved quickly and even found a fixed rope installed on the ice wall crux of the route by an earlier Japanese party. Steps were either chopped or kicked all the way.

On May 17 the four climbers left their 17,200-foot high camp in clear weather for the summit, followed by an Anchorage party who had camped some 400 feet below them. Below Denali Pass the snow and ice surface had been deeply furrowed by the wind but took crampon placements well. Near Archdeacon's Tower the Anchorage party passed the Day party; both teams reached the summit in good form to find two members of a Japanese Meiji University expedition who had set up a camp and decorated the spot with a new plastic pole and various flags.

Descending behind the Anchorage party, the Day party rested at Denali Pass and tied their two ropes together for better security. But on the icy slope-traverse below, Jim Whittaker, who was first on the rope, slipped, and the others were unable to arrest his slide. Schoening recalled the force on the rope: "I apparently flipped and received a blow on the head almost immediately and was knocked unconscious. I don't recall anything for the next 10 or 12 hours. I was, however, still able to walk and climb."[305]

After the party slid and tumbled some 400 feet, the Whittakers were knocked unconscious but soon recovered enough to function. John Day had a broken leg, and Schoening was disoriented (in the confusion of returning to camp, he was dazed and did not realize he had lost a mitten). Because the party had left their radio at base camp, they could not send a distress message.

Most fortunately, the Anchorage party nearby heard their shouts. The leader, Paul Crews, took down their tent and brought it to the accident scene to give John Day some protection from the elements. Schoening and the Whittakers managed to descend to 16,800 feet, where they used the Anchorage party's radio to call for assistance. Concurrently, a member of this party, Helga Bading, contracted pulmonary edema and was in urgent need of evacuation.

The press dramatized the rescue on the front page and brought Mount McKinley, as it has many other times, into the limelight. Meanwhile, on its lower slopes, two rescuers were nearly killed when a helicopter was forced into a partial crash landing in a whiteout. The rescue efforts, in addition to the loss of life and equipment, brought wide repercussions. Army rescue tents, gear, and food boxes littered the icy slopes.

Radio communications soon brought assistance. On May 19 a Cessna 180 flew by Day's tent and made a supply airdrop. On the following day more supplies and a toboggan were dropped. But tragically, a sightseeing plane in the area lost "lift" in executing a sharp turn and plummeted into the hard snow surface. The craft burned, and both the pilot and passenger were instantly killed.

The Anchorage party lost little time placing Bading into the toboggan and lowering her down the ice slope with the help of belays and fixed rope. In an amazing performance, the intrepid Don Sheldon brought his Super Cub to a tiny snow platform at 14,300 feet and evacuated Bading—who was now near death in a coma. The takeoff was a tribute to Sheldon's skill and the high performance of this aircraft.

In another record-setting performance, helicopter pilot Link Luckett landed near 17,200 feet with a stripped-down machine (with only one-quarter hour fuel remaining) and then quickly evacuated Day to a lower altitude. On May 21 Schoening was taken out by helicopter, while the Anchorage party and the two Whittakers in descending met the vanguard of a fifty-man rescue group, many of whom had been flown by army transport from Seattle.

What can be learned from this tragedy? Various reviews have suggested that the John Day party was obsessed with a rapid and light ascent, overconfident of their strength. They certainly moved much faster than the 1,000-feet-per-day yardstick. Certainly with their four-day food supply at high camp and given good weather, there was no great need to make a rapid summit dash. The men had trained on Colorado's heights and on the Pacific Northwest volcanoes, but were they acclimatized to Mount McKinley?

ACCIDENTS IN THE 1970s

Falls near Denali Pass have been too numerous to fully recount. Most of them occur during the descending traverse between the pass and 17,200 feet. Fatigue, hypoxia, and altitude sickness, combined with variable snow conditions, can cause climbers to stumble or make poor crampon placements.

In 1973 a Genet Expeditions group included a client who was unable to descend without assistance because of altitude sickness. Some of the team members decided to be innovative and slide downslope in the self-arrest position. In a procedure confusion, the last person on the seven-man rope team had not been warned of this decision. In the resultant calamity, the entire rope soon lost control—not stopping for some 500 feet. The uppermost man tumbled along, suffering bruises, cuts, and even a concussion. In time he was brought to 14,300 feet and taken off the mountain by an army helicopter.

Three years later, in July 1976, another fall occurred below Denali Pass as a five-man Austrian party was returning from the summit. Because one member was experiencing difficulty breathing, Helmut Linzbichler (the leader) sent Gunter Schmidt (who was using ski poles in his hands rather than an ice axe) to descend quickly to a Canadian party that included a physician. At about 17,800 feet Schmidt apparently slipped when taking a direct line instead of the usual traverse. He then fell 1,200 feet into a crevasse and apparently died from a broken neck. Meanwhile, the member with breathing problems recovered. The leader, unaware of Schmidt's accident, descended the route to tell him that a physician would not be needed.

In 1976 numerous routes on Mount McKinley came into vogue—perhaps the turning point in making alternatives to the West Buttress route. Even Mount Foraker was attempted by three routes. On both mountains, there were twenty Japanese parties and representatives from nine European nations.

Unfortunately the 1976 activity increase brought more tragedies and rescues. Six Japanese climbers died on Mount Foraker, and four mountaineers perished on Mount McKinley. The National Park Service participated in twenty-one rescue missions involving thirty-five climbers. The wilderness experience of mountaineers on both peaks was interrupted by the sights and sounds of helicopters flying nearby during rescues.

The taxpayers' bill that year came to $82,200. Demands came from letters to the press; proposals included that those who needed rescue should pay the costs. Some of the public suggested that mountaineers post bonds, and a minority voice stated that guiding should be disallowed because it brings the less experienced hopefuls to the continent's highest, coldest, and most dangerous mountain.

In June of 1979 a Japanese expedition was attempting a relic technique—fixing ropes on fifty rock pitches on the southwest face of Mount McKinley (4,000 feet of rope remained as litter on the route). They placed no camps on the face but made a summit bid from only 12,000 feet. At the elevation of 16,500 feet, all four climbers became affected by acute mountain sickness. Fortunately they had a radio and were able to make a "Mayday" call.

A helicopter rescue operation saved one man, who was winched upward from his precarious location. An analysis in *Accidents in North American Mountaineering* (1980) reported that a rescue apparently was not needed and that pulmonary edema victims sometimes recover rapidly on evacuation to a lower altitude.

Ascending Mount McKinley at a rapid pace has had other repercussions, although not always with tragic endings. In 1978 Galen Rowell and Ned Gillette, two strong and highly experienced mountaineers, circumnavigated McKinley on skis and then proposed to climb from 10,000 feet to the summit and back in twenty-four hours. Both men were saved from a fatal slide on the ascent near Windy Corner when one of them miraculously managed to grasp a fixed rope.

Gillette remembered the events clearly. When the surface became icy, they were moving together on a nine-millimeter rope and were wearing climbing skins on their skis. Gillette, then ahead, stopped and stepped back to appraise the continuing slope; the nylon "hair" on one skin slid over an uphill ski edge, and he lost control. As he was plummeting downslope, he sighted a section of ¼-inch polypropylene rope sticking out of the frozen surface. Somehow, he managed to grasp it and hang on. In this position, upside down and with skis above him, Rowell (who had been pulled off) slammed into Gillette's sharp ski edges. Fortuitously, the two men hung on and were able to right themselves, dig a platform, and don crampons.

When climbing Mount McKinley became popular with Asians, their accidents and rescues soon gained notoriety. Their first tragedy occurred in late spring 1979 on the upper flank of the West Rib. After two Korean groups joined to climb this route, the six-man team reached the 14,000-foot level without incident. On May 29 Sang-Don Ko, Ii-Kyo Lee, and Hun-Kyu Park elected to make a summit bid while the remaining members moved the camp to 15,500 feet. These three climbers left with light packs, planning to camp at 18,000 feet on the descent. At about 7:00 P.M., they reached the summit and by radio transmission stated that they were descending, but were very tired.

While on the West Buttress route at 8:30 P.M., a guide sighted someone falling down a long, steep snow couloir. Guides Ray Genet and Brian Okonek left their 14,300-foot camp on the buttress and began the ascent in near-whiteout conditions to the presumed accident scene about 1,000 feet higher. Arriving about midnight, they found Ko had died from massive head injuries, but Lee, with limited movement, was still alive; Park was suffering from frostbite and serious injuries. The two guides spent several hours preparing a snow cave for Lee and then took Park to the buttress camp, arriving there at about 5:00 A.M. on May 30.

Okonek and five other climbers then returned to the accident scene to evacuate Lee but found that he had died. Even by this time the remaining members of the Korean party were unaware of the accident, but radio transmission from the West Buttress notified the authorities. Because of the need for quick medical assistance, instead of using commercial helicopters, military assistance was requested.

Two army Chinook helicopters left Talkeetna to fly to the mountain, and by late afternoon that same day Park and the two bodies were flown off. When Park was in an Anchorage hospital with serious frostbite and a severely dislocated knee, more was learned about the tragedy. Park, who was descending the couloir in the lowest and leading position on the rope, stated that the snow slipped from beneath him and he fell. *All three were without crampons.* The two others were unable to arrest the fall, and the entire party slid and fell some 2,000 to 2,500 feet (this 3,500-foot couloir on the north flank of the West Rib, in dark humor, subsequently acquired the name Orient Express because of the continuing accidents of Asians).[306]

Only the expertise of surgeon Dr. William Mills and Park's frostbite and hypothermic condition saved his leg after a complete dislocation, with the popliteal artery severed. *Accidents in North American Mountaineering* surmised that "ascending 6,000 feet in one day took a toll on these climbers. It should also be noted that there were several other climbing groups in the vicinity who were able to assist in the rescue, and, fortunately, a doctor who provided excellent care."[307]

1981 ACCIDENTS

On the afternoon of May 8, 1981, Jim Wickwire and Chris Kerrebrock were descending Peters Glacier at near 6,750 feet just below Jeffrey Point, with the plan of climbing Wickersham Wall. They were roped together, with Kerrebrock in the lead and Wickwire twenty to thirty feet behind. Each man had a short rope tied to a large sled between them.

Kerrebrock broke through a hidden crevasse, while Wickwire felt himself "jerked off his feet and dragged into the crevasse."[308] Although seemingly unhurt, Kerrebrock was tightly wedged some twenty-five feet into the crevasse. His partner climbed out and spent several hours attempting to free him, all to no avail (Kerrebrock was still alive in the early hours of May 9 but apparently died soon after).

Wickwire remained by the crevasse for the following five days, hoping to make CB radio contact with a passing aircraft. During this time he descended into the crevasse once to find food. Then he decided he would attempt to walk out but was unable to move for four days because of a storm. On May 22 as he began to ascend the slopes of a peak near Kahiltna Pass, glacier pilot Doug Geeting flew nearby. Geeting then made a difficult landing on Peters Glacier and flew Wickwire to Talkeetna.

An analysis pointed out that a heavily laden sled can be a dangerous object and that the two mountaineers should have had 50 to 100 feet of rope out. If they had each traveled with a lighter sled and farther apart, Wickwire would probably not have been pulled into the abyss.

In July 1981 three experienced and previously acclimatized Japanese climbers of the Kansei Climbing Club disappeared on the dangerous Kahiltna Glacier's east fork. There is a grave danger in this glacier from hanging glacier sérac discharges; climax avalanches after a heavy snowfall can completely sweep across this glacier arm.

It is surmised that the mountaineers were buried by an avalanche. Guide Mike Covington (who had barely escaped an avalanche) saw them at 9,200 feet, pulling a sled while wearing showshoes, at a time when "the walls were coming down all over the glacier." Given twelve days of snow and high winds, Covington had warned the Japanese of the suicidal nature of continuing upward in this environment, but apparently they persisted despite their awareness of the extreme hazard.

Most likely the Japanese party never even began their planned route of ascent, the American Direct on the south face (whose base camp is a hazardous site between 11,000 and 12,000 feet in a basin). Later a tent was found pitched on the glacier. Continuing storm and avalanche activity would have buried any trace of the expedition. Guides and experienced Alaskan mountaineers have repeatedly warned that even if a storm abates avalanche danger is high after a heavy snowfall. Mountaineers should wait for more than one day after a clearing.

One of the most tragic, painful, and unnecessary accidents on the slopes of Mount McKinley was not one resulting from mountaineering. On December 15, 1981, pilot Ed Homer (who had limited mountain flying experience) flew a Cessna 185 with three passengers from Talkeetna toward Kahiltna Pass. His flight path nearing the pass was low, and, in the face of a strong north wind and downdrafts, he was forced to crash on Kahiltna Glacier near the 10,000-foot level. One passenger died after the impact, and another, Patrick Scanlon, survived the crash but died afterward because of a broken neck. The pilot was incapacitated by the impact—later losing both feet as a consequence of frostbite. In attempting to move Scanlon out of the aircraft because high winds were buffeting it, passenger Michael Clouser lost his gloves, the unfortunate result being partial finger amputations. Although the temperature was mild for the time of year—close to zero—the winds brought a high chill factor. The winds, in fact, created such force that the aircraft was carried over Kahiltna Pass and slid down onto Peters Glacier some distance.

After the impact, an ELT (an electronic device) gave a distress signal that was received by an air force plane. The locator device gave information concerning the downed aircraft's position, which was then plotted on a map by an army rescue group. Another rescue group failed to plot the site in its narrow limits and did not perceive that it was on Kahiltna Glacier. Later, on search, they failed to provide themselves with an adequate map.

The air force had a training flight in the region, and it was diverted by the Rescue Coordinating Center to search for the missing aircraft—later locating the site and sighting flashlights. This led the crew to believe the victims were alive, and flares were dropped.

By 7:20 P.M. that night, the rescue center notified the army helicopter unit at Fort Wainwright—a location that held a number of Chinook helicopters configured for rescue missions; these craft had hoisting capability and hatches that facilitate supply drops. The army had made it a regular practice to perform search and rescue in similar circumstances, undertaking such duty per a national and state plan drawn up for the rescue of both civilians and military personnel.

The weather worsened during the night. The army command, meanwhile, delayed until midnight before making a decision about whether to depart for the impact site or Talkeetna. The decision to wait for the first morning light was apparently made because of the weather conditions. The judge in the later hearing found that this delay was inconsistent with the army's own regulations and policy to deploy assistance to victims believed to be alive and in need of immediate help. The consequences of the delay were indeed grave, for the following two days produced blizzard conditions, during which supplies were not dropped. Clouser's hands and feet froze during this time—a consequence of the Cessna pilot's failure to bring adequate emergency clothing and supplies. Clouser did not have the warmth of a sleeping bag, so vital to preserve his body heat, because he was attempting to save Scanlon's life with the available bags.

The Chinook helicopters did not leave for Mount McKinley until about 9:30 A.M. on December 17, arriving there at 11:30 A.M. Meanwhile the precise location of the crash had been again identified by Doug Geeting of Talkeetna by 8:35 A.M.—with the information transmitted to the two helicopters. Local fixed-wing pilots flew to the crash site in shifts from Talkeetna, hoping to assist the helicopters and to make emergency supply drops. However, their aircraft limitations and weather conditions negated this plan because of dangerous downdrafts. It was brought out later that these pilots were lulled into the belief that the army would be performing a rescue attempt with their more capable equipment.

The weather changed from clear in the morning to cloudiness and severe gusts, which with the lack of shadows impaired hovering. These factors caused the first Chinook pilot not to land and put men on the surface for rescue for the safety of the craft. The second Chinook, in fact, could not even return to its Talkeetna base. Because no supply airdrop had been prepared (including gloves and sleeping bags), neither Chinook dropped survival gear.

Until daylight on December 18, no close approaches were possible in the deteriorating conditions. However, volunteer mountaineers flew to the glacier at a lower elevation. Some hiked in the dark blizzard in order to accomplish a rescue, and they actually reached the site before aircraft landed.

At the trial, *Clouser and Scanlon v. the United States,* it became evident that the case should serve as a prod to various federal agencies to engage in sensible rescue planning. On April 23, 1987, the judge found that the army failed to exercise reasonable care in losing much daylight time on the critical day and that the failure of preparing an airdrop was gross negligence. The failure to land, however, was a reasonable choice. It was brought out that the delay was compounded by an imprudent planning effort. Instead of flying to Talkeetna for refueling and leaving at first light, the Chinooks left in the late morning for the Mount McKinley airstrip, some distance from the crash site. As a consequence, they flew to the site with inadequate fuel to accomplish a useful mission.

With weather changes being unpredictable, it was essential that when the rescue attempt was made, it be made promptly. The judge believed the slow response was due to the army's "chain of command" problems. Other potential rescuers believed the army would conduct the rescue promptly, for there was no request for aid made to Talkeetna's pilots and a private helicopter who had made clear their availability for an airdrop and a landing.

1982 ACCIDENTS

A guided expedition from the German Alpine Club left for the summit of Mount McKinley on May 26, 1982, in quite poor weather. Because they were sick and because of a disagreement about conditions, two of the guides remained at the 17,200-foot high camp. Despite high winds and very bad visibility, the party continued for some time before turning back.

On the descent the guide was roped to only one of the two clients; the unroped woman fell and sustained serious vertebral injuries. Meanwhile, a circus of errors occurred as clients collapsed in the storm. Three climbers fell because they used ski poles instead of ice axes. Later on the descent, in a whiteout, the party was unable to find camp and ended up bivouacking in the open. This expedition did not take a shovel, stove, or radio on the attempt.

Not only the Germans, but also Genet Expeditions seems to have had problems in 1982, a season when both guides and clients required rescue by National Park Service personnel and a helicopter.

Jonathan Waterman related the following events in *Surviving Denali:*

> *The next morning the weather was clear with 70–100 mph winds and the group made it back to 17,200 feet where they asked Ranger Roger Robinson for help. In addition to one client who suffered a back injury, all of the group were hypothermic and two people had frostbitten fingers. Because their tents had blown down, Robinson helped the group to find shelter in caves with other climbers. The next day, when the storm had abated, they descended to 14,200 feet, where three clients were evacuated in a military helicopter along with another client who had suffered frostbite in the same storm.*
>
> *This group made numerous mistakes. The disagreement over the weather should have precluded a summit attempt that day. Also, going to the summit with only one out of three guides showed poor judgment. The head guide should have brought the entire group back down, instead of allowing them to split up and proceed without a guide. All of the clients should have been roped together; they should have carried ice axes, stoves, a radio and a shovel to dig in with. If the weather had been worse, this group would not have survived.[309]*

1985 ACCIDENTS

In the 1985 season there were so many accidents on Mount McKinley's slopes that on reflection it seems amazing there were only two deaths. Although the mountaineering season had a great deal of consistently poor weather, there was a five-day "window" of clear conditions in late May. Groups from Germany, Austria, France, and the United States moved upward as rapidly as possible, causing four individuals to acquire cerebral edema and high-altitude pulmonary edema that required medical attention. Physicians at the rescue camp on the West Buttress had to treat all of them and provide either oxygen or Diamox.

The first serious accident of the year occurred on the afternoon of May 4 when Siegfried Mayer, a member of an unroped German "Schwarzwalder-Alaska-Bergfahrt" expedition, was descending from the summit with his ice axe in his pack. He slipped and fell 600 to 900 feet from the 18,000-foot level below Denali Pass, landing on a snow bridge in a crevasse. Another party member quickly descended to the fixed lines, where a ranger on patrol heard his shouts for help.

Although Mayer was unconscious for a time, he was able to get out of the crevasse when a rope was later lowered to him. Mountaineering physicians at the 17,200-foot camp recommended that Mayer be evacuated by helicopter—perhaps a wise decision because poor weather moved in shortly afterward. A later analysis considered that the victim could have walked to a lower camp and that emergency air evacuation is only appropriate for life and death situations. Mayer later stated that his climbing partners had convinced him to not use his ice axe. It is clear that ski poles are incapable of stopping a fall on steep, hard-packed alpine slopes.

Meanwhile, on the opposite flank of the great ice mountain, an American guided expedition was caught by severe winds on Muldrow Glacier in early May. The climbers were literally blown off their feet—two packs were blown away and travel was impossible.

When a polypropylene rope being used for a fixed line broke, causing the party to fall, they were forced to bivouac. One climber had to remain in the ice-axe–arrest position all night on an open slope, a radical experience that caused serious frostbite on one hand. He was evacuated by helicopter, which also took out another man who had lost all of his equipment.

In mid-May 1985, an American party of four at 18,100 feet on the West Rib lost a member as they were preparing camp. After removing his rope, crampons, and outer boots, the victim slipped while trying to anchor the tent and fell 1,200 feet to his death.

Perhaps the most inexcusable tragedy of 1985 was the one that occurred to the thirteen-man expedition led illegally by the German guide Udo Zeheleitner. Beginning the West Buttress route on May 19, the party made a rapid ascent to the 17,200-foot camp. The expedition left for the summit from this site on May 26, all being unroped and using ski poles instead of ice axes—an obviously flagrant disregard for National Park Service recommendations as well as their safety and that of others on the mountain.

When descending from Denali Pass, Bernard Pfeffer slipped on a small ice bulge, at almost the exact locality of the earlier accident of that month, and cartwheeled downslope an estimated 600 feet. The assistant guide descended to find Pfeffer had died, probably from multiple fractures.

This was Zeheleitner's fourth guided expedition to Mount McKinley. His practice to take seven days to reach the summit and not use ice axes or ropes "is a style that has been contributing to an ever increasing number of accidents," stated a review in *Accidents in North American Mountaineering*.[310] The German party had been briefed at Talkeetna about using ropes and ice axes, especially during the descending traverse from Denali Pass. Zeheleitner is now a *persona non grata* on Mount McKinley—he is no longer authorized to guide there. Rangers sighted him in Talkeetna again in 1990, but he did not linger.

In 1985 a Japanese climber nearly died from life-threatening pulmonary edema because of the irresponsibility of his own party members. Dr. Peter Hackett, Director of the Denali Medical Research Project, pointed out that at the first signs of altitude illness, especially when it became clear that his lungs were involved, the party should have stopped ascending. "When his condition deteriorated to the point that he could not walk a straight line without assistance, his group should have started down with him," Hackett wrote. Had Yoshikatsu Sumimoto descended a mere 1,000 to 2,000 feet when first ill, "he would have made a quick recovery and could have continued on two days later."[311] This man's life was saved by the prudent action of an American team who administered oxygen, Diamox, and fluids and maintained vigil over the victim.

1986 ACCIDENTS

The danger of pulling a sled without sufficient rope between team members was demonstrated again in the 1986 season. In mid-April, four members of the French "Edelweiss" expedition were flown to base camp on the West Buttress route. They chose a route west of that normally taken, where a heavily crevassed area exists near 9,500 feet. Thierry Broisat and Michel Legras were using skis, pulling a sled loaded with an estimated 100 pounds of gear. Both men were tied to the sled with separate lines: Broisat was ahead, with six meters of rope between him and the sled, and Legras was two meters behind him.

Two other party members ahead of them heard a "whump" sound, and "saw a cloud of snow as Broisat and Legras disappeared into a hole in the snow," according to a report made later.[312] The combined weight of the climbers and the sled created an estimated 500-pound force in a small area when the snow bridge over a crevasse collapsed. The two men fell some seventy-five feet to the bottom of the crevasse and were both killed.

Accident reviewers point out that they should have been spaced much farther apart. The leading man was an experienced Chamonix guide, but his chosen method of rope tie-in offered no protection for crevasse falls. It seems that the French expedition members believed the danger of crevasse falls in the area traveled was minimal. Apparently their two teams differed in this opinion and in methods of roping and tying the sled onto the rope.

A tragic case of carbon monoxide poisoning occurred to two Swiss mountaineers in early June 1986 at their 14,300-foot camp. Although they were warned of this danger by other team members and told to leave the two top tent vents open, the victims operated a Bluet stove with cartridges for some time. Being in sleeping bags, they may not have been aware of the odorless gas and simply fallen asleep.

A factor in producing carbon monoxide is the damping effect on the flame in having the pot too close to the burner and having water from the pot's condensation drop onto the flame. Dr. Peter Hackett in a report explained what transpires in carbon monoxide poisoning: "CO [carbon monoxide] combines with hemoglobin in the blood, in preference to oxygen, and therefore reduces the amount of oxygen reaching the brain. In effect, it is like suddenly being taken to a higher altitude. It thus contributes to altitude sickness, and is both dangerous and insidious."[313] A fist-sized ventilation hole guarantees adequate ventilation for poorly operating stoves. This hole can be plugged with snow in an igloo when stove use is completed.

All ice-glazed igloos and snow caves can produce cases of carbon monoxide poisoning. Extra caution should be taken when two stoves are in operation.

Perhaps the most-discussed series of rescues on the upper slopes of Mount McKinley are those of Korean parties on Cassin Ridge. In many ways the rescues of 1986 and 1988 reflect a selfish attitude for accomplishment without the use of good judgement, serious communication problems, and an expected dependency on others for rescue. In both instances, climbers on this difficult technical route went to a high altitude without prior acclimatization.

A seven-member Korean expedition flew to Kahiltna Glacier base camp on June 5, 1986, and then soon separated into groups. A two-man and a three-man party planned to ascend Cassin Ridge. On June 13, Lee Jong Kwan and Chung Seoung Kwon, both in their late twenties, began a rapid ascent, taking only four days to climb from 10,000 feet to a high camp at 19,700 feet. They carried only six days of food, wishing to climb fast to avoid possible poor weather.

On June 16 they radioed their base camp, as planned. Their camp leader recommended that they rest the following day as one man (Kwan) began getting sick. Other problems soon surfaced: On the next day their only stove would not operate. It became apparent that the climbers were in serious trouble when by June 18 Kwan exhibited signs of cerebral edema. Their food was virtually gone, and without a second rope for rappeling, they could not easily descend.

Rescuers Gary Scott, Pete Downing, and Vern Tejas after rescuing a Korean party in 1986 (photo by Roger Robinson)

As the weather became stormy, Kwon was too weak to ascend to the summit ridge. The two men hoped their following group would be able to assist them, but the three men below, unaware of the problems, lost an equipment rucksack, forcing them to descend. On June 19 Kwan and Kwon broadcast an SOS, but with the language barrier, listeners could not decipher the message. On the following day the two Koreans were frantically calling the National Park Service and also their pilot, Cliff Hudson. Nobody could understand.

Rangers Roger Robinson and Scott Gill taped their conversations and played it to the Korean consulate at Anchorage. The consulate, in turn, could not understand their messages because Kwon was trying to speak English instead of Korean. Finally the consulate was convinced there was a problem.

On June 20 pilot Lowell Thomas and a Korean interpreter flew to upper Cassin Ridge in poor weather to assess the seriousness of the situation. Unfortunately the climbers' radio batteries had worn out, and clouds prevented direct visibility.

Mo Anthoine of a British party that had just climbed Cassin Ridge reported that he had seen the two Koreans camped only some 600 feet from the summit ridge. It did not seem that there was a serious problem, but the British party did consider this a strange spot to camp. Since there was no aircraft in Alaska that could land at the camp's location, the only option was to organize an acclimatized ground team to rescue the Koreans by taking them over the summit ridge and then down the West Buttress, where a helicopter could land at the 17,200-foot camp.

Gary Scott, a National Park Service volunteer who had just spent five weeks as camp manager at the 14,300-foot medical rescue camp, was well acclimatized. With the tentative assistance of Anthoine and three of his British partners, and also the guide Vern Tejas, a six-man rescue team was prepared. A Bell 212 helicopter was taken from forest fire fighting to Talkeetna.

Meanwhile, Scott notified ranger Gill that the British climbers, now off the mountain and in Talkeetna, were "passed out" at the Fairview Inn and that there was no possible way they could participate in a rescue of this intensity. Scott and Gill then rounded up Austrians Wolfgang Wippler and Arthur Horied, who had just traversed Mount McKinley. Despite the fact they had only two hours of sleep, they volunteered to help.

Poor weather hindered efforts of the helicopter to land the climbing rescuers at 17,200 feet on the West Buttress, where there was oxygen and a rescue rope. The highest possible landing was at 14,300 feet.

Tejas and Wippler climbed to Denali Pass, and then Tejas continued alone to the summit ridge. At 5:00 P.M. on June 21 he reached 20,100 feet, anchored the rescue rope, and looked down Cassin Ridge. Tejas then descended to the Korean tent and got the two climbers mobilized to ascend the rope. With great effort this was accomplished, but on the summit ridge Kwan collapsed. Tejas now was confronted with a desperate situation. Kwon was still on upper Cassin Ridge, and Kwan was now in a coma. Fortunately, Wippler arrived with oxygen, which they hoped would revive the victim. The two rescuers loaded Kwan into a plastic sled and began to head down—with Kwon stumbling along behind.

Two more days of difficult lowering and hauling by various ground-team rescuers finally got the two Koreans to the 17,200-foot camp. From here, Kwan could be flown to Anchorage by helicopter.

A later analysis of the rescue suggested that once symptoms of acute mountain sickness were present, the two climbers should have either descended or not climbed higher. It appears that the Koreans really had no idea of what would be involved should a rescue be required—apparently they felt that by calling for a rescue, a helicopter would arrive and pick them up. Certainly the use of rescuers being flown from sea level, even when acclimatized, is a dangerous tactic. Many rescuers on this epic turned back because they began feeling altitude sickness symptoms; some began the rescue with a sleep deficit.

Unfortunately the large percentage of accidents and rescues of Koreans indicates a tendency for them to have a poor attitude toward safety and the necessity of maintaining their own self-reliance. Such practices have not only sometimes led to a tumultuous style on Mount McKinley, but they have risked rescue personnel, other mountaineers, and pilots. Much bad feeling has developed in recent years concerning their attitudes and careless behavior.

1988 ACCIDENTS

There were only two deaths on the high arctic mountain in 1988, but some epic and dangerous rescues took place. It was a popular year, with 326 climbers on McKinley's slopes during the first week of June. As usual, the West Buttress was the most popular route (eighty-five percent of the climbers).

Some 103 climbers reported mountain sickness symptoms, with twelve reported as life-threatening cases by the high medical base camp. Of seventeen solo climbers registered for the year, one disappeared and is presumed to have died.

The first serious accident of the year occurred on May 9, as ten Koreans were descending the West Buttress. In attempting to traverse around Windy Corner in high winds, one team slipped, with one man breaking an ankle. He was treated by a physician and sledded to base camp.

On the same day three French mountaineers left high camp for the summit. After one hour, one man's feet became numb because his footgear was inadequate protection for the icy environment: he was wearing ski boots without either overboots or gaiters. Feeling nothing, he assumed that his feet had warmed, so he continued to the summit. After discovering that all of his toes were frostbitten, he thawed them in warm water, but they froze again during the descent on the following day.

On May 18, Lynn Salerno, a client on a Genet Expeditions ascent, began to collapse while descending from the summit. Despite strong assistance from the guides, she began falling and became incoherent and hypothermic.

Because two members of the party experienced difficulties with the cold and altitude, the second guide was sent down with them to keep them alive. The result was that one guide was left alone with three fatigued, cold clients.

This guide and one male client sandwiched the woman between them and tried to move her forward. However, with the wind increasing, they kept tripping over the rough surface and repeatedly fell to the snow. When the group became enveloped in a whiteout, they dug a snow trench.

The guide then descended to 18,500 feet to retrieve clothing and a sleeping bag left lower. By the time he returned, the wind had increased to at least forty miles per hour. He checked the woman's pulse and found none.

A principal problem in this tragedy was the general slowness of the party. They were relatively weak and therefore late in reaching the summit. Other parties that day had long descended; thus, they were alone. Also, warming gear was left lower on the route or taken back to high camp and therefore not available for the hypothermic woman. Once she collapsed at the summit, "her physical deterioration progressed very rapidly.... Even the strongest team would have been hard pressed to reverse her deterioration," wrote ranger Robert Seibert in a later report. The woman client had a high tolerance for pain and suffering and was highly motivated. She focused on reaching the summit and used all of her physical reserves. "Her body was unable to produce the heat necessary to maintain her core temperature,"[314] Seibert added.

In a report to the State Magistrate of Alaska, Dr. Peter Hackett stated that in such an extreme environment an exhausted person who has depleted muscle fuel and who is unable to generate body heat by physical work quickly develops severe hypothermia. Hackett also pointed out that the lack of oxygen at this altitude was a contributing factor. A high heat production is essential for maintaining body temperature on Mount McKinley's high "heatless" environment. Once severe hypothermia develops in such a situation, treatment requires a shelter. The exposure–exhaustion in this case ultimately led to cardiac arrest from hypothermia.

Without question, a high percentage of mountaineers who reach the mountain's summit have pushed themselves toward the outer edge of their personal limits. Seibert's report included the caveat that McKinley is a demanding mountain to climb but is even a more difficult mountain to lead clients under its extreme altitude and climatic conditions. Guides must often rely on a client's assessment of their own physical status and be alert to their limitations. There is a challenge in identifying them at the correct time. "Herein lies the hazard," Seibert wrote. "How many clients on guided expeditions know their physical limits? How many have pushed themselves previously, physically and mentally, to the extent that they do on a Mount McKinley expedition? How many know how their bodies react at the exhaustion threshold?"[315]

A lone Korean, Sung Hyan Back, was flown to Kahiltna Glacier on May 5 to join a Korean Alpine Club expedition that was already headed for Cassin Ridge. Unable to "catch up" with this unit, he climbed solo to about 18,000 feet, where he met them.

On May 26 the ranger station in Talkeetna received a call for help from the party's CB radio—the only English transmittal being "Mayday, Mayday." Apparently Back had altitude sickness and frostbite and was unable to continue upward or descend. The two Koreans reporting the incident stated that they could not lower the man down the route.

The U.S. Army's High Altitude Rescue Team responded, and on May 27 hoisted the Korean. Once examined, his injuries were far less than reported. The Chinook CH 47 helicopter involved conducted the highest hoist operation the army had ever completed.

The rescue location was a dangerous site, and the rescue itself was possible only because of perfect weather conditions and the fact that the group was near one of the few flat areas along Cassin Ridge. As pointed out in *Accidents in North American Mountaineering,* a solo attempt leaves little room for error. "The urgency of this evacuation was questionable due to the minimal medical problems and the sustained risk and expense involved."[316]

An interagency cooperation among the National Park Service, the army, the Denali Medical Research Project, the Mount McKinley guides, and a party of Canadian climbers accomplished a second major rescue of Koreans on Cassin Ridge in 1988 and a repeat of the highest helicopter hoist operation ever made by the U.S. military. This event occurred only seven days after the hoist from the same location!

On June 3 the same two Koreans who had reported the late-May emergency began calling for a rescue for themselves. On May 21 Hyun Young Chung and Lee Jong Kwan (who had been rescued on Cassin Ridge in 1986) began climbing the Japanese Couloir. By May 28 they reached a campsite at 18,600 feet; Chung soon suffered cerebral edema and could not walk. In two days his condition (and the weather) became worse. Two Canadians climbed past but were unable to assist. Meanwhile, guides ascended the West Buttress route from 17,200 feet to the summit ridge to attempt a rescue from above. Here they anchored a 600-foot rope, but due to strong winds and a complete whiteout they were unable to effect a rescue. Dave Staehli descended beyond the full length of the rope, from where he could see the Koreans far below (on the CB radio, they had reported their position to be 19,500 feet).

Communications were a problem because of language barriers and because the Koreans' radio batteries failed early in the rescue operation. On June 2 the Koreans were urged by radio to descend on their own power because an army Chinook helicopter would not be able to conduct a hoist operation at their location. The ground team, subject to extreme danger, had to descend back to their camp.

On the following day two Chinook helicopters flew to 14,200 feet on the West Buttress to obtain assistance from acclimatized mountaineers. Meanwhile, the two Koreans descended to 18,000 feet, the site of the hoist made the previous week. At 10:15 A.M. both men were hoisted in two hover sequences.

This was the third major rescue of Korean climbers from upper reaches of Cassin Ridge within three years. In each case, the parties did not take time to acclimatize on a lesser route prior to beginning a rapid ascent of the ridge. Robert Seibert in a report made on June 20, 1988, summarized a needed wisdom: "The combination of rapid ascents, no prior acclimatization, and inexperience in high altitude arctic mountaineering is a sure formula for disaster."[317] The rangers at Talkeetna commented that parties were climbing on Cassin Ridge without sufficient ropes and anchors to conduct a descent should problems arise.

Most of the severe accidents and fatalities on the crown of North America have occurred because of climbers' rushing the ascent, failure to rope in crevasse fields, or the onset of unexpected storms and the inability of men to survive them.

An exception to competent solo climbers was Ignacio Munoz of Barcelona, who disappeared completely in July 1988. He appears to have chosen his attempt when visiting Alaska and then falsified his experience and equipment list when meeting with park rangers in Talkeetna.

Munoz may have given the rangers misleading information in order to gain permission for a solo ascent, for he had only minor alpine climbing experience. He was not a strong or fast climber, and his equipment (especially his boots) was totally inadequate for extreme cold. Munoz carried insufficient food and fuel and routinely searched caches for food when on the mountain. Perhaps he believed other mountaineers would support him.

The lone Spanish climber was seen and sometimes fed by other parties. After being overdue, an air search failed to locate him, although his tent was found at 16,200 feet and a pack somewhat higher. In the words of National Park Service searchers, Munoz set himself up for a fatal scenario. No trace of him has ever been found.

It should be pointed out that without a stove and shelter to operate from, one will not be able to melt water. Hypothermia, dehydration, and impaired judgement from acute mountain sickness is likely to occur.

1989 ACCIDENTS

Mountaineering events in the 1989 season brought both nostalgia and tragedy. When Jean-Francois Tuveri of Chamonix attempted to mush a dog team to the summit of Mount McKinley in late May, a fifteen-month-old Siberian husky was missing on the sixth day (between 11,000 and 14,200 feet). Apparently the dog fell into a crevasse or became disoriented in poor visibility near Windy Corner. But after eighteen days, the lost dog appeared at the medical research camp—in good condition, although appearing as if it had been through an ordeal. Needless to state, the dog was acutely hungry.

On a more serious vein, the fate of three British mountaineers was not as fortunate (they were among the six deaths that season). According to a May 24 dispatch, they climbed into a storm on the upper West Rib after being warned of the danger of high winds and whiteout conditions by a National Park Service ranger at 18,000 feet. The first British to die on the mountain, they probably fell on the descent while roped together on May 17. All three men fell at near 18,300 feet, tumbling down the icy chute called the Orient Express to 15,800 feet.

Numerous falls have occurred in this couloir over the years, and all on the descent. Each fall could have been arrested if the descending party had put in running belays across the steeper ice sections. A party planning the descent of the West Rib must allow for enough stamina and use caution to safely downclimb the upper ice sections of the route after a long summit day. The 1989 British party would have been wise to spend several extra days at a high camp—this would have enabled a quicker and safer ascent and descent from the summit.

During a winter expedition in 1989, three Japanese climbers, Noboru Yamada, Kozo Komatsu, and Teruo Saegusa, reached the 17,200-foot camp on the West Buttress on February 20—on the same day as three Austrians returned from the summit. The Austrians returned in a blizzard at midnight and could not locate their snow cave. With their chances of survival slim, they searched for three hours and then stumbled upon the tent of the Japanese party that had arrived in their absence. Soon after they found their snow cave but had a desperate time modifying its entrance in the storm.

Terrible weather followed, with wind gusts estimated at 200 miles per hour at times through February 26. On March 10, search flights located the Japanese climbers' bodies on an exposed slope below Denali Pass. It is believed that they attempted the summit during a brief lull and were caught by the storm. The leader, Yamada, was very experienced (with three Everest ascents) and was on a quest to climb the highest peaks of the seven continents in winter.

In May 1989 a dome tent that had been tied to twelve anchors (including four ice axes) at 17,200 feet blew away with its three occupants inside. One man from the guided party involved was freed from the tent as it began to slide. The other two men tumbled some 1,000 feet down the flanking ice slope—dressed only in their underwear and socks. Both climbers were alive but in serious condition when another party came to stabilize them before a helicopter rescue could be made.

This high camp on the West Buttress can be subject to severe winds. It was pointed out in a review that the protecting snow walls were only three feet high and only constructed halfway around the tent.

The second of two nonfatal tent "blow-aways" that occurred to guided groups in 1989 took place at 16,100 feet on July 13. Although the dome tent (one of four pitched there) in concern was anchored with a picket and two ice axes, and protected by three-to-four-feet-high snow walls, the tent floor billowed up from the severe wind gusts. Inside the tent, guide Curt Hewitt of Rainier Mountaineering felt himself roll over a snow wall and slide downslope. He took a tumbling 200-yard fall. He then tried to hold the tent full of gear but had to let go. Without gloves and only an outer boot on one foot, he climbed back to the campsite. Later, he had to be treated for hypothermia.

The tent, a pole-sleeve Oval Intention, did not collapse nor did the poles snap during the fall. The guide believed that he could have held the fall had the tent collapsed instead of acting as a sail.

1990 ACCIDENTS

In contrast to the stormy seasons of 1987, 1989, and 1992, in 1990 heavy winter snows and generally fair weather combined to limit accidents. The dark volcanic ash deposits from Mount Redoubt (150 miles distant in the Aleutian Range) and repeated eruptions caused a greatly accelerated melting of the snowpack and uneven surface ablation. This resulted in early closure of glacier landing strips.

There was a fifty-seven-percent success rate in Mount McKinley attempts, with only three search-and-rescue incidents—the lowest in fifteen years.[318] Medically, 1990 was a relatively inactive year, with only fourteen percent of the climbers getting a serious mountain sickness and three percent receiving frostbite. In other ways it was a typical year, with thirty-four percent of the climbers being guided and thirty-three percent comprising foreigners (representing twenty-nine countries).

Among the foreigners who climbed in early June 1990 was a Japanese expedition to the West Rib. Miroaki Ito, suffering from acute mountain sickness, was left alone at 19,600 feet while the remainder of the party climbed to the summit. During the descent, two of the team became separated from the others in poor visibility and descended the West Buttress route. The others found Ito during the descent and remained at the sick man's location in extreme wind and cold, with little survival equipment, in the hope of locating the two members who had actually bypassed them.

By morning the victim had advanced pulmonary edema, and the three who bivouacked had become severely frostbitten. The National Park Service attempted airdrops of oxygen and equipment as the other climbers attempted to drag Ito downward. He died before a rescue team could arrive from below.

The later analysis concluded that poor judgement was involved when the group reached the top of the West Rib. Ito was ataxic and short of breath. The only solution to save him was to descend immediately (with fixed lines still left on the route, a descent could have been made at that time in good weather). It is curious that Ito's symptoms were apparently not taken seriously by a physician on the expedition who had previous Himalayan experience.

The party's separation during the descent compounded the problem. The climbers returning to Ito's location did not know what had happened to the missing partners. It was felt that a retreat to the last camp on the West Rib would mean deserting the two missing and possibly dooming them.

1991 ACCIDENTS

In July 1991 a Polish solo climber was rescued near the summit of Mount McKinley after spending several days stranded in extremely poor weather with minimal survival equipment. Kcrysztof Wiecha left his 17,200-foot campsite early on the evening of July 3 for the summit after an earlier attempt with a partner. According to a National Park Service report, Wiecha carried no bivouac or survival gear—his light pack including only a few extra clothes, one chocolate bar, and one liter of juice. Typical of Mount McKinley's rapidly changing weather, it began to snow when the Polish climber reached the summit ridge: "The wind started to blow and the visibility was reduced to zero," added the report.[319]

By the time he dug a shallow snow cave with his hands at 20,000 feet to seek shelter, the calendar had moved to a new day. Now disoriented, Wiecha took shelter in several locations. A major storm reached the Alaska Range, and for the following three days and four nights the lone climber suffered from hypothermia, exhaustion, and dehydration.

Rescuers flying in the Aerospatiale Lama helicopter working under contract for the National Park Service first tried to drop a tent and survival gear to the twenty-eight-year-old climber, but the equipment rolled downslope past him. The *Fairbanks Daily News Miner* on July 8 reported, "After the unsuccessful drop, the helicopter flew park service rangers Daryl Miller and Jim Phillips to a landing spot at 19,500 feet. They climbed to 19,800-foot level and lowered Wiecha back down to the drop off point, where the helicopter picked up the injured climber at 12:30 A.M. Sunday." Wiecha, who suffered badly frozen feet (which later required amputation), displayed an incredible will to survive. The consensus of the rangers is that he was caught by unpredictable weather and that it was a miracle that he was able to survive his epic without food and water.

1992 ACCIDENTS

After a relatively benign and tragedy-free 1991 season, some observers believed that mountaineers had finally mastered some of the lessons that Alaska's high places had taught. But not so. The record number of eleven deaths on Mount McKinley in 1992 (and two more on Mount Foraker) would eclipse the sorrowful 1967 and 1980 seasons, each of which claimed eight lives.

The errors of the past—overconfidence, impatience, failure to acclimatize, ignoring bad weather signs, rapid and under-equipped ascent tactics, failure to rope up on glacial terrain, not belaying on steep descents—were often repeated. And there was a bad omen in the air: A jet stream windforce lowered, to bring continual wintry weather for three weeks in late spring. The forecasters at Fairbanks, in fact, on May 11 broadcast warnings, suggesting that possibly the worst tempest to reach the range in years was to arrive. An American climber had just tumbled at 16,000 feet on the West Buttress and broken his shoulder. Fortunately he could be evacuated before the frigid fury struck.

Most mountaineers on the route heeded the meteorological warnings and took refuge in the "tent city" at 14,300 feet—all except a French party of three, who remained exposed at 17,200 feet, while out of food, fuel, and water. Felipe Berthois and Fredric Segment—leaving Edwige Segment behind—finally made a dash to the lower camp for supplies. Then the storm intensified so that the two men could not return, and a helicopter rescue of Segment was out of the question. Her hopes of survival slimmed, but a team of valiant rescuers battled the onslaught all night to escort her down safely, barely averting a fatality as the wind and a whiteout continued for seven more days.

The first deaths on Mount McKinley since 1990, however, were not French, or Korean as one might speculate, but two skilled Italians, Roberto

Piombo and Giovanni Calgagno. They had fallen far down the exposed Cassin Ridge on May 15, possibly after being blown off their feet; one man's body was later found at 15,000 feet and another at 11,800 feet. Gary Bocarde, a guide who met the two Alps experts at base camp, related that the wind "sounded like a freight train" even low on the mountain (he estimated the wind at over 100 miles per hour!).

Denali by the weekend of May 16 to 17 was a prime candidate for an alpine disaster site. A count showed 422 climbers on its slopes. Who would prompt the next rescue?

A Korean was seriously injured from a fall while ascending the 15,000-to-16,000-foot West Buttress headwall. A minor lull in the wind fortunately permitted a helicopter rescue—the fifth man to be flown off alive this season. Then, without much warning, a Swiss guide, Alex von Bergen, died, not directly by the elements but by a cerebral hemorrhage while he was in a tent at the 14,300-foot camp.

On the same day, May 17, a Korean climber from a Je Ju University expedition arrived at the medical tent, frenetically shouting that his two companions had just fallen into a deep crevasse. Rescuers rushed upslope 1,200 feet in a whiteout and found the slot, partially covered with a collapsed snow bridge. John Roskelley and Matt Culberson rappelled sixty feet into an open hole and found a man buried to his waist and another buried by ice blocks. Both were still alive. They dug both free, fearing that one would soon succumb from injuries and hypothermia in the icy jumble. To release the victim from his tomb, it became necessary to cut the ice with a saw. A seemingly hopeless survival turned into release: the climber was alive (although he had a broken back) after being trapped for hours in the subzero cold. It was a risky rescue because the outward-leaning, uphill snow wall threatened to collapse. Later the rescue team learned that the Koreans had halted on the snow bridge—not the wisest location for a rest—although others had apparently stopped there previously. Postcript: Later others from this university expedition continued their bad judgement by returning to the crevasse to search for lost equipment without the safety of a rope.

Meanwhile, the outlook for another Korean expedition, at 17,700 feet on Cassin Ridge, worsened as three men encountered their seventh day without food and fuel. On May 15, after their tent had blown away, the climbers began a series of desperate radio calls. Although not top-rank mountaineers, the Koreans were as competent as many others who had climbed Cassin Ridge. They were victims as much as anything of the severity and length of the tempest, but they did "cut it thin" in the opinion of the National Park Service rangers. A news release on May 19, in fact, stated that they had packed only enough food for a three-day trip to the summit and ate dry rice powder the first two days and then just melted snow.

At first, the Lama helicopter could not reach the stranded climbers, who were now in a dire predicament, huddled in their emergency snow cave. Terrible winds prevented the stripped-down Lama from landing, but while hovering above Cassin Ridge, Jim Phillips, the ranger on board, spotted the body of one of the Italians hanging in a rope tangle. On May 18 the Lama's pilot, Jim Ramsey, dropped an emergency food bundle, but it plummeted off the precipitous ridge flanks. Finally daring to land, he sighted a flat rock some fifty feet below the Koreans' snow cave. The three men rushed for a lift-off rescue, but Ramsey dared only rescue one person at a time. In the cabin Phillips waved one finger at the desperate others as the machine circled away for the first run to the 14,300-foot medical camp with the leader, Hyun Do Kang.

When the last man, Bong Kue Chung, was retrieved, he attempted to hook the climbing packs on the Lama's skid apparatus. Phillips kicked them off because of the excess weight and load imbalance. But at the medical camp the malcontent demanded that the helicopter return for the packs, which included his wallet and passport. Not even thanking anyone for saving his life, the Korean became belligerent when rescuers suggested he could climb back and retrieve the equipment. Insisting that he was not leaving Denali for Anchorage with the larger army helicopter until the Americans returned with his money and passport, he turned combative. Roskelley and Jim Wickwire, perhaps to the delight of ringside bystanders, subdued the argumentative foreigner and wrestled him with a full-nelson into the Chinook.

This episode did little to warm relations between Americans and Korean mountaineers. This rescue alone cost the public taxpayers for use of the high-altitude helicopter, two army Chinook helicopters as backup, Air National Guard helicopters to take the Koreans to Anchorage, and a Hercules C-130 aircraft to coordinate the entire operation.

But at the Anchorage hospital's emergency room, there was no hint of local self-righteousness as the climbers were treated for frostbite and altitude sickness. Reportedly, the Asians were in good spirits as they dined on breaded pork chops, vegetables, scalloped potatoes, macaroni salad, rolls, pie, milk, and juice.

Another Korean expedition on Mount McKinley did not have such a pleasant farewell. The *Anchorage Daily News* on May 21 reported three more deaths on Denali, as three Koreans fell on the deceptively easy Orient Express ice couloir—the single most dangerous location on the mountain. Part of the same JeJu University expedition that had been rescued from the crevasse three days earlier, the climbers had rationed food and water for one week while marooned near 18,000 feet on the West Rib during the intense winter-storm pattern. They undoubtedly were weak from exhaustion, dehydration, and hypoxia. Falling some 2,500 feet, the tragedy continued a disastrous trend for Koreans on North America's highest peak. As Dr. Peter Hackett stated later, the snow in this couloir is usually hard, and climbers short of oxygen have slow reactions. When one climber falls, the others, instead of stopping him, are pulled from their positions.

The seventh fatality on Denali in seven days occurred on May 21 when Terrance ("Mugs") Stump dropped into a crevasse while descending near 14,400 feet on "The Ramp"—a thirty-degree jumble of ice blocks and crevasses on the South Buttress route. On May 24 the *Daily News* headlined, "Lifeline vanished into the ice. Companions say crevasse swallowed Stump quickly, silently."

When the lead man of two clients halted because he saw a "dropoff" in the veiled visibility, Stump moved forward to investigate. About two feet from the crevasse lip, its edge let go, and he tumbled down, pulling the loose rope behind. Why there was some ninety feet of slack in the rope is not clear. Nelson Max later recalled that there was "a slight sound, like snow settling" before he was pulled off his feet. Attempting an ice-axe arrest, he was pulled some fifteen feet toward the chasm before stopping. An attempt at rescuing Stump by rappeling into the crevasse was futile. Sixty feet down, Max could see the bottom of a wedge of snow and ice that plugged the crevasse, but no rope emerged from it.

With difficulty the two survivors made their way down the glacier, missing a stove and radio that had been in Stump's pack. They credited a pair of unknown Seattle climbers ascending the route with helping them to safety. That an expert noted for his success on difficult and dangerous routes should die in a simple crevasse fall "shook the Alaska climbing community to its very soul," stated the press. Stump, considered to be an extraordinary alpinist, had boldly solo-climbed Cassin Ridge in a record fifteen hours during the previous spring.

Storms really did not affect the accident of the Swiss guide and perhaps not even the three Koreans who slid down the Orient Express couloir, but the violent weather did kill the two Italians and necessitated the many rescues. At the end of May the worst spring storms in many years, which had led to seven deaths on Denali, subsided. But by the night of the 30th, climbers and rangers at the West Buttress patrol camp saw huge snow plumes flying off the summit ridge. There was a distinct concern for a group of four Quebec Canadians, who carried only one-day packs on a summit bid and had not yet returned.

On the following day Roger Robinson accompanied a pilot to search for the overdue Quebec team. Through radio communication, the rescue patrol on the West Buttress was relieved to learn that he had sighted them descending near 19,000 feet, making their way roped together across the upper end of Messner Couloir (an hour-glass–shaped ice gully—an unexpected descent position for the team).

The four men, Simon Proulx, Christian Proulx, Alain Potvin, and Maurice Grandchamp, had bivouacked near 19,000 feet and undoubtedly were fatigued. On a traversing descent toward the West Buttress, they kept below the cornice, probably to avoid the fierce wind that was whipping the upper ridges. But less than fifteen minutes after they had been reported safely in motion, the ranger patrol and others in the 14,300-foot camp saw the last man on the rope stumble. As the horrified onlookers (and others at the 17,200-foot camp) watched, the Canadians began tumbling on the forty-five-degree slope—all of them ripped off their stances and now out of control.

Falling an estimated 3,000 feet in the icy gully, the accident brought the seasonal death toll to eleven. Patrol members climbed to the victims, but the "loaded" slope cracked and settled—threatening to slide. They would have to return later. "They made a decision to go to the summit without, in my opinion, proper equipment," mountaineering ranger J. D. Swed reported to the press. "When weather did hit them, they weren't able to stick it out. They were forced to move." While crossing the exposed couloir near 19,000 feet, they did not place any pickets or other belay anchors.[320] As

Swed commented, "Where they were, if you don't self-arrest in the first two seconds, you won't be able to self-arrest."[321]

In a sequel to the deadliest year in Alaska Range alpine history, two mountaineers died on Mount Foraker. On June 26, an injured Colby Coombs completed his struggle back to Kahiltna Glacier base camp, reporting that his two companions, Tom Walter and Rick Kellogg, had died in an avalanche six days earlier. The team had virtually ended their difficulties on the Pink Panther route, near the top of the east face, as the snow surface broke loose. When the leader fell, self-arrests failed, and the men were swept off. However, the rope between them was stopped by a rock. When Coombs awoke from trauma the following day, he found that his companions had not survived, and he now faced a difficult six-day descent alone.

The three competent climbers had chosen this technical route because of its steepness, presuming it would have firmer snow conditions than the Southeast Ridge. Although fewer than thirty mountaineers attempt Mount Foraker each year, unstable snow and ice often aborts attempted ascents; four men were killed by avalanches in 1987.

CONCLUSIONS

Numerous conclusions have been drawn from the accidents and rescues on Mount McKinley. In *Surviving Denali,* Jonathan Waterman summarized the fatalities from 1902 to 1982. Although now one decade outdated, his statistics are still relevant. The greatest cause of death on Mount McKinley was falls (thirty-four percent), with hypothermia next at twenty-two percent. Crevasse falls (twelve percent) and pulmonary edema (twelve percent) accounted for the other known causes, and twenty percent of the victims died from unknown causes.

That fatigue and carelessness play a serious factor in the Mount McKinley tragedies is shown by these illuminating figures; during this same period, while there were fourteen fatalities on the ascent, there were twenty-seven on the descent.

The Mount McKinley tragedies have been compared to those on Mount Everest. By Memorial Day in 1992, a total of 7,172 persons had reached the highest point in North America, and 75 persons from thirteen nations have now died since the first victims sixty years earlier. Mount Everest has been climbed by 386 mountaineers, with 115 deaths, and Aconcagua in South America, climbed many thousands of times, has had about 57 deaths.

Without question, many mountaineers underestimate Mount McKinley. Many appear to be lulled by a false sense of security because of the large numbers on the popular routes and the likelihood of helicopter rescue. The recent tragedies reflect some of the changes that have affected mountaineering. Easy access provided by the airlines and local air services may well affect the number of accidents and rescues in Denali National Park and Preserve.

Styles have changed in mountaineering, and, on Mount McKinley, Roger Robinson believes there is more emphasis on rapid ascents, going "thin" on supplies to save overall weight, and individuals not properly acclimatizing. Eventually these tactics catch up with the practitioners, he feels. But, despite all the precautions taken by most expeditions, luck is still a prevailing factor in keeping alive.

Today's problems in high Alaska are partly a result of impatience, a human trait hard to subdue. Bradford Washburn has suggested that it is often wise to wait two days after a storm in order to obtain more settled weather and superior snow conditions. The traditional technique on big mountains—to make additional relays, thus stocking camps while becoming acclimatized—is now often replaced by the practice of carrying a minimum of food and fuel.

There does seem to be a difference in attitudes among many of the foreign expeditions, especially in the willingness to accept risk and a willingness to rely on rescue. Foreign rescues in the past decade have been on the rise: In 1991 less than one-half of the mountaineers were foreign, but they were involved in ten out of eleven helicopter rescues! Since 1986 (through 1992) all but five of twenty-eight who died were foreigners, and in the 1992 tragedies only one death was an American.

In many instances, it appears to be a clear and conscious decision on the part of foreign climbers to adopt travel modes, techniques, and ascent rates that are not recommended for proper acclimatization. This irresponsibility may in part stem from the insurance and rescue tendencies prevalent in Europe.

Accidents on Mount McKinley have occurred largely to Asians and Europeans, many of whom have obtained their experience in the Alps. There is a certain similarity: easy access, probable helicopter rescue, and a new fashion of quick, light ascent. Many climbers simply assume that Mount McKinley cannot be that much different—but it is! Denali is wrapped in a frigid environment, with often higher winds than the Himalaya. The drain on the human body from its extreme conditions and altitude leads to weakness and human error.

In the August 1992 issue of *Outside*, Jon Krakauer pointed out, "Those who have mastered the Alps are lulled into thinking that Denali is essentially the same kind of mountain, just a little bigger. But there is nothing like it."[322] Even when compared to Mount Everest, K2, Kanchenjunga, and other mountain giants, the arctic, windy aspect of North America's highest point should never be taken lightly.

The two Italians on Cassin Ridge in 1992 apparently underestimated the severity of the elements and the effects of a rapid ascent on the human body. These men, highly expert in the Alps, probably believed the climb would be trifling compared to harder technical routes they had done successfully. Reportedly, at Talkeetna, they scoffed at ranger warnings of the seriousness of Alaskan weather. They were impatient and did not wish to hear out the briefing. They decided to "blitz" the route—lightly loaded and without acclimatization—and omitted tent and shovel. Instead, they were literally blown off by jet-stream-force winds.

Certainly in recent years Asians have troubled the mountaineering world, which has agonized over the speed tactics and often seemingly careless disregard for their own members and, consequently, rescuers.

Most puzzling is the Korean problem, which Krakauer stated "is that the overwhelming number of those who have gotten into serious trouble on the slopes of Denali in recent years have hailed from a single country: South Korea."[323] Koreans were only five percent of the 1991 aspirants on Mount McKinley, yet they were involved in a disproportionate sixty-six percent of the rescues. The 1992 accident on the Orient Express couloir raised the figure to nine Asians killed on this dangerous topographic feature.

Korean mountaineers do appear to possess a propensity to err on Mount McKinley and other high mountains. In a country where mountaineering is prestigious, the lore of the Alaskan giant rises as more of them become rescued or killed. Their culture places a high value on success, with a greater willingness to accept risk—always an ingredient of high-altitude mountaineering. The pressure of homeland sponsors reminds Korean climbers that Denali is virtually a prerequisite for acceptance on a Himalayan expedition.

The *Alaska Daily News* on June 5, 1992, heralded, "Bad year for Korean climbers. Non-English speakers at a disadvantage on McKinley, physician [Dr. Peter Hackett] says." There is more than a mite of truth in this, for Asians tend to keep to themselves in Talkeetna and on the mountain, and they do not hear the "scuttlebutt" and warnings circulated in casual conversation.

National Park Service rangers spend more time and money on the controversial Koreans than on any other nationality. Rangers and guides (all of whom are American) resent having to risk their lives because of carelessness and ill-planned ventures—some with a high-risk philosophy. The taxpaying public, too, is jarred by the expense of rescues—one on Cassin Ridge alone costing over $100,000, this being the fourth time in six years that a Korean party had been helicoptered off the upper ridge. One climber, Jong Kwan Lee, in fact, was rescued twice (in 1986 and 1988) from virtually same location!

▲▲▲

CHAPTER 20

High-Altitude Medical Problems

HIGH-ALTITUDE ILLNESSES

High-altitude illness, although recognized for centuries, was relatively rare until modern times. A quicker and easier access to mountain ranges and greater leisure time have dramatically increased the number of unacclimatized individuals who suffer the consequences of rapid ascent. Thousands of transient winter skiers in the Alps and Rocky Mountains are afflicted by some degree of high-altitude illness. Most of these persons travel from altitudes near sea level to resorts in one day—which does not allow time for acclimatization.

The threshold of where altitude-related illness occurs is regarded as a moderate 8,000 feet. Physicians have noted that the altitude at which one sleeps is a more important determinant of high-altitude illness than the altitude attained during a day of skiing or climbing.

Even moderate altitudes result in a decrease in maximal physical performance and a progressive decrease in maximal oxygen consumption. The effects can be very striking at extreme altitude. The physiological effects of ascent to high altitude are as follows:

1. Decrease of oxygen in the blood (secondary to both low oxygen in the air and finite capacity of the lung to transfer oxygen from air to the blood).
2. Increase in breathing.
3. Increase in red blood cell production.
4. Decrease in cardiac output and heartrate, especially at extreme altitude.
5. Decrease in plasma volume.

During the first few days at high altitude, humans experience unpleasant symptoms and an abrupt decrease in physical performance. Improvement, however, occurs during continued exposure. In the process of acclimatization, physical adjustments occur. The most important is an increase in breathing—which persists for the duration of stay at a given altitude.

Acclimatization can be achieved by staging a gradual ascent and making transitional stays at intermediate levels before a higher altitude is attempted. When climbing to elevations of 10,000 to 14,000 feet, a visit of two to four days at an intermediate altitude of 6,000 to 8,000 feet provides significant protection against high-altitude illness at greater elevations. Above 14,000 feet (4,270 meters) a daily ascent of no more than 1,000 feet is prudent, and a rest day after one to two days of climbing is advisable.

Because it is located well above 60° north latitude, Mount McKinley's barometric pressure is lower for a given altitude, and altitude effectively higher, than peaks closer to the equator. Barometric pressure varies with latitude, due to the centrifugal force of planetary spin and temperature differences that cause compression of the atmosphere near the poles and an expansion toward the equator. The barometric pressure at the summit of Mount McKinley is equivalent to altitudes 1,000 to 2,500 feet higher in the Himalaya at 27° north; the effects of cold are also more severe. This harsh environment is only equaled by the highest peaks of Antarctica.

A study by Dr. Peter Hackett of the Denali Medical Research Project in 1984 showed that sixteen percent of climbers on Mount McKinley suffered cold injury. Thirty percent of climbers studied suffered acute mountain sickness (AMS) of varying degrees: headaches were present in fifty-two percent. Loss of appetite was also common above 15,000 feet.

While it is certain that the lack of oxygen (hypoxia) is the underlying cause of AMS, high-altitude pulmonary edema (HAPE), and high-altitude cerebral edema (HACE), it is suspected that the extreme cold of Mount McKinley and Mount Foraker, together with heavy physical exertion, are additive factors to altitude illness. Dr. Hackett has observed that the incidence of pulmonary edema on Denali seems to be higher than in other locations, striking approximately 1 in 30 to 1 in 50 climbers.

The initiating event of HAPE is probably an accentuated degree of hypoxic pulmonary precapillary constriction, which elevates pulmonary artery pressure. This high pressure may lead to fluid leakage from the small blood vessels to the air sacs of the lung. Typical HAPE symptoms are weakness, coughing, undue fatigue, a resting heartbeat exceeding 100 beats per minute, shortness of breath (a respiratory rate of over twenty breaths per minute), and signs of fluid in the lungs or air passages. Nausea and vomiting may occur.

These symptoms (weakness, shortage of breath at rest, rapid pulse, and dry cough) usually begin twenty-four to forty-eight hours after a too-rapid ascent for proper acclimatization, but they may occur in just a few hours, with no advance warning. Loss of coordination may occur quickly. As the condition progresses, the victim may become delirious and unable to stand up. Once consciousness is lost, death may occur within six to twelve hours unless oxygen is administered or a descent is made. Mortality usually is the result of a failure to diagnose the condition in stages early enough to prevent progression. The wisest course of action is to descend to a lower camp for one to two days and then take more time to ascend again.

Some persons acclimatize more slowly than others and are susceptible to HAPE because of genetic and other predisposing factors. Individuals who have had previous episodes of HAPE are likely to have recurrent episodes on return to high altitudes. There is a great variance among individuals, and there seems to be no way of predicting who will or will not develop altitude illness. Some individuals experience the same symptoms during repeated high-altitude exposures. It has been shown that a strenuous program of physical fitness at sea level does not prevent AMS. Gender seems to make no difference. Repeated exposure during a period of many years, however, may provide some adaptive protection. What is still unclear is the point at which simple AMS turns into HACE, but it is certain that all three disorders involve abnormal shifts of fluids to the lungs and brain.

Accident reviews show that a large percentage of falls occur above 14,000 feet on Mount McKinley and mostly during the descent. Certainly hypoxia, cold, fatigue, and AMS are factors in these critical situations.

A number of learned opinions have stated that mental functions at higher altitudes can be impaired by fifty percent. Certainly hypoxia impairs judgement and mobility. Falls and stumbling are more common as a result of slower reactions. Self-arrest is therefore more difficult to perform.

FROSTBITE

Frostbite cold injury is characterized by ice crystals forming in intercellular spaces; this occurs when there is insufficient heat and decreased blood flow in the local area—usually the fingers and toes. Pain in the affected localized tissues is the first symptom, but pain and sensation are lost as tissues freeze. The danger lies in that such numbness may not be noticed.

Frostbitten tissues are usually pale because of blood vessel constriction; they may become firm or hard. Because they are usually covered by gloves or socks, frozen tissues may not be readily noticed. Blisters will form during tissue thawing. Pain, tissue loss, and discoloration may occur.

A cooling of the body's core temperature contributes to both frostbite and, by definition, hypothermia. If you begin the day being cold, and soon feel nothing in your feet, this is a warning of cold injury or deep frostbite. Action must be taken to reverse the damage immediately. Some controversy exists regarding the best thawing methods: Rapid rewarming in warm water, when possible, is favored (100 to 106 degrees Farenheit). Excessive heat thawing may be disastrous and result in serious injury to tissues. Never attempt thawing where there is danger of refreezing the injured part; it may be safer to walk out on frozen feet than damage them while walking after thawing.

To minimize the frostbite danger, mountaineers should be careful to maintain foot circulation in the toes. Be certain that the inner boot insulation is dry. And remember, rehydration increases the frostbite danger. The arctic temperatures on Alaska's high peaks during April and May require that fully insulated overboots, even for plastic double boots, be worn.

DEHYDRATION

Body fluid loss is the result of exhaling and strenuous exercise in dry, cold air. Dehydration is a major hazard of high-altitude mountaineering. It compounds the problems of any illness or injury, making recovery more difficult. The effects of frostbite are much worse when the body is dehydrated.

Rehydration is vital. All experts state that drinking four quarts of fluid each day is important. This fluid input can help prevent altitude sickness, exhaustion, and frostbite.

Note that Lasix is a diuretic that causes severe dehydration. It should not be used in the field setting. Also, diarrhea can be fatal above 14,000 feet because it aggravates dehydration.

▲▲▲

CHAPTER 21

The Climbing Challenge

After his expedition in 1903, Dr. Frederick Cook described the challenge of scaling Mount McKinley:

> *The area of the mountain is far inland, in the heart of a most difficult and trackless country, making the transportation of men and supplies a very arduous task. The thick underbrush, the endless marshes, and the myriads of vicious mosquitoes bring to the traveller the troubles of the tropics. The necessity of fording and swimming icy streams, the almost perpetual cold rains, the camps in high altitudes on glaciers in snows and violent storms bring to the traveller all the discomforts of the arctic explorer.*[324]

The long approach that Dr. Cook described is not ordinarily experienced by today's mountaineers; however, the ascent above the snow line can indeed be a polar experience, given the potential of bitter arctic temperatures and unexpected, violent storms. In consideration of the high altitude of the mountain and potential dangers of snow-covered crevasses, Mount McKinley must be climbed with care and respect by even a strong team. Rescues are uncertain, even with a radio available. The lack of technical difficulties on some routes has made the climb possible for parties with minimal mountaineering experience who have used care, effort, and persistence, coupled with benevolent weather. But, as the caveat in the National Park Service mountaineering booklet reminds, the combined effects of cold, wind, and altitude may well present one of the most hostile climates on earth. It may well be as hostile as the poles.

Mount McKinley's ascent requires hard work, patience, and endurance. Much of the effort is more akin to farm labor than aerobic exercise, but with the odors gone and oxygen reduced. Because much of the activity on the mountain is plain drudgery and suffering in the cold, many initially underestimate its challenge. But it is a fact that most mountaineers returning from the mountain have gained rather than lost respect for the challenge.

Peter Habeler, in writing of his experience in *Alpinismus,* cautioned readers on the consequences of underestimating Mount McKinley. He stressed that its sudden high-altitude storms overshadowed by far those of

Snow blowing off summit ridge of South Peak (photo by Olaf Sööt)

the Himalaya. In 1976, the British climber Doug Scott vividly described his storm experiences on the south face:

> *Just as the murky sun was dropping over Mt. Foraker, a tremendous blast of wind tore across the face, all but dislodging us.... In the midst of removing boots, brewing up and getting into the bivi-bag, we suddenly found ourselves fighting for survival, groping amongst particles of ice for*

our boots, gloves and everything else. The wind continued unabated for the next three hours—the worst few hours that either of us had spent in the mountains. There, at 15,000 ft., we manoeuvered ourselves back into the bag and put the brew back on. Strangely, though, we fell asleep with 80 m.p.h. winds threatening to pluck us clean off the mountain.[325]

Another gripping experience with the elements was given in the journal of guide Michael Covington on June 5, 1980:

Today we descend from our camp on the West Rib at 16,000 feet (4,876 m) to 11,200 feet on the West Buttress in what was one of the most terrifying days I have ever spent in the mountains. By the time we arrived at camp below Windy Corner (12,500 feet / 3,810 m), the gusts were in excess of one hundred miles per hour and gusting once every twenty seconds. The effort and likelihood of getting a wall up was equivalent to the risk and effort of getting to a lower elevation, so we continued to descend. The winds continued to increase as we continued down. One of the gusts knocked all nine of us to the snow. I got up quickly during a brief lull and completely to my surprise I was swept into the air and flew until my rope came tight. That gust must have been in excess of 150 mph (240 km / h). I don't ever recall a feeling of such helplessness in the mountains. Had it not been for the fact that most of the rest of the team were still trying to get up, it's quite possible we all could have been swept off the mountain and down onto the Peter's Glacier several thousand feet below.[326]

▲ ▲ ▲

Mount McKinley is less than 200 miles from the Arctic Circle. Spring and summer temperatures may drop to minus forty degrees Fahrenheit, and winds to 100 miles per hour may last for several days. The mountain is 35° north of Mount Everest in latitude, and it has a snow and glacier cover extending 16,000 feet in height. Large glaciers descend to low levels: Kahiltna Glacier is forty-six miles in length, and the Muldrow, Ruth, Eldridge, Tokositna, and Yentna (south of Mount Foraker) are all over twenty-six miles in length. The melting of these glaciers only takes place below about 13,000 feet in the summer months. At this altitude an abrupt climatic change takes place, with subzero temperatures possibly occurring both day and night. The glaciers on the upper third of Mount McKinley are polar in nature, and the snow surface at the higher altitudes is almost always hard and wind-packed.

Mount McKinley generates its own weather, and the mountain is seldom completely clear. It has often been pointed out that most clouds hovering on the mountain produce snow. This is in contrast to many other cloud-capped peaks, where the precipitation may fall as rain, not snow.

Weather cycles tend to be both good and bad. Generally it is either clear or it is snowing. There are great variables, even in summer. Changes for the worse can be sudden: It may be eighty degrees Fahrenheit in the sun and then quickly change to intense wind and a whiteout. Mountaineers should always be on the watch for storm signs, such as cirrus clouds to the south and southwest and lenticular cloudcaps over high peaks. One should also be alert to temporary changes in a poor weather interlude—these lulls have accounted for some of Mount McKinley's worst tragedies. The violence of storms can endanger anyone on the moutain.

In winter, extreme cold is often accompanied by high northerly winds. February and March may have clear conditions, but it is almost always very cold. While April and May can be cold and windy, April often has clear days, and in late May the local storms often subside to bring clear spells. These two months also have an advantage in that the crevasses on the lower glaciers are more filled. During May, however, there tends to be avalanche danger, especially on steep, lower slopes.

Low clouds that shroud glaciers in the summer and interfere with flight landings may be merely "creepers" from marine air; it may be clear at higher elevations. Summer temperatures can be torrid in the daytime but frigid in the dry night air. Throughout June and until mid-July, there are twenty-four hours of daylight—providing flexibility in climbing tactics, particularly for night climbing on lower, avalanche-prone slopes. The most stable conditions on the upper portion of Mount McKinley are in July, but even then the wind typically streams upward to form a lenticular cloudcap that produces precipitation; such cloudcaps, however, can clear rapidly. The typical cloud activity begins in the early morning when cumulus clouds form at the lower altitudes. These clouds fuse into a more solid ceiling and thicken, and by evening they reach an altitude of from 7,000 to 12,000 feet. Sometimes a great anvil rises to 20,000 or 25,000 feet. The night's cooling dissipates the overcast and then in the morning the warming and cloud process resumes. In August the weather tends to become progressively worse, with snow falling regularly. September is generally a wet month. Overall, the best time to climb Mount McKinley is from May to July—with July having the highest success rate.

▲ ▲ ▲

Excellent conditioning, stamina, willpower, and the ability to withstand severe arctic conditions are vital for survival, let alone success, in reaching Mount McKinley's summit. Expeditions should travel and climb fully prepared, as though no rescue were available. Those who depend on rescue efforts or the strength and expertise of others to extricate themselves from difficult positions are inviting disaster. Acclimatized rescuers are often not available, and a helicopter may not be able to reach an accident scene. Mountaineers should be mindful that rescues can involve grave danger to pilots and rescue personnel.

On Mount McKinley, impatience is a sin. A fundamental rule of self-preservation is proper acclimatization: the tactics of sleeping low and climbing high are critical for proper acclimatization. It is a mistake to push for the summit until the entire party contemplating the ascent is in condition for the high altitude. When this is done, party members should not separate. Certainly the fact that 0.5 percent of Mount McKinley climbers have died (ten times the rate at Mount Rainier and on the Grand Teton) is a grim reminder that some expeditions have not acclimatized and with blunted judgement have made poor decisions. At higher elevations on this mountain, Peter Habeler has warned that the mind and body can deteriorate rapidly.

To minimize the danger from frostbite, never permit yourself to become dehydrated. Dr. Peter Hackett and other high-altitude medical experts have repeatedly warned that dehydration decreases physical performance and the ability to generate muscular heat, contributing to fatigue as well as hypothermia and frostbite. Exercising the toes is important; hand circles—swinging the arms in circles—helps eliminate dangerous fingertip numbness. Short rests (even resting on ski poles or an ice axe) are a wiser plan than long breaks that involve sitting down; short rests after thirty to fifty steps can be very beneficial.

On Mount McKinley, it is important to plan for the campsite shelter before a storm arrives. If tents are used, build proper and adequate snow-block walls. Igloos or snow caves should be used at higher altitudes, and even at lower altitudes they are often preferable.

Mountaineers must always be aware of the dangers of Alaskan crevasses. While most routes are safe from crevasses in their upper portions, never travel unroped on the large, lower glaciers. All party members must be familiar and prepared for crevasse rescue. Because of this crevasse hazard, solo climbing is very dangerous on these lower glaciers. Solo climbers have no rescue ability where a belaying rope is important for safety.

The recommended number of persons for a Mount McKinley ascent is a minimum of four. It is important to make up a group of members who have climbed together, not one organized by mail or phone calls. The consensus of those familiar with the mountain is to allow a minimum of two full weeks, with at least one week of spare supplies in the event of hostile weather. Ray Genet, who climbed or attempted Mount McKinley twenty-seven times, never believed in rushing the ascent. While some mountaineers have set records, such accomplishments are quite specialized and generally made possible by prior acclimatization. In 1986 Gary Scott climbed from base camp to the summit in 18½ hours, but he had spent considerable time at the medical camp above 14,000 feet. Charles Porter climbed Cassin Ridge solo in 1976, taking only thirty-six hours; Mugs Stump climbed the ridge in June 1991, taking only fifteen hours from bergschrund to the "Football Field" (not far below the summit ridge), but, again, he was already acclimatized. And in descending the Orient Express, snowboarders have now made it to the 14,000-foot basin in remarkably short time, a feat not to try either by sliding or by descending with crampons.

▲▲▲

CHAPTER 22

The Logistics of Exploring and Climbing Mount McKinley: Travel, Backpacking, and Mountaineering Suggestions

TRAVEL TO AND WITHIN ALASKA

Major airlines serve both Anchorage and Fairbanks from air terminals in the United States, Canada, Europe, and Japan. A scheduled flight network serves many other Alaskan cities and towns, and numerous flight services can be chartered for wilderness destinations.

The Alaska Highway

The historic highway through western Canada to Alaska is today much improved over the era of muddy tracks and flying gravel from opposing vehicles, but one should anticipate sections under repair. To avoid continual driving and "jet lag," one should allow a minimum of four days from the United States–Canada border in Alberta or British Columbia. Approach routes converge at Dawson Creek, British Columbia, where the Alaska Highway begins (with the Cassiar Highway to the west being an optional and even shorter route). The distance from Dawson Creek to Tok Junction in Alaska, where the highway divides, is 1,314 miles: the northern branch continues to Fairbanks (1,523 miles), and the Glenn Highway connects with Palmer (1,592 miles) and Anchorage (1,634 miles).

Much of the Alaska Highway is a somewhat monotonous vista of boreal forest, but when passing Summit Lake, crossing through Stone Mountain Provincial Park, and near Muncho Lake, all in British Columbia, watch for Stone sheep and spectacular folded limestone formations. Whitehorse, in Yukon Territory, is worth savoring for its historical frontier legacy. Near Haines Junction and Kluane Lake there are fleeting glimpses of the high mountains of the Icefield Ranges, a region hosting the world's largest glaciers outside of Greenland and Antarctica. High summits of the Alaska Range and Wrangell Mountains can be seen when continuing along either branch of the highway in Alaska, but Mount McKinley is not visible until near Fairbanks or Anchorage (the mountain is 135 miles from Anchorage and 135 miles from Fairbanks).

The Alaska Ferry System

An automobile or passenger alternative to the Alaska Highway is to combine ferry and highway travel. The Alaska Ferry route begins from Bellingham, Washington, or from Prince Rupert, British Columbia, to Haines or Skagway, Alaska; from here one can continue by auto or bus. The distance from Haines to Anchorage is about 750 miles.

Ferry reservations are required for both automobiles and passengers. It is recommended that reservations be placed well in advance of planned travel, especially during the summer months. On the summer schedule (subject to change), a ferry departs from Bellingham on Tuesday and Friday, arriving at Haines and Skagway on Saturday and Monday. The southward sailing is on Monday and Saturday, to arrive in Bellingham on Friday and Tuesday.

The Prince Rupert to Haines and Skagway summer schedule is currently five days weekly, in both directions. At Haines and Skagway, a shuttle bus to town meets all ferries at the terminal. The Haines Visitor Bureau can be reached at (907) 766-2234 or (800) 458-3579. For current ferry schedules, reservations, and rates, contact Alaska Marine Highway, P.O. Box 25535, Juneau, AK 99802; (907) 465-3941 or (800) 642-0066; in Canada call (800) 665-6414. Information is also available in Bellingham at (206) 676-8445 and in Prince Rupert at (604) 627-1744. Tickets may be purchased at the ferry terminals of departure or in Anchorage at 4th Street and C.

Connecting Bus Service

The Alaskan Express (Grey Line of Alaska) leaves Haines four times weekly in spring and summer for both Anchorage and Fairbanks, from where connections can be made to Denali National Park and Preserve. The return bus leaves both Anchorage and Fairbanks four times weekly. Allow two days for this bus transit. There is also connecting bus service via Skagway and Whitehorse. For current schedules and prices, call (907) 277-5581 or (800) 544-2206 (both in the U.S. and Canada).

Alaska Direct Busline connects Whitehorse, Anchorage, and Fairbanks, with connections to Skagway and Haines. This busline also serves the Anchorage–Talkeetna–Denali National Park–Fairbanks route. For information call (800) 770-6652; (907) 277-6652 in Anchorage; or (403) 668-4833 in Whitehorse.

Alaska Denali Transit currently serves Haines, Anchorage, Talkeetna, Denali National Park and Preserve, and Fairbanks by van service; for information, call (907) 276-6443.

The Alaska Railroad

The Alaska Railroad links Anchorage, Talkeetna, Denali National Park and Preserve, and Fairbanks. Current schedules and price information can be obtained by writing to P.O. Box 107500, Anchorage, AK 99510; (907) 265-2494 (Anchorage), (907) 456-4155 (Fairbanks), or (800) 544-0552. Local ticket offices are at 411 West 1st Avenue in Anchorage and at 280 North Cushman Street in Fairbanks.

As of this writing, the schedule from May through September is as follows: Leaving Anchorage station at 8:30 A.M. daily, arrive at Talkeetna at 11:30 A.M., arrive at Denali National Park and Preserve at 3:45 P.M., and arrive at Fairbanks at 8:30 P.M; leaving Fairbanks at 8:30 A.M. daily, arrive at Denali National Park and Preserve at 12:15 P.M., arrive at Talkeetna at 4:15 P.M., and arrive at Anchorage at 8:30 P.M. In winter, trains operate twice weekly. Current fares are as follows: Anchorage to Talkeetna, $69; Anchorage to Denali National Park and Preserve, $85; Anchorage to Fairbanks, $115; Fairbanks to Denali National Park and Preserve, $45; and Fairbanks to Talkeetna, $66.

It should be noted that passengers must have reservations or board on a standby basis. Bicycles can be taken provided space allows.

Crews building the Alaska Railroad began work in 1917 after the completion of surveying the line, pushing up the Susitna River valley and through its canyon. Two years later, in 1919, the rails reached Talkeetna. That same year Alfred Brooks assisted in study of the Nenana River valley with Alaska and Interior Department officials. At Nenana, at milepost 411.7, on July 15, 1923, President Warren G. Harding drove the golden spike that signified the completion of the historic transportation corridor.

Anchorage to Talkeetna Transportation

ERA Aviation operates a regular shuttle flight between Anchorage and Talkeetna; call (907) 243-3300 or (800) 426-0333 for current schedules and rates. Other air services at Anchorage and Talkeetna can make charter flights (see Air Services section later in this chapter).

For van service, try one of the following: Denali Overland Transportation, P.O. Box 330, Talkeetna, AK 99676; (907) 733-2384 (also serves Denali National Park and Preserve); or Tri-River Charter, P.O. Box 312, Talkeetna, AK 99676; (907) 733-2384. Current prices are $40 each way, including equipment, but be sure to contact a service for the latest price information.

Anchorage Resources

It should be noted that the Anchorage International Airport is located six miles from downtown and that visitor facilities and resources are somewhat scattered.

The Alaska Public Lands Information Center (National Park Service) is located in the Old Federal Building, 605 West 4th Avenue, Anchorage, AK 99501. Map sales are in room G 84; for telephone information, call (907) 271-2737. During the summer months, this information center is open seven days a week, 9:00 A.M. to 7:00 P.M.

The Anchorage Visitor Information Center is located at 527 West 4th Avenue; (907) 274-3531 (open daily June through August). For general Alaska information, contact Alaska Division of Tourism, P.O. Box E, Juneau, AK 99811; (907) 465-2010.

There are many accommodations in Anchorage, the most reasonable of which is the International AYH Hostel at 700 H Street; (907) 276-3635.

Some expeditions bring food to Alaska, especially freeze-dry items. Food purchases in Alaska are best made in the larger population centers, such as Anchorage, Palmer, Wasilla, and Fairbanks.

Mountaineering and backpacking equipment can be found at Alaska Mountaineering and Hiking, 2633 Spenard Road, Anchorage, AK 99503; (907) 272-1811; or R.E.I., 1200 West Northern Lights Boulevard; Anchorage, AK 99503; (907) 272-4565.

FM radio rentals can be made at Surveyor's Exchange, P.O. Box 111037, Anchorage, AK 99511; (907) 345-6500.

Fairbanks Resources

The Fairbanks Visitor Bureau is located at 550 1st Avenue; (907) 456-5774 or (800) 327-5774. Maps can be found at U.S. Geological Survey, 101 12th Avenue, Fairbanks, AK 99701; (907) 456-0244. The Fairbanks Youth Hostel is located at 2895 Mack Road; (907) 479-2034. Mountaineering and backpacking equipment can be found at All Weather Sports, 3875 Geist Road, Fairbanks, AK 99709; (907) 474-8184.

Maps

Mount McKinley National Park and Preserve (1:250,000)—U.S. Geological Survey

Mount McKinley (1:250,000): Maps A2 and A3 include Mount McKinley; Maps A3 and A4 include Mount Foraker; Map A2 includes Ruth Gorge (all 1:63,500)

Talkeetna (1:250,000): Maps D3 and D4 include Mount Foraker; Maps D2 and D3 include Mount Hunter; Map D2 includes Mount Huntington and Ruth Gorge; Map D4 includes Mount Russell; Map C3 includes Little Switzerland; Map B6 includes the Kichatna Spires (all 1:63,500)

U.S. Geological Survey maps are available from Map Distribution Center, Denver Federal Center, Denver, CO 80225. Maps are also available at regional offices in Anchorage and Fairbanks, at some outdoor retail stores, and at National Park Service offices at Denali National Park and Preserve and Talkeetna. Mount McKinley (1:50,000—showing climbing routes) by Bradford Washburn and the Museum of Science (Boston) and aerial photographs are available from Museum of Science, Science Park, Boston, MA 02114; (617) 723-2500. This map is also available in Anchorage, Fairbanks, Talkeetna, and Denali National Park and Preserve.

The George Parks Highway

The George Parks Highway connects Anchorage and Fairbanks (358 miles) to Denali National Park and Preserve at 237 miles from Anchorage. The exit to Talkeetna is at ninety-nine miles (fourteen miles more on spur road to Talkeetna); the Petersville road exits at milepost 115 (this rough and narrow road extends thirty-three miles to mining and homestead locations and wilderness backpacking). Denali State Park flanks the highway southeast of Denali National Park and Preserve; it is essentially a wilderness with some fifty miles of hiking trails.

Denali National Park and Preserve

The headquarters of Denali National Park and Preserve can be written at P.O. Box 9, Denali National Park, AK 99755; (907) 683-2294. The Visitor Access Center, which can provide information on campground permits, can be reached at (907) 683-1266.

The Visitor Access Center, Riley Creek campground, and Denali Park Hotel are located a short distance on the branch road into the Park. At 1.4 miles on this road there is a gas station and grocery store, and at 1.6 miles is the Alaska Railroad station.

To register for camping, go to the Visitor Access Center (there are seven campgrounds within the Park; four of these are for tents only). Reservations for campgrounds cannot be made by mail or phone.

Denali National Park Road

Private automobiles are allowed on the first fifteen miles of the ninety-one-mile Denali National Park road. Tour and shuttle buses provide visitor transportation during the summer season. Shuttle buses start at the Visitor Access Center (allow eight to ten hours round trip to Wonder Lake). The shuttle bus is free, but there is a small Park entrance fee. Bicycles are permitted on Park roads; users are requested to check with the Visitor Access Center.

Polychrome Pass (3,700 feet) is reached at milepost 46 on the Park road. Huge alluvial fans resulting from Pleistocene Ice Age glacier meltwater flows are visible here. There is an extensive alpine tundra and wildflower area. One may see the Toklat grizzly, Dall sheep, and caribou on the tundra and golden eagles soaring on thermal currents.

Eielson Visitor Center is located at milepost 66 on the Park road. One passes near the terminus of Muldrow Glacier at milepost 71 and arrives at the Wonder Lake campground at milepost 84. The ranger station is two miles farther, and the road-end (milepost 91) is at Kantishna—an old mining town.

BACKPACKING

Back-country permits must be obtained in person at the Backcountry Desk at Eielson Visitor Center. These permits can be obtained a day in advance (no charge) and must be obtained for overnight hiking. Note that some areas are restricted to protect the wildlife habitat, and these are subject to change.

Camping is not allowed within ½ mile or in sight of the Park road and developed areas. Minimum impact is encouraged. Campfires are not permitted in most sections of the Park. A stove and fuel are recommended, and water should be treated by boiling or filtering.

Hikers should note that the landscape's scale is enormous. Because of spongy tundra, brush, and riverbar travel, even hiking five miles per day can be tiring. Plan a route carefully and study maps. Because much of the Park is above treeline, navigation is often easy, but river crossings may be difficult and dangerous. For such fords, select wide, gravelly spots, and cross where the stream is divided into several channels, if possible. Choose a crossing that offers a retreat. A ski pole or long pole is very helpful in keeping balance. Release the pack's waist strap and be ready to jettison it if necessary.

When crossing streams, wear tennis shoes, neoprene booties, or boots without socks (never cross barefoot). During crossings, seal off clothing and sleeping bag in watertight plastic bags. At a difficult crossing, angle downstream, and use a pole or link arms for more steadiness; a triangular link that points upstream or a huddle formation are other methods used in crossings.

Hikes

Numerous hikes are possible within the Park; these are covered in detail on maps, in hiking books, and at visitor and ranger stations. Four hikes are listed here.

Eielson Visitor Center Ridge is a popular and easy 2-mile walk with stunning views; begin at 65.2 miles on the Park road.

For experienced hikers, the hike to Toklat River is a several-day round trip from Eielson Visitor Center. The route crosses a glacier, so a rope and mountain boots should be taken.

The Polychrome Trail loop from Polychrome Pass (six miles, moderately difficult) involves tundra vistas, some stream fords, and possible bear sightings.

Historic McGonagall Pass (5,720 feet) is a scenic three-to-four-day round trip (approximately forty-five miles) that ends near Muldrow Glacier. Begin this hike near Wonder Lake. Crossing the McKinley River is not for novices: there are numerous cold and swift channels to ford.

Fishing

Suspended silt from glacier runoff is difficult for fish to tolerate and, of course, interferes with fishing. Arctic grayling can be caught in a few clear streams, and lake trout may be caught in some lakes. No license is needed to fish within the Park, but other restrictions do apply. Obtain a current copy of fishing rules and regulations at the Visitor Access Center.

Camping and Food Storage

Always keep a clean camp and carry out all trash. Camp must be made 100 feet or more from any water source. Avoid camping on animal trails, on riverbars, and in thick brush or near berry patches. Use double-layer plastic bags to pack food, because this reduces odors. Never store food in tents, and sleep well away from food storage and the cooking area. It is important that bears do not learn to associate humans with food. Bear-resistant food containers are required in most Park backpacking areas; obtain these free of charge at the Visitor Access Center.

Bears

It is estimated that there are about 35,000 brown and grizzly bears and 50,000 black bears in Alaska. Grizzlies once occupied a vast range from the central United States to the West Coast, but now nearly all are found in Canada and Alaska. The Far North is one of the last places on earth where a healthy grizzly population still exists.

When sighting a grizzly from a distance, move slowly, pray, and get away quietly. Avoid surprising a grizzly. Keep your distance (use a telephoto lens for photography). If visibility is limited, shouting or singing or ringing a bell will help alert a bear of your presence. In this case a bear will usually run off before a party notices its presence.

When moving, travel in pairs and remain alert. Grizzly tracks are unmistakable, with the five-toed footprint and claws extending well beyond the toes. Leave an area if you notice tracks, droppings, or dead animals.

Avoid thick brush areas, both on the upland tundra and along riverbars. If you do encounter a bear, never run away. Make a noise, but do not approach the animal. Remain calm. If you are charged, do not run. Wave your arms and stand facing the bear. Most bear charges are bluffs, and the bear will likely stop, turn, and run off. As a last resort, drop to the ground, lie face-down, and play dead. Bear attacks on humans are usually a result of the bear feeling threatened. By playing dead during an approach, you may alleviate that threat.

Defensive aerosol sprays have been used with some success for bear protection at a range of six to eight yards. Do not discharge these sprays against the wind.

MOUNT MCKINLEY AND DENALI NATIONAL PARK AND PRESERVE EXPEDITION, GUIDE, AND SUPPORT SERVICES

Guide Services

Alaska Denali Guiding (Brian Okonek), P.O. Box 326, Talkeetna, AK 99676; (907) 733-2649; FAX (907) 733-1362.

American Alpine Institute, 1212 24th Street, Bellingham, WA 98225; (206) 671-1505.

Fantasy Ridge Alpinism (Mike Covington), P.O. Box 1629, Telluride, CO 81435; (303) 728-3546; FAX (303) 728-3546.

Mountain Trip (Gary Bocarde), P.O. Box 91161, Anchorage, AK 99509; (907) 345-6499.

Rainier Mountaineering, 535 Dock Street, Tacoma, WA 98402; (206) 627-6242; FAX (206) 627-1280.

National Outdoor Leadership School, Box AA, Lander, WY 82502; (307) 332-6973.

Support Services

Denali Dog Tours and Wilderness Freighters (dogsled support), P.O. Box 670, Denali National Park, AK 99755; (907) 683-2644.

Sheldon Mountain House (at 5,710 feet, one mile west of Mount Barrille;

reservations are required), P.O. Box 292, Talkeetna, AK 99676; (907) 733-2414.

Air Services

Doug Geeting Aviation, P.O. Box 42, Talkeetna, AK 99676; (907) 733-2366.
Hudson Air Service, P.O. Box 82, Talkeetna, AK 99676; (907) 733-2321.
K2 Aviation, P.O. Box 545, Talkeetna, AK 99676; (907) 733-2291.
Talkeetna Air Taxi, P.O. Box 73, Talkeetna, AK 99676; (907) 733-2218.

As of 1992, round-trip flights, including gear (no baggage limit for most expeditions) cost the following: Kahiltna Glacier, $230 per person; Ruth Glacier, $200 per person; and Little Switzerland, $210 per person. The Kahiltna base camp fee was $5 per person. Anchorage to Talkeetna flights (maximum three persons with gear) were $345 per trip.

Air services usually can rent CB radios (in 1991, $50), sleds ($5), and Coleman fuel ($8 per gallon). It should be noted that the portable CB radios (2½ pounds) can generally contact radio operators at the Kahiltna base camp and on Ruth Glacier. They may also communicate with the National Park Service and with radio operators at the 14,300-foot ranger camp, in Talkeetna, in aircraft, in homes with radio, in trucks, and at visitor centers. The ranger station and all glacier-flying services monitor CB radios during flight. The air services operate a joint radio telephone and CB set at the Kahiltna base camp. It is recommended that climbers use the channel 19 crystal on the south flank and the channel 7 crystal on the north flank of Mount McKinley.

Weather Service

The Anchorage forecast number is (907) 936-2525 or (907) 271-5105. Continuous VHF radio transmissions are available from Anchorage and can be received over most of the Cook Inlet region and at times on Mount McKinley and peaks of the Alaska Range. The broadcast frequency for Anchorage is 162.55 megaHertz (most VHF weather radios can receive this frequency).

Talkeetna Resources

The Talkeetna Ranger Station is staffed from April to September and can be contacted at P.O. Box 588, Talkeetna, AK 99676; (907) 733-2231; FAX (907) 733-1465.

Accommodations include the following: Fairview Inn, (907) 733-2423; Latitude 62°, (907) 733-2262; Swiss Alaska Inn, (907) 733-2424; Talkeetna Motel, (907) 733-2323; and Talkeetna Roadhouse, (907) 733-2341. Campsites are also available. The K2 bunkhouse, with kitchen and shower, was $11 per person in 1993.

River trips can be scheduled with the following: Denali Floats, P.O. Box 330, Talkeetna, AK 99676; (907) 733-2384; Up the Creek, P.O. Box 31, Talkeetna, AK 99676; (907) 733-2601; and Talkeetna River Boat, Village Arts and Crafts, (907) 733-2281.

Talkeetna is renowned for its excellent fishing spots; ask the locals for some of their favorites.

COSTS, TRENDS, AND STATISTICS

As of this writing, it has been estimated that the typical Mount McKinley mountaineer spends $2,000 to 3,500, not counting equipment purchases. Food and community equipment usually amount to $300 to 400 each (if food is purchased at Carr's in Anchorage, it runs about $160 each). Motel charges, taxis, and rental cars are other possible costs. Allow at least $40 a person or more to travel from Anchorage to Talkeetna and roughly $230 for the round trip flight to base camp. Guides, if used, will cost about another $1,500. It is wise to research the latest price information prior to arrival.

▲▲▲

One analysis showed that most guided clients are male, American, white-collar professionals with almost no experience at high-altitude climbing. Most of them are seeking a great adventure, perhaps the biggest in their lives. Rather than spending years accomplishing the mountaineering arts and then making the ascent, a guided climb is the sensible answer to what one guide has stated is the test of a lifetime. There are no guarantees of reaching the summit, of course, and guides can really only promise high adventure.

Because the new age of Mount McKinley mountaineering depends on bush pilots for quick access, perhaps ninety-eight percent of the parties begin at Talkeetna, which has taken over the role of staging area. The northern approaches offer special challenges because a party cannot use aircraft for either a supply drop or landing. The approach from Wonder Lake must be made either by skis, by snowshoes, or on foot—though one can use a dog team for packing in the early season.

▲▲▲

With over 7,000 persons now having ascended Mount McKinley, it seems in order to review briefly the changes in popularity and trends. American mountaineers pioneered the mountain, and the first European ascent was by a Spanish party in 1952 (the ninth ascent). The first Japanese ascent came in 1960 (the sixteenth ascent).

Except for 1976, the number of climbers has increased steadily since the early 1970s. In 1973 the summit was reached by more than 100 climbers. By 1975 there were more than 400 attempts, and by 1992 there were 1,070 attempts.

A profile in the 1984 *American Alpine Journal* provided the following insights: The typical group size on the mountain is five members, and the success rate is forty-six percent. Guided parties account for twenty-five percent of the total numbers on the mountain.

The average age of the Mount McKinley climber is twenty-eight, and eighty-nine percent are male. Of these climbers, sixty-five percent come from North America, twenty-five percent from Europe, and ten percent from the Far East. Between 1903 and 1988, there were 7,354 American climbers, 919 Japanese, 411 Germans, 277 Swiss, 248 Canadian, 202 French, 172 Austrian, and 158 British. A tabulation by the National Park Service indicated that in 1990 some twenty-nine nations were represented.

One may wonder why Mount McKinley is so popular with the Japanese and Koreans. The reasons include the relative geographic proximity, the strength of their currencies against the U.S. dollar, and appropriate vacation time (most Alaskan visits last about one month).

A few statistics from the year 1989 are relevant. Of a total number of 1,009 climbers, 524 were successful. On May 13 there were 367 climbers on the mountain's slopes. The West Buttress had the most climbers (eighty-five percent), and the West Rib was second in popularity. Foreigners accounted for thirty-six percent of the climbers and, overall, twenty-six percent were guided.

On the darker side, fifty-four climbers reported frostbite with hospitalizations. Twenty-three climbers had severe acute mountain sickness, with another twenty-three moderate cases.

MOUNTAINEERING REQUIREMENTS AND SUGGESTIONS ON MOUNT MCKINLEY AND MOUNT FORAKER

When organizing an expedition, and before arrival in Alaska, choose an expedition or group name. Use this name on all correspondence, for all liaisons, with support services, and for radio communications. The National Park Service and all air services monitor with this group name. The wisdom of this policy will make immediate sense when a team joins the parade on the mountain and makes radio calls.

The current mountaineering regulations are simple and are really for the benefit of all concerned. Each climber must register at a National Park Service ranger station (Talkeetna or Denali National Park and Preserve headquarters) before leaving for an ascent and check in upon returning. During climbing registration, one can expect a brief but graphic film presentation that depicts the perils of combat at the high Alaskan altitudes. This required viewing likely has its cynics but probably has never dissuaded anyone from carrying out an expedition plan.

For other peaks within Denali National Park and Preserve or in the Alaska Range, parties are requested, but not required, to check in and check out. Rescue insurance may be required in the future.

The Talkeetna Ranger Station is staffed from April to September. The address is P.O. Box 588, Talkeetna, AK 99676; (907) 733-2231; FAX (907) 733-1465. The other mountaineering entry is at Denali National Park and Preserve, P.O. Box 9, Denali National Park, AK 99755; (907) 683-2294. Recorded National Park information (updated) is given at (907) 683-2686.

EQUIPMENT AND CLOTHING

The choice of climbing rope (from nine to eleven millimeters in diameter and 120 to 165 feet in length) varies among climbers and the nature of the ascent route. In any event there should be ample spacing between climbers (at least fifty feet). It is vital that each climber carry ascenders and is attached to them so that these mechanisms will operate efficiently. Be certain that you can use an ascender while wearing gloves. Each climber should bring a minimum of one locking carabiner, five standard carabiners, and three webbing slings, rescue slings with footloops, a pulley, and prusik-knot loops or Jumar-type ascenders. The climbing harness should have a chest-harness capability or adaptation. It is a wise plan to practice crevasse rescue methods before reaching base camp; any fall into a crevasse is potentially a serious problem.

Dome-shaped tents with three- to four-person capacity are used by at least eighty percent of expeditions. This shape is the most stable, is the least likely to drift in, and has the most interior space. Any tent used at high altitudes in the Alaska Range must be first class and be able to withstand eighty-mile-per-hour winds. When encountering extremely windy conditions, a good choice is to build an igloo or snow cave rather than rely on a tent.

Take two aluminum shovels for a four-person party, and two snow saws for snow wall, cave, and igloo construction.

It is suggested that an expedition carry 50 to 100 wands of four feet in length for the most used routes (take more [100–200] for routes that have not seen a party during the season visited). Some wands should be double-length or bound together to mark caches. Wands are especially useful in poor visibility and to mark dangerous crevasse areas.

The suggested ice axe length is seventy or more centimeters. This length is useful for glacier walking, crevasse probing, and rope anchoring. Use an ice axe with a regular alpine pick.

Plastic sleds are standard usage for load-shuttling on glacier approaches. One person can pull a thirty- to forty-pound load with little difficulty on gradual slopes. Tie sleds into the climbing rope (using a prusik-knot loop) behind you, not to the individual climber. In this manner, as the rope becomes taut after a fall, the sled will stop and remain suspended above the fallen climber. It is most comfortable to sled-haul with separate lines clipped to carabiners at the back of one's pack.

All mountaineers undertaking Mount McKinley, Mount Foraker, or Mount Hunter should plan on using either skis or snowshoes for the lower glaciers; snowshoes are the best choice for individuals of unequal skiing ability. If using skis, bring climbing skins. Regardless of the equipment used, always carry a set of ski poles for balance; however, one ice axe and one ski pole may be more suitable on steep terrain.

The flexible type of crampon is best for the West Buttress and Muldrow Glacier routes and the rigid type for the more technical routes.

Despite their proven warmth, the military-type ("bunny") vapor-barrier boot has been largely replaced by the insulated plastic double-boot (with either overboots or supergaiters). In April and May it is recommended that climbers wear a fully insulated overboot that completely covers the boot sole. Keep in mind that it will be necessary to adjust crampons and strap fittings so that the boot and overboot fit snugly (always perform this fitting before you arrive at a glacier base camp).[327]

For maximum warmth and comfort, socks should be layered, usually in a thinnest-to-thickest fashion. Begin with a synthetic layer, followed optionally by a vapor-barrier sock. Vapor-barrier socks can be dangerous, especially after feet have perspired heavily and are then subjected to extremely cold temperatures. The outer layers should be heavy wool, or blended wool and synthetic.

Keep in mind that frequent sock changes and keeping socks and feet dry at night are most important. It is a wise procedure to test out the boot, overboot, gaiter, and sock system before beginning an expedition. Consider wearing a light "half" gaiter on the lower glaciers—just sufficient to keep snow out of the boots—and saving dry overboots for the colder, higher altitudes.

It is important that clothing units fit in a practical manner and that they can be readily altered in amount. Patience can be severely tested by clothing system adjustments needed because of temperature changes brought on by sunny periods followed by snow squalls and by the wind's variance from calm periods to gusts that may knock you down. All of this may occur within an hour. While some clothing combinations seen on Mount McKinley recently seem like sartorial indulgences, the styles all relate to a good fit and a layering system that permits freedom of motion as well as easy adjustment.

A useful lower-body combination is synthetic or wool underwear, pile pants, and water-repellant bibs or wind overpants (be certain this outer unit has full side zippers so that it can be donned and removed over boots and crampons).

For the upper body, various synthetic and wool combinations, including a pile sweater, are favorites. The windproof jacket should have a good-fitting hood and roomy, easily accessible pockets. A down or synthetic-fill parka with hood is the final outer layer (be certain that it fits over all other apparel). Remember to tie long nylon loops through all zipper pulls to facilitate operation with gloves.

Alaska mountaineering clothing is incomplete without a good balaclava hat and neoprene face mask, light finger gloves, pile or wool mittens (always carry a spare set), and long-sleeved insulated mittens.

A clear or amber "snow" goggle is important in blizzards and drifting snow; a visor hat with a scarf reduces sunburn and reduces glare at the lower altitudes. Sunglasses must have side-shields to minimize glare (carry a spare set per group). The intensity of burning rays on a glacier, even on a cloudy, snowy, or foggy day, is so great that protection is mandatory. Apply sunscreen and lip chapstick regularly; keep applying sunscreen to sensitive skin areas, as one sweats it off.

Pack selection is generally guided by individual choice, but a large-capacity internal-frame pack is used by most mountaineers.

A three-pound (1.4-kilogram) sleeping bag of down with a water-repellant cover is the general choice; however, take precautions to prevent the down from becoming wet. A synthetic-fill bag is also good, but the fill has a lower loft-to-weight ratio. Vapor-barrier liners are often added for sleeping bag warmth. Bring both a good foam-filled inflatable air mattress and a closed-cell foam pad as a backup and for additional insulation.

Carry two stoves for four people and bring spare parts. Many climbers feel that a stove with a fuel pump is essential for pressurization due to the cold.

If a butane (cartridge) stove is taken, figure one cartridge per day for two persons. One advantage of these stoves is that they can be hung in the tent ceiling and are spill-proof, but butane stoves need prewarming under a jacket or in a sleeping bag for about ten minutes. Once heated, the boiling time is nearly the same as a good gasoline stove. Remember to carry down all disposable cartridges. Take sufficient fuel to burn at least two hours daily. Plan to carry one-quarter to one-half pints of fuel per person per day—this is to provide three to four quarts of water daily for each individual. Should a storm or illness occur, it is imperative to have sufficient fuel.

An Alaskan mountaineering party should carry two nesting pots (1½- to 2½-quart capacity) for each cooking group; bring pot grips and pocket lighters.

A repair kit should include pliers, wire, patching material, glue, tent-pole repair items, extra stove parts, duct tape, and a sewing kit.

A mosquito net is an essential addition if one plans any tundra or forest entry or exit during the bug season.

A portable CB radio is highly recommended for any expedition in the Alaska Range. These radios have saved many lives and reduced injuries by allowing prompt calls for assistance. These CB radios are line-of-sight. Consequently, their usefulness depends on a party's position: they generally do not work well below 14,000 feet on Mount McKinley but may be efficient on other mountains at a lower altitude. Fortunately, messages are often relayed by other expeditions on Mount McKinley and nearby peaks—instilling a sense of camaraderie into the chilly and often lonely wilderness. It is recommended to use an external battery pack that can be kept warm next to the body (warm the batteries before using). It is also wise to carry spare batteries.

Channels 19 and 11 are the most commonly used; channels 7 and 19 may be monitored on the north flanks of Mount McKinley and Mount Foraker. It is suggested that expeditions review radio procedures with the Kahiltna Glacier base camp operator or their air service.

MEDICAL KIT

The following items for a medical kit that is portable and practical provide treatment for a party of four to six climbers. Such a kit requires that a party have some wilderness skills of improvisation; it is not feasible or reasonable, for example, for a party to carry an entire selection of splints, stretchers, or surgical kits. An experienced party should be able to improvise the former two items and accept the risk of the absence of the latter. The party must also have the knowledge of how and when to use medications and not just the ability to carry them up and down the mountain. If this knowledge is not available within the party, then a person well versed in wilderness and altitude medicine should be sought for advice. The following items are covered on a "systems" basis. These items can easily be fit into a small stuff bag and add less than a couple of pounds to a rucksack.

Item	Use
Benadryl	Allergies, sleep
Phenergan	Nausea, vomiting
Ibuprofen	Headache, muscle aches and pains, burns
Afrin	Nasal congestion
Codeine	Painkiller, cough suppressant
Decadron	Severe AMS or HACE
Diamox	AMS prevention or treatment
Keflex or similar	Antibiotic
Ophthalmic ointment	Snow blindness
Labiosan	Lip protection
Immodium	Diarrhea
Polysporin ointment	Skin infections and prevention
Sun block	Sunburn prevention
Throat lozenges	Sore throat

Other items

Gauze, bandages, pads
Adhesive tape
Suture kit
Space blanket
SAM splint
Thermometer
Small scissors
Spare sunglasses
Safety pins

Skin problems include sunburn and infections. Prudent and liberal use of one or several of the excellent sunscreens on all exposed parts of the body is essential. Infections include bacterial ones that are usually secondary to trauma (abrasions, cuts) and should initially be treated with topical antibiotics (e.g., Neosporin) and dressings. If the infection worsens, then an antibiotic that will treat staph infections is necessary. Infections of covered areas are usually fungal and often occur in areas of heat and moisture—the groin, armpits, or feet. They can be prevented by careful attention to drying off at the end of the day, rotating clothing, and using cornstarch or body powder. Antifungal creams or powders (Desinex, mycosatin) are also available once an irritating infection has set in.

Eye problems include corneal abrasions, conjunctivitis, and corneal sunburn. Gauze eyepatches and ophthalmologic steroid and antibiotic ointment should suffice for all of the preceding problems.

Adequate numbers of sterile 4x4s and 2x2s, Kerlex or Clings, and a couple of 4" Ace bandages are required. A good antibacterial soap or small bottle of betadine surgical soap should also be taken. Cloth slings are useful for many purposes, and the party can decide whether or not they feel comfortable and knowledgeable to carry and use a small suture setup.

Upper respiratory infections and/or irritation from the cold, thin air can be treated with throat lozenges, cough suppressants, nasal sprays (e.g., Afrin), systemic decongestants (such as Actifed or Sudafed), and antihistamines for people with allergies.

Lower respiratory problems include bronchitis and pneumonia. The former can often be treated symptomatically with some of the above-mentioned items, but if the cough develops into a productive one with thick or yellow sputum, there is a possibility of pneumonia developing, in which case antibiotics are necessary. Depending on allergies, prescription drugs such as ampicillin, amoxicillin, Septra, and second-generation cephalosporin are all useful. Individuals with asthma should have their own personal drugs available.

Gastrointestinal problems may include heartburn, diarrhea, or constipation. The former is best treated by simple antacids. Immodium or Lomotil are effective for treating diarrhea that may be incapacitating. The latter is usually a blessing but can be avoided with good hydration and treated with milk of magnesia tablets.

Urinary tract infections in women are a common problem. The symptoms can be treated immediately with Pyridium, and the infection with an antibiotic (a second-generation cephalosporin can cover respiratory, urinary tract, and most skin infections).

Tylenol, aspirin, or Tylenol with codeine usually is enough for pain. If a more potent pain reliever is sought, then a prescription for injectable morphine or Demerol is necessary.

Some individuals are known to be susceptible to altitude illness (acute mountain sickness [AMS], high-altitude pulmonary edema [HAPE], and high-altitude cerebral edema [HACE]). The best treatment is prevention by slow ascent to allow time for acclimatization. Those who often get sick should take low doses of Diamox (125 mg twice a day) for prevention. This drug is also effective for treatment of symptoms once they start and helps to prevent the irregular breathing that often occurs at night in sojourners who ascend quickly. Decadron (steroid) prevents and treats AMS and HACE but should be reserved for people who are very ill, particularly in rescue situations when getting a person ambulatory may make the difference between life and death. In climbers who have had HAPE in the past, nifedipine prevents its development. All of these drugs are prescription drugs. For more information on altitude sickness, see chapter 20, "High-Altitude Medical Problems."

Sleeping pills are not recommended: as a respiratory depressant, they can invite HAPE.

FOOD

An expedition should figure a menu with 4,000 to 5,000 calories per person per day. Before leaving for base camp, repackage food into plastic bags to minimize packaging garbage on the glaciers. Plan a base camp food cache and mark it for identity. Remember, extra food is important, especially during storm waits.

Very popular for lunch snacks is gorp—a mix of nuts, chocolate chips, raisins, sunflower seeds, and candies. Cookies and figbars have a relatively high caloric count per pound and are a morale booster.

While high-calorie snacks give an energy boost during the day, when this is needed most, some thought should be given to breakfast (usually the dullest meal). Certainly include cocoa and coffee for the morning drink. A thermos with a hot drink is excellent for restoring energy. Insulate water and sugary drinks to prevent them from freezing.

For dinners, freeze-dry foods are good because they can be prepared quickly and are lightweight. Also, pasta, rice, and cereals are nutritious and easy to prepare. Soup, tea, cocoa, milk, and powdered fruit drinks are excellent supplements. It is important to drink four or more quarts of fluid daily to help rehydrate from fluid loss due to strenuous exercise in the dry, high, and cold atmosphere. This fluid intake reduces the risk of exhaustion, altitude sickness, and frostbite.

Above 14,000 feet in altitude, use a high-carbohydrate diet. At the lower altitudes, fats and proteins are usually not difficult to digest, and such items as cheese, butter, peanut butter, and nuts are excellent to ward off the cold. Cakes, meat, and canned fruit are desirable items at the lowest camps.

TRASH AND SANITATION

The leaving of trash appears to be a worldwide phenomenon—one sees glaring examples in former war zones, in the wreckage of auto yards, forgotten manufacturing plants, abandoned mining equipment, oil pipes in a fragile desert, high-altitude mountain camps worldwide, and even scientific cache remnants at Denali Pass on Mount McKinley.

As early as 1913 a pile of "not neededs" were left at 18,000 feet on Mount McKinley. At the time, the party thought nothing of this, reasoning that it would be a long time before others would camp in that grand basin. But this gear will eventually be churned up in the crevasses and moraines of Muldrow Glacier; tins eventually rust, but glass, plastic, and foil do not.

The immensity of the mountain seemed to overwhelm any garbage problem in the first half-century of mountaineering. High winds on the upper slopes reveal trash rather than bury it in the snows and stagnant ice. The waste simply remains. By 1964 the National Park Service enacted new rules for Mount McKinley, an attempt to solve some of the certain aesthetic problems and hopefully bring about a more well-regarded wilderness environment. Between 1973 and 1976 a project evolved to clear the West Buttress of junk dumps, this becoming a stimulus to a greater environmental awareness.

On the mountain, take great care where you obtain snow for melting. Old latrines melt out. For your health and that of others, follow these waste disposal guidelines:

1. Use an existing public pit latrine where available. Otherwise, when making camp, first dig a deep latrine, preferably near a crevasse, or at

least below camp. Mark the pit with wands so it can be found in a storm.

2. Line the hole with a biodegradable plastic bag and stake its corners with wands. In fair weather, doubled paper grocery bags may be used. When not in use, close the top of the bag (use the bag for the entire party).

3. When the bag is full, or when moving camp, tie it off and throw it into a crevasse or return it to base camp for removal from the mountain. On steep routes, shovel the bag off the route.

A few other rules and good practices are as follows:

- Remove fixed lines; they are trash.
- When leaving a camp, carry out all trash. Use sleds to tow back non-burnables.
- Do not abandon caches. They become trash.

If an expedition leaves a cache for later usage, mark the location with wands and bury the bags under snow blocks; otherwise, ravens, whose tracks have been seen as high as 18,000 feet, will peck apart food bags and scatter the litter. It is not unusual for two to three feet of snow to melt off at lower elevations during an expedition; therefore, bury bags deeply. Caches in the lowlands and on moraines should be protected or placed in special plastic containers to prevent bears, wolverines, and ravens from breaking into them.

▲ ▲ ▲

CHAPTER 23

The Mount McKinley Experience: What to Expect

Mountaineers who arrive in Alaska's Susitna River lowland for their first Mount McKinley experience may be in for a surprise. As the George Parks Highway courses its way northward along the western flank of the Talkeetna Mountains, the countryside is a boreal forest, with birch predominating. There may be glimpses of the ice-clad Alaska Range, but often Mount McKinley and its alpine court are locked in cloud. If the summits are open, the view from Ski Hill, the last rise before reaching Talkeetna, is simply stunning. Cameras are put to duty, generally focusing with a telephoto lens. After the beginning of June, rampant mosquitoes may well frustrate the photographer.

THE TALKEETNA SPIRIT

Talkeetna is little more than an offbeat village close to the Susitna River and adjacent to a waterlogged muskeg. A turn-of-the-century mining and trapping settlement 114 miles from Anchorage, it has a fluctuating population of some 400, featuring a variety of small businesses that cater to the outdoor trade. Most of them are found in log cabin–style buildings with moose antlers above the doorways. An immediate informality will be apparent: swearing is not unknown, hitchhikers generally obtain rides, dogs have the right-of-way, and anyone wearing a necktie will be greeted with suspicion unless he is a foreigner. Moose (*Alces alces*) wandering in from the forest fringe may leave their prints on the town's few streets, and the mosquitoes will leave their own special impact. More likely, however, the first fauna a visitor will meet is the tail-wagging dog (*Canis familiaris*).

The usual stops of call in the little town are the ranger station, the post office, the trading post (for postcards and bug dope), one of the casual eating spots along the main street, and one of the flight services at the airport, just across the train tracks.

Talkeetna is the past of the gold prospector and now the center of tourist flights and the base for Mount McKinley mountaineers. For local color, the weekend of Miner's Day (in May) and the Moose Dropping Festival (in July) are unforgettable. The celebrants of these events, many who hail from some

Quaint sign greets newcomers at edge of Talkeetna (photo by Jim Balog)

distance, are likely to bring their own accelerating activities onto the street—which may include dancing in the Far North's twilight, the rapid emptying of beer bottles for hydration, and the uttering of various barbaric sounds. More than one moral rule has been broken during these (and other) convivial weekends. But Talkeetna is generally harmless: there tends to be a pretentious rowdyism, but motorcycle gangs and thieves do not find this a welcome destination.

During the frigid season, to thaw Talkeetna's informal mood and expand the short daylight hours of early December, there is the annual Bachelor's Ball and Alaskan Wilderness Woman Contest. The festivities include a Bachelor's Auction—where men are bid upon by women for a drink and dance (up to $30), with proceeds to local charity. One year, a man arrived in a tuxedo—and was bid upon for $140. But dress is usually less formal: one individual came dressed in a rabbit-skin G-string.

During the Wilderness Woman Contest, which has not yet received the press coverage of the 1,049-mile Iditarod dogsled race, some twenty to thirty participants compete in snowshoe and snow-machine races and a "bunny boot" race, mush and feed dogs, clean fish, split wood, and climb a tree to escape a potential moose attack. This event, in which contenders display abilities that might lure an Alaskan bachelor, includes a handicap race—the carrying of filled water buckets on a pole across the shoulders. The winner's reward is a trip to London. The more physically strenuous Outhouse Race is deferred until the warmer time of Miner's Day.

The Fairview Hotel, which can hardly be missed, is probably the most famous in the world for its size (seven rooms and approximately 3,500 square feet on its two floors). During a typical night, dancing in the crowded

Competitors in the Talkeetna Outhouse Race during Miner's Day, May 1984 (photo by Dave Johnston)

barroom takes place, stray ladies from Anchorage have been spotted seeking a climbing guide, and, on occasion, pilot Doug Geeting sings and plays the guitar. Some long-hair types who arrived at the Fairview in the 1970s found a backwoods greeting sign: "Hippies Use Side Door." Walking around to this entry, they found a notice stating, "This Door Locked."

MOUNT McKINLEY BY AIR

About 1,000 mountaineers fly from Talkeetna to Mount McKinley each season, and there are others who seek a glacier landing near Mount Hunter, Mount Huntington, Mount Foraker, or in the Ruth Amphitheatre. There are now eleven ski-equipped aircraft that operate all year, a charter business that was begun by the renowned bush pilot Don Sheldon in 1954 with one Super Cub. Today the usual aircraft for the mountain flights is the Cessna 185, which with its 1,000-pound payload and versatility can normally take three passengers and their gear to the 7,200-foot base camp on Kahiltna Glacier, some forty miles distant.

In May and June there is pressure to get mountaineering parties to base camp, for with the usual time limits and impatience, cloudy and rainy weather are greeted with disdain. The pilots often have to wait in Talkeetna to be on call while waiting for a clearing to fly a party to or from the glacier base camp.

The small, maneuverable aircraft are fitted with skis made of a tough aluminum, some four feet long and about fifteen inches wide. The ski-wheel aircraft's versatility depends on a simple hydraulic system: the pilot uses a double-action pump to manually lower the skis into the low mode for a snowfield or glacier landing. After the mountain takeoff, the skis are pulled up, so as not to interfere with the ground landing (except in winter, when the airstrips are snow-covered).

For a smooth arrival on a snowfield or glacier, it helps if the pilot has a packed runway and markers (only possible if there is an existing strip or a party already on site). The pilot must seek visual clues to determine how far above the surface the craft is. The featureless glacier seems to rapidly "come up" on the aircraft—and here experience is essential, for the pilot with a load must land with full power and flaps down. The rule is, as veteran Jim Okonek of K2 Aviation says, "The steeper the gradient, the shorter the distance for takeoff and landing." To help determine the aircraft's height above the snow at an unmarked glacier landing, Don Sheldon and his successors would often drop alder branches, spruce boughs, or light stuffed sacks to mark the surface.

The takeoff from a glacier, especially on a short runway and with a crevasse field not far distant, can be distinctly frightening. The flying lore is replete with epics of these situations and stuck planes in deep snow. The latter situation is not just the pilot's problem: numerous expeditions have found their first chore after landing was to free the aircraft by pushing, rocking the plane, and holding onto one wing while the engine power and

Ski-wheel aircraft on Ruth Glacier's Great Gorge, near Mooses Tooth and across from Mount Barrille (photo by Jim Okonek, K2 Aviation)

turning technique is used to bring an "about face." Hermann Geiger, the pioneer of Piper Cub flying in the Alps in midcentury, was probably fortunate not to have the deep powder snow of the Alaskan glaciers to contend with for such takeoff epics.

All of the Mount McKinley pilots can tell classic stories about being stuck in deep snow, but none may be more memorable than the events that took place during Bradford Washburn's expedition of 1937 to Mount Lucania in the Icefield Ranges.

Pilot Bob Reeve, flying a single-engine Fairchild 51 equipped with large wooden skis (with stainless steel bases), made three trips in May from the Valdez mudflats to Walsh Glacier to cache equipment at about 8,600 feet. But in mid-June, the glacier landing took place on a very slushy surface—so soft that once out of the aircraft the men plunged through to well above the knees. Reeve refueled and then used ropes tied to the wings and the help of Washburn and Robert Bates to turn the craft about.

All takeoff efforts failed: the plane got forward but soon stuck in the bottomless snow with a wingtip into the slush. Efforts at digging out the plane were to no avail. For four days of rainy weather, Reeve was cooped up with the mountaineers, completely stranded. Fortunately there was enough space in the tent.

On the fifth day, colder air moved in, and a thin crust formed—just enough for Reeve to bring the stranded airplane into motion. There was a brief shout of hope from the mountaineers, but after about 100 feet of travel the plane nosed into a crevasse. But the engine power kept Reeve chugging along—though at a speed too slow to get airborne. For the next mile he bumped along more crevasses, but now a crisis was imminent, for ahead were large crevasses. Finally, in all desperation, Reeve made a sharp turn to the left, applied full power, and, aided by a downslope, dove the Fairchild over a potentially fatal icefall—just in the nick of time. Almost on empty tanks, he made it back to the mudflats to end a miraculous flight.

In 1951 pilot Terris Moore installed aluminum skis on his Super Cub to ferry Washburn's expedition to the West Buttress of Mount McKinley. The skis were smaller and more flexible than Reeve's and were retractable with the use of a hydraulic pump operated within the cabin.

Flight services at Talkeetna have shown a threefold increase in the past few years, mainly because of sightseeing flights. These airlifts are in vogue, mainly through word-of-mouth and because the public feels they are safe. For sightseeing and mountain reconnaissance, the pilots generally use a Cessna 206. The smallest craft, the light Super Cub with its 150-horsepower engine, is favored for limited or uncertain landings on dirt strips, sandbars, and glaciers.

One of the Talkeetna pilots is Doug Geeting, a Californian who once taught aerobatics. Business has been good, and he now owns several Cessna 185s. With almost two decades of experience, he has become a legend as a daring rescue pilot, sometimes landing in zero visibility with no way out or space to turn about.

But as any of Talkeetna's glacier pilots will confirm, flying is somewhat like teaching: one needs to spend two hours in preparation for every hour in the air. There is much boredom before the excitement, and careful maintenance and checkup in the hangar are neverending—none of which the public sees.

Unfortunately, Alaska mountaineering is sometimes accompanied by tragedy. When this occurs, the glacier pilots are usually the first to see the events of grim disaster, either by reconnaissance flights or when being called into a rescue. Lowell Thomas, Jr., tells of the poignant experience he had in the winter of 1984 when he was the last person to talk to Naomi Uemura by CB radio, during his descent from the summit of Mount McKinley on February 12.

Today, flights to Mount McKinley glaciers are largely a legacy of the legendary Don Sheldon, a daring and rugged individualist who made the ski-wheel approach a reality in the 1950s after working with Bradford Washburn on logistics during an extensive mapping project. Sheldon, once a Wyoming ranchhand and cowboy, and who earned a Distinguished Flying Cross in World War II, made some of his most brazen landings on and near the great white mountain. Taking his Super Cub to 14,200 feet on the West Buttress in May 1960, he made a risky landing on a tiny flat area to rescue a woman mountaineer in a coma from cerebral edema. This record-setting mission to save a life padded his fame.

Sheldon's most notable rescue, in July 1955, did not take place on alpine glaciers but in the swirling, dangerous waters of the Susitna River canyon, saving eight men whose fifty-foot boat had broken into pieces.[328] Aware that the U.S. Army Scouts were engaged in a risky boating adventure through Devil's Canyon, Sheldon was curious enough about their safety to make an overflight with his Aeronca Sedan. Some sixty miles above Talkeetna, he sighted wreckage of the yellow raft and gasoline barrels floating in the watercourse. On closer investigation, he saw the men trapped on wet rock ledges of the canyon palisades, seemingly with little hope of escape.

The veteran pilot now faced a dilemma: He knew that a small aircraft does not operate at its manufactured efficiency on water, for the surface designs are made for aeronautics. On floats in a swift current, the craft's efficiency is even less than on the ground. But Sheldon made a quick decision—save the men without waiting for additional help. Carefully gauging his planned upstream landing, he leveled his aircraft against the foaming, thirty-mile-per-hour current. Somehow he managed to keep the nose pointed forward, a difficult tactic while keeping the throttle on full power and while floating rapidly backward. In a skilful tactic with poor cabin visibility, Sheldon powered the Aeronca close to the rock wall, brought one wingtip to the nearest man, and held his position while he could jump onto the pontoon and make his way to the cabin. He then floated 1½ miles downcanyon, carefully keeping pointed upstream until reaching flat water.

Sheldon then returned three times, on each landing picking up two survivors and conducting the same "float" down the Susitna. Later he found and rescued the eighth man, who had been carried far below the canyon in the icy, muddy waters.

Throughout his career, Sheldon relied on what he referred to as "good hunches." This was certainly true in another episode that brought Sheldon into the news, when in winter 1958 a military C-54 transport was overdue while crossing the Alaska Peninsula. Following his "hunches" Sheldon searched the volcano Mount Iliamna with his Super Cub and found the wrecked transport.

Not surprisingly, Sheldon's name is constantly revived. Known for his youthful exuberance and chatty manner, he seemed to thrive on adversity, joking even when he later was faced with a terminal illness. Sheldon gained his early Alaskan flying experience by transporting workers and supplies for the Alaska Road Commission and then, during the sheep season, landing hunters on small sandbars with his Super Cub. The moose season followed: here a challenge was to shove the vital portions of the huge game animal into a small aircraft and still get airborne.

It is said that Sheldon survived thirty-nine crashes in his thirty years of busy bush flying and air-taxi business. He owned forty-five airplanes, most of them wearing out from old age while he logged some 800 hours annually (mostly in a Super Cub or Cessna 180). To mountaineers his flights became legendary, as men and bags of equipment and food were crammed into a small aircraft cabin. Sheldon sometimes created a bit of vaudeville with his looping "cowboy" turns near a serrated rock ridge as he told stories about close encounters.

But the Talkeetna veteran was a master at the controls, and he knew his alpine topography better than did his mountaineering clients. In 1964 I flew through a cloudbank on Ruth Glacier with Sheldon, close to the immense rock walls of the Mooses Tooth while he seemed to defy gravity by hugging the glacier. During momentary glimpses of the glacier gorge walls, I became convinced that we would land on a snow bridge and become stuck—but Sheldon intimately knew the nuances of the terrain better than any of us.

Flights to Mount McKinley became important by the Bicentennial Year; there was much publicity about the great Icy Crown, and climbers arrived in greater numbers. Ray Genet began guiding large groups on the West Buttress, and in the falls and winters he took hunters to search for sheep and moose—all these events giving the pilots considerable business.

After Sheldon's death, Cliff Hudson became the dean of Talkeetna pilots. When both of them were flying, there was considerable rivalry—the subject of regular chitchat. They had their grudges, air buzzings, and once even a tomato-throwing episode (on the ground, of course).

After Sheldon's time, pilot Jim Sharp of K2 Aviation landed a Cessna 185 at 14,300 feet on Mount McKinley for rescues a number of times. While ski-equipped aircraft could land at this spot in good conditions, as Sheldon had demonstrated earlier, the small flat area was hardly ideal for such landings; when rescues are needed, they are now done by helicopter.

The flight to see the Mount McKinley area glaciers is an alien and little-understood "spellbinder" for the usual tourist passenger. Even for many first-time mountaineers, flying close to the great granitic forepeaks can be a traumatic shock. The normal flight path from Tokositna Glacier to Kahiltna Glacier is through One Shot Pass, a 7,450-foot gap (named by Don Sheldon) east of Avalanche Spire. A wise pilot does not aim the nose head-on for the gap because there is a serious downdraft danger with virtually no spare room to turn back between the narrowing rock walls. The name is not inappropriate.

STARTING FROM KAHILTNA BASE CAMP

The Kahiltna Glacier base camp is perhaps the world's most unique of its type. As I flew in for a direct landing with Jim Okonek of K2 Aviation in June 1991 onto the packed-out runway (always done upslope), I counted sixteen markers on each flank—plastic bags wrapped around a wand bundle and rows of red-flagged markers. Colorful tents were dug-in behind snow barricades, and a European party was scurrying about with their packs, readying for the outbound flight.

Operated as a joint air-services arrival, departure, and communications camp, a large weatherport canvas dome structure houses the camp manager and the radio networking equipment. There is a radio–phone link to Talkeetna. The camp manager broadcasts the weather forecast each evening on the CB radio network; depending on topographic interference, the manager may be able to speak to a number of parties on Mount McKinley, Mount Foraker, and Mount Hunter.

Mountaineering parties customarily leave a cache at this base camp for their return, marking and packing it carefully. Almost immediately on leaving with a load for the first camp, each individual is thrust into the labor of packing and load-pulling a heavy sled. During this stage of the West Buttress ascent, one's mind may wander to reflect what slaves en-

Mount Foraker from Kahiltna Glacier camp, April 1973 (photo by Dave Johnston)

dured in Roman and Egyptian times. One consolation for modern against ancient times is that on Alaska's glaciers, the scenery is spiritually rewarding and the labor is not politically forced.

During these laboring sessions, climbers often daydream, replaying favorite basketball and football games and television serials, participating in romances, or reflecting on their friends currently vacationing on a tropical beach. After returning from the West Buttress in 1963, Frances D. Chamberlain, the second woman to climb Mount McKinley, offered a few of her thoughts: "There are certain advantages on this climb, which shouldn't be overlooked to compensate for the hardships. There wasn't a single mosquito or any other bug, no bushwhacking, it doesn't rain (though it may snow plenty), it's clean (no dust or soot) and the world situation and everyday problems are completely forgotten, which affords a certain peace."[329]

The graphic problems of the slow ascent usually begin to strike within a few hours. The glaring sun may blister the skin and chap the lips. Or, if it is cold and windy, one will need to remove the pack and make clothing adjustments. Some advice from the guides and Mount McKinley survivors follows:

1. Begin the expedition with complete rest from travel to Alaska.
2. Always rope up on the glaciers. Keep slack out of the rope, and probe with a ski pole.
3. Even if it is a cloudy day, regularly apply sunscreen and chapstick; cracked lips and a burnt face become more painful in the drier air at higher altitude.
4. If it is sunny, do not strip to shorts and T-shirt; the consequences of a crevasse fall would be chilly.
5. In late June and July, it is safest to travel at night at the lower altitudes; in May, this is not usually necessary.
6. Keep a physiological safety margin against cold and fatigue. Maintain a respectable reserve.

While pulling sleds on skis or snowshoes, it will become evident that the literature and ranger advice has merit: common sense and self-sufficiency is vital to survive and keep healthy on large Alaskan mountains.

It should be remembered that the average relative humidity at the higher altitudes is similar to that of a dry desert region (such as the Colorado Plateau, the Mojave Desert, and the Sahara Desert). The hard work under stress and consequent deep breathing in addition to the dry rarified air (with its diminished oxygen at higher altitude) leads to a serious fluid loss. Adequate fluid intake to replace this loss not only increases personal performance, it is vital to life. Do not skimp on fluids! Dehydration compounds any illness, morale problem, and frostbite. If you do not leave your share of yellow snowspots on the mountain, perhaps you are not taking sufficient fluid. Exceed or a similar preparation is an excellent energy replacement.

When nearing Windy Corner, remember the stories about the possible blowouts and cold. Numerous experts advise parties not to camp between 11,000 and 14,300 feet.

When making camp, anchor all gear, including packs and sleds. An expedition may need to anchor tents with slings and pickets (sometimes even with the climbing rope). Buried stuff sacks, food bags, etc., also make useful tent anchors. Never leave tents unanchored when away from camp.

In addition, be certain to keep shovels away from the tent fly to avoid ripping it. When cooking, be careful while handling fuel; white gasoline is very volatile. Attempt to make a walled kitchen enclosure or use a cook tent pitched over a snow pit for cooking purposes. One danger of cooking in a sealed tent, aside from spilled gasoline, is asphyxiation.

The unceasing nighttime cold in the tent creates a blanket of frost; when the wind strikes, the condensed frost falls on occupants (this is most annoying when one is reading a borrowed book and has promised to keep it clean). Anything not stowed in a sleeping bag at night (especially water and sunscreen) will certainly freeze solid. It is best to keep filled water bottles, covered with duct tape, in an insulated liner or in a sleeping bag. Experienced mountaineers take pains to keep all clothing and gear dry when possible—especially socks, inner boots, and liner gloves, which can be put in sleeping bags; many persons wear their inner boots in the bag when sleeping.

Food caches should be dug three to four feet deep and then marked with a long wand and flag. Place gear bags atop food to discourage the raven forays. Place fuel cans so that they cannot contaminate food should they leak.

When building an igloo or snow-wall blocks, cut the blocks in a rectangular shape, large enough to carry easily. Slide the shovel blade beneath the block to pry it loose, being careful not to exert undue force; shovel blades can break.

EARTHQUAKES AND AVALANCHES

What besides storms, high winds, heavy snowfall, hypothermia, altitude sickness, logistical problems, and poor morale can occur during a Mount McKinley ascent? The answer comes from tectonic forces—the movement of basalts once part of the Pacific Ocean floor, slipping farther into the earth's mantle. During the night of April 30, 1991, an earthquake whose origin was determined to be some seventy miles beneath the earth's surface and some fifty miles southwest of Mount McKinley released energy equal to that of an atomic bomb and rocketed upward at three miles per second. The earthquake registered 6.0 on the Richter scale, jolting the Alaska Range with such force that immense avalanches released and icefalls and cornices collapsed. Not only did the quake break free séracs and create havoc in the mountains, it broke free the Tanana River ice in two hours. Near the epicenter, a witness reported spruce trees lurching to and fro, as if struck by an intense gale.

Southcentral Alaska is one of the world's most earthquake-prone regions. As the North American continental plate slides over the North Pacific oceanic plate, forcing it deeper into the mantle, the forces become incalculable. The compressional shock waves from tremors that night jolted millions of tons of ice loose from Mount McKinley and neighboring peaks. Cornices that stood seemingly as permanent fixtures quickly collapsed and sped their chaos downslope.

At the time, some 250 climbers were in the area. Ann Lowry, manager of Kahiltna Glacier base camp, reported that "spindrift" clouds of pulverized ice crystals driven by high winds pounded the camp for a half hour. Climbers watched agape as ice faces on nearby ridges and Mount Hunter loosened, plummeting to the lower glaciers. Most of them believed other climbers, including some friends, would be buried alive by the billowing clouds of ice. On Cassin Ridge, guides Matt and Julie Culberson reported seeing avalanches thundering into Kahiltna Glacier's northeast fork—a glacier valley famed for its deathly potential. In the *Anchorage Daily News,* they related, "In seconds, the snow slides overran the floor of the valley. When they met in the middle, the two slides rose upward, forming an eerie, mushroom-shaped cloud of crystal."[330]

A German couple camped near 15,000 feet on Harper Glacier in a snow-filled crevasse crawled out of their tent, which had dropped some fifteen feet, and were stunned to find that a large crevasse had formed nearby. Their tent and its poles crumpled, they hastily descended in the middle of the night with only the bare essentials. Pilot Jim Okonek flew past the north flank of Mount McKinley, spotting the debris that littered Karstens Ridge and saw that the gargantuan Wickersham Wall underwent vast change.

Yet for all the superficial destruction, there providently were no mountaineering injuries or deaths. At the time, guide Gary Bocarde and a party of five were camped on the corniced west ridge of Mount Hunter. When he heard the tent doors unzipping, the *Anchorage Daily News* account related, he "scrambled out into the icy wind of an exposed ridge wearing only wool socks and long johns. From all around him came the deafening sound of avalanches.... We heard noises, like cracks. Right below us, a lot of big ice faces were going." Later he reflected with friends on the possibility of freezing to death had the tents disappeared. On the descent, Bocarde's party found their tracks leading directly into chasms where cornices had plunged off the ridge.

ORIENTATION AT THE WEST BUTTRESS CAMP

The campsite location in the basin on the West Buttress route at 14,300 feet has a National Park Service ranger stationed all summer and an emergency hut with radio. It is here that a large assembly of colorful mountaineers may greet the new arrival, for most expeditions try to get away from base camp quickly and move to the higher altitude for acclimatization. Very often the first-time Mount McKinley climber at this stage will admit that he or she has greatly underestimated the mountain. The misery and physical labor will likely have caused some exhaustion, and the warnings of cold and storms may strike the survival instinct.

The tents and igloos, barricaded behind snow walls, give the impression of a fortified establishment. The occupants who greet new arrivals—the alpine version of the miners of the Klondike gold rush—likely have lips cracked and bleeding and have possibly just experienced a night of shivering.

The congregation at this camp on the West Buttress route on June 1, 1989, was typical of the past years. A sequence of storms and the need to acclimatize led to a well-populated site when Jim Nelson and Mark Bebie of Seattle arrived. With fine weather, the encamped climbers were outside of their barricades, ready to appraise the new arrivals during their idle hours. According to some of the climbers, Korean parties had recently aroused hilarity with their camp-moving tactics in hoisting sleds with ropes on the steeper slopes. Apparently it proved effective for them.

Nelson and Bebie had come up from a lower camp that day, arriving early. Their goal was to become acclimatized for a forthcoming ascent of Mount Foraker's Infinite Spur, with an ascent to McKinley's summit in the plans only if the weather was ideal. Before making camp, they dropped their loads and ski-climbed upslope some 1,000 feet (to the base of Messner Couloir) to take advantage of what appeared to be an excellent powder snow cover.

With the entire camp as observers, they laced together a long series of linked turns on their mountaineering skis in a fashion they did not anticipate would be possible because of the usual wind's effect on the surface. Among the 75 to 100 climbers in the camp was a female threesome, Charlotte Fox and Kim Reynolds of the Aspen ski patrol and Kathy McCarthy, a Utah ski instructor. All three women were well qualified for the ascent, wishing to focus on self-reliance and not rely on male support for direction and experience. Fox and Reynolds had climbed together in Peru, and McCarthy had been an Outward Bound instructor in Colorado and had guided clients on Mount McKinley. The motto of the threesome was to be serious about safety, but not at the risk of camaraderie and fun. Earlier in the season, when planning their expedition and choosing its identifying name, the slogan "Chicks on Pricks" (meaning crampons) was adopted—the name derived from an informal women's Friday ski group at Aspen, "Chicks on Sticks."

With the entire camp cheering after the two new arrivals finished their well-executed turns, the impressive ski descent prompted Fox to ask Bebie, "Can I feel your thighs?" In the next few days of inclement weather, the five socialized, relaxing with rewarding chatter and chess in the women's tent. As Fox later explained, they enjoyed a certain exclusivity by being some of the few women up there.

Gradually attaining higher altitudes is accepted as the best method to acclimatize. Numerous expeditions have profited from rest days, even from storms at 14,300 feet, before moving higher. Carrying loads high and returning to sleep at a lower camp is a traditional technique, whether it be in Alaska, South America, or Asia. A National Park Service report in 1985 by ranger Scott Gill is relevant to this important policy: He asserted that an ascent rate of 7,000 feet in 4 or 5 days may be fine for some individuals but that other climbers may become seriously ill at such a rate. A slower ascent rate tailored to the person who is having the most difficulty can prevent the onset of serious altitude problems. It is difficult to catch up on rest while on Mount McKinley. Adequate sleep is vital and should be planned to fit the climbing program, yet inactivity at high camps can be dangerous. It is necessary to keep up morale and motivation as well as the will to succeed. It is important to cook hot meals and melt water regularly.

WHAT DOES THE FUTURE HOLD?

The Alaska Range has unique mountaineering and wilderness-travel resources found in few other locations on earth. Not only are there nearby unlimited mountaineering challenges that are bound to continue for centuries, but the majestic range also offers a unique challenge for discovery, for the unexplored, and for an isolated wilderness that cannot be equalled even in Asia. Persons entering the range are forced to call upon all their skills and good sense as mountaineers and explorers in order to travel and climb safely.

There are no guidebooks to the Alaska Range to replace research, although a combination of books (including this one) now document the past ascents and established routes on Mount McKinley, Mount Foraker, and Mount Hunter.

There is a validity in not providing vast detail about a particular route, because such detail diminishes an attitude for self-reliance. It has been noted that, while telling people everything about a route before they start may make them safer climbers, such detail could backfire in Alaska. Certainly to describe the mere technical difficulties of a pitch (or route) ignores the fact that a mountaineer may make an ascent in winter conditions, in a bitter wind, with heavy packs, and at an altitude far higher than one spends most of his or her life.

The popular West Buttress route can provide a rewarding personal achievement, but today it is seldom a lonesome experience. Fortunately, Denali's environment (together with Mount Foraker, Mount Hunter, and other important peaks in the range) is grandiose and can provide alternate adventures.

Certainly Mount McKinley will continue to fascinate mankind. The number of mountaineers is increasing; there will be more guided parties and more adventure travelers. With a projected increase in numbers, there will be a need for a greater environmental awareness and probably a louder chorus of self-righteousness. To keep alert for problems and possible rescues, the National Park Service plans to continue a rescue presence at the 14,300-foot campsite.

Because guiding is projected to increase, the National Park Service has a contractual responsibility to ensure a high degree of judgement and capability. In 1992 Genet Expeditions' permit was revoked. This was the largest and oldest of the guide services, yet a series of problems and questionable client decisions (with two fatalities in twenty-four years) arose. Some Alaskans and the Genet owners criticized this decision, pointing out that a competitor has lost eleven clients worldwide during their twenty-seven years in business.

Forecasting the future has its imperfections. But the predictions indicate that in the quest for the summit there will be more solo climbers, that more of the technically difficult routes will be climbed, and that there will be a greater emphasis on rapid alpine-style ascents. The result of these practices and tactics may well be more accidents, rescues, frostbite, and acute mountain sickness. In the obsession for success, hopefully the many lessons of the past will be remembered.

▲ ▲ ▲

Chronology of Events Related to Exploration and Ascents of Mount McKinley

1778   Captain James Cook, on a mission for the British Admiralty to search for a Northwest Passage, discovered Cook Inlet on the southern Alaska Coast. Between May 26 and June 3, he explored the inlet in generally cloudy weather, making no mention of what could have been Mount McKinley.

1794   On May 6, Captain George Vancouver, during a month-long exploration of Cook Inlet, undoubtedly sighted Mount McKinley and Mount Foraker when he alluded to distant and stupendous mountains covered with snow.

1839   Governor Ferdinand von Wrangell of the Russian–America Company published the first volume of his new encyclopedia of the Russian Empire. The company's map included the names *Tenada* and *Tschigmit,* the first clear positioning of Mount McKinley and the Alaska Range; the "Sushitna" River is also shown.

1866   The American scientist William H. Dall and English artist Frederick Whymper canoed up the Yukon River to the Fort Yukon trading post, noting the range of huge snowy peaks to the south. Although it was some 150 miles distant, they probably saw Mount McKinley.

1867   The United States purchased Alaska from Russia for just over $7 million. Many political leaders and the press referred to this purchase as "Seward's Folly" (for Secretary of State William H. Seward who negotiated the transaction) and Alaska as "Walrussia." Even Seward, who championed Alaska, had no real idea of the natural resources, economic potential, and scenery within this immense territory.

1878   The first confirmed sighting of Mount McKinley ("a great ice mountain") from the Alaskan interior came during an ascent of the Tanana River by Arthur Harper and Alfred H. Mayo.

1885   Lieutenant Henry T. Allen of the U.S. Army may have seen Mount McKinley as he descended the Tanana River.

1889   Frank Densmore, noted Alaska pioneer, described Mount McKinley after portaging from the Tanana River to the Kuskokwim River. This was to result in its informal designation as "Densmore's Mountain."

1894   Hundreds of prospectors probed the Cook Inlet shores and nearby Susitna River lowlands for gold, this terrain being in full sight of Mount McKinley.

1896   William A. Dickey, a prospector of the Susitna and Chulitna rivers, named Mount McKinley for the future twenty-fifth president of the United States. Dickey made a rough survey of the mountain, quite accurately stating it to be over 20,000 feet in height.

1897   Dickey described his visits to Alaska in the *New York Sun* on January 24. He narrated how and why he named the mountain (ignoring Native American names) and included a sketch map. Dickey's naming was influential with the press and the various categories of mapmakers, while proponents of traditional names had no such clout.

1898   Robert Muldrow of the U.S. Geological Survey, a topographer for the George H. Eldridge exploring expedition, determined Mount McKinley's altitude at 20,464 feet through a professional instrumental determination, which included its precise position by latitude and longitude.

1898   Josiah E. Spurr led an extraordinary U.S. Geological Survey exploration from May 7 to October 31 across the Alaska Range. This first crossing of the range, just north of Rainy Pass, followed the Yentna and Skwentna rivers to Simpson Pass and then down the Kuskokwim River.

1899   Lieutenant Joseph S. Herron led a four-man army party across the Alaska Range via Simpson Pass. Here they were abandoned by their Native American guides and nearly died from starvation. In traversing over 1,000 wilderness miles in 167 days, Herron named Mount Foraker.

1902   Alfred H. Brooks and his U.S. Geological Survey expedition made a thorough exploration of the western and northern flanks of Mount McKinley in a 105-day expedition. Brooks contributed vast knowledge of the entire region and produced a most useful map that became a bible to explorers, prospectors, and mountaineers for the next five decades.

1903   Judge James Wickersham and a party of four colleagues made the first attempt to climb Mount McKinley. This Fairbanks party reached perhaps 8,100 feet in altitude on July 20, this position being on a spur of what became known as Wickersham Wall.

1903   Dr. Frederick A. Cook and his party of five followed the Brooks route across the Alaska Range and then attempted to climb Mount McKinley from Peters Glacier. On August 31 the party reached perhaps 10,900 feet on the Northwest Buttress of the North Peak. Dr. Cook's party, which began and ended on Cook Inlet, completed the first "circumnavigation" of Mount McKinley.

1906   The Kantishna gold stampede resulted in the establishment of a village north of Wonder Lake, in full sight of Mount McKinley.

1906   The eight-man expedition with Dr. Frederick A. Cook, Belmore Browne, and Herschel Parker was the first to explore the southern and southeastern approaches to Mount McKinley between June and August. Their highest point was on a knoll near the Tokositna Glacier, twenty-five miles from the mountain's summit.

1906   Dr. Cook and Edward N. Barrill made a rapid and mysterious attempt to climb Mount McKinley via Ruth Glacier, immediately after the conclusion of the preceding expedition. Cook alleged that the pair reached Mount McKinley's highest summit on September 16, an absurd claim that has been fully discredited by the evidence. They did reach a small rock peak of some 5,300 feet and fifteen miles from the true summit.

1910   The North Peak of Mount McKinley was climbed on April 3 by William R.

("Billy") Taylor and Pete Anderson of the Sourdough Expedition. The expedition, organized by Thomas Lloyd, proceeded via Muldrow Glacier, Karstens Ridge, and upper Harper Glacier.

1910   The Mazama Club expedition from Portland, Oregon, on July 12 entered the Sheldon Amphitheatre of Ruth Glacier during an investigation of Dr. Cook's claims and an attempt to climb Mount McKinley from its southeast flank.

1910   The Browne–Parker Expedition reached about 10,300 feet on Mount McKinley on July 13, approaching by the Northwest Fork of Ruth Glacier. During the expedition Dr. Cook's "fake peak" was discovered and photographed.

1912   On March 30 the *Fairbanks Times* Expedition, led by Ralph H. Cairns, climbed to about 9,200 feet on Pioneer Ridge, a long spur of Mount McKinley's North Peak.

1912   An expedition with Belmore Browne, Herschel Parker, and Merl LaVoy nearly climbed to the highest summit of Mount McKinley on June 29. They followed the Sourdough Expedition route, only to be turned back by a most severe blizzard.

1913   Reverend Hudson Stuck led the first ascent of Mount McKinley, again following the Sourdough Expedition route. His party members were Harry P. Karstens, Walter Harper, and Robert G. Tatum.

1917   Mount McKinley National Park was established on February 26 by an Act of Congress.

1923   The Alaska Railroad was completed, with President Warren G. Harding driving the final gold spike.

1932   Pilot Joe Crosson made the first glacier landing of an airplane in Alaska, at 5,700 feet on Muldrow Glacier. His landing on April 25 for Allen Carpé's cosmic ray expedition was by ski-equipped Fairchild monoplane.

1932   The second ascent of Mount McKinley's South Peak was made on May 7 by Alfred D. Lindley, Harry J. Liek, Erling Strom, and Grant Pearson. They climbed the North Peak two days later.

1932   Mount McKinley's first fatalities occurred on May 9 when Allen Carpé fell into a deep crevasse near 10,000 feet on Muldrow Glacier and Theodore Koven died in an attempt to rescue him.

1934   The first ascent of 17,400-foot Mount Foraker, the second highest peak in the Alaska Range, was made on August 6 by Charles S. Houston, Thomas Graham Brown, and George C. Waterston.

1938   The Denali Highway was completed to Wonder Lake.

1942   The United States Army Alaskan Test Expedition made the third ascent of Mount McKinley's South Peak, again using the Sourdough Expedition route via Muldrow and Harper glaciers. Seven members of the expedition reached the summit on July 23 and 24, after extensive testing of cold weather equipment and clothing.

1947   Bradford Washburn led a party of seven to the summit of the South Peak via Muldrow and Harper glaciers on June 7. During this filming and scientific expedition, Barbara Washburn became the first woman to climb Mount McKinley.

1951   A new route to the summit of the South Peak of Mount McKinley was established via the West Buttress by Bradford Washburn's eight-man party. The route from Kahiltna Glacier is now considered the standard route. The summit was reached July 10, 13, and 14; party members were James Gale, Captain William D. Hackett, Barry Bishop, Dr. John Ambler, Dr. Henry A. Buchtel, Dr. T. Melvin Griffiths, and Jerry More.

1954 The first ascent of Mount McKinley via the South Buttress (and south–north traverse) from Ruth Glacier was made on May 15. Elton Thayer, the leader, died on Karstens Ridge during the descent.

1954 The first ascent of Mount McKinley's North Peak via the Northwest Buttress was made on May 27 by Dr. Donald H. McLean, Captain William D. Hackett, Henry Meybohm, Charles R. Wilson, and Fred Beckey.

1954 The first ascent of Mount Hunter, the third highest peak in the Alaska Range, was made on July 5, by Heinrich Harrer, Henry Meybohm, and Fred Beckey. Pilot Don Sheldon made his first commercial glacier landing on Kahiltna Glacier during this expedition.

1957 The first observed surge of Muldrow Glacier was made by the British Parachute Brigade Expedition during June 1956. This cataclysmic advance created a sea of pinnacles and crevasses throughout the glacier in 1957 below 8,000 feet and resulted in a vertical surface drop of some 250 feet.

1959 The first ascent of the West Rib of the South Peak of Mount McKinley was made on June 19 by John E. ("Jake") Breitenbach, William J. Buckingham, Barry Corbet, and Leon Sinclair.

1960 The first party to camp on the summit was the Japanese team of Koji Kobayashi and Susumu Takahashi on May 14 to 15.

1960 The John Day Expedition's rescue in late May, on the West Buttress, resulted in the most complex to date. This rescue involved a 14,300-foot aircraft landing by Don Sheldon and a record helicopter landing by Link Luckett at 17,200 feet.

1960 Bradford Washburn's new topographic map of Mount McKinley, printed by the Swiss Federal Institute of Topography, was completed. This map was the result of fifteen years of field exploration and cartographic labor.

1961 The first ascent of the central buttress on the south face of Mount McKinley, known as Cassin Ridge, was climbed by the Italian party of Riccardo Cassin, Giancarlo ("Jack") Canali, Romano Perego, Annibali Zucchi, Luigino Airoldi, and Gigi Alippi on July 19.

1961 The first ascent of Pioneer Ridge on Mount McKinley's North Peak was made on July 23 by the German–Canadian party of Sev Heiberg, Adolf Baur, Donald Lyon, Larry Fowler, and Dietrich Haumann.

1962 The first ascent of the Southeast Spur of Mount McKinley was made on June 29 by the Boyd N. Everett, Jr., Expedition.

1963 The first ascent of the south face of the East Buttress was made on May 25 by William A. Read, Peter Lev, and Rod Newcomb.

1963 The first ascent of the North Peak of Mount McKinley via Wickersham Wall's western flank, known as the Canadian Route, was climbed on June 13 by Hans Gmoser, Gunther Prinz, and Hans Schwarz.

1963 The first ascent of the North Peak of Mount McKinley via the central Wickersham Wall, known as the Harvard Route, was made on July 16 by Henry L. Abrons, Peter Carman, Christopher Goetze, Donald C. Jensen, David S. Roberts, Richard Millikan, and John A. Graham.

1963 The first traverse of Mount McKinley from the Muldrow to Kahiltna Glacier and ascent of Mount Hunter was made between July 19 and 31 by J. Vincent

Hoeman, David P. Johnston, Thomas S. Choate, and Clifford D. Ellis.

1965   The first ascent of the South Buttress via the Northwest Ramp was made on July 3 by Shiro Nishimae, Masatsugu Kajiura, and Hisazumi Nakamura of Japan.

1967   The first winter ascent of Mount McKinley was made on March 1 by Arthur ("Art") Davidson, David P. Johnston, and Ray Genet.

1967   The worst disaster on Mount McKinley occurred when seven members of a Muldrow Glacier expedition died high on the South Peak on July 18 to 19.

1967   The first ascent of Mount McKinley via Centennial Wall on the south face was made on August 4 by Dennis Eberl, Graham ("Gray") Thompson, Roman Laba, and David Seidman.

1969   The first ascent of Catacomb Ridge, the East Ridge of the East Buttress, was made on July 13 by Niels-Henrik L. Andersen, Joseph K. Davidson, James B. Given, Dr. Gordon A. Benner, Robert H. Fries, and Peter L. Reagan.

1970   The first complete ski descent of Mount McKinley (via the West Buttress) was made on July 5 by Kazuo Hoshikawa and Tsuyoshi Ueki of Japan.

1970   The first all-female ascent of Mount McKinley (via the West Buttress) was made on July 6 by Margaret Young, Grace Hoeman, Dana Isherwood, Faye Kerr, Arlene Blum, and Margaret Clark.

1970   The first solo ascent of Mount McKinley was made by Naomi Uemura of Japan on August 26.

1972   The first ascent of Mount McKinley via Traleika Glacier and Traleika Spur was made on May 25 by Jock Jacober, William Ruth, David Pettigrew, John G. Johnson, Craig Schmidt, and Pat Stewart.

1975   The first ascent of Reality Ridge on Mount McKinley, via the South Fork of the Southeast Spur, was made by Peter Metcalf, Lincoln Stoller, Henry Florschutz, and Angus Thuermer on July 24.

1976   A major variation of the Centennial Wall route on the south face of Mount McKinley was made on May 12 by the British pair Doug Scott and Dougal Haston.

1976   The first solo ascent of Cassin Ridge was made on May 20 by Charles Porter.

1976   The first helicopter landing on Mount McKinley's summit was made on June 3 by pilot Bud Woods, who with Ray Genet carried out a critical mountaineering rescue.

1978   The first "circumnavigation" on skis of Mount McKinley was made from April 7 to April 28 by Ned Gillette, Galen Rowell, Alan Bard, and Doug Weins via Kahiltna Pass, Peters Glacier, Muldrow Glacier, Traleika Glacier, and Ruth Glacier.

1979   The first ascent of Mount McKinley by dog team was made on May 28 by Susan Butcher, Joe Reddington, Ray Genet, Brian Okonek, and Robert Stapleton.

1980   A new route on the eastern flank of Mount McKinley's south face was made by a Czechoslovakian team on June 13. The climbers were Michal Orolin, Daniel Bakos, Vladmir Petoik, and Philip Johnson.

1980   A new route, the Direct Southwest Face, was climbed on July 1 by Jack Roberts and Simon McCartney.

1980   The name of Mount McKinley National Park was changed to Denali

National Park and Preserve on December 2. The park's size was enlarged by 3,353 square miles.

1982   The first winter ascent of Cassin Ridge was made between February 28 and March 6 by Roger Mear, Jonathan Waterman, and Michael Young.

1982   During May the Denali Medical Research Project began its operations at the 14,300-foot level on the West Buttress.

1982   The first ascent of the Isis Spur to the crest of the South Buttress was made from May 8 to 16 by Jack Tackle and David Stutzman.

1983   The first climb of the Denali Diamond route on the southwest face was made on June 7 by Bryan Becker and Rolf Graage.

1984   The first solo climb of Mount McKinley in winter was made on February 12 by Naomi Uemura of Japan. He disappeared on the descent and was never found.

1984   The first ascent of the Ridge of No Return to the crest of the South Buttress was made on May 11 by Renato Casarotto of Italy.

1984   A new route on the south face of Mount McKinley, to the east of Cassin Ridge, was made by the Czechoslovakian party of Adam Blasej, Anton Krizo, and Frantisek Korl on May 23.

1984   A French army climbing party traversed Mount McKinley from Kahiltna Glacier to Wonder Lake, via the West Buttress route, in five days.

1986   The rescue of two Koreans from Cassin Ridge at 19,700 feet on June 20 was the most complex and dangerous since 1960.

1988   The rescue of a Korean climber on Cassin Ridge at 18,200 feet on May 27 was the highest hoist operation ever performed by U.S. Army helicopters. Vernon Tejas made the first solo winter ascent, with survival, on Mount McKinley.

1988   The first complete ascent of Pioneer Ridge from Gunsight Pass to the North Peak of Mount McKinley was made July 8 by Randy Waitman, Charles Maffei, Tim Cancroft, and Rowan Laver.

1992   Eleven mountaineers died on Mount McKinley in one season, a tragic record.

BIBLIOGRAPHY

American Alpine Club. *Accidents in North American Mountaineering.* Published annually.

Anderson, H. D., and W. C. Sells. *Alaska Natives.* Stanford, Calif.: Stanford University Press, 1975.

Banks, Michael E. B. "Two North American Expeditions." *Alpine Journal* 71, no. 312 (May 1966): 19–22.

Barrill, Edward N. "Barrill's Mount McKinley Affidavit" (Bradford Washburn, ed.). *American Alpine Journal* 31 (1989): 112–22.

Bassett, Digby. *The Mammoth and Mammoth-Hunting in North-East Siberia.* London: H. F. & G. Witherby, 1926.

Bates, Robert H. "Mount McKinley, 1942." *American Alpine Journal* 9, no. 2 (1955): 31–36.

———. *Mountain Man: The Story of Belmore Browne.* Clifton, N.J.: The Amwell Press, 1988.

Beckey, Fred. "Climbs in Alaska, 1954." *Alpine Journal* 60 (May 1955): 1–13.

———. "Mt. Deborah and Mt. Hunter: First Ascents." *American Alpine Journal* 9, no. 2 (1955): 39–50.

Beckwith, Edward P. "The Mount McKinley Cosmic Ray Expedition." *American Alpine Journal* 2 (1933): 45–68.

Bright, Norman. "Bill Taylor Sourdough." *American Alpine Journal* 3, no. 3 (1939): 274–86.

Broecker, Wallace S., and George H. Denton, "What Drives Glacial Cycles?" *Scientific American,* January 1990, 49–56.

Brogan, Hugh. *The Longman History of the United States of America.* New York: William Morrow and Company, 1985.

Brooks, Alfred H. "An Exploration to Mount McKinley." *Journal of Geography* 2 (1903): 441–69.

———. "The Mount McKinley Region, Alaska." *Professional Paper,* no. 70. Washington: U.S. Geological Survey, 1911.

———. *Blazing Alaska's Trails.* Fairbanks: University of Alaska Press, 1973.

Brooks, Alfred H., and D. L. Reaburn. "Plan for Climbing Mt. McKinley." *National Geographic* 14 (January 1903): 30–35.

Brown, T. Graham. "Mount Foraker." *Alpine Journal* 46 (1934): 393–402.

Browne, Belmore. "The Struggle up Mount McKinley." *Outing* 50 (1907): 257–76.

———. *The Conquest of Mount McKinley.* 1915. Reprint. Boston: Houghton Mifflin Company, 1956.

Buckingham, William J. "The Western Rib of Mount McKinley's South Face." *American Alpine Journal* 12 (1960): 1–9.

Buskirk, Steve. *Denali (Mount McKinley): The Story Behind the Scenery.* Las Vegas: K.C. Publications, 1978.

Cassin, Riccardo. "The South Face of Mount McKinley." *American Alpine Journal* 13, no. 1 (1962): 27–37.

———. *Fifty Years of Alpinism.* London: Diadem Books, 1981.

Chadwick, Douglas H. "Denali, Alaska's Wild Heart." *National Geographic,* August 1992, 63–87.

Chamberlain, Frances D. "Second Woman up Mt. McKinley." *Canadian Alpine Journal* 46 (1963): 61–65.

Chevigny, Hector. *Russian America: The Great Alaska Venture 1741–1867.* New York: Viking Press, 1965.

Cole, Terrence, ed. *The Sourdough Expedition: Stories of the Pioneer Alaskans Who Climbed Mount McKinley in 1910.* Anchorage: Alaska Northwest Publishing Company, 1985.

Cook, Dr. Frederick A. "America's Unconquered Mountain." *Harper's Monthly Magazine* 108 (1904): 335–44.

———. "The Conquest of Mount McKinley." *Harper's Monthly Magazine* 114 (1907): 821–37.

———. *To the Top of the Continent.* London: Hodder & Stoughton, 1909.

Culberson, Matt. "In the Eye of the Beholder." *Climbing,* October–November 1992, 62–68, 132–35.

Dalby, Ron. *The Alaska Highway: An Insider's Guide.* Golden, Colo.: Fulcrum Publishing Company, 1991.

Dall, William H. *Alaska and Its Resources.* Boston: Lee and Shepard, 1870.

Davidson, Art. *Minus 148°: The Winter Ascent of Mt. McKinley.* New York: W. W. Norton & Company, 1969.

Dean, David. *Breaking Trail—Hudson Stuck of Texas and Alaska.* Athens: Ohio University Press, 1988.

"Denali." *Alaska Geographic* 15, no. 3 (1988).

Denton, George H., and Terence J. Hughes. *The Last Great Ice Sheets.* New York: John Wiley & Sons, 1981.

Du Fresne, Jim. *Alaska: A Travel Survival Kit.* Australia: Lonely Planet Publications, 1991.

Dunn, Robert. *The Shameless Diary of an Explorer.* New York: Outing Publishing, 1907.

Everett, Boyd N., Jr. "The Southeast Spur of Mount McKinley." *American Alpine Journal* 13, no. 2 (1963): 381–89.

———. *The Organization of an Alaskan Expedition.* Pasadena, Calif.: Gorak Books, 1984.

Fisher, Raymond H. *Bering's Voyages: Whither and Why.* Seattle and London: University of Washington Press, 1977.

Fodor, R. V. *Frozen Earth: Explaining the Ice Ages.* Hillside, N.J.: Enslow Publishers, 1981.

Freedman, Lewis. *Dangerous Steps: Vernon Tejas and the Solo Winter Ascent of Mount McKinley.* Harrisburg, Penn.: Stackpole Books, 1990.

Freeman, Andrew A. *The Case for Doctor Cook.* New York: Coward-McCann, 1961.

Gilbert, Wyatt. *A Geologic Guide to Mount McKinley National Park.* Anchorage: Alaska National Parks and Monuments Association, 1978.

Golder, Frank A. *Russian Expansion in the Pacific 1641–1850.* Cleveland: Arthur H. Clark Company, 1914.

Greiner, James. *Wager with the Wind: The Don Sheldon Story.* Chicago: Rand McNally and Company, 1974.

Hackett, Peter H. *Mountain Sickness: Prevention, Recognition, and Treatment.* New York: American Alpine Club, 1980.

Hackett, Peter H., et al. "Preliminary High Latitude Center Study Report, Mount McKinley (Denali)." *American Alpine Journal* 26 (1984): 134–38.

Haenington, C. R. "Ice Age Mammal Research in Yukon Territory and Alaska." In *Early Man and Environments in North America,* 35–51. Calgary: University of Calgary Archaeological Association, 1970.

Hamilton, Thomas D., et al. *Glaciation in Alaska: The Geologic Record.* Anchorage: Alaska Geological Society, 1986.

Heacox, Kim. *The Denali Road Guide.* Anchorage: Alaska Natural History Association, 1986.

Heller, Christine. *Wild Flowers of Alaska.* Portland, Oreg.: Graphic Arts Publishing Company, 1966.

Herron, Lt. Joseph S. *Explorations in Alaska, 1899.* Washington: U.S. War Department, Adjutant General's Office, 1901.

Herschman, Fred. *Bush Pilots of Alaska.* Portland, Oreg.: Graphic Arts Publishing Company, 1989.

Hopkins, David, ed. *The Bering Land Bridge.* Stanford, Calif.: Stanford University Press, 1967.

Hulten, Eric. *Flora of Alaska and Neighboring Territories.* Stanford, Calif.: Stanford University Press, 1968.

Imbrie, John, and Katharine O. Imbrie. *Ice Ages: Solving the Mystery.* Cambridge, Mass.: Harvard University Press, 1986.

Jones, Chris. *Climbing in North America.* Berkeley: University of California, 1976.

Karstens, Harry. "Diary of the First Ascent of Mount McKinley, 1913." *American Alpine Journal* 16, no. 2 (1969): 339–48.

Krakauer, Jon. "Daredevil Pilots Take Glacier Flying to New Heights." *Smithsonian,* January 1989, 96–107.

———. "Mean Season on Denali." *Outside* 27, no. 8 (August 1992): 54–60, 121.

Kurtén, Björn. *The Ice Age.* New York: Putnam, 1972.

Kurtén, Björn, and Elaine Anderson. *Pleistocene Mammals of North America.* New York: Columbia University Press, 1980.

Langbauer, Del, and Roman Laba. "Mount McKinley's South Face—1967." *American Alpine Journal* 16, no. 1 (1968): 10–20.

Lindley, A. D. "Mount McKinley, South and North Peaks, 1932." *American Alpine Journal* 2, no. 1 (1933): 34–44.

London, Jack. *The Call of the Wild.* New York: The Macmillan Company, 1903.

McLean, Donald H. O. "McKinley, Northwest Buttress." *American Alpine Journal* 9, no. 2 (1955): 70–77.

Mear, Roger. "Cassin Ridge in Winter." *Mountain* 92 (July–August 1983): 24–29.

Mills, James. *Airborne to the Mountains.* London: Thomas Yoseloff Ltd., 1961.

Montague, Richard. *Exploring Mount McKinley National Park.* Anchorage: Alaska Travel Publications, 1973.

Moore, Terris. *Mt. McKinley: The Pioneer Climbs.* Seattle: The Mountaineers, 1984.

Murie, Adolph. *A Naturalist in Alaska.* Old Greenwich, Conn.: Devin-Adair Company, 1961.

———. *Mammals of Mount McKinley National Park.* Anchorage: Alaska National Parks and Monuments Association, 1962.

———. *The Grizzlies of Mount McKinley.* Scientific Monograph Series No. 14. Washington: National Park Service, 1981.

Murie, Olaus. *Alaska–Yukon Caribou.* Washington: Bureau Biological Survey, 1935.

National Park Service. *Mountaineering: Denali National Park and Preserve, Alaska.* Washington: National Park Service, 1981.

Oberholtzer, Ellis Paxson. *A History of the United States since the Civil War 5.* New York: The Macmillan Company, 1937.

Pearson, Grant. *My Life of High Adventure.* Englewood Cliffs, N.J.: Prentice-Hall, 1962.

Péwé, Troy L. "Quaternary Geology of Alaska." *U.S. Geological Survey Professional Paper* 835. Washington: U.S. Geological Survey, 1975.

Porter, Russell W. *The Arctic Diary of Russell William Porter.* Charlottesville, Va.: University Press, 1976.

Potter, Louise. *Wildflowers along Mount McKinley Park Road.* Hanover, N.H.: privately published, 1972.

Pruitt, William O., Jr. *Animals of the North.* New York: Harper and Row, 1967.

Randall, Frances. *Denali Diary: Letters from McKinley.* Seattle: Cloudcap Press, 1987.

Randall, Glenn. *Breaking Point.* Denver: Chockstone Press, 1984.

———. *Mt. McKinley Climber's Handbook.* Talkeetna, Alas.: Genet Expeditions, 1984.

Reed, John C., Jr. "Geology of the Mount McKinley Quadrangle, Alaska." *U.S. Geological Survey Bulletin* 1108-A. Washington: U.S. Geological Survey, 1961.

Roper, Steve, and Allen Steck. *Fifty Classic Climbs of North America,* 19–24. San Francisco: Sierra Club Books, 1979.

Rowell, Galen A. *High and Wild.* San Francisco: Sierra Club Books, 1979.

Ruggles, Richard L. *A Country so Interesting: The Hudson's Bay Company and Two Centuries of Mapping 1670–1870.* Montreal and Kingston: McGill-Queen's University Press, 1991.

Rusk, Claude E. "On the Trail of Dr. Cook." *Pacific Monthly,* January 1911, 48–62.

Schwatka, Frederick. *Along Alaska's Great River.* London: Cassell & Company, 1885.

Scott, Douglas. "Adventure on McKinley." *Mountain* 52 (1976): 18–21.

Selters, Andy. *Glacier Travel and Crevasse Rescue.* Seattle: The Mountaineers, 1990.

Sheldon, Charles. *The Wilderness of Denali.* New York: Charles Scribner's Sons, 1960.

Sherwonit, Bill. *To the Top of Denali: Climbing Adventures on North America's Highest Peak.* Bothell, Wash.: Alaska Northwest Books, 1990.

Sherwood, Morgan B., ed. *Alaska and Its History.* New Haven and London: Yale University Press, 1965.

Simmerman, Nancy. *Alaska's Parklands: The Complete Guide.* Seattle: The Mountaineers, 1983.

Snyder, Howard H. *The Hall of the Mountain King.* New York: Charles Scribner's Sons, 1973.

Spurr, Josiah E. *A Reconnaissance in Southwestern Alaska in 1898,* 31–264. 20th Annual Report. Washington: U.S. Geological Survey, 1900.

Stewart, T. D. *The People of America.* New York: Charles Scribner's Sons, 1973.

Stuck, Hudson. *Ten Thousand Miles with a Dog Sled.* New York: Charles Scribner's Sons, 1914.

———. *The Ascent of Denali (Mount McKinley): A Narrative of the First Complete Ascent of the Highest Peak in North America.* New York: Charles Scribner's Sons, 1914. Reprint. Lincoln: University of Nebraska Press, 1989.

Tebenkov, Mikhail, Capt. *Atlas of the Northwest Coast of America, from Bering's Straits to Cape Corrientes and the Aleutian Islands.* St. Petersburg: 1852.

Thompson, Graham R. "McKinley's Centennial Wall." *Summit Magazine,* March 1968.

Troyer, Will. *Movements of the Denali Caribou Herd.* Anchorage: National Park Service, 1981.

Viereck, Leslie, and Elbert L. Little. *Alaska Trees and Shrubs.* Washington: Government Printing Office, 1972.

Ward, Michael. *Mountain Medicine: A Clinical Study of Cold and High Altitude.* London: Crosby, Lockwood, Staples, 1975.

Washburn, Bradford. "Mount McKinley from the North and West." *American Alpine Journal* 6 (1947): 283–93.

———. "Operation White Tower." *American Alpine Journal* 7, no. 2 (1948): 40–58.

———. *Mount McKinley and the Alaska Range in Literature.* Boston: Museum of Science, 1951.

———. "Mount McKinley: The West Buttress, 1951." *American Alpine Journal* 8, no. 2 (1952): 212–26.

———. "Mount McKinley Conquered by New Route." *National Geographic,* August 1953, 219–48.

———. "Mount McKinley, History and Evaluation." In *The Mountain World 1956–1957,* edited by Malcolm Barnes. New York: Harper Brothers, 1957.

———. *A Tourist Guide to Mount McKinley National Park.* Anchorage: Alaska Northwest Publishing Company, 1976.

———. "Barrill's Mount McKinley Affidavit." *American Alpine Journal* 31 (1989): 113–22.

Washburn, Bradford, Adams Carter, and Ann Carter. "Dr. Cook and Mount McKinley." *American Alpine Journal* 11, no. 32 (1958): 1–30.

Washburn, Bradford, and David Roberts. *Mount McKinley: The Conquest of Denali.* New York: Harry N. Abrams, Inc., 1991.

Waterman, Jonathan. *Surviving Denali: A Study of Accidents on Mount McKinley 1903-1990.* New York: American Alpine Club, 1991.

———. *High Alaska: A Historical Guide to Denali, Mount Foraker, & Mount Hunter.* New York: American Alpine Club, 1988.

Webb, Melody. *The Last Frontier: A History of the Yukon Basin of Canada and Alaska.* Albuquerque: University of New Mexico Press, 1946.

Wickersham, James. *Bibliography of Alaskan Literature 1724–1924.* College, Alas.: University of Alaska, 1927.

———. *Old Yukon Tales, Trails, and Trials.* Washington: Washington Law Book Company, 1938.

Wilcox, Joe. *White Winds.* Los Alamitos, Calif.: Hwong Publishing Company, 1981.

Wilkerson, James A. *Medicine for Mountaineering.* Seattle: The Mountaineers, 1985.

Wilson, William H. *Railroad in the Clouds: The Alaska Railroad in the Age of Steam, 1914–1915.* Boulder, Colo.: Pruett Publishing Company, 1977.

Wood, Morton S. "The First Traverse of Mt. McKinley." *American Alpine Journal* 9, no. 2 (1955): 51–69.

Wren, Christopher. "We Climbed Our Highest Mountain." *Look* 26, no. 21 (October 9, 1962): 60–69.

NOTES

1 George Vancouver, *Voyage of Discovery to the North Pacific Ocean, and Round the World,* vol. 3 (London, 1798), 124.

2 Alfred H. Brooks, "The Mount McKinley Region, Alaska," *Professional Paper,* no. 70 (Washington: U.S. Geological Survey, 1911), 11.

3 *Terrane* is a term that refers to a rock formation characterized by a unique sequence of geological events, whereas *terrain* refers generally to a geographical area or its physical features.

4 The average age of biotite from nine granodiorites of the Mount McKinley sequence is 57.3 million years.

5 The ice depth in the gorge was determined to be 3,770 feet in a 1992 study. Ruth Glacier's great mass has been shown to currently move 3.3 feet per day, compared to a Muldrow Glacier flow rate of five inches daily.

6 Troy L. Péwé, "Quaternary Geology of Alaska," *Geological Survey Professional Paper* 835 (Washington: U.S. Geological Survey, 1975), 15.

7 Wisconsin time as used here encompasses the interval between approximately 70,000 to about 10,000 years ago. The maximum Wisconsin ice advance was attained early in this time.

8 Austin S. Post, "The Exceptional Advances of the Muldrow, Black Rapids and Susitna Glaciers," *Journal of Geophysical Research* 65, no. 11 (November 1960), 3703.

9 For a period of at least fifty years, the lower Muldrow has been wasting away with little or no movement.

10 Of the Muldrow's 152 square miles of ice, only 64 square miles advanced.

11 The widespread wooly mammoth is the best-known Pleistocene mammal; the mastodon was a related cousin. In 1821 the Russian admiral Kotzebue published an account regarding Ice Age mammals after he examined fossils in the permafrost along the eastern Bering seacoast. Specimens were later collected by Captain Beechey of the Royal Navy and given to the British Museum.

12 Alaska's aboriginal inhabitants fall into three groups: Indians, Aleuts, and Eskimos—together they number about 53,000 today.

13 Dr. Frederick A. Cook, *To the Top of the Continent* (London: Hodder & Stoughton, 1909), 50.

14 Ibid., 44.

15 Rather than risk the *Discovery* to the strong tidal currents and dangerous, moving ice floes of the inlet, Vancouver sent Joseph Whidbey in boats to examine the Turnagain Arm of Cook's third voyage and then himself led a boat expedition to trace the northern part of the inlet. He found great tide flats, extensive shoals, and a background of high mountains—exploding the theory that the inlet could connect to the sought-after Northwest Passage.

16 Terris Moore in *Mt. McKinley* states that both Kolmakov and Lukeen reached the Takutna River.

17 Terris Moore, *Mt. McKinley: The Pioneer Climbs* (Seattle: The Mountaineers, 1984), 3. Moore is uncertain how far Glazunov went when he sighted Mount McKinley.

18 In his 1870 map, von Wrangell labeled the range as the Alaska Range but did not single out Mount McKinley.

19 Doroshin came to the colony for the Russian–American Company in 1848 and remained four years.

20 Moore, *Mt. McKinley,* 3.

21 Frederick Whymper, *Travel and Adventure in the Territory of Alaska* (London: John Murray, 1868), 214–15.

22 Morgan Sherwood, *Exploration of Alaska 1865–1900* (New Haven and London: Yale University Press, 1965), 1.

23 Seward was a former New York State governor and United States Senator, a tough politician, and a skilful orator with surprising intellect. He insisted that the United States had imperial obligations and that Alaska's dominating position in the North Pacific was a vital geopolitical acquisition.

24 William McKinley, an Ohio Republican, was touted as a loyal American, Christian gentleman, statesman, patriot, and soldier. McKinley, who believed in a "Chinese wall of tariffs" to protect industry, had endeared himself to the American public. With the worst of a great depression behind, a period of great prospects for America began.

    McKinley addressed a convention at the Pan-American Exposition in Buffalo on September 5, 1901, but on the next day he was fatally shot by an anarchist. With his death, the whole outlook on American politics was changed. To come was the versatile Theodore Roosevelt's reform movement and political realism.

25 Hudson Stuck, *The Ascent of Denali (Mount McKinley): A Narrative of the First Complete Ascent of the Highest Peak in North America* (New York: Charles Scribner's Sons, 1914; Lincoln: University of Nebraska, 1989), vii.

26 Alfred H. Brooks, "The Mount McKinley Region, Alaska" *Professional Paper,* no. 70 (Washington: U.S. Geological Survey, 1911), 27.

27 Israel C. Russell, *Glaciers of North America* (Boston and London: Ginn & Company, 1897), 107.

28 Ibid., 74.

29 Brooks, "Mount McKinley Region," 22.

30 Muldrow's theodolite measurements produced an error of only 0.7 percent, one due to atmospheric refraction. Possible errors arise from the bending of light rays, this refraction depending on the density and temperature of the air. The plumb line deflection from the gravity of a mass may also affect theodolite measurements.

31 Spurr would later become renowned for his mining studies and appraisals in the Cascade Range and South America.

32 After reelection in 1902, Foraker was exposed by the press for accepting fees from Standard Oil Company and was driven from public life.

33 Ibid., 30.

34 Ibid.

35 Ibid., 32

36 Ibid., 33–34.

37 Ibid., 35.

38 Ibid., 37–38.

39 Ibid., 41.

40 Ibid.

41 Ibid.

42 Ibid., 42.

43 Ibid.

44 Alfred H. Brooks, "An Exploration to Mount McKinley," *Journal of Geography* II, no. 9 (1903), 450.

45 Ibid., 452–53.

46 Ibid., 461–662.

47 Stoughton, 1909, 96.

48 Hudson Stuck led the first successful ascent of Mount McKinley's South Peak, which is described in chapter 7, "A Missionary Leads the First Complete Ascent."

49 In early 1903 federal Judge Wickersham moved his court from Eagle on the

Yukon to the new town of Fairbanks because of gold strikes and its likelihood to become the interior's commercial center. The new court session did not begin until late July.

50 James Wickersham, *Old Yukon Tales, Trails, and Trials* (Washington: Washington Law Book Company, 1938), 428–29.

51 Ibid., 204.

52 Ibid., 217.

53 Ibid., 218.

54 Ibid., 220.

55 Ibid., 221.

56 Ibid., 222.

57 Ibid., 225–27.

58 Ibid., 241–42.

59 Ibid., 256.

60 Ibid., 258.

61 Ibid., 260.

62 Ibid., 260–62.

63 Ibid., 262.

64 Ibid., 268.

65 Ibid., 275.

66 Ibid., 276.

67 Ibid., 278–79.

68 The party had been following the Muddy River (Wickersham's middle fork of the Kantishna River) to where it emanates from Peters Glacier.

69 Wickersham, *Old Yukon Tales*, 282.

70 Ibid., 283.

71 Ibid., 283–4.

72 Wickersham named the glacier for Ohio Senator Marcus A. Hanna. Dr. Cook adopted this name, but Alfred Brooks had already named it Peters Glacier in 1902 for topographer Willard J. Peters, with whom he was associated during his first Alaskan expedition.

73 Wickersham, *Old Yukon Tales*, 284.

74 Ibid., 292.

75 This is the small Jeffrey Glacier later named for a Wickersham party member; some maps spell it "Jeffery."

76 Wickersham, *Old Yukon Tales*, 286.

77 Ibid., 288–89. The Wickersham party actually climbed only to about 8,000 feet, in the opinion of both Terris Moore and Bradford Washburn. Aneroid barometers were subject to large errors for obtaining altitude at that time.

78 Ibid., 294.

79 Ibid., 294–95.

80 Ibid., 296.

81 Ibid., 312.

82 Terris Moore, *Mt. McKinley: The Pioneer Climbs* (Seattle: The Mountaineers, 1984), 31.

83 *Harper's* paid Dr. Cook $1,200 for story rights, but the amount has been reported to be considerably more. Henry W. Disston of Philadelphia may also have provided financial support.

84 Dr. Frederick A. Cook, *To the Top of the Continent* (London: Hodder & Stoughton, 1908), 2.

85 Robert Dunn, *The Shameless Diary of an Explorer* (New York: Outing Publishing, 1907), 40.

86 Cook, *To the Top*, 19.

87 Ibid.

88 Ibid., 93.

89 Ibid., 131.

90 Ibid., 152.

91 Cook, *To the Top*, 61.
92 Ibid., 65.
93 Dunn, *The Shameless Diary*, 227–28.
94 Cook, *To the Top*, 65–66.
95 Ibid., 66.
96 Ibid., 67.
97 Ibid., 70.
98 Ibid., 72.
99 Dr. Frederick A. Cook, "America's Unconquered Mountain," *Harper's Monthly Magazine* 108 (1904), 335.
100 Cook, *To the Top*, 77.
101 Ibid.
102 In *Harper's*, Cook stated that he had required $28,000 to finance the 1903 and 1906 expeditions.
103 Belmore Browne, *The Conquest of Mount McKinley* (1915; reprint, Boston: Houghton Mifflin Company, 1956), 32.
104 Robert H. Bates, *Mountain Man: The Story of Belmore Browne* (Clifton, N.J.: The Amwell Press, 1988), 108.
105 Cook, *To the Top*, 131.
106 Ibid., 132.
107 Bates, *Mountain Man*, 109.
108 Ibid., 111.
109 Ibid., 113.
110 Cook, *To the Top*, 154.
111 Ibid., 168.
112 Browne, *The Conquest*, 53.
113 Ibid., 69.
114 Ibid., 190.
115 Cook, *To the Top*, 196.
116 Ibid., 205.
117 Ibid., 207.
118 Ibid., 232.
119 Terris Moore, *Mt. McKinley: The Pioneer Climbs* (Seattle: The Mountaineers, 1984), 54.
120 Browne, *The Conquest*, 71.
121 Stuck to Brooks, National Park Service files, Talkeetna Ranger Station, Alaska.
122 Dr. Frederick A. Cook, "The Conquest of Mount McKinley," *Harper's Monthly Magazine* CVX (1907), 830.
123 Browne, *The Conquest*, 72.
124 Moore, *Mt. McKinley*, 59.
125 Ibid., 64.
126 Ibid., 65.
127 Ibid.
128 Bradford Washburn, "Barrill's Mount McKinley Affidavit," *American Alpine Journal* 31 (1989), 118–22.
129 Browne, *The Conquest*, 72.
130 Additional photographs were taken between August 1 and 15, 1956, by Bradford Washburn, whose surveys yielded convincing new facts about the false peak. He confirmed its altitude and estimated the point to be 19.48 miles southeast of the summit of McKinley's South Peak. Adams Carter conducted additional surveys a decade later in this row of small granitic summits that Vincent Hoeman termed Sleuth Peaks. Cook's "ring of rocks" camp, which supported the light Shantung silk tent, was found by Hoeman in the 1960s on the 4,220-foot hump between lower Ruth Glacier and the Tokositna ablation moraines.
131 Browne, *The Conquest*, 141–43.

132 Ibid., 164.

133 Hudson Stuck, *The Ascent of Denali (Mount McKinley): A Narrative of the First Complete Ascent of the Highest Peak in North America* (New York: Charles Scribner's Sons, 1914; Lincoln: University of Nebraska, 1989), 166.

134 Robert Service's *Songs of a Sourdough* (1907) popularized the term sourdough, which arose during the Yukon gold rush and refers to the sourdough carried for emergency food and used as a yeast in making bread. Old-timers took the sourdough to bed with them during the extreme cold.

135 The Kantishna placers, discovered in 1905, are located in crystalline schist along several gold-producing creeks.

136 This pass is twenty-six miles from the terminus of Muldrow Glacier.

137 W. F. Thompson, "First Account of Conquering Mt. McKinley," *New York Times,* June 5, 1910.

138 The upper ridge east of Muldrow Glacier was eventually named Karstens Ridge for Harry Karstens, who climbed Mount McKinley in 1913 with Hudson Stuck. The northern ridge leading to the North Peak, to the west of the Muldrow, was later named Pioneer Ridge in honor of the Sourdoughs.

139 Norman Bright, "Bill Taylor: The Youngest Sourdough," in Terrence Cole, ed., *The Sourdough Expedition: Stories of the Pioneer Alaskans Who Climbed Mount McKinley in 1910* (Anchorage: Alaska Northwest Publishing Company, 1985), 56.

140 Apparently Taylor and Anderson were not aware that the South Peak was the true summit, the bane of not having topographic maps and mountaineering experience; they wished to have the flag seen from either Kantishna or Fairbanks. While both McKinley peaks are visible from Fairbanks, Terris Moore pointed out that because of atmospheric interference the pole could not possibly have been seen through even the best of available telescopes.

141 Francis P. Farquhar, "The Verdict of History," in Cole, ed., *The Sourdough Expedition,* 59.

142 Norman Bright, "Billy Taylor Sourdough," *American Alpine Journal* 3, no. 3 (1939), 277.

143 Hudson Stuck, *The Ascent of Denali (Mount McKinley): A Narrative of the First Complete Ascent of the Highest Peak in North America* (New York: Charles Scribner's Sons, 1914; Lincoln: University of Nebraska Press, 1989), 170.

144 Robert H. Bates, *Mountain Man: The Story of Belmore Browne* (Clifton, N.J.: The Amwell Press, 1988), 49.

145 Belmore Browne, *The Conquest of Mount McKinley,* (1915; reprint, Boston: Houghton Mifflin Company, 1956), 282.

146 Ibid., 299–300.

147 Ibid., 300.

148 Ibid., 319.

149 Ibid., 332.

150 Ibid., 336.

151 Ibid., 340.

152 Ibid., 342.

153 Ibid., 344.

154 Bradford Washburn and David Roberts, *Mount McKinley: The Conquest of Denali* (New York: Harry N. Abrams, Inc., 1991), 80. Washburn studied Browne's account and the party's photographs. With the assistance of a National Outdoor Leadership School party in 1977, who surveyed this locale, he concluded that Browne was only 125 vertical feet below the summit (or 650 feet distance), with Parker and LaVoy close behind.

155 Browne, *Conquest,* p. 346.

156 Bates, *Mountain Man.*

157 Stuck recounted his experiences in his narrative, *Ten Thousand Miles with a Dog Sled* (New York: Scribner's Sons, 1914).

158 Hudson Stuck, *The Ascent of Denali (Mount McKinley): A Narrative of the First

Complete Ascent of the Highest Peak in North America (New York: Charles Scribner's Sons, 1914; Lincoln: University of Nebraska Press, 1989), 3.
159 Ibid., 9.
160 The boom burst the next summer, and the miners deserted the towns during a mass exodus.
161 Stuck, *Ascent of Denali,* 28–29.
162 Ibid., 31.
163 Ibid., 40.
164 Ibid., 43.
165 Ibid., 45.
166 Ibid., 61.
167 Ibid., 94.
168 Ibid., 99.
169 Ibid., 103.
170 Ibid., 102–103.
171 Ibid., 128–29.
172 Ibid., 130.
173 Ibid., 133–34.
174 Liek was then superintendent of Mount McKinley National Park.
175 Edward P. Beckwith, "The Mount McKinley Cosmic Ray Expedition," *American Alpine Journal* 2 (1933), 48.
176 Ibid., 51.
177 Terris Moore, *Mt. McKinley: The Pioneer Climbs* (Seattle: The Mountaineers, 1984), 135–37.
178 Grant Pearson, *My Life of High Adventure* (Englewood Cliffs, N.J., 1962), 162.
179 Bradford Washburn and David Roberts, *Mount McKinley: The Conquest of Denali* (New York: Harry N. Abrams, Inc., 1991), 17.
180 In 1960 Washburn produced his magnificent Mount McKinley map, and throughout the decades he photographed the mountain from the air, producing unexcelled detailed images.
181 Captain William D. Hackett, personal diary, unpublished.
182 Bradford Washburn, "Mount McKinley: The West Buttress, 1951," *American Alpine Journal* 8, no. 2 (1952), 219.
183 Ibid., 222.
184 Ibid., 223.
185 Bradford Washburn, "Mount McKinley Conquered by New Route," *National Geographic,* August 1953, 248.
186 James Wickersham, *Old Yukon Tales, Trails, and Trials* (Washington: Washington Law Book Company, 1938), 289.
187 Charles R. Wilson, personal diary, unpublished.
188 Wilson, diary.
189 Donald H. O. McLean, "McKinley, Northwest Buttress," *American Alpine Journal* 9, no. 2 (1955), 71–72.
190 Captain William D. Hackett, personal diary, unpublished.
191 Dr. Frederick A. Cook, *To the Top of the Continent* (London: Hodder & Stoughton, 1908), 70.
192 Charles R. Wilson, personal communication to Beckey, 1992.
193 McLean, "Northwest Buttress," 73.
194 Camp II was set up in the cirque at 13,000 feet.
195 Ibid., 74–75.
196 Ibid., 76.
197 Ibid., 77.
198 Ibid.
199 Wilson to Beckey, 1992.
200 Wilson to Beckey, 1992.
201 McLean, "Northwest Buttress," 77.

202 Jonathan Waterman, *High Alaska: A Historical Guide to Denali, Mount Foraker, & Mount Hunter* (New York: American Alpine Club, 1988), 92.

203 Morton S. Wood, "The First Traverse of Mt. McKinley," *American Alpine Journal* 9, no. 2 (1955), 53.

204 Ibid., 55.

205 Ibid., 57.

206 Ibid., 57–58.

207 Talkeetna Ranger Station, National Park Service, accident reports.

208 Wood, "The First Traverse," 61–62.

209 Ibid., 63.

210 In 1954 modern harnesses of broad straps of nylon webbing were not available. Climbers tied directly into the climbing rope, often with a single bowline knot.

211 Wood, "The First Traverse," 67.

212 Ibid., 69.

213 Bradford Washburn, "Mt. Hunter via the West Ridge: A Proposed Route," *American Alpine Journal* 8, no. 3 (1953), 478–84.

214 Heinrich Harrer, personal correspondence to Beckey, unpublished.

215 Fred Beckey, "Mt. Deborah and Mt. Hunter: First Ascents," *American Alpine Journal* 9, no. 2 (1955), 44.

216 Ibid.

217 Ibid., 45.

218 Ibid., 45–46.

219 Ibid., 46–47.

220 Ibid., 47.

221 Ibid., 50.

222 James Mills, *Airborne to the Mountains* (London: Thomas Yoseloff Ltd., 1961).

223 Ibid., 44–45.

224 Ibid., 83.

225 Ibid., 85.

226 Ibid., 201.

227 Ibid.

228 Ibid., 211.

229 Bradford Washburn, "Mount McKinley, History and Evaluation," in *The Mountain World 1956–1957,* ed. Malcolm Barnes (New York: Harper Brothers, 1957), 79.

230 Riccardo Cassin, "The South Face of Mount McKinley," *American Alpine Journal* 13, no. 1 (1962), 31.

231 Riccardo Cassin, "McKinley, versant Sud," *La Montagne et Alpinisme,* trans. and ed. Félix Germain (Paris: Club Alpin Français) (April 1962): 202–10.

232 Ibid.

233 Ibid.

234 Paul Stoliker, "Denali, the Lion, Sleeps," *Canadian Alpine Journal* 72 (1989), 57–60.

235 Dennis Eberl, personal correspondence to Beckey, November 24, 1992.

236 Christopher Wren, "We Climbed Our Highest Mountain," *Look* 26, no. 21, (October 9, 1962), 69.

237 Boyd N. Everett, Jr., "The Southeast Spur of Mount McKinley," *American Alpine Journal* 13, no. 2 (1963): 381.

238 Don Sheldon damaged his landing gear while skimming over a crevasse. He informed Everett that the ensuing pickup would be made eight miles down-glacier.

239 Wren, "We Climbed," 69.

240 Everett, "Southeast Spur," 383.

241 Wren, "We Climbed," 69.

242 Everett, "Southeast Spur," 384.

243 Ibid., 384.

244 Wren, "We Climbed," 69.
245 Ibid.
246 Everett, "Southeast Spur," 386.
247 Wren, "We Climbed," 69.
248 Ibid.
249 Art Davidson, *Minus 148°: The Winter Ascent of Mt. McKinley* (New York: W. W. Norton & Company, 1969), 14.
250 Ibid., 24–25.
251 Ibid., 31.
252 Ibid., 42.
253 Ibid., 45.
254 Ibid., 66.
255 Ibid., 93.
256 Ibid., 98–99.
257 Ibid., 99.
258 Ibid.
259 Ibid., 109.
260 Ibid., 115.
261 Ibid., 151.
262 Ibid., 192.
263 Talkeetna Ranger Station, National Park Service, accident reports.
264 Jonathan Waterman, *High Alaska: A Historical Guide to Denali, Mount Foraker, & Mount Hunter* (New York: American Alpine Club, 1988), 131.
265 His party's Cassin Ridge ascent would eventually be the third; a Japanese party made the second ascent a month earlier.
266 Anthony Horan, "Mt. McKinley Conquered," *Dartmouth Alumni Magazine,* November 1967, 11.
267 Ibid.
268 Ibid.
269 Ibid., 12–14.
270 Ibid., 12.
271 Ibid.
272 Ibid.
273 Ibid., 13–14.
274 Ibid., 14.
275 Del Langbauer and Roman Laba, "Mount McKinley's South Face—1967," *American Alpine Journal* 16, no. 1 (1968), 13.
276 Dennis Eberl to Beckey, 1992.
277 Langbauer and Laba, "Mount McKinley's South Face," 15.
278 Eberl to Beckey.
279 Graham Thompson to Beckey, unpublished.
280 Langbauer and Laba, "Mount McKinley's South Face," 16.
281 Eberl to Beckey.
282 Thompson to Beckey.
283 Eberl to Beckey.
284 Graham Thompson, "McKinley's 'Centennial Wall'," *Summit* 14, no. 2 (March 1968), 3.
285 Eberl to Beckey
286 Ibid.
287 Thompson to Beckey.
288 Ibid.
289 Thompson, "McKinley's 'Centennial Wall'," 4.
290 Eberl to Beckey.
291 Ibid.
292 Ibid.
293 Ibid.
294 Bill Sherwonit, *To the Top of Denali: Climbing Adventures on North America's*

Highest Peak (Bothell, Wash.: Alaska Northwest Books, 1990), 177.

295 Howard H. Snyder, *The Hall of the Mountain King* (New York: Charles Scribner's Sons, 1973), 95.

296 Joe Wilcox, *White Winds* (Los Alamitos, Calif.: Hwong Publishing Company, 1981), 157.

297 Ibid.

298 Boyd Everett, expedition report, Talkeetna Ranger Station, National Park Service.

299 Bill Sherwonit, *To the Top of Denali: Climbing Adventures on North America's Highest Peak* (Bothell, Wash.: Alaska Northwest Books, 1990), 214.

300 Glenn Randall, "Over the Edge," *Anchorage Daily News,* August 14, 1983.

301 Glenn Randall, *Breaking Point* (Denver: Chockstone Press, 1984), 215.

302 Talkeetna Ranger Station, National Park Service, accident reports.

303 Craig Medred, "Naomi Uemura: Final Days of a Climbing Legend," *Anchorage Daily News,* May 12, 1985.

304 Jonathan Waterman, *Surviving Denali* (New York: American Alpine Club, 1983).

305 Pete Schoening, accident report, Talkeetna Ranger Station, National Park Service.

306 In a similar accident, in June 1972 three Japanese women slipped and died in this gully; there were other tragedies in 1982, 1989, and 1992. Now nine of twelve deaths have been Japanese or Korean mountaineers.

307 *Accidents in North American Mountaineering,* 1980, 21.

308 *Accidents in North American Mountaineering,* 1982, 22.

309 Waterman, *Surviving Denali.*

310 *Accidents in North American Mountaineering,* 1986, 24.

311 Ibid., 19.

312 Talkeetna Ranger Station, National Park Service, accident reports.

313 *Accidents in North American Mountaineering,* 1986, 25.

314 Ibid., 22.

315 Ibid., 23.

316 Ibid., 26.

317 Seibert, accident report, Talkeetna Ranger Station, National Park Service.

318 As a comparison, in 1975 there were 363 climbers reported on Mount McKinley, whereas in 1990 there were 998 climbers.

319 Talkeetna Ranger Station, National Park Service, accident reports.

320 Messner Couloir rises from near the Denali West Buttress camp at 14,300 feet nearly to a 19,400-foot plateau. It is named for the world-renowned mountaineer Reinhold Messner, who pioneered the couloir as a steep route variant. Since Messner's ascent, the couloir has been the site of several major accidents.

321 J. D. Swed, *Anchorage Daily News,* June 17, 1992.

322 Jon Krakauer, "Mean Season on Denali," *Outside* 27, no. 8 (August 1992), 59.

323 Ibid.

324 Dr. Frederick A. Cook, *To the Top of the Continent* (London: Hodder & Stoughton, 1909), 96.

325 Douglas Scott, "Adventure on McKinley," *Mountain* 52 (1976), 20.

326 Michael Covington, accident report, Talkeetna Ranger Station, National Park Service.

327 If using insulated overboots, modify them so that the crampon's bail and heel clip fit and cinch on the boot welt. It may be necessary to cut small slits at the overboot toe and heel to ensure a proper fitting.

328 See James Greiner, *Wager with the Wind: The Don Sheldon Story* (Chicago: Rand McNally and Company, 1974); and Jon Krakauer, "Daredevil Pilots Take Glacier Flying to New Heights," *Smithsonian,* January 1989.

329 Francis D. Chamberlain, "Second Woman up Mt. McKinley," *Canadian Alpine Journal* 46 (1963), 64.

330 Doug O'Harra, "The Night Denali Shook," *Anchorage Daily News,* June 9, 1991.

INDEX

THE MOUNTAINEERS, founded in 1906, is a nonprofit outdoor activity and conservation club, whose mission is "to explore, study, preserve, and enjoy the natural beauty of the outdoors...." Based in Seattle, Washington, the club is now the third-largest such organization in the United States, with 12,000 members and four branches throughout Washington State.

The Mountaineers sponsors both classes and year-round outdoor activities in the Pacific Northwest, which include hiking, mountain climbing, ski-touring, snowshoeing, bicycling, camping, kayaking and canoeing, nature study, sailing, and adventure travel. The club's conservation division supports environmental causes through educational activities, sponsoring legislation, and presenting informational programs. All club activities are led by skilled, experienced volunteers, who are dedicated to promoting safe and responsible enjoyment and preservation of the outdoors.

The Mountaineers Books, an active, nonprofit publishing program of the club, produces guidebooks, instructional texts, historical works, natural history guides, and works on environmental conservation. All books produced by The Mountaineers are aimed at fulfilling the club's mission.

If you would like to participate in these organized outdoor activities or the club's programs, consider a membership in The Mountaineers. For information and an application, write or call The Mountaineers, Club Headquarters, 300 Third Avenue West, Seattle, Washington 98119; (206) 284-6310.

Send or call for our catalog of more than 200 outdoor books:
The Mountaineers Books
1011 SW Klickitat Way, Suite 107
Seattle, WA 98134
1-800-553-4453